Software Measurement

*A Visualization Toolkit for Project Control
and Process Improvement*

Dick B. Simmons
Texas A&M University

Newton C. Ellis
Texas A&M University

Hiroko Fujihara
Hewlett–Packard Company

Way Kuo
Texas A&M University

To join a Prentice Hall PTR Internet mailing list, point to:
http://www.prenhall.com/mail_lists/

ISBN 0-13-840695-2

90000

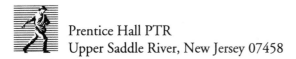

Prentice Hall PTR
Upper Saddle River, New Jersey 07458

9 780138 406950

Library of Congress Cataloging-in-Publication Data

Software measurement : a visualization toolkit for project control and
   process improvement / Dick B. Simmons . . . [et al.].
      p. cm.
   Includes index.
   ISBN (invalid) 01308406952
    1. Computer software—Quality control. 2. Computer software—
Development—Management. I. Simmons, Dick B.
QA76.76.Q35S568   1997
005.1′068′4—dc21   97–18173
                                         CIP

Acquisitions Editor: Bernard M. Goodwin
Editorial Assistant: Diane Spina
Editorial/Production Supervision: James D. Gwyn
Cover Designer: Design Source
Cover Design Director: Jerry Votta
Manufacturing Manager: Alan Fischer
Marketing Manager: Betsy Carey
Compositor/Production Services: Pine Tree Composition, Inc.

© 1998 by Prentice Hall PTR
Prentice-Hall, Inc.
A Simon & Schuster Company
Upper Saddle River, New Jersey 07458

Prentice Hall books are widely used by corporations and government agencies for training, marketing, and resale.
The publisher offers discounts on this book when ordered in bulk quantities. For more information contact: Corporate Sales
Department. Phone: 800–382–3419; FAX: 201–236–7141; E-mail: corpsales@prenhall.com; or write: Prentice Hall PTR,
Corp. Sales Dept., One Lake Street, Upper Saddle River, NJ 07458.

Printed in the United States of America
10 9 8 7 6 5 4 3 2 1

ISBN 0-13-840695-2

Prentice-Hall International (UK) Limited, *London*
Prentice-Hall of Australia Pty. Limited, *Sydney*
Prentice-Hall Canada Inc., *Toronto*
Prentice-Hall Hispanoamericana, S.A., *Mexico*
Prentice-Hall of India Private Limited, *New Delhi*
Prentice-Hall of Japan, Inc., *Tokyo*
Simon & Schuster Asia Pte. Ltd., *Singapore*
Editora Prentice-Hall do Brasil, Ltda., *Rio de Janeiro*

Contents

Preface

"Software, like wind, is invisible yet powerful. We can 'see' wind only by observing its effect, as it sways branches and swirls sand. And we can 'see' software only by observing its functionality. Invisibility is what makes software development so difficult to manage—it is hard to monitor the construction of something you can't see."

Pei Hsia
[Hsia96]

Indeed, software is difficult to visualize. Managers typically rely on staff to describe the status of a software product. Software development projects often fail for lack of knowledge about the software being developed. Experts agree that software is hard to visualize. Fred Brooks, who wrote the article stating there is no silver bullet that by itself promises even one order-of-magnitude improvement in productivity, in reliability, in simplicity, says that invisibility is an inherent software property and that software is invisible and unvisualizable [Brooks87]. In our opinion, Brooks is overly pessimistic. The purpose of this book is to show the reader how to visualize software which experts like Brooks have said is unvisualizable. We not only show that software attributes can be visualized but that they can be unobtrusively measured and the measurements can be used to drive volume, complexity, rework, efficiency, effort, productivity, schedule, reliability, reuse, speedup, and usability prediction models.

Over the past 35 years, administrators have spent large sums of money producing documents to describe a software product. Large government projects may require contractors to produce from 30 to 50 separate documents for each software product. With all these documents available, it is clear that people may still not know the status of a project. Many companies still use document-driven development to produce software that is over budget, behind schedule and then deliver it to a dissatisfied customer. In 1995, Capers Jones stated that the failure or cancellation rate of large software systems is over 20% [Jones95]. Of the 80% that are completed, approximately two thirds are late and experience cost overruns as much as 100%. Roughly two thirds are also plagued by low reliability and quality problems in the first year of development.

During the 1990s, forward-looking companies have turned away from documentation driven development and turned toward metric driven process improvement methodology. While some documentation is necessary, software measurement can replace documents that really do not help you visualize software. In Chapter 1 we cite examples of successful software development projects from AT&T Bell Laboratories, AT&T Network Systems, Boeing, Bull, CSC, DEC, IBM Santa Teresa Laboratory, Microsoft, NASA, Raytheon, Toshiba, and University of Maryland. Process improvement activities at these organizations have resulted in annual defect reduction of up to 32%, cost reduction of up to 8.4%, productivity gains of up to 32% and customer satisfaction gains of up to 7.8%. All of these successful projects apply some form of software measurement as part of their process improvement activities. But many other major organizations still do not have process improvement activities and many of these have ended up with failed projects. Often the management of these software projects were not aware that there were any problems until it was too late to salvage the project or to prevent cost over runs, extended outages, or major delays in scheduled delivery. Management was not able to see that problems were developing. In 1996, Norm Brown, Executive Director of the Department of Defense Software Acquisition Best Practices Initiative, stated, "In many cases, the true nature and pervasive extent of underlying project problems remains invisible to the project management until it is too late"[Brown96]. Metric based software project management helps you dynamically track software product development so you can apply management control early in a project cycle where adjustments can be effective.

This book has been written for practicing software developers, team leaders, project managers, top administrators and others interested in software measurement, project control, and process improvement. Also, it can serve as a reference text for advanced undergraduate or graduate classes in software engineering and as the main text for a course in software metrics, models, and process improvement.

The book is divided into three parts: Software Process Visualization, Models and Metrics, and Visualization Tool. Part 1 on software process visualization contains five chapters. Chapter 1 shows how software has become the high cost item for most computer projects. We explain how management has difficulty visualizing software during development and maintenance. Examples are presented where industry has learned how to improve the software development process by applying software improvement methodology. Also, major failures are described where they were not able to visualize the software development process. Project technologies deployed in successful software projects and the Department of Defense PRINCIPAL BEST PRACTICES are introduced to show how they contain planning based on accurate measurements to improve project visibility. Chapter 2 examines the criteria and standards for quality systems.

Chapter 3 introduces a set of project object classes for describing an arbitrary software development project. A view of the project world is introduced that uses objects, relationships, attributes, and properties. The objects are defined to be easily understandable by both managers and software developers. Once the object world is presented, the project personnel can use it to view the effect of changes in resources, schedules, or software product features from historical, status, compliance to plans, and prediction perspectives. We also introduce a dual project control/process improvement cycle where common visualization stages help you efficiently and objectively gather object attributes for analysis and prediction.

In Chapter 4, we partition the evolution of the software life cycle (SLC) into three time periods: Early SLC, Black Box SLC, and Process SLC. We start with simple SLCs for small projects and proceed to complex SLCs for large software products. For the Black Box SLC period, we examine waterfall, V, prototype, and incremental SLCs. For the Process SLC period we examine spiral and the natural milestone SLCs. We also describe the IEEE SLC Process Model, which contains development, management, and integral processes.

In Chapter 5 we describe the object classes that can be used to portray a software project. You can use the objects to see exactly what is happening in a software development project. All activities of SLC processes can be made visible to you. After we describe the object classes, we give a few examples of the object attributes. Detailed descriptions of all software project object classes, attributes, relationships, and properties are presented in Appendix A.

Part 2 on models and metrics, contains nine chapters. Chapter 6 describes size metrics, including volume, structure, rework, and reuse. Models that use amount of new code and recycled code to predict equivalent amount of new code are included. Chapter 7 describes effort prediction models that range from models based on a single cost driver to complex composite models based on many cost drivers. Cost dominators are introduced which are project attributes that can have a 10:1 affect on project cost. These dominators often cause projects to fail. Chapter 8 explains how you can estimate development time. Development schedule compression is examined from a team viewpoint and then from the overall project perspective. Chapter 9 shows how to predict productivity based on effort and volume models. Eighteen cost drivers are examined to see their affect on productivity. Efficiency and speedup up prediction models are introduced to show how communications, work breakdown structure, and number of team members affect productivity. In Chapter 10, we examine the many factors that contribute to overall software product quality. We then show that software reliability and usability are the main contributors to overall software product quality. Chapter 11 presents a review of some well-known reliability models, both stochastic and nonstochastic (static) models, to pave the way for the future development and evaluation of highly reliable software and of systems involving software and hardware. Important issues like software life-cycle costs, software safety, and the necessity of documents are also addressed. Chapter 12 explains how to validate that the correct features have been built into a software product and to verify that the design is properly implemented. In this chapter, we cover the software test process, test categorization, test management systems, test tools, defect management, and test process measurement. Chapter 13, on usability, addresses the problem of user frustration because they have difficulty operating software. We first define usability, explain how to design for usability, usability models, and summarize recent studies in usability. Chapter 14 shows how to test for usability. We explain the purpose of testing; we then describe usability test variables, scenarios, and procedures.

Part 3, on visualization tool, contains a single chapter describing the Project Attribute Monitoring and Predicting Associate (PAMPA) tool. The PAMPA tool is being developed to unobtrusively gather metrics from any software development project. The information is preserved as objects with attributes, relationships, and properties. The objects are recognizable and understandable by a typical software developer or manager. PAMPA analyzes the information and presents it in a variety of formats including management reports, 2-dimensional graphs, 3-dimensional graphs, radar graphs, histograms, and Pareto diagrams. Intelligent agents can be developed to monitor projects and alert management of anomalies.

An initial version of the PAMPA tool is included on a compact disk (CD) in the cover of this book. With it, after you transfer your files to your workstation, you can gather project information from any software development project and then save it in an understandable object/attribute format. You can then view the projects using an inexpensive workstation that runs *Microsoft* Windows 95 or NT and Office 97. Included is an Object Editor to view detailed attributes and relationships of project objects. Also, there is a Metric Plot Generator that allows you to view 2-dimensional graphs and bar charts, 3-dimensional charts, and radar charts. Sorting features are available that allows you to create a Pareto chart from bar charts. This simple version of PAMPA gathers information on a software product written in C or C++ program languages. Later versions will gather information for any arbitrary language that is developed in an arbitrary development environment. Also they will gather information from defect manage systems, feature tracking systems, planning systems, suppliers, and customers. A PAMPA Users Manual is included in Appendix B. The manual contains information for installing and configuring PAMPA, a PAMPA tutorial, an Object Editor reference section and a Metric Plot Generator section.

The authors gratefully acknowledge the contributions of numerous individuals whose assistance and support were invaluable to the development of this book and the software that is included with the book. Jamileth Holtfrerich made an indispensable contribution by coordinating tasks and organizing all draft versions of the book. Hewlett Packard (HP) provided financial support to the Software Process Improvement Laboratory at Texas A&M University where the PAMPA tool was developed. Art Lane, the HP representative to the Computer Science Department Development Council Committee, was a key individual in helping to establishing a working relationship between HP and the Software Process Improvement Laboratory at Texas A&M University. We would like to thank the following managers at HP for their support: Von Hansen, Bob Deely, Don Wadley, Gary Johnston, Mark Brown, Ming-Zen Kuo, and Tommy Mouser. There were many students who directly and indirectly worked on the many projects within the Software Process Improvement Laboratory. While we cannot recognize every student, we would like to thank the following students for their contribution to development of the PAMPA tool: David Aldridge, John Burton, Chris Chapman, Travis Chow, Clayton Daigle, Mark Fleming, Mario Garcia, Gunawan, Mark Hashimoto, Jason Jaynes, Doug Keegan, Gunadi Lauw, Jeremy Mayhew, Steve Mazzucco, Ryan Moran, Anh Nguyen, David Quick, Balaji Rathakrishnan, Saravjit Rihal, Michael Schmidlkofer, Jeffery Sharp, Linda Thai, Jason Thompson, Glen Weinecke, and Matthew Wilson.

REFERENCES

[Hsia96] Hsia, P., "Making Software Development Visible," *IEEE Software,* March 1996, pp. 23–25.

[Jones95] Jones, C., "Patterns of large software systems: Failure and success," *IEEE Computer*, March 1995, pp. 86–87.

[Brooks87] Brooks, Jr., F. P., "No silver bullet essence and accidents of software engineering," *IEEE Computer*, April 1987, pp. 10–19.

[Brown96] Brown, N., "Industrial-Strength Management Strategies," *IEEE Software*, July 1996, pp. 94–103.

Part One

SOFTWARE PROCESS VISUALIZATION

1
Introduction

Does software development truly constitute a black art, wherein programs are crafted by artisans with not a little black magic? Or, can software be engineered and truly managed in the same way we manage the construction of lofty bridges over the Chesapeake and Oakland Bays, in the same way we manage the erection of skyscrapers that extend a hundred stories into the sky, in the same way we manage the manufacture of the airplanes, ships, and tanks that have made us a superpower?

The answer is an unqualified "Yes!" Software can *be engineered; software development* can *be managed.*

Lloyd K. Mosemann, II
Deputy Assistant Secretary of the Air Force
[Mosemann94]

INTRODUCTION

We are convinced that the software development process can be continually improved by all organizations that develop software. We will describe examples that show organizations that have realized annual

- defect reduction of up to 32%,
- cost reduction of up to 8.4%,
- productivity gains of up to 32%, and
- customer satisfaction improvement of up to 7.8%.

To improve a process, you must be able to visualize the attributes of all activities, inputs, and outputs. In initiating a process improvement activity, you should select the correct practices to predict software process attributes during planning stages and to gather, save, track and trace attribute values during other stages. When you measure process attributes, these attributes are often called metrics. In this book, we will explain how you can cost effectively accomplish software process visualization by transforming process attributes into tables, two-dimensional graphs, three-dimensional graphs, radar diagrams, and other forms of information presentation that can be used to control projects and improve processes.

To introduce software process improvement, we will first review the evolution of hardware and software cost trade-offs and technology advancements. We will then discuss examples of organizations that have successful software process improvement activities and have developed successful products. We next will examine a number of notable recent software project failures. We will then provide suggestions on the best practices that have been used by successful software organizations. At the end of this chapter, we will discuss how to use this book.

HARDWARE/SOFTWARE EVOLUTION

From the beginning of the computer era, cost has been of concern to everyone. Close to 100% of the cost of the vacuum tube ENIAC computer built by the University of Pennsylvania during the 1940s was hardware, as shown in Figure 1.1. Computer projects were sponsored by the government. Software for these computers was an afterthought. Delay lines and storage tubes were used for memory. They were programmed directly in machine language using wired plug boards, paper cards, and punched paper tape. These machines had very small memories and were unreliable by today's standards.

In Figure 1.1 we show how the circuitry, memory, and architecture of computer hardware and the languages, operating systems, communications, and databases of computer software have evolved over time. By the late 1960s, the hardware/software percentages of computer system costs were approaching 50:50 [Boehm87]. Many of the software projects were over budget, and the resulting software products were delivered behind schedule to dissatisfied customers.

Many people felt that proper engineering methodology was not being used by software project staff. They felt sound engineering principles and practices applied to complex hardware systems were equally applicable to software projects. The North Atlantic Treaty Organization (NATO) Science Committee held conferences on software engineering concepts and techniques in Garmisch, Germany, in 1968 and in Rome, Italy, in 1969. The conferences were held to shed light on the problems in software engineering and to discuss possible techniques, methods, and developments that might lead to their solution. Since that time a considerable amount of effort has been expended in trying to solve software engineering problems.

Processor hardware size in transistor count has continued to grow. In the early 1970s, the microprocessor arrived on the computer scene. Intel manufactured a 4-bit microprocessor as a single integrated circuit, as shown in Figure 1.2. The semiconduc-

Milestone Events

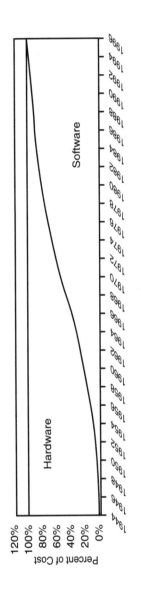

	ENIAC computer	Commercial tube computer	Minicomputer	Microcomputer	Personal computer	High-performance workstation
Hardware						
Circiut	Vacuum tube	Transistor	IC MSI	LSI		VLSI
Memory	Delay line Storage tube	Magnetic core Magnetic Tape Magnetic Disk	Virtual Cache Removable Disk		Floppy Disk	Optical Disk
Architecture	Wired program Card program Stored program SISD, MISD streams	I/O Channel (4 M bytes/sec) Micro Programs SIMD streams	Family with byte, half-word, word, double-word members	CISC RISC		Fiber Channel (20 M byte/sec, 1 kilometer) MIMD streams
Software						
Language	Machine Macro assembler	Assembler Interpreter Simulator Compiler Application Generator	Vendor Independent	Object oriented Spread Sheets	Query Framework Graphic icons	Middleware
Operating System		Control Monitor Multi	Timesharing Virtual Portable environment Personal I/O Spooling		Windows Client/server	
Communications		Asynchronous Synchronous	Bisynchronous Packet networks Communications controller LAN		Distributed systems	World-Wide Web Intelligent software agents
Database	Direct Access	Sequential	Indexed Sequential Relational Database management Distributed		Knowledge base	Object oriented Very large heterogeneous
Software Engineering		Waterfall Model Top Down Constr. Reuse Chief Programmer Teams Tool Environments Productivity, Schedule, Reliability, & Usability Models and Metrics Libraries Quality Assessment & Evaluation			Metric-based management Process Improvement Intelligent Associates	

NATO Software Engineering Conference

Software systems wre often delivered over budget, behind schedule to dissatisfied customers.

Figure 1.1   Hardware/Software Evolution

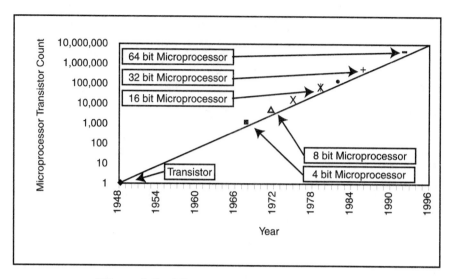

Figure 1.2   Microprocessor Size in Transistor Count

tor manufacturers have continued to produce higher and higher density of transistors as part of a single microprocessor until we have data paths of 32 bits as part of the CISC architecture. By producing reduced instruction set computers (RISC), manufacturers have built faster and simpler microprocessors with 64-bit internal architecture. As the density of transistors in a microprocessor increased, processor cost has fallen. System architectures have expanded to process multiple instruction streams and multiple data streams (MIMD). For large computer systems, channels have increased in speed from the 4 megabytes per second per channel, which could only be used over short distances, to 20 megabytes per second, which can connect over a kilometer away to mainframes. Computer professionals began to use workstations directly on their desks. Small personal computers (PCs) have become pervasive and soon will be located in as many homes as telephones or television sets. The PCs and professional workstations talk directly to each other over local area networks (LANs) or to computers distributed at a distance using the standard telephone networks.

Software tools have become commonplace. Applications generators have been built to easily create high-level language programs for specific application domains. Many high-level languages have become independent of the vendor that produced the language compilers. Spread-sheet and database query tools are available for noncomputer professionals to directly implement simpler applications. Software reuse continues to be a major goal of software developers, and object-oriented, framework, middleware, and graphic languages have been produced to aid in reuse. Portable operating systems such as UNIX have helped to free software from dependence on a specific machine architecture. Distributed software systems are being created with intelligent software agents that can travel among the clients and servers interconnected by communication networks.

Software applications have continued to grow in size, functionality, and complexity. The original computer users were professional scientists and engineers. When computers were first used commercially, technicians and office workers were trained to operate and use information-processing applications. As the cost of computers continued to drop, more and more people began to use computers until, today, the software must be usable by everyone. Today, software is expected to be reliable. The software application is expected to be defect free and easy to use. Software applications are expected to operate in distributed environments where computer servers communicate with each other, as well as interacting with clients that require their services. By 1985 the cost of a typical computer project was 15% hardware and 85% software [Boehm87]. The relative cost of software with respect to hardware has continued to increase.

We must find ways to improve the productivity of software development while at the same time improving the reliability and usability of software systems. Since the early 1970s when major emphasis was placed on engineering software, a great deal has been learned about how to improve software development. Figure 1.1 lists many of software engineering advancements that have been applied over the past 30 years. We are now at the point where computers are available worldwide. All companies spend a considerable amount on software. Software developers must continue to improve the software development process or they will be forced out of business by competition. We are optimistic that the typical company can realize major gains in software productivity, reliability, and usability by applying continuous process improvement methodology to their software development process. We will now look at some companies that have successfully improved their software development process.

SUCCESSES

Some organizations are very successful in developing large, complex software systems and in improving software development processes. We will now cite examples of software process improvement initiatives by NASA/Goddard; University of Maryland; Computer Sciences Corporation; Toshiba; AT&T Bell Laboratories; Raytheon; IBM Santa Teresa Laboratory; Bull; AT&T Network Systems; Digital Equipment Corporation; Microsoft; and Boeing.

NASA/University of Maryland/CSC

In 1976, the Software Engineering Laboratory (SEL) was established as a cooperative effort among NASA/Goddard, University of Maryland, and Computer Sciences Corporation (CSC) with the goal of improving (1) quality by reducing defect rate,

(2) productivity by reducing costs, and (3) schedules by reducing the average time to produce mission support software [Basili95]. They conducted experiments on about 125 NASA projects by applying, measuring, and analyzing software process changes. As a result, SEL has adopted and tailored processes to significantly improve software production. The result of their effort has been a 75% reduction in defects, 59% reduction in costs, and a 25% reduction in cycle time.

Toshiba

The Japanese began to introduce software factories during the late 1970s [Matsumoto89]. They defined a software factory as an environment that allows software manufacturing organizations to design, program, test, ship, install, and maintain commercial software products in a unified manner. As an integral part of their factories, they would continually measure, analyze results, implement improvements, and then continue the improvement cycle. In the Toshiba Fuchu Software Factory, they measured productivity every 6 months. They achieved an average yearly productivity improvement of between 8% and 9%. At this rate, their productivity would double every 9 years.

AT&T Bell Laboratories

In 1986, AT&T Bell Laboratories established a software process improvement program with the goal of tripling software productivity within 3 years [Factor88]. They expected that productivity increases would be accompanied by an increase in quality. Many of the productivity increases would result from reductions in complexity in all stages of the development process. The reduction in process complexity would also improve quality. They also believed that improvements in quality would increase productivity, which would result directly from reduced rework. They hypothesized that their near-term gains would result from product administration and configuration management, software reuse, languages, and improved project management. Two years after the start of the initiative they had almost tripled productivity from 1984 [Belanger90].

Raytheon

In 1988, Raytheon Equipment Division started a process improvement initiative that has improved its bottom line, increased productivity, and changed the corporate culture. Much of the improvement resulted from reducing rework [Dion93]. Between 1988 and 1993, the improvement initiative resulted in a $7.70 return on every dollar invested, a twofold increase in productivity, a fourfold reduction in rework costs, and an overall improvement in the predictability of the software development process.

IBM

In 1989, IBM began a process improvement initiative at their Santa Teresa Laboratory, the largest software development site in the world [Kaplan95]. In fact, in 1989 the Santa Teresa Laboratory produced more revenue than all but one independent software company. Their products already had fewer defects than the industry average. After implementing process improvements, their average number of defects dropped 46%, service costs dropped 20%, revenue per employee rose 58%, and customer satisfaction increased 14%.

Bull

In 1989, Bull's Enterprise Servers Operation in Phoenix, Arizona, used a software process that was unpredictable in terms of product quality and delivery schedule [Weller94]. Over a 5-year period, they developed a process that is repeatable and manageable and that delivers higher-quality products at lower costs.

AT&T Network Systems

In August 1990, the AT&T Network Systems Silver Bullet Project was initiated to optimize and accelerate the software development process by incrementally improving business, organizational, and technical processes [Deutschen96]. As a result of their process improvement effort, they kept costs one-third lower than the rest of the business unit, developed more than 14 products, reduced the average product interval from 25 to 15 weeks; they have been evaluated as one of the top three software organizations in AT&T. They concluded that gains in accelerating software development can be achieved incrementally on many fronts. A key to the process improvement was submitting to the discipline of meticulously measuring and explicitly defining the layout and execution of each step in a development project.

DEC

In 1992, Digital Equipment Corporation (DEC) completed the Alpha AXP program where they delivered their product on schedule with high quality [Conklin96]. The Alpha AXP program was the most complex program that DEC has ever attempted. The project management developed an Enrollment Management Model that is similar to the continuous process improvement cycle. The cyclic stages of the model are (1) vision enrollment based on business goals and project objectives, (2) commitment delegation based on trust and accountability, (3) inspection support based on review and encouragement, and (4) inspection support based on what was learned and how they could do better. The project team learned as the project progressed and identified areas needing strengthening for future programs.

Microsoft

The Languages Group is the oldest group at Microsoft. By 1992 the original languages business was dwarfed as the company moved into operating systems and applications. At that time there were numerous complaints about the products from the Languages Group and the Group's inability to ship a product on time [McCarthy95]. From 1992 on, the upper management mostly pursued a policy of empowerment and accountability, which led to a turnaround of the fortunes of the Languages Group. Their process improvement efforts resulted in the Microsoft Visual C++ product, which has become a market leader. In 1995, Jim McCarthy, one of the senior managers over the Visual C++ project, wrote a book describing 54 rules for delivering great software on time [McCarthy95]. We apply many of his rules to the natural milestone software life cycle that we describe in detail in Chapter 4.

Boeing

The recent success of the Boeing 777 aircraft was the result of a large complex software development project [Gillette96]. The Boeing project used 30 different suppliers, expended 9 million person hours, coded 2.5 million lines of new software, reused 1.6 million lines of commercial off-the-shelf (COTS) software, and delivered on schedule with 95% of the initially promised functionality. Five percent of nonessential functionality was deferred at initial delivery. The first flight of the Boeing 777 aircraft was on schedule in June 1994, and the aircraft was certified for passenger flights in June 1995. The project required biweekly reports on software planning, coding, and test planning and passage. The metric related to software test completion correlated best with successful code delivery. Metrics were gathered and analyzed by the 70 people required to monitor the project. Progress monitoring and reporting were also shared by hundreds of software engineers drawn from both Boeing and the suppliers.

In summary, there are many examples where process improvement methodology has been applied to improve productivity, quality and usability. In the above examples, we saw defect reduction that ranged from 7.2% to 32%, annual cost reduction that ranged from 5% to 8.4%, annual productivity gains between 8.5% to 32%, and an annual customer satisfaction increase of 7.8%. We also reviewed the very successful Boeing 777 airplane project, which was delivered on time with all essential functionality. We thus know continuous improvement can be applied to the software development process. But there are still many projects that are delivered over budget, behind schedule, to dissatisfied customers. We will now examine some recent failed projects.

FAILURES

In 1995, Capers Jones stated that the failure or cancellation rate of large software systems was over 20% [Jones95]. Of the 80% that are completed, approximately two-thirds are late and experience cost overruns as much as 100%. Roughly two-thirds are also plagued by low reliability and quality problems in the first year of development.

While some organizations have instigated successful software process improvement programs, most have not. Norm Brown, executive director of the Department of Defense (DoD) Software Acquisition Best Practices Initiative, claims that organizational improvement has been occurring at a glacial rate [Brown96]. The DoD Software Engineering Institute (SEI) has developed a five-level software capabilities maturity scale (see Chapter 2 for more detail on the SEI capabilities maturity model). Brown says that, according to the SEI, of 379 organizations at 99 companies that have process improvement programs in place and have conducted SEI maturity assessments, 73% do not rate higher than level 1. Thus, one should not be surprised that many projects fail. We will now look at recent projects that were unsuccessful.

Ashton–Tate

A 1990 *Wall Street Journal* article reported how Ashton–Tate lost its leadership in the PC software arena [Zachry90]. Edward Esber, CEO of Ashton–Tate Corporation, makers of dBASE IV, said in 1986 that delays in completing the program had been helpful because they gave the programmers time to ensure that it would meet "quality standards" and would be "everything we'd said it would be." The product was marred by thousands of errors that Ashton–Tate's management did not know existed. Within weeks, irate customers complained that dBASE lacked important features, was too slow, and frequently crashed. To quiet critics, Esber promised a corrected version within 18 months. When it did not appear, he stopped trying to predict when it would appear. At the time the article was written in 1990, Ashton–Tate IV still had not shipped the corrected dBASE version.

American Airlines

In 1992, American Airlines fell on its sword trying to develop a state-of-the-art, industry-wide airline reservation system that could also handle car and hotel reservations [*San Jose Mercury News*92]. It stopped development of its new Confirm reservations system shortly after it was supposed to take care of transactions for partners Budget Rent-A-Car, Hilton Hotels Corporation and Marriott Corporation. This cancellation of the 4-year-old project resulted in a $165 million pretax charge against earnings. The main pieces of the massive project had been developed separately by different methods. When put together, they did not work with each other. AMR, the parent company of American Airlines, fired eight senior project members, including team leader John Mott, saying it had "determined that information about the true status of the project appears to have been suppressed by certain management personnel."

Denver Airport

In 1995, the Denver Airport was delayed because of the software that controls the automatic baggage system [Bernstein95]. The delay caused by the software cost Denver $1.1 million a day in interest and operating costs.

Toronto Stock Exchange

In July of 1996, the Toronto Stock Exchange canceled their project to create an all-electronic trading floor [Hayes96]. Some brokers who deal with the exchange said, "It was a $35 million fiasco." The reported reason for the failure were internal and technical problems. Those problems included an overly ambitious schedule, glitches in the proposed UNIX-based client/server technology, and difficulties matching the exchange's internal messaging format with those of trading firms.

America On Line

During August 1996 the America On Line computer network service was unusable for 19 hours due to a software problem.

FAA

One of the biggest software failures is a software project to replace a system that must not fail. The U.S. Federal Aviation Administration (FAA) Advanced Automation System (AAS) project [Charette96] is supposed to replace the current air traffic control system, which is an overtaxed and breakdown-beset 1960s era system. We only hope that the new system is ready before the old out-of-date system causes a catastrophic accident. The Initial Sector Suite System (ISSS) part of the proposed replacement system was initially defined in 1981. The AAS project started in 1984. In 1990, the FAA granted an AAS contract for $4.3 billion. In 1992, the Government Accounting Office stated that continuing delays in the deployment of ISSS, a key component of the AAS, could "have the potential for affecting FAA's ability to handle safely the predicted increases in traffic into the next century." Toward the end of 1992, the FAA blamed a 19-month delay on underestimating the development and testing time for the ISSS software, as well as on unresolved differences in the system specifications caused by changes to the requirements. An additional 14-month delay announced in 1993 was blamed on ISSS-related software problems. By April 1994, another 31-month schedule slip was anticipated with the cost of AAS completion estimated to be $7 billion. The FAA declared the AAS project "out of control" and effectively suspended the AAS program. In 1996 the FAA announced a reduced-functionality AAS program called the Display System Replacement (DSR) project, which is proposed to be operational in 1998. If the DSR program meets its current schedule, the replacement air traffic control system will be 6 years late and will cost an estimated $5.6 billion. The system will be delivered 17 years after originally defined and 14 years after the project started.

IRS

The Internal Revenue Service (IRS) may have caused the most expensive systems development fiasco in history. A *Computerworld* investigation found that delays in overhauling the federal tax systems are costing the U.S. Treasury as much as $50 billion per year [Anthes96]. Representative Jim Lightfoot recently said, "The IRS has spent $4 billion on TSM (Tax Systems Modernization) and has nothing to show for it." The *Computerworld* investigation reported that the IRS has done the following:

- Failed to do much needed business process redesign before it began its systems development.
- Neglected to develop an overall systems architecture or development blueprint.
- Employed primitive and at times chaotic software development methodologies.
- Failed to manage information systems as investments.
- Neglected information security.

In December 1995, the National Research Council found "serious deficiencies" in the IRS technical management, systems architecture, process improvement, and systems security. A later GAO report stated that the IRS has "provided little tangible evidence that actions being taken will correct the pervasive management and technical weakness that place TSM, and the huge investment it represents, at risk."

In summary, most of the above projects failed either directly or indirectly from management problems. Management was not able to visualize the software systems that were being developed. They did not know the status of the systems until it was too late. The above projects failed because of breakdowns in their software development process. Many other smaller projects fail and never make the newspapers.

We believe that software project failures can be prevented through the use of superior practices that have been proved effective by successful organizations. In the next section, we will focus on practices that will help you to visualize the software development process.

PROCESS IMPROVEMENT PRACTICES _____

We can learn from both the successful projects and the unsuccessful projects. Successful projects indicate practices that we should adopt, and unsuccessful projects help us to learn of practices that we should avoid. A number of groups have developed lists of best practices from studying successful software projects. Jones lists 10 project technologies that have been deployed by unsuccessful projects and 10 that have been deployed by successful projects [Jones95].

The 10 technologies associated with successful software projects are the following:

1. Accurate software measurement
2. Early use of estimating tools
3. Continuous use of planning tools
4. Formal progress reporting
5. Formal design reviews
6. Formal code inspections
7. Specialists used for critical tasks
8. Automated design and specifications
9. Automated configuration control
10. User requirements creep <15%

Brown describes the following nine *principal best practices* that create a framework for managing the acquisition of large-scale software development and maintenance programs that are an essential part of increasingly complex DoD weapons systems [Brown96].

Practice 1.	Formal risk management
Practice 2.	Agreement on interfaces
Practice 3.	Formal inspections
Practice 4.	Metric-based scheduling and management
Practice 5.	Binary quality gates at the inch-pebble level (this is interpreted to mean that the detailed activity network requires that each task be no more than 5% of the duration and effort of the release and be performed at least 95% of the time by a single, lowest-level organization)
Practice 6.	Program-wide visibility of progress versus plan
Practice 7.	Defect tracking against quality targets

Practice 8.   Configuration management

Practice 9.   People-aware management accountability

The above project technologies deployed in successful software projects and the principal best practices contain planning based on accurate measurements to improve project visibility. We take the approach to successful software product development that software visualization is a major problem and that tools and practices to improve visualization are necessary for software process improvement. In the next section, we will describe how you can use this book to help you to improve the software development process.

HOW TO USE THIS BOOK

This book has been written for practicing software developers, team leaders, project managers, top administrators, and others interested in software process improvement. Also, it can serve as a reference text for advanced undergraduate or graduate classes in software engineering and as the main text for a course in software metrics, models, and process improvement.

The book is composed of 16 chapters partitioned into three parts, which should be read in the order described in Figure 1.3.

Part 1 explains the software life cycle process and describes an object-oriented representation of the software project. Part 1 is composed of Chapters 1 through 5.

Chapter 1   *Introduction* shows how both computer hardware and software have evolved since the early 1950s. Software has become the high-cost item for most computer projects. We explain how management has difficulty visualizing software during development and maintenance. Examples are presented in which industry has learned how to improve the software development process by applying software improvement methodology. In contrast to successful projects, several software project examples are described that show major software projects that have failed. Best practices for visualizing projects are shown.

Chapter 2   *Quality Systems Criteria and Standards* examines the criteria and standards for quality systems. Chapter 2 can be skipped by readers already familiar with quality criteria and standards. We start out by reviewing Deming's 14 points. Then we present the Software Engineering Institute's capabilities maturity model for assessment and evaluation, the Malcolm Baldrige

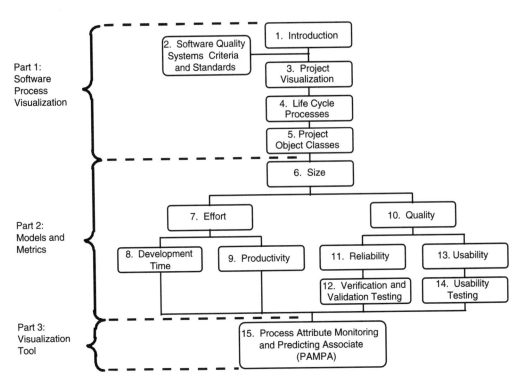

Figure 1.3   Book Organization

National Quality Award criteria, the ISO 9000 standards for quality systems, and the IBM Santa Teresa Laboratory methodologies for software quality improvement.

Chapter 3 *Project Visualization* introduces a set of project object classes for describing an arbitrary software development project. A view of the project world is introduced that uses objects, relationships, attributes, and properties. The objects are defined to be easily understandable by both managers and software developers. Once the object world is presented, the project personnel can use it to view the effect of changes in resources, schedules, or software product features from historical, status, compliance to plans, and prediction perspectives. We also introduce a dual project control/process improvement cycle in which common visualization stages help you to efficiently and objectively gather object attributes for analysis and prediction.

Chapter 4   *Life Cycle Processes* shows how all software products have a beginning (project initiation) and an end (project termination). The evolution of a software product between the beginning and end of a process is called the software life cycle (SLC). For a specific software project, the SLC is a sequenced map of activities (or tasks). From the very beginning, the SLC of large software development projects has been tracked as sequential phases. In this chapter we partition the evolution of the SLC into three time periods: Early SLC, Black Box SLC, and Process SLC. For the Early SLC period, we look at a number of straightforward types of SLC models. We start with simple SLCs for small projects and proceed to SLCs for large, complex software products. For the Black Box SLC period, we examine Waterfall, V, Prototype, and Incremental SLCs. For the Process SLC period, we examine Spiral and the Natural Milestone SLCs. We also contrast the differences between industrial and government software projects.

Chapter 5   *Project Object Classes* explains a notation that will be used to portray the relationships between object classes. Then we describe the object classes that can be used to portray a software project. You can use the objects to see exactly what is happening in a software development project. All activities of SLC processes can be made visible to you. After we describe the object classes, we give a few examples of the object attributes. Detailed descriptions of all software project object classes, attributes, relationships, and properties are presented in Appendix A.

Part 2 explains software metric prediction models and the testing methodology used to gather test data. Readers who are only interested in software models and metrics can read this part of the book independently of the other two parts. Also, the chapters on development time, productivity, reliability and usability can be read independently of each other. Part 2 is composed of Chapters 6 through 14.

Chapter 6   *Size* shows how size metrics are used to describe physical magnitude, extent, or bulk. A size metric can represent relative or proportionate dimensions. We classify software size metrics as volume, structure, and rework. You can use volume metrics to predict the amount of effort required to produce a system, defects remaining in a system, and the time required to create a system. Structure metrics indicate software complexity. Complex software is harder to understand and create than simple software. Examples of structure metrics are the number of unconditional branches, depth of control loop nesting, and module fan-in and/or fan-out. Rework metrics describe the size of adds, deletes, and changes that are made to a system between versions. When rework metrics are combined, they measure the amount of turmoil in a file.

Chapter 7   *Effort* describes effort prediction models and what causes effort to vary. These models range from simple effort prediction models based on a single cost driver to complex composite models based on many cost drivers.

Chapter 8   *Development Time* takes a brief look at how development time is estimated under the software science model. Next we examine development schedule prediction using well-known, empirically developed models. The relationships among product size, effort, time, and staff required to produce a product are explored. Development schedule compression is examined from a team viewpoint and then from the overall project perspective.

Chapter 9   *Productivity* shows how to improve the process by which we create a software product. Projects overrun budgets because productivity is inaccurately estimated for a specific project. In this chapter we will define productivity. We will then show how to estimate productivity based on volume and effort models. Then we will explore how cost driver attributes affect productivity and how each of the cost drivers can contribute to a budget overrun.

Chapter 10   *Quality* discusses quality from an global point of view. We examine the many factors that contribute to overall software product quality. We then show that software reliability and usability are the main contributors to overall software product quality.

Chapter 11   *Reliability* presents a review of some well-known reliability models, both stochastic and nonstochastic (static), to pave the way for the future development and evaluation of highly reliable software and of systems involving software and hardware. Important issues like software life cycle costs, software safety, and the necessity of documents are also addressed.

Chapter 12   *Verification and Validation Testing* explains how to validate that the correct features have been built into a software product and to verify that the design is properly implemented. In this chapter we cover the software test process, test categorization, test management systems, test tools, defect management, intelligent test advisors, and test process measurement.

Chapter 13   *Usability* addresses the problem of user frustration when they have difficulty operating software. We first define usability, explain how to design for usability, describe usability models, and summarize recent studies in usability.

Chapter 14   *Usability Testing* shows how to test for usability. We explain the purpose of testing and then describe usability test variables, scenarios, and procedures.

Part 3 describes the PAMPA computer tool that can be used to gather metrics and visualize a software project. A version of the tool that operates under Microsoft Windows 95 is included in the back of the book. Part 3 consists of Chapter 15.

Chapter 15   *Project Attribute Monitoring and Prediction Associate (PAMPA)* describes the computer tool that we have developed to unobtrusively gather, preserve, analyze, and portray a software project. We explain how the tool can be used to provide many views of a software project and how the conformance to plans can be tracked. We explain how PAMPA can define intelligent agents for tracking progress and alerting managers to anomalies that occur. We also show how PAMPA can provide multiple views of a software product that supports software process improvement. A CD containing a version of the PAMPA tool is included in the back of the book.

REFERENCES

[Anthes96]   Anthes, G. H., "IRS Project Failures Cost Taxpayers $50B Annually," *Computerworld*, Vol. 30, No. 42, October 14, 1996, pp. 1, 28–29.

[Basili95]   Basili, V., Zelkowitz, M., McGarry, F., Page, J., Waligora, S., and Pajerski, "SEL's Software Process-Improvement Program," *IEEE Software*, November 1995, pp. 83–87.

[Belanger90]   Belanger, D. G., Chappell, S. G., and Wish, M., "Evolution of Software Development Environments," *AT&T Technical Journal*, March/April 1990, pp. 2–6.

[Bernstein95]   Bernstein, L., "Software in the Large," *AT&T Technical Journal*, January/February 1996, pp. 5–14.

[Boehm87]   Boehm, B. W., "Industrial Software Metrics Top 10 List," *IEEE Software*, September 1987, pp. 84–85.

[Brown96]   Brown, N., "Industrial-Strength Management Strategies," *IEEE Software*, July 1996, pp. 94–103.

[Charette96]   Charette, R. N., "Large-Scale Project Management Is Risk Management," *IEEE Software*, July 1996, pp. 110–117.

[Conklin96]   Conklin, P. F., "Enrollment Management: Managing the Alpha AXP Program," *Digital Technical Journal*, Vol. 4, No. 4, 1992, pp. 193–205.

[Deutschen96]   Deutschen, N. R., Bowers, E. J., and Lankford, J. W., "ASCC: The Impact of a Silver Bullet," *AT&T Technical Journal*, January/February 1996, pp. 24–34.

[Dion93]   Dion, R., "Process Improvement and the Corporate Balance Sheet," *IEEE Software,* July 1993, pp. 28–35.

[Factor88]   Factor, R. M., and Smith, W. B., "A Discipline for Improving Software Productivity," *AT&T Technical Journal*, July/August 1988, pp. 2–9.

[Gillette96]   Gillette, W., "Managing Megaprojects: A Focused Approach," *IEEE Software*, July 1996, pp. 28–30.

[Hayes96]   Hayes, F., "Toronto Stock Exchange: Going, Going, Gone," *Computerworld*, July 22, 1996, pp. 1, 16.

[Jones95]   Jones, C., "Patterns of Large Software Systems: Failure and Success," *IEEE Computer*, March 1995, pp. 86–87.

[Kaplan95]   Kaplan, C., Clark, R., and Tang, V., *Secrets of Software Quality*, McGraw-Hill, Inc., New York, 1995, 383 p.

[Matsumoto89]   Matsumoto, Y., "An Overview of Japanese Software Factories," Japanese Perspectives in Software Engineering. Addison–Wesley Publishing Company, Reading, MA, 1989, pp. 303–320.

[McCarthy95]   McCarthy, J., *Dynamics of Software Development*, Microsoft Press, Redmond, WA, 1995.

[Mosemann94]   Mosemann, II, L. K., "Let's Write *Finis* to the Black Hole Syndrome," *CrossTalk: The Journal of Defense Software Engineering,* published by the Software Technology Support Center, Vol. 7, No. 10, October 1994, p. 2.

[*San Jose Mercury News*92]   "Software Nightmare Comes Alive for Airline—American Finds the Pieces of New Reservation System Do Not Fit Together," *San Jose Mercury News*, Monday, July 20, 1992, p. 9F.

[Weller94]   Weller, E. F., "Using Metrics to Manage Software Projects," *IEEE Computer*, September 1994, pp. 27–33.

[Zachry90]   Zachry, G. P. "How Ashton–Tate Lost Its Leadership in PC Software Arena," *Wall Street Journal*, April 11, 1990, pp. A1, A4.

2
Quality Systems Criteria and Standards

As with any parable, there is a moral. The parable of the beads has several:

- *Variation is part of any process.*
- *Planning requires prediction of how things and people will perform. Tests and experiments of past performance can be useful, but not definitive.*
- *Workers work within a system that—try as they might—is beyond their control. It is the system, not their individual skills, that determines how they perform.*
- *Only management can change the system.*
- *Some workers will always be above average, some below.*

W. Edwards Deming
[Walton86]

INTRODUCTION

Until after World War II, people conducted quality inspections at the end of an assembly line after manufacturing a product. When defective products were found, they were either discarded or reworked. Deming introduced continuous quality improvement methodology to the Japanese after the war and to U.S. companies during the early 1980s. In 1951, to honor Deming, the Japanese established a Deming Prize for accomplishments in statistical theory. In 1987 the United States established a similar award called the Malcolm Baldrige National Quality Award. Continuous quality improvement methodology has proved effective in improving quality and productivity for both manufacturing and service organizations. During the late 1980s, the U.S. government and industries began to apply continuous quality system improvement methodology to software development.

The U.S. Department of Defense has established a capabilities maturity model (CMM) to assess and evaluate their software contractors. The International Standards Organization has established the ISO 9000 series of quality systems standards, which is being applied to software development. IBM Santa Teresa Laboratory has combined the Baldrige award criteria and the ISO 9000 standard requirements to develop a very effective software quality improvement program.

In this chapter we examine the criteria and standards for quality systems. We describe the Deming management method, the Software Engineering Institute's capabilities maturity model for assessment and evaluation, and the Malcolm Baldrige National Quality Award criteria. Then we will discuss standards in general and the ISO 9000 standards for quality systems in particular. Finally, we will show how IBM Santa Teresa Laboratory used the above methodologies in their software quality improvement program. We will find that the criteria and standards will tell us *what* must be done, but they do not tell us *how* to implement the criteria and standards. In succeeding chapters, we will look at how software metrics can be gathered and used to visualize software status and predict effort, schedules, productivity, reliability, and usability. By improving the visibility of software, the software professional can do a better job of controlling a software development project and improving software life cycle processes.

DEMING METHODOLOGY

Since the beginning of the industrial revolution during the late nineteenth century, industry has been very concerned with both productivity and quality improvement. Productivity is the amount of product produced for resource used. When software productivity is measured, the product source lines of code is produced by the resource people. Thus, a popular measure of software productivity is the number of source lines of code per person-month. Industry measures quality as the number of defects in products that are produced. In the software field, quality is often measured as defects per thousand source lines of code. In the past, quality was measured at the end of a production process. Statistical methods were used to determine if a product met the desired level of quality, and products that failed to meet quality standards were usually rejected and reworked before they were accepted. In the field of software production, a software product was tested until management felt the product was ready for release. In the case of a software product, management frequently is not able to visualize the status of the product.

Modern manufacturing process improvement began after World War II with W. Edwards Deming's work with the Japanese in about 1950. He was born in the United States in 1900 and had worked his entire career as a statistician. In 1947, Deming was recruited by the Supreme Command for the Allied Powers (SCAP) to help prepare for the 1951 Japanese census. During this early visit, he befriended many Japanese and met many Japanese statisticians. A number of them were members of a group called the Union of Japanese Scientists and Engineers (JUSE) that had been organized to aid the reconstruction of Japan. In March 1950, the JUSE managing director wrote Deming, asking him to deliver a lecture course to Japanese research workers, plant managers, and engineers on quality control methods. He accepted their invitation and gave a dozen lectures throughout Japan. The success of his lectures resulted in a meeting between him and an association of Japan's chief executives from their top companies.

He made many points with the chief executives that would later be included in what has become known as his 14 points. He convinced the executives that they could produce quality. He encouraged them to perform customer research that emphasized looking toward the future and to produce goods that would have a market years from then, which would allow them to stay in business. He told them not to put up with poor quality in incoming materials. He emphasized that the customer was the most important part of any production line. Since in the past they had sold their products to a captive market, this concept was new to them.

In 1951 the Japanese established the Deming Prize to be given in two major categories: to an individual for accomplishments in statistical theory and to companies for accomplishments in statistical application. The award was established with proceeds from Deming's published lectures. He donated the proceeds to the prize. Since 1951 the Deming Prize has been awarded annually and has become a prestigious, sought after award; the presentation ceremony is nationally televised in Japan.

Deming made many more trips to Japan, and JUSE initiated training courses for tens of thousand of Japanese engineers within the next 10 years. Improvement in quality control has become pervasive throughout Japan. The Japanese found increased productivity followed the improved quality. The improved quality with lower rework costs resulted in Japan dominating the world markets for radios and parts, transistors, cameras, binoculars, and sewing machines. By the early 1980s, Japan had begun to gain market share in the automobile industry.

The Deming management method was discovered in the United States as a result of an NBC television documentary titled "If Japan Can . . . Why Can't We?", which was broadcast on June 24, 1980. His telephone literally began to ring off the wall with calls from people who wanted to know more about his methodology and how to apply it to their companies here in the United States. He began presenting 4-day seminars at companies throughout the United States. The companies ranged from the small companies to the largest corporations, which included AT&T and Ford Motor Company.

Deming's 4-day seminars, which explained his management method, emphasized the following 14 points [Walton86]:

1. *Create constancy of purpose for improvement of product and service.* Deming suggested that the role of a company should be to stay in business and provide jobs through innovation, research, constant improvement, and maintenance.

2. *Adopt the new philosophy.* Deming felt that poor workmanship and sullen service should not be tolerated. A new philosophy should be adopted where mistakes and negativism are unacceptable.

3. *Cease dependence on mass inspection.* Deming said that American firms typically inspect a product as it comes off the line or at major stages. The defective products found are very expensive because they must be either thrown away or reworked; both result in lost productivity. He felt that quality comes from process improvement, not inspection, and that workers could be enlisted in this improvement.

4. *End the practice of awarding business on price tag alone.* Purchasing supplies from the lowest bidder often results in supplies of inferior quality. A quality supplier should be selected in a long-term relationship to supply each item.

5. *Improve constantly and forever the system of production and service.* Management is obligated to continually look for ways to reduce waste and improve quality.

6. *Institute training.* Often, workers learn their jobs from other workers who were never trained properly.

7. *Institute leadership.* Leading consists of helping people to do a better job and of learning by objective methods who is in need of individual help. Objective meaningful measurements should be gathered as a basis for process improvement.

8. *Drive out fear.* Fear may result in employees not asking questions or taking positions even when they do not understand their job or what is right or wrong. Deming felt that the economic loss from fear is appalling.

9. *Break down barriers between staff areas.* Teamwork should be encouraged, and barriers that cause conflict and unnecessary competition should be eliminated.

10. *Eliminate slogans, exhortations, and targets for the work force.* Deming felt that people should be allowed to put up their own slogans.

11. *Eliminate numerical quotas.* To hold a job, a person will try to meet a quota at any cost without regard to the negative effect on a company.

12. *Remove barriers to pride of workmanship.* Deming felt that people are eager to do a good job and are distressed when they cannot. Barriers such as misguided supervisors, faulty equipment, and defective materials should be removed.

13. *Institute a vigorous program of education and retraining.* Management and workers must be educated in teamwork, statistical methods, and the like.

14. *Take action to accomplish the transformation.* A top management team with a plan of action is necessary to carry out the quality mission. Neither workers nor managers can do it on their own.

Many top American corporations have applied Deming methodologies to successfully create high-quality products at lower costs. For example, at the request of Ford Motor Company President Donald Petersen, Deming came to Ford in the spring of 1981 to meet with Petersen and other high-ranking officials. He was hired as a consultant to Ford and helped them to develop a new mission, values, and guiding principles statement (see [Walton86]). At a time when Ford was losing money, they committed to the new quality program, which resulted in development of the Ford Taurus automobile for $400 million less that the original $3.25 billion budget. In the mid-1980s, the Taurus became a big seller for Ford and is still one of the most successful automobiles in the world.

There is wide agreement that Deming methodology can be applied to improve a manufacturing process like the one that produced the Taurus. Manufacturing processes require large investments in capital equipment, but the labor costs can be relatively low. Industries like the software industry require large staff costs to develop software. Can the Deming methodology be applied to the life cycle process when the main cost is personnel? To answer this question, we will examine a case study of the Ford Motor Company service organization in Windsor, Canada. A software product development organization has many of the characteristics of an organization that provides a service.

In 1984, Deming served as a consultant to a Ford installation called Windsor Export Supply. The installation was the overseas supply arm for parts from North American plants. The approximately 250 employees that worked there in 1984 took orders from Ford's foreign manufacturing and assembly plants and from outside suppliers. In response to orders, Windsor purchased parts from Ford supply plants, arranged for their shipment, and collected payment. About 150 Windsor employees were then members of the United Autoworkers Union. At this time, things were not looking good for Windsor. Due to competition from Japan, overseas sales were slipping. Also, former customers were now supplying the United States, and the devaluation of the dollar had caused problems. As a result, sales were down 40%.

Many of the problems at Windsor resulted from the excessive bureaucracy that evolves in a people-intensive service organization. A detailed description of how the Deming method was applied to the service organization at Windsor is described by Walton [Walton86]. By streamlining the ordering process and attracting a Ford parts-and-accessories export operation, the fortunes of the Windsor plant were turned around. A decision was made that no one would be fired. Even though fewer managers were required in the streamlined organization, they were either brought along to the new methodology immediately, given some time to adapt, or accepted already scheduled retirement. Streamlining the ordering process resulted in a reduction in the work force by 43 workers. New work was found for Windsor, which resulted in an increase of 31 new jobs. The net loss in positions was mainly the management positions that were no longer needed in the new streamlined organization.

The Windsor project proved that Demings methodology can be applied to a service organization where no product is actually manufactured.

The Deming methodology is statistically based. Critical to his methodology is the need to base decisions as much as possible on accurate and timely data, not on wishes or hunches or experience. For a successful software process quality improvement program, accurate and timely data are a must. To improve the life cycle, we must be able to measure process attributes, predict the effect of process modifications, and access the results of process alterations.

DEPARTMENT OF DEFENSE SOFTWARE PROCESS ASSESSMENT AND EVALUATION PROGRAMS

During the late 1980s, based on work by Deming, Crosby, Juran, and other quality gurus, the U.S. Department of Defense (DoD) initiated software process assessment and evaluation programs [Bollinger91].

SEI Software Process Assessment Program

The assessment program is a voluntary one that helps an organization determine how various parts of a project (such as people, tasks, tools, standards, and resources) interact to produce software. The DoD Software Engineering Institute (SEI) promotes a well-defined process assessment approach that emphasizes self-evaluation by organizations. SEI process assessments are usually done at the request of the assessed organizations, not the government. The SEI provides training of personnel and various levels of on-site assistance. The results of SEI assessments are kept confidential. Employees often react very positively to these voluntary assessments. Many organizations are interested in SEI process assessment program because of its very close relation to the SEI Software Capability Evaluation (SCE) program.

SEI Software Capability Evaluation (SCE) Program

SEI developed the SCE program in parallel with the SEI process assessment program. The two programs share many concepts and materials. Unlike the assessment programs, the evaluation programs are neither voluntary nor confidential. A government agency may require that all its potential contractors undergo an SCE. The SCE results can then be used to eliminate low-scoring organizations from future bidding on contracts. Frequently, interest in the SEI assessment program is a result of the need for government contractors to receive a high SCE rating. An SEI assessment is like requesting a tax consultant to advise you on your tax strategy. An SCE evaluation is like a being audited by the U.S. Internal Revenue Service. Both the process assessment program and the SCE program are based on the DoD software process maturity framework.

SEI Software Process Maturity Framework

In 1989, Watts Humphrey described the SEI software process maturity framework [Humphrey89]. The SEI software process is the set of tools, methods, and practices used to produce a software product. The objectives of software process management are to produce products according to plan while simultaneously improving the organization's capabilities. Many SEI concepts are based on the work of Deming. Humphrey asserts that, if the process in not under statistical control, sustained progress is not possible until it is. He goes on to state that the basic principle behind statistical control is measurement.

The process maturity framework has five levels:

1. *Initial.* This is the level before the software process activities are the same for more than one software development project. To progress to the next level, the process must be repeatable between projects.
2. *Repeatable.* Once the process is repeatable, the next objective is to define all the activities, tasks, inputs, and outputs that make up the software process.
3. *Defined.* Once all parts of the process are defined, then the next goal is to introduce comprehensive measurements.
4. *Managed.* Once measurements have been introduced, then process measurement and analysis are possible.
5. *Optimizing.* After a foundation of measurement and analysis has been established, then continuous process improvement and optimization can be attained.

In promoting the SEI software process maturity framework, Humphrey had to adapt the Deming methodology to the realities of the bureaucratic infrastructure of the government contracting process. While Deming based his methodology on fourteen points, Humphrey based his on the following six basic principles:

1. Major changes to the software process must start at the top.
2. Ultimately, everyone must be involved.
3. Effective change requires a goal and knowledge of the current process.
4. Change is continuous.
5. Software process changes will not be retained without conscious effort and periodic reinforcement.
6. Software process improvement requires investment.

Only principles 1, 4, and 5 are directly from Deming's 14 points. Humphrey's principle 1 is similar to Deming's point 14; principle 4 is similar to point 5; and principle 5 is similar to points 6 and 13. Deming's points 1 through 4 and 7 through 12 are not directly included in Humphrey's principles.

Principles 2, 3, and 6 would probably not be endorsed by Deming. Humphrey's principle 2 states that "everyone must be involved." The word "must" probably is too strong for Deming. Deming's approach is to "drive out fear" and "institute leadership." Humphrey's principle 3 says "Effective change requires a goal and knowledge of the current process." Deming's point 1 says "Create constancy of purpose for improvement of product and service." The "constancy of purpose for improvement" is more than just a goal. Humphrey's point 6 states that process improvement requires investment. Walton [Walton86] cited a case study at Ford where the Deming methodology was applied to the Taurus project that came in $400 million under the budgeted $3.25 billion. The Deming methodology can reduce cost during its initial application without requiring transitions from initial level to repeatable level to defined level to managed level.

Software Capabilities Evaluation (SCE) Grading

The SCE numeric grade is derived using three components: (1) process maturity framework, (2) SEI process maturity questionnaire, and (3) SEI grading templates. The process maturity framework was described above.

The SEI process maturity questionnaire consists of 101 yes/no questions in three topic areas [Bollinger91]. The subjects by topic area are listed in Table 2.1. The SEI assessments program only uses the questionnaire as a tool for introducing management, process, and technical issues that are of undisputed importance to developing an efficient software development organization. The SEI evaluation program uses 85 of the 101 questions to compute the SCE score. The 16 technology questions are not used to compute the SCE score. The unfortunate result is that the effect of technology on the software process in very nearly ignored when an organization receives an SCE audit.

An SEI grading template and a simple algorithm are used for the 85 yes/no questions that are scored to determine the SCE grade. A yes answer must be scored in 11 out of a possible 12 questions to progress from SEI level 1 (Initial) to level 2 (Repeatable Process). The algorithm says that if only 10 questions are answered yes then an organization would remain at the lowest level. This is true even if the organization had answered yes to the other 73 question. This is an obvious flaw to the grading process. A similar procedure is used to determine progression to other levels. Many people believe that this simplistic algorithm with severe grading consequences for a few no answers is a flawed process that does not accurately reflect the true maturity level of an organization.

Table 2.1   SEI Process Maturity Questionnaire Topics [Bollinger91]

Topic Area	Topics	Questions per Topic	Questions per Topic Area
Organization and resource management	Organizational structure	7	
	Resources, personnel, and training	5	
	Technology management	5	
			17
Software engineering process and its management	Documented standards and procedures	18	
	Process metrics	19	
	Data management and analysis	9	
	Process control	22	
			68
Total graded questions			**85**
Tools and technology (not graded for SCE score)			16
Total questions			**101**

SEI Assessment and Evaluation Programs Effectiveness

When you compare the acceptance of the SEI assessment and evaluation programs, the assessment program is truly an outstanding contribution to the software industry [Bollinger91]. The confidential, in-depth assessments are very useful aids in developing software process improvement programs.

Many organizations feel that the SCE evaluation program is a seriously flawed program that places too much emphasis on a simple questionnaire to determine who should be eliminated from the government software development process. Bollinger and McGowan stated that, while they do not feel there is anything fundamentally wrong with the idea of a government program for accrediting software organizations, the SCE effort clearly is not such a program, nor will it easily be transformed into one [Bollinger91].

SEI Measurement, Prediction, and Improvement

The SEI recognizes the need for measurement as a foundation for their maturity framework. To progress from the initial level 1 to the repeatable level 2, 11 out of 12 questions must receive yes answers. Four of the questions deal with management controls, three deal with configuration controls, three with project estimation, and two with data collection. Since only one question may be answered no to progress from level 1 to level 2, then data collection and project estimation activities must be present.

To receive a high grade on questions required to progress from level 1 to level 2, project configuration controls must be in place to control changes to requirements and code. A project must use prediction models for estimating software size, development schedules, and software development costs. Software size data must be collected for each software configuration item as a function of time. Also, statistics on software code and test errors must be gathered.

Levels 2 and 3 show a strong emphasis on collecting data about product and development trends and on data traceability. Level 3 also includes the formation of a software engineering process group to take a proactive approach to improving the software process and inserting new software technologies. Bollinger and McGowan state that "The process group is one of the more innovative recommendations of the first three levels, and one that clearly has merit as a means for increasing the long-term awareness of process issues in an organization or project" [Bollinger91].

Level 4 focuses on data collection and data analysis. The data are used to estimate, track, and control software quality.

Level 5 is the optimizing level. Emphasis is placed on defect prevention.

MALCOLM BALDRIGE NATIONAL QUALITY AWARD

The success of the Deming methodology in the United States has led to a need for recognition similar to the Deming Prize that is awarded annually in Japan. In 1987 the Malcolm Baldrige National Quality Award (often referred to as Baldrige) was established for the purpose of recognizing U.S. companies that excel in quality management and quality achievement. Baldrige has been adopted by the U.S. Government National Institute of Standards and Technology (NIST).

The Baldrige award criteria consists of seven categories that are related by the four-element framework described in Figure 2.1. The four basic elements of the framework are *driver, system, measures of progress,* and *goal.* The *driver* is the senior executive leadership that must create the values and goals of the organization and must guide pursuit of the goals. The *system* consists of all the processes used for meeting the goals. *Measures of progress* provide the references to determine whether an organization is heading toward its goals. The *goal* states the desired objectives of an organization. The Baldrige categories and items are listed in Table 2.2. Notice that out of a maximum of 1,000 possible points, the focus is on the quality and operational results (worth 180 points) and customer focus and satisfaction (worth 300 points).

STANDARD PROCESS MODELS

Whoever develops software uses a software process model. There are probably as many process models as there are software developers. Many of the Fortune 500 companies whose primary business is related to computers and software development

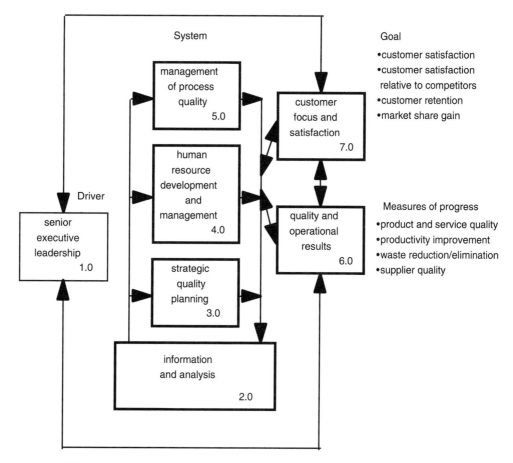

Figure 2.1 Baldrige Award Criteria Framework with Dynamic Relationships (*U.S. Department of Commerce, NIST*)

consider the software process model that they use to be proprietary. They do not publish their exact software process model because they believe that they have a competitive advantage by not doing so.

When a customer contracts with a supplier to develop a software system, the customer often would like assurance that the supplier is qualified to fulfill the contract. Too often, software projects result in low-quality software systems that do not meet customer expectations and, in some cases, produce nothing at all.

Manufacturing criteria have been developed that have resulted in high-quality electronics, cameras, and automobiles. In Japan, the Deming Award Criteria developed by JUSE indicate that a supplier who wins the Deming Award has a high-quality manufacturing process. In the United States, the Malcolm Baldrige National Quality Award was adopted by the U.S. NIST for the purpose of recognizing U.S. companies that excel in quality management and quality achievement. The Baldrige

Table 2.2 Baldrige Categories and Items

Category	Item	Maximum Points	Maximum Points
1.0	**Leadership**		100
	1.1 Senior Executive Leadership	40	
	1.2 Quality Values	15	
	1.3 Management for Quality	25	
	1.4 Public Responsibility	20	
2.0	**Information and Analysis**		70
	2.1 Scope and Management of Quality Data and Information	20	
	2.2 Competitive Comparisons and Benchmarks	30	
	2.3 Analysis of Quality Data and Information	20	
3.0	**Strategic Quality Planning**		60
	3.1 Strategic Quality Planning Process	35	
	3.2 Quality Goals and Plans	25	
4.0	**Human Resource Utilization**		150
	4.1 Human Resource Management	20	
	4.2 Employee Involvement	40	
	4.3 Quality Education and Training	40	
	4.4 Employee Recognition and Performance Measurement	25	
	4.5 Employee Well-being and Morale	25	
5.0	**Quality Assurance of Product and Services**		140
	5.1 Design and Introduction of Quality Products and Services	35	
	5.2 Process Quality Control	20	
	5.3 Continuous Improvement of Processes	20	
	5.4 Quality Assessment	15	
	5.5 Documentation	10	
	5.6 Business Process and Support Service Quality	20	
	5.7 Supplier Quality	20	
6.0	**Quality Results**		180
	6.1 Product and Service Quality Results	90	
	6.2 Business Process, Operational, and Support Service Quality Results	50	
	6.3 Supplier Quality Results	40	
7.0	**Customer Satisfaction**		300
	7.1 Determining Customer Requirements and Expectations	30	
	7.2 Customer Relationship Management	50	
	7.3 Customer Service Standards	20	
	7.4 Commitment to Customers	15	
	7.5 Complaint Resolution for Quality Improvement	25	
	7.6 Determining Customer Satisfaction	20	
	7.7 Customer Satisfaction Results	70	
	7.8 Customer Satisfaction Comparison	70	
		Total	**1,000**

criteria also serve as indicators of high quality. While the Deming and Baldrige criteria are widely recognized, they are not standards, but standards do exist. In the following we will examine standards in general and then investigate the ISO 9000 series of quality systems standards. We will discuss the IEEE standard for developing life cycle processes later in Chapter 4.

Standards

Before we discuss specific standards, we will examine how they come into being and how they are categorized [Bernt93]. There are three different ways to create standards. One way is free interplay of market forces, which result in *de facto standards*. The second way is for a government body to create a standard, which is called *de jure standards*. The third way is for standard setting bodies to set standards, resulting in *voluntary consensus standards*.

Many software standards have been de facto standards. The Microsoft DOS and the IBM OS 360/370 operating systems are examples of a de facto standards. Each of these products was produced by a market leader and widely accepted by the public. As acceptance among users increased, other firms began to produce software that operated under these standards.

The SCE described earlier is an example of a de jure standard used to restrict the DoD software project awards to contractors that have high SCE scores. In contrast to de facto standards, the choice of users in the marketplace is largely irrelevant to the establishment of de jure standards. Only the political interests and strengths of the interested parties are relevant. In the case of the SCE audit described earlier, the political interest is the U.S. Department of Defense, and the users of the standard are software contractors that want to do business with DoD.

An example of a voluntary consensus standard is the International Standards Organization (ISO) 9000 series of standards for quality systems. Manufacturers and users in accredited standards committees [such as ISO or American National Standards Institute (ANSI)] develop voluntary consensus standards. After the standard is approved, companies build products under the standard. In the case of the ISO 9000, a company requests that its quality system be assessed by an independent, accredited third party for the purpose of confirming its conformance to the ISO 9000 series of standards and attesting to it in writing. In the United States this procedure is known as registration.

We have looked at how standards come into being. Now we will examine different classifications of standards. This will help us to focus on the standards that are most useful to software professionals. David has proposed the standards classification system explained by Table 2.3 [David87]. Standards are separated into reference, minimum attribute, and compatibility standards that can be applied to technical design or behavior. An example of technical reference standards are weights and mea-

Table 2.3   Classifications of Standards [David87]

Standard	Technical Design	Behavioral
Reference	Weights and measures	Etiquette Accreditation
Minimum attribute	Strength of materials	Professional licensure
Compatibility	Nuts and bolts Modems Data communications	Language Protocols

sures like those defined by the ISO and maintained by NIST in the United States. An example of a minimum attribute standard is the minimum necessary strength of a material, such as aluminum. ISO, the American Society for Testing and Materials (ASTM), and the Institute of Electrical and Electronic Engineers (IEEE) frequently develop standards such as these. In contrast, you can consider the registration of a company under ISO 9000 as a reference because it is compared to an absolute reference. In communication systems, a key problem is the interoperability of systems, so many of the telecommunications industry standards pertain to technical compatibility.

Standards Organizations

Three types of voluntary organizations involved in standards are international, national, and professional society. ISO is an example of an international standards organization, ANSI an example of a national standards organization, and IEEE an example of a professional society. We will now explain the structure of these three types of organizations.

International Standards Organization (ISO)

ISO is a nongovernmental organization that was established in 1947 to develop worldwide standards to improve international communication and to promote smooth and equitable growth of international trade. The membership currently includes about 90 countries. Since its inception, ISO has prepared and approved many thousands of standards, covering topics from screw threads to data processing.

The ISO is divided into 160 technical committees, each containing several subcommittees. Each Technical Committee (TC) is responsible for developing standards in a relatively broad area. TC176, for example, was formed in 1979 to formulate an international standard for quality systems.

American National Standards Institute (ANSI)

Any country that wishes to participate in ISO can be represented by their representative standards organization. The United States is represented by ANSI. The ISO certifies bodies such as ANSI to carry out standards activities. Each of these member bodies is entitled to participate and exercise voting rights on any Technical Committee of the ISO. Nations that do not have standards organizations are considered correspondent members. Six of the 90 ISO member organizations are listed in Table 2.4.

Institute of Electrical and Electronics Engineers (IEEE)

Professional societies work with standards organizations to develop standards. We mentioned earlier that that the ASTM and IEEE professional societies worked with ISO to establish the minimum necessary strength of a material, such as aluminum. The IEEE Standards Board is very active in Telecommunications and Computer Standards activities. Although mainly a U.S. organization, the IEEE has over 300,000 members worldwide. Standardization historically has been an important activity of the IEEE. Over 530 currently active standards are published through the Standards Board, with new or revised publications approved at the rate of about 45 per year.

We will now explain the ISO 9000 software quality standards.

ISO 9000 Quality Standards

ISO 9000 is a series of international quality standards that applies to the quality management system and the process used to produce a product. A basic set of quality systems requirements are established that are necessary to ensure that your process is capable of consistently producing products that meet the expectation of your cus-

Table 2.4 ISO Member Organizations

Country	ISO Member	Abbreviation
Canada	Canadian Standards Association	CSA
France	Association Française de Normalisation	AFNOR
Germany	Deutsches Institut für Normung	DIN
Japan	Japanese Industrial Standards Committee	JISC
United Kingdom	British Standards Institute	BSI
United States	American National Standards Institute	ANSI

tomers. The standards provide an excellent base upon which to extend and improve your process, thereby improving the quality of your product or service.

While the ISO 9000 series of standards was originally developed for the manufacturing environment, it is not written for any specific industry or business, The standards have been implemented by the electronics, chemistry, automobile, transportation, health care, banking, and many other industries [Schmauch94]. By January 1993, 56 nations and the European Economic Community had adopted ISO 9000. The United States version of the standard is known as ANSI/ASQC Q90-Q94.

The ISO 9000 series of standards for quality systems is built on the premise that if the production and management system is right the product or service that it produces will also be right. Strong emphasis is placed on control, auditability, verification/validation, and process improvement. Control means that you are able, at all times during the process, to identify each item, who owns each item, its status, where it is, its currently valid version, proposed changes, and so on. Auditability means that you can always show objective evidence of what has been done, how it was done, the current status of the project and product, and what is planned to be done. The standards rely heavily on verification that a product is properly produced and validation that customer requirements are met. The standards require that you continually improve your process, which should lead to improved products and services.

Benefits of ISO 9000

If quality software products are your objective, then ISO 9000 should be of interest to you. The benefits are numerous to having ISO 9000 conforming quality systems. The benefits include the following:

- *Registration.* Your quality system can be registered as conforming to the IS0 9000. The European Community (EC) has adopted quality management as a key strategic element in its drive to improve the competitiveness of European suppliers, and the EC has chosen ISO 9000 as its series of standards for quality assurance. The registration approach is to request an on-site audit by a third-party assessment team. Registering your quality system tells the world that you have a quality system that conforms with the ISO 9000 standards. It reduces the need for your customers to do their own assessment of your quality system.
- *Foundation of quality.* Today, many people agree that you need a quality system to produce quality products. ISO 9000 provides the quality system to ensure that your software development process has the level of control, discipline, and repeatability necessary for you to build consistent quality into your products.

- *Increased productivity.* Improved quality can eliminate the need for costly after-the-fact inspections, software usability problems, rework, and redesign. The reduced costs result in improved quality.

- *Consistency.* An ISO 9000 conforming quality system will ensure your customers that you will likely produce the quality product that you set out to produce and that you will continue to produce continually improved products.

- *Improved competitiveness.* An ISO 9000 conforming quality system will provide a competitive advantage in the increasingly competitive global marketplace. Potential customers will know that your products will be more likely to meet the claims made about them than products with similar claims made by non-ISO 9000 competitors.

- *Customer demand.* Already European customers often favor suppliers that conform to ISO 9000. As ISO 9000 becomes prevalent, more and more customers will demand it.

- *Corporate image.* ISO 9000 conformance requires a demonstrated continuing commitment to quality.

The standards specify a minimum set of required activities that must be done during the development of a product. We will now look in more detail at the structure of ISO 9000.

ISO 9000 for Software Development

We are interested in how ISO 9000 can be applied to improve the software processes along the entire life cycle. The ISO 9000 series consists of the following five sections:

1. *ISO 9000 Quality systems—Quality management and quality assurance standards—guidelines for selection and use.* ISO 9000 provides guidance for selection of ISO 9001, ISO 9002, or ISO 9003. ISO 9000-3 provides guidelines for the application of the standards to the software development process.

2. *ISO 9001 Quality systems—Model for quality assurance in design/development, production, installation, and servicing.* This standard applies to an organization that develops a software product that it designs.

3. *ISO 9002 Quality systems—Model for quality assurance in production and installation.* This standard applies to an organization that produces a software product designed by a different organization.

4. *ISO 9003 Quality systems—Model for quality assurance in final inspection and test.* This standard applies to a software test organization.

5. *ISO 9004 Quality systems—Quality management and quality systems elements— guidelines.* This standard provides guidance on the interpretation of ISO 9001, ISO 9002, and ISO 9003.

The relationship of the ISO 9000 standards to the life cycle process is shown in Figure 2.2. Notice that ISO 9001 covers more aspects of the life cycle and more elements of the standard apply to ISO 9001 than to ISO 9002 and ISO 9003. Also, some of the elements that apply to ISO 9002 and ISO 9003 are less stringent than the corresponding elements in ISO 9001. ISO 9001 is a superset of ISO 9002, which in turn is a superset of ISO 9003.

ISO 9000 Standards Elements

Schmauch [Schmauch94] states that to meet the ISO 9000 series of standards, your quality system must be

- documented,
- controlled,
- auditable,
- monitored,
- improved, and
- effective.

He simply states that if your processes are documented, controlled, auditable, effective for you, continually monitored, and improved and your management is committed and your employees are involved, then you are well on your way to meeting the requirements of the ISO 9000 series of standards.

The ISO 9000 series of standards contains the 20 standards elements listed in Table 2.5. ISO 9001 requires conformance to all 20 elements. ISO 9002 requires conformance to 18 elements. ISO 9003 requires conformance to only 12 elements.

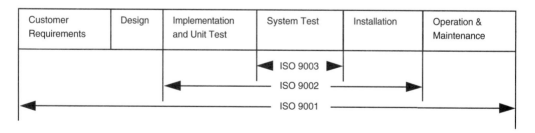

Figure 2.2   Relation of ISO 9000 Standards to the Life Cycle

Table 2.5   ISO 9000 Standards Elements versus Standards Levels*

ISO 9000 Standards Elements	ISO 9001	ISO 9002	ISO 9003
1 Managing responsibility	✓	✓	✓
2 Quality system	✓	✓	✓
3 Contract review	✓	✓	
4 Design control	✓		
5 Document control	✓	✓	✓
6 Purchasing	✓	✓	
7 Purchaser-supplied product	✓	✓	
8 Product identification and traceability	✓	✓	✓
9 Process control	✓	✓	
10 Inspection and testing	✓	✓	✓
11 Inspection, measuring, and test equipment	✓	✓	✓
12 Inspection and test status	✓	✓	✓
13 Control of nonconforming product	✓	✓	✓
14 Corrective action	✓	✓	
15 Handling, storage, packaging, and delivery	✓	✓	✓
16 Quality records	✓	✓	✓
17 Internal quality audits	✓	✓	
18 Training	✓	✓	✓
19 Servicing	✓		
20 Statistical techniques	✓	✓	✓
Number of elements in each standard level	20	18	12

*ISO 9000 Elements That Are Related to Measurement and Prediction for Software Development Process are Shaded

Software professionals frequently have difficulty visualizing how ISO 9000 can be applied to improve the quality and productivity of the software development process. As mentioned earlier, management commitment and involved employees are necessary. We agree that commitment and involvement are necessary to improve the software development process. We will now explore the ISO 9000 standards elements to determine how measurement and prediction can lead to improvement.

ISO 9000 Measurement, Prediction, and Improvement

Continuous process improvement requires constant monitoring, measurement, analysis, and prediction. The ISO 9000 series of standards specifies what, at a minimum, must be done to comply with the standards. While the elements of the standards do not tell you how things should be done, this book will explain in detail how measurement and prediction can be integrated into your quality system. Even though we believe all ISO 9000 standards elements listed in Table 2.5 are important, we will concentrate only on those that directly relate to measurement and prediction. These are the shaded elements (elements 3–5, 8–14, 16, 17, and 20) in Table 2.5. In the following, the owner of an item is the person responsible for its status.

The customer review element requires you to have procedures for ensuring that what is expected from you is adequately defined and documented and that you have the capability to satisfy the requirements. For a software product, the customer requirements should be under a configuration control system to keep track of customer requirements document owner, to track modifications and changes, to trace defects back to a customer requirement, and as a reference base for product validation during testing.

The design control element requires you to have procedures for controlling and verifying the design output to ensure that customer requirements will be met. For a software product, the design specifications should be under a configuration control system to keep track of the specification document owner, to track modifications and changes, to trace defects back to a design specification, and as a reference base for product verification during testing.

The product identification and traceability element requires you to have procedures for identifying and tracing the software product during all stages of production, delivery, and installation. The best application of this requirement to the software development environment is that you control the content and status of all parts of your software product during development and later when the product is used by a customer.

The inspection and testing element requires you to have procedures for all levels of inspection and testing that you have identified as being required. A log should be kept of all test activities. The log should reflect the owner of the test, the test hardware and software configuration, the time and duration of the test, the staff that ran the test, and the test results. Test failure information should be fed to a defect tracking system.

The inspection, measuring, and test equipment element requires you to control, calibrate, and maintain inspection, measuring, and test equipment. For a software development process, you must demonstrate that tools for test coverage, test tracing, verification, validation, measurement, and the like, can serve their intended purpose and that they are under control.

The inspection and test status element requires you to be able to identify the test status of the product throughout the process. You can use software tools to gather and filter data, capture measurements, analyze and chart results, and measure and predict status.

The control of nonconforming product element requires you to have procedures for controlling a product that does not conform to its specifications and requirements.

For a software product, a defect management system must be used to track software product defects both before and after a product is delivered to customers.

The corrective action element requires you to have procedures for investigating the causes for nonconforming products and ensuring corrective actions to prevent recurrences. This element addresses the software development process, not the product. Measurements should be gathered and records kept of software development process metrics.

The quality records element requires you to identify and keep records to demonstrate achievement of product quality and effective operation of your quality system. Records of metrics should be kept to demonstrate the quality, safety, reliability, usability, productivity, and customer satisfaction. These records will be useful in improving the quality of both software process and product.

The internal quality audits element requires you to plan and carry out internal quality audits, by qualified individuals, to verify that you are doing what you say you are doing and to determine the effectiveness of your quality system. A comprehensive metrics system and a computerized intelligent auditor assistant can perform many of the functions and duties of the internal auditor.

The statistical techniques element requires you to show that any statistical techniques that you use are correct. You must show that all measurements, metrics, and predictor models are correct and accurate. You must be able to show the validity of a predictive algorithmic or heuristic predictor.

These ISO 9000 elements can be applied to the software development environment. Some may require considerable interpretation, but others can be applied with little or no interpretation. We will now look at a quality improvement effort a the IBM Santa Teresa Laboratory in San Jose, California, that is compliant with the ISO 9000 series of standards.

IBM SOFTWARE QUALITY IMPROVEMENT PROGRAM _____

Kaplan, Clark, and Tang describe a journey of quality improvement at IBM Santa Teresa Lab that began in 1989 [Kaplan95]. By 1993, the quality improvement efforts resulted in a 46% decline in defects, lab service costs declined 20%, productivity in terms of revenue per employee increased 58%, and customer satisfaction had increased by 14%. We will now examine some of the high points of their methodology, which is based on an iron triangle, four-stage maturity framework, and the Baldrige criteria.

The Iron Triangle

Kaplan et al. feel that only when they began to focus on the three areas of technology, process, and leadership shown in Figure 2.3 did they begin to make sustainable quality progress. These three focus areas make up a triangle with technology at one point of the triangle and leadership and process at the other two. The triangle can be

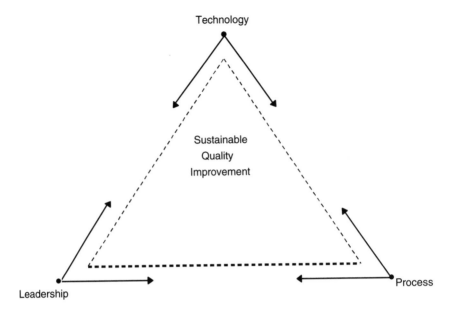

Figure 2.3 The Iron Triangle

visualized as an iron spearhead to penetrate business as usual and to introduce the ingredients for sustainable quality improvement to an organization. We will now look at how the focus areas can be combined with the Baldrige criteria to create a four-stage maturity framework.

Four-Stage Maturity Framework

IBM Santa Teresa Lab bases their four-stage maturity framework on the score computed using the Baldrige criteria. The highest Baldrige score that an organization can attain is 1,000. An organization progresses from the lowest level to the highest level of the maturity framework based on improving their Baldrige scores. The four stages of quality maturity are awareness, coping, management, and integration. The awareness stage objectives are listed in Figure 2.4. You know that you are in the awareness stage when most of the organization ignores quality issues altogether. Those who are aware of quality tend to view quality as management's latest fad. These organizations would usually receive a Baldrige score of 500 or less. The cost of poor quality is like a leak in a dike that has not been discovered. The first action is to sound the alarm.

During the awareness stage, the leader should increase awareness of the quality crisis through communication and education. The process objectives should be first to understand and document the process. Then immediate progress should be made toward cost reduction. The technology objective should be to make immediate

Awareness stage (Baldrige score ≤ 500)

Objectives	
Leadership:	quality awareness and education
Process:	immediate cost reduction and process understanding
Technology:	tools for customer understanding and process modeling
Management focus:	cost control

Figure 2.4 Awareness Stage of Quality Maturity

progress toward cost reduction. All these areas are essential to establishing your foundation for quality improvement.

The coping stage of quality maturity marks the transition from activities that are primarily aimed at raising quality awareness to activities that are aimed at bringing quality under some measure of control. The coping stage objectives are listed in Figure 2.5. Organizations that are coping receive a Baldrige score of between 500 and 625. The goal in the coping stage is to do something immediately to improve the quality of products and processes, while laying the foundation for innovation that will lead to quality breakthroughs in following stages.

During the coping stage, your leadership challenge is to influence more of the organization to buy into quality. Systems must be created that ensure that people act to improve quality. These systems act as catalysts for change, facilitating the exchange of quality-related information. The process challenge is to continue to understand and contain the quality problems through assessment and process improvements. Enhanced testing and defect detection techniques can be used at this point. These techniques are reactive since they do nothing to prevent defects. The plus side of improved testing is that defects are prevented from reaching customers, and it allows organizations at this stage of quality maturity to realize immediate results. The technology objective should be to apply tools that will produce immediate results with a minimum of restructuring of the organization. Better use of existing information is one of the highest-leverage quality activities possible. This is realized from the fact that analysis of existing data and the resulting information can greatly improve an organization's effectiveness.

Coping stage (500 < Baldrige score ≤ 625)

Objectives	
Leadership:	organizational catalysts for quality improvement
Process:	process assessment and enhancement through improved defect detection
Technology:	analysis of defect and customer satisfaction data
Management focus:	defect detection

Figure 2.5 Coping Stage of Quality Maturity

Management stage (625 < Baldrige score ≤ 750)

Objectives

Leadership:	strategy from the top; innovation and empowerment at all levels
Process:	defect prevention and benchmarking
Technology:	computerizing team development and new technological paradigms for software development
Management focus:	defect prevention

Figure 2.6 Management Stage of Quality Maturity

To reach the management stage, an organization must began to take a proactive approach to quality. Some of the quality problems must already be under control. The organization should understand its processes and have made efforts to improve quality through process improvements. An example of improvements would be enhanced testing or rigorous code inspections. The management stage objectives are listed in Figure 2.6. Organizations that are in the management stage receive a Baldrige score of between 625 and 750. During lower stages, incremental gains in quality can be obtained by doing the same things and concentrating on quality. The goal of the management stage of quality maturity is to make quantum improvements in quality. To make quantum improvements, you may have to make radical process change along with unprecedented levels of teamwork and innovation.

In the management stage, the leadership challenge is no longer to focus attention on the organization's quality problems, but to support innovative and proactive approaches to these problems. The process objectives shift from the coping stage focus on defect detection to the management stage focus on defect prevention. The shift is from doing the existing process better to analyzing and changing the existing process. The technology objective should be to introduce technology to assist teams in developing more efficient and error-free code.

In the integration stage, quality values are embedded in the culture and daily operations of the organization. Continuous improvement should be a reflective response requiring a minimum amount of stimulus from top management. The integration stage is the time to expand quality horizons to include suppliers, business partners, customers, and the community at large. The integration stage objectives are listed in Figure 2.7. Organizations that are in the integration stage receive a Baldrige score of over 750.

During the integration stage, the objectives for leaders are to continually improve the organization's process and technologies through innovation while simultaneously wielding influence beyond the boundaries of the organization. The process objective is to create quality partnerships with customers and suppliers. Highest levels of quality can only be attained when the improved processes are shared with customers and suppliers. The technological objective is to increase the rate of ex-

Integration stage (750 < Baldrige score ≤ 1,000)

Objectives

Leadership:	sustainable; continuous improvement and grass-roots leadership; expanding the scope of quality outside the organization
Process:	quality partnerships with customers and vendors
Technology:	inventing tools for the future
Management focus:	customer satisfaction

Figure 2.7   Integration Stage of Quality Maturity

perimentation and innovation. Otherwise, an organization can loose ground to competitors who have accelerating rates of experimentation.

Innovations

The IBM Santa Teresa Lab classifies each of their quality innovations into one of the focus areas of the iron triangle. Kaplan, Clark, and Tang list 40 innovations that they have developed that have helped reach the integration stage of the maturity framework [Kaplan95]. A detailed description of each of their innovations can be found in their book.

SUMMARY

In this chapter we have discussed quality systems. We have examined the major criteria and standards and given an overview of all aspects of the methodology. We have shown how measurement and prediction are a integral to quality improvement. In the following chapters, we will shift gears and concentrate only on the measurement, prediction, and improvement aspects of process improvement. Process improvement requires data gathering, filtering, analysis, and prediction. We will now proceed to define the life cycle process, show what data can be gathered, and to explain the models for data analysis and metric prediction.

REFERENCES

[Bernt93]   Bernt, P. W., and Weiss, M. B. H., *International Telecommunications*, Sams Publishing, A Division of Prentice Hall Computer Publishing, Carmel, IN, 1993, 446 p.

[Bollinger91]   Bollinger, T. B., and McGowan, C., "A Critical Look at Software Capability Evaluations," *IEEE Software*, July 1991, pp. 25–41.

[David87]   David, P. A., "Some New Standards for the Economics of Standardization in the Information Age," *Economic Theory of Technological Policy*, eds. P. Dasgulpa and P. L. Stoneman, Cambridge University Press, New York, 1987.

[Humphrey89]   Humphrey, W. S., *Managing the Software Process*, Addison–Wesley Publishing Company, Reading, MA, 1989, 494 p.

[Kaplan95]   Kaplan, C., Clark, R., and Tang, V., *Secrets of Software Quality*, McGraw-Hill, Inc., New York, 1994, 383 p.

[Schmauch94]   Schmauch, C. H., *ISO 9000 for Software Developers*, ASQC Quality Press, Milwaukee, WI, 1994, 156 p.

[Walton86]   Walton, M., *The Deming Management Method*, Putnam Publishing Group, New York, 1986, 262 p.

3
Project
Visualization

You software guys are too much like the weavers in the story about the Emperor and the new clothes. When I go out to check on a software development the answers I get sound like, "We're fantastically busy weaving this magic cloth. Just wait a while and it'll look terrific." But there's nothing I can see or touch, no numbers I can relate to, no way to pick up signals that things aren't really all that great. And there are too many people I know who have come out at the end wearing a bunch of expensive rags or nothing at all.

An Air Force Decision Maker
[Boehm73]

INTRODUCTION

During the late 1960s and early 1970s many software projects failed due to the inability of management to see exactly what was being developed. In Chapter 1 we cited examples of successful software development projects from AT&T Bell Laboratories, AT&T Network Systems, Boeing, Bull, CSC, DEC, IBM Santa Teresa Laboratory, Microsoft, NASA, Raytheon, Toshiba, and the University of Maryland. But many major organizations still do not have process improvement activities and end up with failed projects. Because of negative publicity, failed projects are not usually known outside of the organization responsible for the project. Until a project evolves into a financial disaster or has major operational problems, it does not make the national newspapers. In Chapter 1 we cited national news media accounts of major software project failures of American Airlines, American On Line, Ashton–Tate, Denver Airport, FAA, IRS, and the Toronto Stock Exchange. Often the management of these software projects was not aware that there were any problems until it was too late to salvage the project or to prevent cost overruns, extended outages, or major delays in scheduled delivery. Management was not able to see that problems were developing. In 1996, Norm Brown, executive director of the Department of Defense Software Acquisition Best Practices Initiative, stated, "In many cases, the true nature and pervasive extent of underlying project problems remains invisible to the project management until it is too late."

In this chapter we will introduce a set of project object classes. By measuring attributes in these classes, you will be able to visualize what is happening internal to a project. We then introduce a dual control/improvement cycle where common visualization stages help to efficiently and objectively gather measurements for analysis and prediction.

SOFTWARE PROJECT

To help visualize software products, we will represent items, which we will call objects, that we would like to visualize in bold Microsoft Arial font. Thus, we will represent a software product as **SoftwareProduct**. It is developed by a software development **Project**. A software **Project** is initiated as soon as a budget and plan are approved. The software **Project** shown in Figure 3.1 is shown to be composed of the

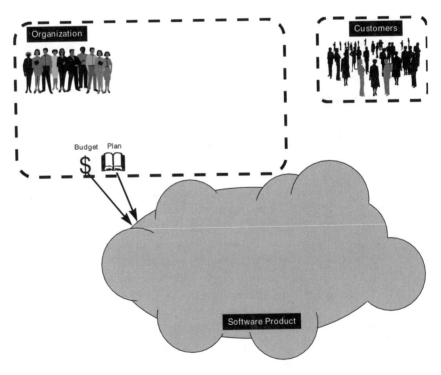

Figure 3.1 Software **Project**

- **Organization** of people that work on the **Project,**
- **SoftwareProduct** that is produced by the **Project,** and
- **Customers** that use the **SoftwareProduct** produced by the **Project**.

Notice that the **SoftwareProduct** is represented by a dark cloud. Sadly, the **SoftwareProduct** often remains encapsulated in a cloud throughout its entire existence. We will show you how to penetrate this cloud to understand the attributes of important objects that compose the **SoftwareProduct** and the software process that creates it.

People are the major cost involved in software development. Figure 3.2 shows how we will visualize the **Individual** people within the **Project Organization**. Each **Individual** may have many different **Assignment**s. An individual may receive different **Salar(y)**ies due to raises, promotions, or position changes. From these we can determine the people costs. As part of process improvement, an **Activity** accounting system can be set up. The **Individual**'s **Activity** objects describes each activity owned or performed by the **Individual**.

Individuals are organized into **Group**s or teams. Even though each **Individual** may report to more than one person, we will assume that everyone has only one main boss. We next assume that the **Group**s are organized into **Area**s and the **Area**s are part of the **Organization**. A software development **Project** with three levels of management would be a fairly large development effort. But there is no reason that there cannot be more than three levels. In this book, we will assume that there are only three levels. In later chapters, you will see that **Individual** and **Group** productivity can be dominated by many different cost drivers. Often it is difficult to control everything that affects productivity. There is general agreement among software productivity researchers that one of the most effective ways to keep costs low and to im-

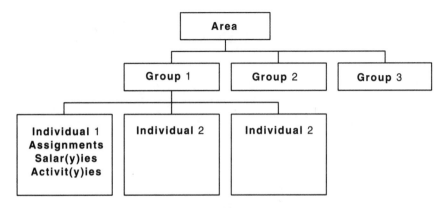

Figure 3.2 An **Area** within an **Organization**

prove productivity is to reuse software. Figure 3.3 shows the **Supplier**s that provide software for reuse. The two main types of reused software are commercial off-the-shelf (COTS) software, which are stored as **LicensedRunFile**s and software files from past **Project**s that you modify and then reuse, which are stored as **Reusable-SoftwareFile**s. You will realize the greatest gains from software that you can reuse without modification. Once you know how much software is to be reused, gross estimates can be made on the size of the **SoftwareProduct**. From **SoftwareProduct** size and other cost drivers, you can predict the effort and time required to create the **SoftwareProduct**.

Before you can create a **SoftwareProduct**, you must decide on exactly what is to be accomplished. You or your marketing staff may interact directly with **Customers** to determine the **SoftwareProduct** requirements or **Feature**s shown in Figure 3.4. If the desired **Feature**s are relatively stable, it will be easier and less expensive to create the **SoftwareProduct**. If they are allowed to continually change, then costs will rise and delays will result.

Once you know what **Feature**s you want to have in the **SoftwareProduct**, you decide how the system will be built. In the same way that you would decide on the

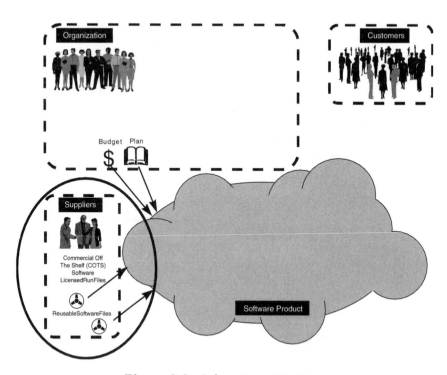

Figure 3.3   Software **Project Suppliers**

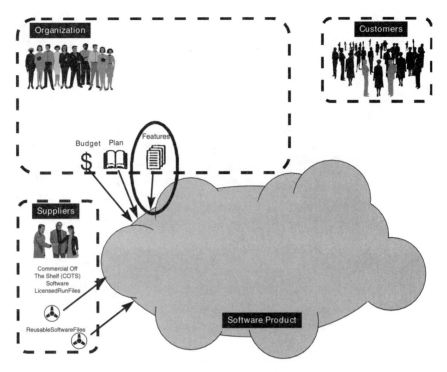

Figure 3.4 SoftwareProduct Features

architecture of a new house, you must decide on the software system architecture and then the system design. Figure 3.5 shows the system **DesignFile**s opening the dark cloud as if we know exactly how the system will be built to implement the **Feature**s. In actual practice, the system design is an abstract representation of how we think that we can build the system.

Once we have completed the system design contained in the system **Design-File**s, we then must decide exactly how the smaller units will be implemented. The unit design is contained in the unit **DesignFile**s shown in Figure 3.6. The system and unit designs provide guidance for implementing **SoftwareProduct Feature**s. The implementation process consists of producing documentation, source code, and many other activities. The source code is stored in **SourceFile**s, as shown in Figure 3.7. **SourceFile**s contain smaller cognitive **Chunk**s of code, such as subroutines, spread sheets, query commands, packages, scripts, or subprograms. Each of the **Chunk**s has **Volume**, which describes the overall size and **Structure**, which is related to the complexity of what is being built. You would like to build the software once and not have to continually **Rework** the software units because of mistakes that have been made or **Feature**s that have increased or changed. Measurement of **Rework**

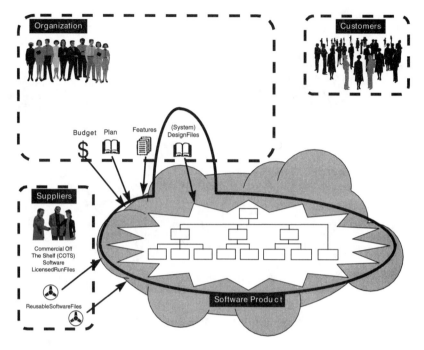

Figure 3.5 **SoftwareProduct** System Design

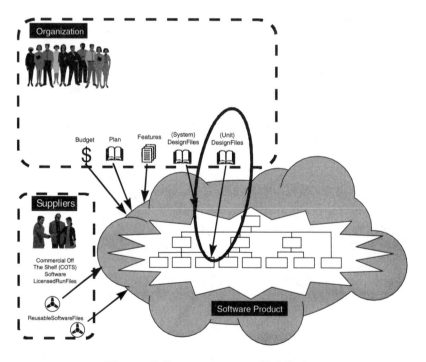

Figure 3.6 **SoftwareProduct** Unit Designs

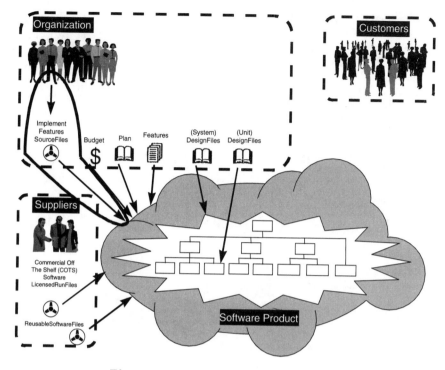

Figure 3.7 **SoftwareProduct** Implementation

helps us to visualize the effectiveness of the software development process. The relationships between **SourceFile**s, **Rework**, **Chunks**, **Volume**, and **Structure** is described in Chapter 5.

Until the source code is created, there is no recognizable **SoftwareProduct**. After the source code is implemented, there may still not be any recognizable **SoftwareProduct**. You may not have produced the correct **Features** or built the system in a sound manner. You must inspect and test the system to determine the state of the software.

In Figure 3.8, we introduce the inspection and testing processes. The goal of these processes is to determine where software will fail. A software failure is a departure from the expected result or of software output from the expected **Feature** output. **Defect**s in software cause failures. **Defect**s that cause software to fail are created when any **Individual** in the **Project Organization** makes a mistake or an error. The mistake could have been made while determining customer requirements, creating system and unit designs, specifying or implementing **SoftwareProduct Feature**s, and so on. Inspections to locate **Defect**s should be conducted throughout the software development life cycle process. **Defect**s found early by inspection cost much less to correct than those found later by verification and validation testing or by the

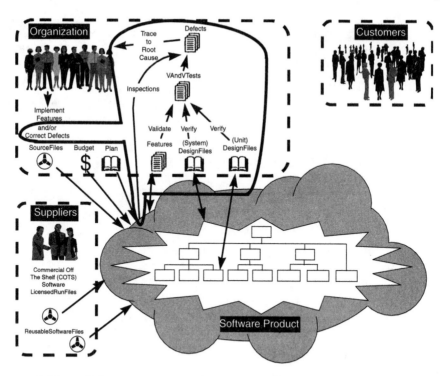

Figure 3.8   **SoftwareProduct** Testing and **Defect** Gathering, Tracking, and Correction

customer. After you have implemented the **Feature**s, run validation tests to assure that you have created the correct **Feature**s and regression tests to validate that **Feature**s that were working correctly in the past are still working.

You run system tests to verify that you have correctly implemented the system design and unit tests to verify that you have correctly implemented each unit design. You should keep records of (or have the computer record) all tests. For each test that is run, you should create a validation and verification test (**VAndVTest**) record. Those tests that fail are analyzed, and an open **Defect** should be created. The testing process is discussed in detail in Chapter 12. Once the **Defect** is traced back to the root cause and corrected, the **Defect** record should be closed. Management is interested in the number of open **Defect**s, the time it takes to correct **Defect**s, the number of **Defect**s per thousand lines of code, the rate at which **Defect**s cause failures, and the like. By keeping track of all **Defect**s, you can use reliability models to predict failure rates, number of **Defect**s remaining in software, and so on. Reliability will be discussed in Chapters 10 and 11.

If you create a **SoftwareProduct** that has all the desired **Feature**s and no **Defect**s but it is not usable by the intended user, the **Customer** will not be satisfied.

The **Customer** and the user may or may not be the same person. A **Customer** is one that purchases the **SoftwareProduct**. A user is someone that uses the **SoftwareProduct**. To make the **Customer** happy, you must deliver a **SoftwareProduct** that is on schedule, within budget, full **Featured, Defect** free, reliable, and usable. If all these criteria are met, then we predict that the **Customer** has a high probability of being satisfied.

Usability prediction models and methods can be used relatively early in the software development process to predict usability. Usability measurements can unobtrusively be gathered to assess usability. By testing for usability, you can find usability **Defect**s before a **SoftwareProduct** is delivered to a **Customer** (see Figure 3.9). Records should be kept of all usability tests (**UsabilityTests**). Usability will be discussed in detail in Chapters 10, 13, and 14.

Once a **SoftwareProduct** is complete and delivered to a **Customer** and he or she begins to use it, problems are often found. Figure 3.10 shows that when a customer reports trouble you should formally track trouble reports that provide input to the **Defect** management, tracking, and correction process. For failed **Project**s, management often does not even know the status of **Defect**s or **Feature**s before delivery. Some do not

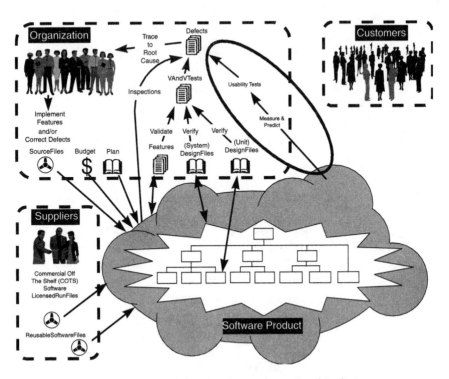

Figure 3.9   Usability Tests (**UsabilityTests**) and Prediction

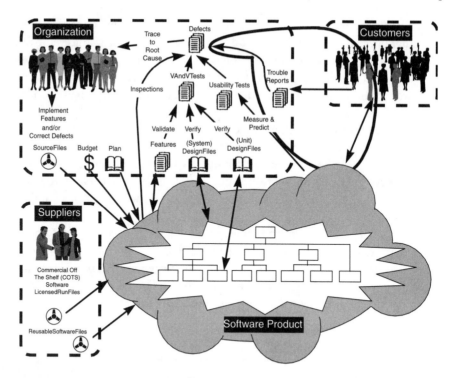

Figure 3.10   **Customer** Problems

even know that there is a flawed design that cannot be corrected without a major re-design. We feel that you should continually focus on gathering measurements through-out the entire software development life cycle. We will now look at how you control software development and implement software process improvement.

PROJECT CONTROL

Control of a software development **Project** requires an understanding of the software professional. A successful software developer is a job motivated **Individual** who, given the proper tools, training, and environment, wants to do a good job. The job of **Project** management is to establish a plan, select the right personnel for a **Project**, assign them to the appropriate tasks, empower them to make decisions within their domain of competency, track and review results, and modify the plan when appro-priate. Management can control the direction of a **Project** by applying the control triangle shown in Figure 3.11. If a **Project** is behind schedule, you can add resources (that is, people) or decrease **Features** (by removing them from the **SoftwareProduct**

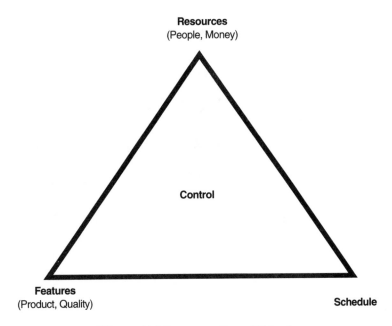

Figure 3.11 Project Control Triangle

or relaxing quality goals). If a **Project** is ahead of schedule, you may decide to decrease resources or add **Features**. The trade-off between schedule (that is, development time) and resources is discussed in detail in Chapter 8. If you want to add **Features**, you must lengthen the schedule or add additional resources. If you want to reduce resources, you must decrease **Features** or lengthen the schedule. If any one of the triangle vertices is adjusted, one or both of the other vertices must be modified for a **Project** to stay on track.

Oversight of a **Project** should be continuous. Figure 3.12 shows what we call the four-stage software development control cycle. During the first stage of the first cycle you implement and test **Features**. In later cycles you will implement and test **Features** and correct and test **Defects**. In the second stage of a cycle, you gather measurements. You can gather measurements on a monthly, weekly, daily, or continuous basis. We recommend that you continuously gather metrics and report them to **Project** personnel upon request. During the third stage you should analyze the measurements to determine how close you are to your plan and if you will finish on time. You can use models to predict the effort and time required to complete a software **Project**. Effort and development time predictor models are described in detail in Chapters 7 and 8. You can also predict reliability and usability with the models described in detail in Chapters 10, 11 and 13. In the fourth stage, after you have completed your analysis and predictions, you can apply management control to modify

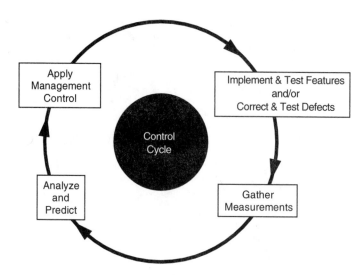

Figure 3.12 Software Development Control Cycle

your plan. The development cycle should be continuous, with management periodically applying control to keep a **Project** on track. Bernstein at AT&T [Bernstein96] says that when developing software you should make it

- work,
- work right, then
- work better.

McCarthy at Microsoft [McCarthy95] believes that you should start this cycle as soon as you can. He says that you should "engage the team in building the product *frequently, regularly, throughout the development cycle,* with *the highest possible quality,* and in a *public place* where all team members can have access to it."

Conklin at Digital Equipment Corporation [Conklin92] applied what he calls the Enrollment Management Model, which contained the following four stages: vision enrollment, commitment delegation, inspection support, and acknowledgment learning. His model can be applied as part of the software development control cycle. In the vision enrollment stage, **Project** management tries to enroll teams in the set of goals and **Project** objectives envisioned by management. The **Project**'s vision should be expressed in the terms and language of the **Group** being enrolled. The vision has to be large enough to encompass all commitments made by the **Project**. Commitment delegation is when **Project** management delegates planning tasks to **Group**s and solicits specific commitments to content and schedule. A key element of the delegation process is the explicit specification of task outputs such that they are measurable and identified with an **Individual** owner. The owner is empowered by the committing **Group** and is held accountable for the task outputs. The owner may or may not be the **Individual** who actually does the work. Inspection support is the measurement and analysis of the **Project** to ensure delivery on schedule. This support should be in the form of supportive feedback that encourages **Individual**s to disclose potential problems before they become actual problems. At the acknowledge learning stage, management acknowledges progress both personally and publicly. For each event, management asks what was learned and how managers and **Group** members can do even better next time.

Bernstein of AT&T [Bernstein96] points out that problems inevitably will occur in every **Project**. He states that "the mantra of fix the problem, then fix the process, but don't fix the blame" establishes an environment of trust. Under such an environment, **Group** members are willing to take appropriate risks.

When you pass through the software development cycle, the cost of the **Project** will increase with each cycle. A software development control cycle spiral is shown in Figure 3.13. With each pass through a control cycle, costs increases as an ever expanding spiral. Boehm of TRW [Boehm87] introduced the spiral model of software development and enhancement in 1987. Boehm's spiral model is described in detail in Chapter 4. Each cycle of Boehm's spiral begins by identifying and resolving risks.

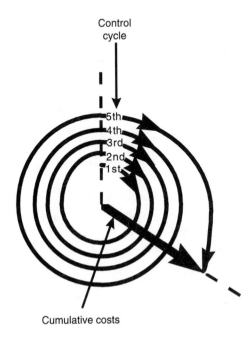

Figure 3.13 Software Development Control Cycle Spiral

Then a prototype is built. After each prototype is completed and reviewed, the objectives, alternatives, and constraints of a another prototype are planned. Then the spiral continues until an operational prototype is achieved. The radial dimension represents the cumulative cost incurred in accomplishing the steps to date; the angular dimension represents the progress made in completing each risk-prototype-based cycle of the spiral.

Instead of linking each cycle to a prototype, we suggest that a cycle should be linked to continuous monitoring and analysis, with each cycle terminated by a controlled modification of your plan based on the control triangle. Like Boehm's prototype-based spiral model, the spiral radial dimension represents the cumulative cost incurred in accomplishing the steps to date, but the angular dimension represents progress made through the software development control cycle. We recommend that the control cycle continue throughout the life of a **SoftwareProduct** and only terminate when the **SoftwareProduct** is no longer supported.

IMPROVEMENT

As the size and complexity of software continues to increase, you must do everything possible to keep up with the competition. In the early 1990s, AT&T initiated an effort to improve the productivity of software development and the quality of **SoftwareProduct**s [Belanger90]. They based their improvement on three forces that drive change: **Organization**, which represents the software development personnel; Process, which represents how improvement will be implemented, and Technology, which represents what tools can be used to implement change. These forces can be represented by a triangle as in Figure 3.14, which we will call the process improvement triangle (Belanger et al. called it the development triangle). In Chapter 2 we discussed a variation of this triangle used at IBM by Kaplan et al. [Kaplan95], which they called the iron triangle, to focus on areas for sustainable quality improvement. They replace the **Organization** vertex of the triangle with one they label Leadership. Both of these triangles emphasize that people, process, and technology are key to process improvement.

You should continuously focus on process improvement by looking for areas to improve. Shown in Figure 3.15 is the continuous process improvement cycle. You must first implement process changes that you think would improve the software development process. Next you gather measurements to see the results of the changes. Then you analyze these results and predict the effect of permanently adopting the changes. Finally, you examine the process and propose additional changes to further improve the process. After selecting the most promising improvements, you should start the cycle again by implementing the selected improvements.

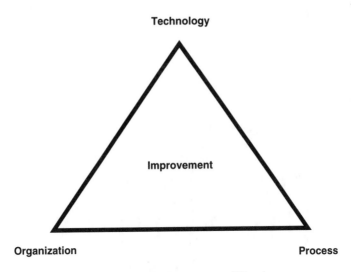

Figure 3.14 Improvement Triangle

You can represent successive passes through the software process improvement cycle by the software process improvement cycle spiral in Figure 3.16. When you successfully apply changes that improve the process, you should realize cost reductions, productivity improvements, **Defect** reductions, shortening of development time, and so on. These improvements are represented by the radial dimension of the spiral, which becomes smaller with each improvement. The angular dimension of the spiral represents progress made through the software improvement cycle.

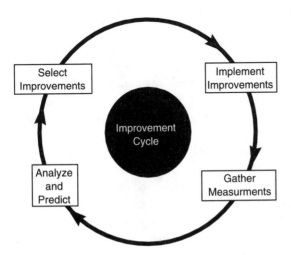

Figure 3.15 Software Process Improvement Cycle

Improvement
cycle

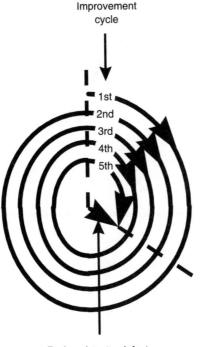

1st
2nd
3rd
4th
5th

Reduced costs, defects,
development time, etc.

Figure 3.16   Software Process Improvement Cycle Spiral

VISUALIZATION

The software development control cycle in Figure 3.12 passes through a measurement gathering stage. The process improvement cycle in Figure 3.15 passes through the same two stages. In Figure 3.17 we combine the gather measurements and analyze and predict stages of the software development control cycle and the software process improvement cycle and call these the visualization stages of the combined dual control/improvement cycle shown as branch 1 in Figure 3.17. Branch 2 is for the software development control, and branch 3 is for software process improvement.

Gathering of measurements and subsequent analysis and prediction should be continuous, which is represented by branch 4, the metric gathering cycle. Output from these visualization stages need only be performed once, with results being used by both the software developers and the process improvement staff. Computerized tools should be applied during the visualization stages to accurately gather and present quantitative development and process information in a form that is easy to use by everyone involved in the software development process. There is no technical rea-

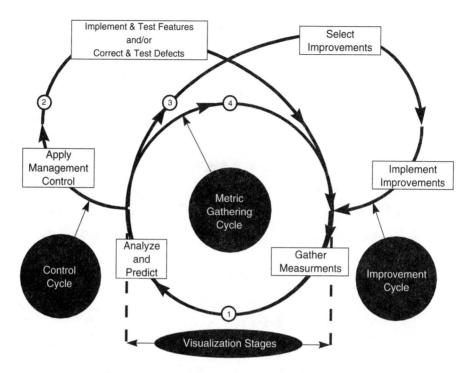

Figure 3.17 Dual Control/Improvement Cycles

son why everyone from top management to beginning programmers should not be able to directly see all aspects of the software development. With everyone continually informed, there should be fewer failed software development **Project**s.

SUMMARY

A dual control/improvement cycle was introduced in which both the control and improvement cycles shared what we described as the visualization stages. The dual cycle will result in lower overhead for gathering measurements and the resulting analysis and predictions. In Chapter 2 we described quality systems criteria and standards in support of process improvement. We will discuss the evolution of software development life cycles in Chapter 4.

We have introduced the concept of software project visualization by pointing out objects in a project that are of interest to management. The objects we introduced were **Area, Assignment, Chunk, Customer, Defect, DesignFile, Feature, Group, Individual, LicensedRunFile, Organization, Project, ReusableSource-File, Rework(SourceFile), Salary, SoftwareProduct, SourceFile, Structure,**

Supplier, UsabilityTest, VAndVTest, and **Volume(Chunk).** In Chapter 5 we will introduce additional objects and show how we can group them into classes to describe any arbitrary project. Also, we will describe how you will be able to unobtrusively gather measurements that reflect the attributes of the objects. You can use these measurements to support the software development control cycle and the software process improvement cycle.

REFERENCES

[Belanger90]   Belanger, D. G., Chappell, S. G., and Wish, M., "Evolution of Software Development Environments," *AT&T Technical Journal,* March/April 1990, pp. 2–6.

[Bernstein96]   Bernstein, L., "Software in the Large," *AT&T Technical Journal,* January/February 1996, pp. 5–14.

[Boehm73]   Boehm, B. W., "Software and Its Impact: A Quantitative Assessment," *Datamation,* May 1973, pp. 48–59.

[Boehm87]   Boehm, B. W., "A Spiral Model of Software Development and Enhancement," *Tutorial: Software Engineering Project Management,* Thayer, R. H. (ed.), IEEE Computer Society Press, Washington, DC, 1987, pp. 128–142.

[Conklin92]   Conklin, P. F., "Enrollment Management: Managing the Alpha AXP Program," *Digital Technical Journal,* Vol. 4, No. 4, 1992, pp. 193–205.

[Kaplan95]   Kaplan, C., Clark, R., and Tang, V., *Secrets of Software Quality,* McGraw-Hill, Inc., New York, 1995, 383 p.

[McCarthy95]   McCarthy, J., *Dynamics of Software Development,* Microsoft Press, Redmond, WA, 1995, 184 p.

4
Life Cycle
Processes

Instead of rushing out to buy the latest and greatest equipment for every employee, managers in a company of any size should first step back and think about how they would like their business to work. What are its essential processes, and its key databases? Ideally, how should information move?

Bill Gates
[Gates95]

INTRODUCTION

In Chapter 3 we looked at criteria, standards, and frameworks for quality systems. We know that quality and productivity can be improved. Continual improvement of processes will give you a competitive advantage over other software developers.

Software **Project**s create software following accepted software life cycles (SLCs). In this chapter we will define SLC by showing how the SLC has evolved over time. We will also contrast the DoD SLC with the industrial (nongovernment) SLC. We will then define process and show the relationships between software processes and the SLC. Software processes can be mapped to your SLC as a basis for understanding how your software processes function. When you understand the processes you are using, you can measure process activities in support of continual process improvement.

SOFTWARE LIFE CYCLE MODELS

All creatures on the earth have a life cycle. They are born, they evolve through various phases, and in the end they die. **SoftwareProduct**s are similar. All **Software-Product**s have a beginning (**Project** initiation) and an end (**Project** termination).

The evolution of a **SoftwareProduct** between the beginning and end of a process is called the software life cycle (SLC). For a specific software **Project,** the SLC is a sequenced map of activities (or tasks). From the very beginning, the SLC of large software development **Project**s has been tracked as sequential phases. The evolution of the SLC can be divided into three time periods: Early SLC, Black Box SLC, and Process SLC.

Early SLCs (Presoftware Engineering to 1968)

Early computer developments were expensive, with at least 90% of a computer development project being hardware cost. Software was considered an afterthought. Most of the design and development time went into the hardware development, with the software developed to make use of the hardware. The Early SLC period began with the development of the first large **Project**s and ended with the first software engineering conferences that were held in Europe during 1968.

The development process for large systems is usually divided into smaller manageable phases, each of which follows the previous. Early large software systems were organized in this manner. As early as 1956 [Agresti86], experience gained during the development of the Semi-Automated Ground Environment (SAGE) led to the suggestion of a phased development model containing nine phases. Also, Agresti [Agresti86] reported that in 1956 Canning proposed a phased SLC applied to electronic data processing for business [Canning56]. In 1963, Laden and Gildersleeve identified a seven-phase development SLC [Laden63]. Conferences on software engineering were held in Garmisch, Germany, in 1968 and Rome, Italy, in 1969 [Buxton69]. One of the participants at those conferences was J. D. Aron, who described an SLC of eight phases [Aron70]. For his ideas concerning the SLC, Aron credited previous work by A. M. Pietrasanta of IBM and V. LaBolle and others of Systems Development Corporation. Pietrasanta [Pietrasanta70] directly related **Project** costs to the time and resource trade-off of the SLC. He described development programmers as those who specify and code the programs that become part of the final operational system and technical support personnel as everyone else who contributes to system development, including managers, secretaries, and personnel involved in test case development, documentation, modeling, machine operations, plans and controls, recruitment and training, support programs, system integration and conversion, and so on. He stated that for different **Project**s the ratio of development programmers to technical support was 1 to 1, 1 to 2, and even as high as 1 to 3. The increase in the ratio of development personnel to support personnel indicates that the productivity decreases for large, complex software development **Project**s. Toward the end of the Early SLC period, companies began to realize that software was an expensive, complex process that was required to be engineered separately by software engineers. Also, people realized that software was hard to visualize and that something had to be done to give customers early warnings of possible software **Project** disasters. We will now look at a number of straightforward types of SLC models similar to those used in the Early SLC phases. We will start with simple SLCs for small **Project**s and proceed to SLCs for large, complex **SoftwareProduct**s.

Single-phase SLC. We will first look at the SLC of the very simple software development **Project** shown in Figure 4.1 to introduce the important concepts of SLC phase, milestone, and deliverable. We assume that the **SoftwareProduct** is so simple that you are both the developer and the user. In this chapter we will expand the definition of **SoftwareProduct** when we introduce additional SLCs.

You first have an idea for creating a piece of software. You then convert your idea into **Features** that will be built into the **SoftwareProduct**. The first milestone is to initiate a **Project** to create a simple **SoftwareProduct**. You then create the source code, compile and test the software, and then use the software for its intended purpose. We will call this part of the SLC the Code, Test, & Use phase. The software can be delivered as a run file stored on a tape, disk, or some other storage media. The **SoftwareProduct** can then be kept in storage for later use by you, or you can give it to an associate as a deliverable. When you no longer find the **Software-Product** useful and you may need more memory space on your computer, you

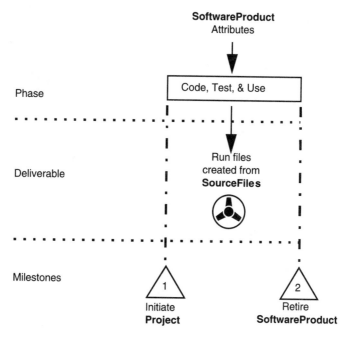

Figure 4.1 Single-phase SLC

would retire it from active use. The SLC of the simple **Project** example consists of the two milestones: (1) initiate **Project,** and (2) retire **SoftwareProduct,** and a single phase: Code, Test, & Use. You are in your highest productivity mode when you create small software systems for your own use.

Two-phase SLC.   When you produce a **SoftwareProduct** for a customer, the simplest SLC consists of at least two phases, as shown in Figure 4.2. A **Project** is initiated when a customer contacts you with an idea for a **SoftwareProduct.** From your past experience you would decide how much it would cost to create and inform the customer. If the customer disagrees with the budget, then the **Project** would terminate. If the customer agrees with the budget, you would allocate resources of people and computers to the **Project.** The activity of reviewing a **Project** at a milestone is

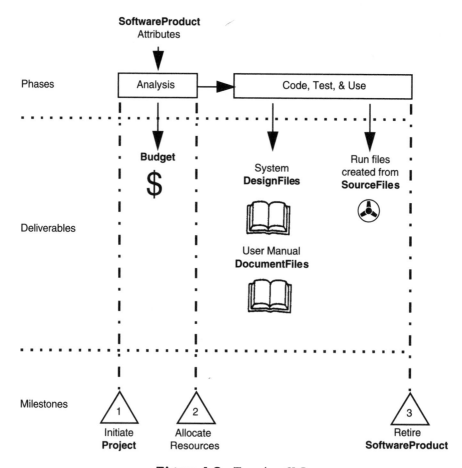

Figure 4.2   Two-phase SLC

called a milestone review. A **Project** must successfully pass a milestone review to proceed to the next phase of the SLC. During the Code, Test, & Use phase, you produce a system design specification that you save in **DesignFile**s and a user manual that you save in one of the **DocumentFile**s. The computer program is built in **SourceFile**s. At delivery time, the **SourceFile**s are translated into a run file that is delivered to the customer.

Three-phase SLC.   In two-phase SLC, you initiate implementation as soon as the budget is approved. Often, misunderstandings can arise between you and the customer over exactly what is to be designed and produced. A three-phase SLC is shown in Figure 4.3. The three-phase SLC adds a Design phase to the SLC. You should produce and deliver a design specification to the customer that describes exactly what is to be produced in a form understandable to the customer. If you and the customer do not mutually agree on what is to be produced, you can terminate the software at this point. If the customer approves the design specifications, then

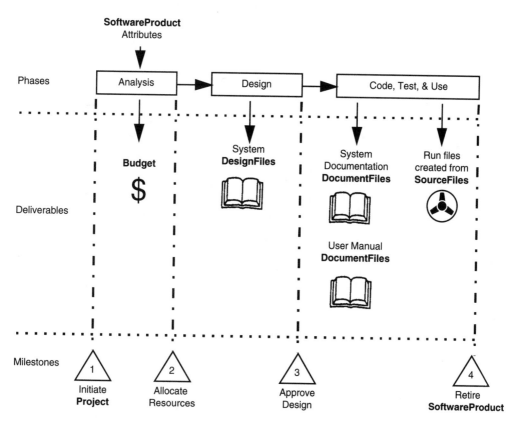

Figure 4.3   Three-phase SLC

the **Project** can proceed to the Code, Test & Use phase. During the Code, Test, & Use phase, system documentation is produced that explains exactly what is being built. The documents are saved as part of the **DocumentFile**s.

Four-phase SLC.   Software is often delivered with **Defect**s. The customer may want you to correct the **Defect**s and add new **Feature**s to the software by maintaining it after it goes into operation. Figure 4.4 shows a four-phase SLC with an added Operation & Maintenance phase. Thus, after the software is coded, tested, and installed and you and the customer agree on a maintenance budget and plan, you then maintain the software by correcting **Defect**s and adding simple enhancements during the Operation & Maintenance phase.

Black Box SLC (1968 to 1985)

The Black Box SLC period began with the NATO Software Engineering Conferences in Europe in 1968 and ended in about 1985 when process improvement methodology started to be applied to software **Project**s. At the beginning of this period, software accounted for approximately 50% of the costs of a computer project.

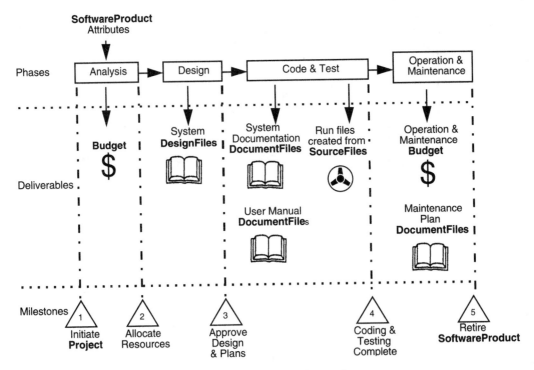

Figure 4.4   Four-phase SLC

By the end of this period, software had reached 85% of the cost of a typical computer project. During this period, software was recognized as a major problem. The software development process was treated as a black box where the customer would not interfere with how the contractor developed software. The customer would follow the software development by observing the deliverables that were produced during each phase of the SLC. Since the customer was not involved with the development process, this period will be called the Black Box SLC period.

In 1970, Royce [Royce70] described contractor problems that occur while managing large system DSLCs (Development SLCs) of the type sponsored by the U.S. government. In this book, we will define a large project as one that is larger than 75 KSLOC (thousands of source lines of code). Contractor problems could be reduced by using Royce's seven-phase DSLC. This approach emphasizes a documentation-driven development process where the customer is involved early in a formal way [through documents such as a Statement of Work (SOW)] so that the customer is committed to the **SoftwareProduct** before final delivery. Royce suggested that the customer pay for extensive personnel-intensive documentation and commit to the **Feature**s of the software prior to the delivery of the final **SoftwareProduct.** This approach has led to tying the government customer to paying for deliverables and milestone reviews, rather than tying the contractor to satisfying the customer and to delivering a working system.

During the Black Box SLC period, two different methodologies for software development process began to develop: industry methodology and government methodology. Industry methodology is used when a contractor develops software for a commercial firm. The contractor considers a **Project** successful when it is completed on time, within budget, and to customer satisfaction.

Government methodology is used when a contractor develops software for a government agency. A contract is initiated when a contractor responds to a Request for Proposal (RFP), which contains an SOW. Numerous contractors respond to the RFP with proposals. One of them is selected as prime contractor. The development process proceeds through a document-driven government DSLC where the contractor must meet milestones and produce standard government predetermined deliverables. The contractor may base expected profit on inevitable changes that always occur after development begins. The contractor considers a government **Project** a success if he makes a profit based on the original RFP and negotiated changes and produces all required deliverables according to government standards. The government decouples the Operation & Maintenance phase from DSLC phases, which allows the contractor that develops a system to leave at the end of the DSLC. While many systems perform according to government needs, some systems that perform according to the RFP may perform no useful function to the government, leaving an obviously dissatisfied customer. The following will examine industry **Project**s and government **Project**s in more detail.

Industry Projects

In 1973, Robert Gholson [Gholson73], administrative assistant to the vice-president of Information Systems at IBM, stated that, even though IBM was deeply committed to common systems development, they discovered one basic fact that made them consider abandoning that approach. The fact was that their programming process lacked a disciplined management system. He described the following management techniques and disciplines used by IBM:

- *Phase review process.* This allowed them to be sure that function was not deferred or dropped because of cost and schedule pressures.
- *Program estimating techniques.* New estimating techniques were developed because new programming technology had made their estimating techniques obsolete.
- *Predictive capability.* They needed an early warning system to allow them to concentrate their efforts on programs in trouble at a time when corrective action could be effective.
- *Measuring productivity.* They felt it was important to know about productivity before they could worry about changing it. They felt that they had to have some consistent way of measuring the effect of implementing new techniques.

IBM became committed to a software measurement program that involved not just quantity but also quality, cost, installability, serviceability, and maintainability. Gholson described their Development SLC in terms of percent of total effort and percent of total time, as shown in Table 4.1. Their distributions were compared with those of programming Projects at an IBM manufacturing plant in Mainz, Germany. The result was that they were so close as to be almost identical. This and other comparisons led them to believe that the distributions of effort and time were probably

Table 4.1   IBM Information Systems SLC

Phase	Effort (%)	Time (%)
Feasibility phase	2.2	4
General design	5.5	8
Detail design	14.4	16
Code and unit test	44.5	40
Systems test	25.6	21
Installation	7.8	4

Table 4.2   Individual Productivity versus Complexity

Difficulty	Productivity
Easy	10,000 SLOC per person-year
Medium	5,000 SLOC per person-year
Hard	1,500 SLOC per person-year

universal for IBM internal application development. They were able to estimate their major programs within 5% variance from actual.

In 1977, Alvin Kustanowitz [Kustanowitz77] of the IBM Data Processing Division described an SLC Estimation (SLICE) procedure for estimating software development resources. From an earlier work by Aron [Aron70,71], Kustanowitz partitioned program complexity into three classes as shown in Table 4.2: *easy* programs are those with very few interactions with other system elements, such as data-processing application programs; *medium* programs are those with some interactions with other system elements, such as utilities and language compilers; and *hard* programs are those with many interactions with other system elements, such as monitors and operating systems. Kustanowitz stated that the percentage of effort expended on each phase of the DSLC is a function of **Project** size as expressed in the Table 4.3.

Many authors working in the commercial environment have shown that as the size of a **Project** increases the average productivity per individual decreases. We will explore productivity in greater detail in Chapter 9.

The more complex industrial **Project**s are those that produce programming systems products [Brooks75]. Another name for this type of software is heavy-duty software, which was described by Gunther [Gunther78] of Amdahl Corporation as software to be installed at more than one site, for use by people not known by the developers, in ways not anticipated by the developers. In this book, we say that a **SoftwareProduct** is any programming system that is produced by a **Project**. **SoftwareProduct**s are usually designed for a marketing window of opportunity, which is defined by demand for the **SoftwareProduct** created for the commercial market-

Table 4.3   Effort Expended versus Project Size

DSLC Phase	Size (%)		
	Small	Intermediate	Large
Design	10–20	20–30	30–45
Code	80–60	60–40	40–10
Test	10–20	20–30	30–45

Table 4.4   SoftwareProduct **SLC**

SLC Phase	Range	Percent of Maximum DSLC (%)	Percent of Maximum SLC (%)
Analysis	4 to 10 weeks	8.6	2.3
Feasibility	1 to 10 weeks	8.6	2.3
Design	1 to 10 weeks	8.6	2.3
Programming	2 to 10 months	37.1	10.1
Evaluation	2 to 10 months	37.1	10.1
Use	2 to 6 years		72.8

place. These windows of opportunity were described by Gunther to vary from 2 to 6 years, as shown in Table 4.4. When the DSLC exceeds the planned schedule, the schedule overrun reduces the marketing window of opportunity.

In 1979, Albrecht [Albrecht79] described a methodology used by IBM Data Processing (DP) Services organization to develop contract software for customers. The DP Services organization consisted of about 450 people simultaneously engaged in approximately 150 application development **Project**s. While some **Project**s required an many as 40 DP Service and customer people, the average **Project** size was 3 people. Albrecht used the SLC shown in Table 4.5.

Prior to initiation of a DP Service contract, a need must be identified and **Project** objectives described. For a typical **Project**, system design requires about 20% of effort and implementation requires about 80%. The DP Services organization measures the success of an application development **Project** by their basic criteria that **Project**s should be finished on time and within budget and delivered to a satisfied

Table 4.5   IBM DP Services SLC

Phase	Subphase	Percent of total effort
Identify need		
Describe **project** objectives		
System design	Requirements External design Internal design	20%
Implementation	Unit design Code Unit test System test	80%
Operation and maintenance		

customer. An extensive measurement program was initiated to assure that the criteria were met.

In the industrial (nongovernment) area, successful software contractors learned how to produce software that was on time, within budget, and delivered to satisfied customers. If they did not, they would not have repeat customers.

Government Projects

The government software development methodology of the mid-1970s was influenced by W. W. Royce, who observed that when you develop software for a customer the only two essential phases common to all SLCs are the Analysis and the Coding phases [Royce70]. He felt that, when you create a plan to develop a large software system with an SLC keyed only to these two phases, your software development **Project** is doomed to failure. He felt that many additional development phases are required, but none contribute as directly to the final **SoftwareProduct** as Analysis and Coding, and all drive up the development costs. When you create additional phases and deliverables, customer personnel typically would rather not pay for them, and development personnel would rather not implement them. Royce felt that the prime function of management is to sell these concepts to both groups and then enforce compliance on the part of development personnel. Based on work by Royce and others, rigorous versions of complex SLCs were developed that were made up of multiple phases, deliverables, and milestone reviews. This complex model of successive overlapping phases, deliverables, and milestone reviews became known as the Waterfall SLC Model. Royce believed that you should have a lot of documentation. In fact, you should have more than most programmers, analysts, or program designers are willing to do if left to their own devices. One of his rules of managing software development is ruthless enforcement of documentation requirements. Another of his rules was that if the **SoftwareProduct** in question is being developed for the first time arrange matters so that the version finally delivered to the customer is actually the second version insofar as critical design/operations areas are concerned. The Royce Waterfall SLC is a document-driven management approach where deliverables and milestones are used to reflect progress.

In 1976, Alberts [Alberts76] analyzed the SLC to determine where in the cycle the application of quality assurance would be most beneficial. Large software development **Project**s, all of which would have cost over a billion dollars, in terms of 1990 dollars, were reviewed. He computed the average cost and time for known very large development **Project**s (that is, SAGE, NTDS, GEMINI, SATURN V, OS/360) and presented the composite four-phase SLC shown in Table 4.6 based on a 16-year length. He analyzed the cost of design, logic, and syntax errors and determined that design errors account for 80% of the total cost of errors. The high percentage cost of design errors can probably be traced to the costly document-driven

Table 4.6   Proportion of SLC Cost and Time for Very Large Development Projects

SLC Phase	Idealized SLC (%)		Composite Actual Data (%)	
	Cost	Time	Cost	Time
Conceptual	4	15	1	31.2
Requirements	4	8	1.5	9.4
Development	60	40	47.5	9.4
Operations	32	37	50	50

DSLC, where manually created multiple deliverables are very expensive. Developers began to place more effort and time on reduction of design errors that occur during the earlier phases of the SLC.

In 1976, Boehm of TRW [Boehm76], while discussing the field of software engineering, presented a cascaded SLC that emphasized validation during each phase of the SLC. At the Second Annual Software Engineering Conference, Patrick [Patrick76] reported that Boehm described the cost distribution as shown in Table 4.7. In 1987, Boehm reported that the amount of effort spent in coding should be approximately 15% and that two out of every three dollars spent on a software **Project** are spent on software maintenance [Boehm87a].

In 1977, Walston and Felix [Walston77] of IBM Federal Systems Division presented the results of a study of 66 completed **Project**s that contained from 4,000 to 467,000 SLOCs and with effort that ranged from 12 to 11,758 person-months. A least-squares fit to their data resulted in the effort estimation equation:

$$E = 5.2L^{0.91}$$

where E = total effort in person-months and L = thousands of SLOC (KSLOC). The average productivity based on **Project** size would then be

TABLE 4.7   Boehm's SLC Cost Distribution

SLC Phase	Percent of DSLC Cost [Boehm76]	Percent of SLC Cost [Boehm76]	Percent of DSLC Cost [Boehm87a]	Percent of SLC Cost [Boehm87a]
Design	40	12	60	20
Code	20	6	15	5
Test	40	12	25	8
Maintenance		70		67

$$P = 0.19L^{0.09}$$

where P = average productivity in KSLOC per person-month.

Most authors report that productivity declines as the size of **Project**s increases [Boehm81][Hester81][Jones77][Jones86][Wolverton74]. After examining actual empirical data, both Walston and Felix [Walston77] and Nelson [Nelson78] found that productivity for government **Project**s actually increased as the size and complexity of **Project**s increased. The only explanation for the low productivity of small **Project**s is that military standards and other government policies forced small **Project**s to carry the same documentation and other government-dictated overhead as large **Project**s. Evidence for this explanation can be found in the Walston and Felix equation [Walston77] for documentation:

$$D = 49L^{1.01}$$

where D = pages of documentation. This equation says that a 4-KSLOC software system had an averages of 50 pages per KSLOC, while a 400-KSLOC software system had 52 pages per KSLOC. In other words, they required essentially the same amount of documentation for small government systems as for large government systems.

Banker and Kemerer [Banker89] describe the apparent contradiction of productivity decreasing or increasing as either economies or diseconomies of scale. They hypothesize that, for most software development production processes of a given SLC, there exist increasing returns to scale for smaller **Project**s and decreasing returns for very large **Project**s. That is, average productivity is increasing as long as the **Project** size is smaller than the most productive scale size (MPSS) and is decreasing for **Project**s that are larger. The actual MPSS will be different for different SLCs.

The SLC for a software **Project** is usually chosen depending on the size of a **Project** and the organizational culture of an organization. Each SLC requires a fixed investment in **Project** management overhead, and average productivity increases initially as the fixed overhead is spread over a larger **Project.** Productivity increases on progressively larger **Project**s may also come from the greater use of specialized personnel and tools and possibly greater management attention. Banker and Kemerer hypothesized that eventually the larger **Project** size generally makes it more difficult to manage, and the marginal productivity of the **Project** team is likely to decline.

The economies of scale described by Banker and Kemerer and those observed by Walston and Felix occur when an SLC optimized for a very large software **Project** is used for a small **Project.** Since government standard SLCs are designed to be used for very large software **Project**s, it is not surprising that productivity decreases when these same SLC methodologies are applied to smaller **Project**s. The low-overhead, high-productivity SLC for small programs would not be effective in removing the increasing number of **Defect**s per KSLOC that are found in the larger projects. Thus, the high-productivity $SLC_{small\ programs}$ cannot be effectively used for larger categories. For similar reasons, the high overhead $SLC_{very\ large\ programs}$ demonstrates low productivity when used for small programs. The selection of an SLC is a trade-off between productivity and quality. As the size and complexity of a software system increase, the SLC overhead increases to control quality, which results in a decrease in productivity.

Walston and McHenry [McHenry78] point out that the typical Department of Defense (DoD) procurement is divided into at least two procurement life cycles (PLCs) because DoD Directive 5000.29 contemplates a separate development and maintenance contractor. Some software development **Project**s are divided into more than two separate procurements. Each contract is preceded by a period of preproposal, proposal, evaluation, and selection activities during which the contractor is operating at least in part with his own discretionary funds. Total SLC cost estimates are difficult to compute because of unknown government personnel and facility costs. During the PLC, the government does not follow the accounting practices imposed on its contractors, and personnel and facility costs may not be accurately known.

In 1979, Jensen, Randall, and Tonies of Hughs Aircraft Company [Jensen79] discussed the SLC, which included a discussion of the PLC. Before an RFP is advertised to potential contractors, the government must prepare a Program Management Directive, Decision Coordination Paper, Program Management Plan, Determination and Findings, Advance Procurement Plan, Computer Resources Integrated Support Plan, Statement of Work, Procurement Specification, and a Contract Data Requirements List. Some bidding companies, realizing that adjustments or overruns are inevitable no matter who does the job, submit proposals to do the work more or less as called for in the RFP. The logic is [Jensen79] "let's win the contract first; then we'll show the customer where his requirements are unreasonable, and together we'll draft a new plan." In all such cases, cost and schedule overruns become apparent to both customer and contractor, and disagreements on the **SoftwareProduct** definition usually develop. Salvaging the **Project** is painful, expensive, and embarrassing to all parties. The preproposal, proposal, and postproposal activities performed by government personnel are expensive, but are many times hidden because of government agency accounting procedures.

Hester, Parnas, and Utter [Hester81] discuss using documentation as a medium for developing and expressing software designs. Parnas and Clements [Parnas86] go further and propose that we ought to document software development as though we followed conventional SLC models, even though we often do not follow such models. This would cause deliverables to be produced by the contractor and paid for by the customer even though the DSLC methodology is not followed.

If the deliverables actually helped in the visualization and understanding a **SoftwareProduct** and its status, they might be worth the effort. Dorfman [Dorfman90] describes a typical Jet Propulsion Laboratory software development **Project** that had

10 phases, 38 separate documents as deliverables, and as many as 13 major milestone reviews. Government milestone reviews can last up to a week and cost as much as $580,000 per review [Shere88]. That number of expensive deliverables and milestone reviews is not found in the development of commercial software for industry.

In 1982, Simmons et al. [Simmons82] examined under government contract a large multibillion dollar flight computer software development contract to determine what deliverables and nondeliverables should be retained to monitor and predict software complexity and programmer productivity for future **Project**s. From the deliverables provided, the government customer personnel felt that the **Project** was visible to them and they knew the status of all software. The **Project**'s feasibility, design, development, verification, validation, and operational testing phases had taken 10 years and cost hundreds of millions of dollars at the time the study was performed. A total of 1,600 person-years of development effort had been expended to produce 2,010 program modules that contained 700,000 lines of code. Approximately 85% of the modules were written in a higher-order language, and approximately 15% were written in assembler language. The government thought that they had all releases of their software system on magnetic tape. While a run version of their system was all that was required as an official deliverable, the government assumed that a source code version was available for the asking and that it could be compiled and linked to create a run version. To the surprise of the government, the study found the following:

- Even though the **Project** was 10 years old, accurate changes to the specifications (that is, CRs) and discrepancies found during testing (DRs) were only available for the previous 5 years from the contractor.

- Units of measurement were not consistent between software releases. The units to measure personnel and cost were changed, and the functions of the departments were also changed between releases.

- The contractor would deliver run versions to the customer. Source modules and the module linkage or compilation sequence information were not deliverables. If a source module did not change between releases, only the changed modules were recompiled. Over time, the system software was changed, which meant that modules that were not recompiled actually were out of phase with modules that were compiled using up-to-date system software.

- Statistical information was supplied with each release of the software. The software that produced statistics only gave a partial set of possible statistics.

- The error information available in the DRs was incomplete. A consistent error classification system was not used. While the customer thought that all the release information was available from the very first release, complete release information was found for only the most current release.

- The most surprising problem encountered was a result of a government economy drive. A request had been issued to reuse magnetic tapes that no longer contained current information. Most of the software release information that was more than 1 year old had been erased. The government had erased 9 years of historical data.

From the numerous deliverables and milestone reviews, the government personnel thought that they knew the status of all current and past releases. The many official deliverables through which the contractor communicated with the customer masked the actual status of the system. A large number of deliverables can mask actual system status.

During the Black Box SLC period, a lot was learned about the software development process that would be very useful during the Process SLC period. We will now look at a number of versions of the SLCs used during the Black Box period. We examine a Waterfall SLC, V SLC, Prototype SLC, and an Incremental SLC.

Waterfall SLC.   A version of the Waterfall Model is shown in Figure 4.5. Input to the Waterfall SLC is **SoftwareProduct** attributes. The Waterfall SLC **SoftwareProduct** is a computer program plus all the planning, documentation, testing, publications, training, distribution, maintenance, and control that comprise the aggregate heavy-duty software—software that will be replicated many times and installed at many different sites; software that will be used by many different people in different ways not anticipated by the developers; software whose users will not have access to the developers. Ideas for a **SoftwareProduct** often are gathered by marketing representatives who analyze them and propose to develop a **SoftwareProduct** with a given set of attributes. Once a **Project** is budgeted, the feasibility of the **SoftwareProduct** is determined. In the feasibility phase you determine technical, operational, economic, and marketing feasibility. When you determine that a **SoftwareProduct** is feasible, you produce a set of **Features** that, when implemented, will emulate the attributes of the desired **SoftwareProduct.**

Testing becomes a major consideration for a **SoftwareProduct.** Notice that a System Test phase is added after the Coding & Unit Test phase. The coding and testing of all modules and units within a system happens during the Coding & Unit Test phase. An actual working system must exist before the **SoftwareProduct** is passed from the development team to the test team.

The test that must be passed before formal system test begins is the α test. Once the α test has been successfully passed. The system developers give the **SoftwareProduct** to the test team for the System Test phase (often called the β test phase). Software is tested to verify that the software properly implements the system design specifications (that is, you verify that you have built the **SoftwareProduct** right) and to validate that **Features** have been implemented (that is, you validate

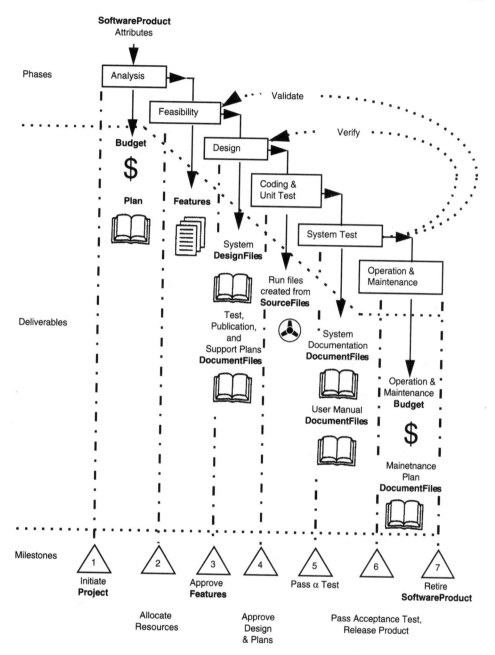

SoftwareProduct
Attributes

Phases

Analysis

Validate

Feasibility

Verify

Budget

Design

$

Coding &
Unit Test

Plan

Features

System Test

System
DesignFiles

Operation &
Maintenance

Run files
created from
SourceFiles

Deliverables

Test,
Publication,
and
Support Plans
DocumentFiles

System
Documentation
DocumentFiles

Operation &
Maintenance
Budget

User Manual
DocumentFiles

$

Mainetnance
Plan
DocumentFiles

Milestones

1   2   3   4   5   6   7

Initiate
Project

Approve
Features

Pass α Test

Retire
SoftwareProduct

Allocate
Resources

Approve
Design
& Plans

Pass Acceptance Test,
Release Product

Figure 4.5   Waterfall Model

that you have built the right **SoftwareProduct**). A final acceptance test must be passed; then the **SoftwareProduct** is released for the Operation & Maintenance phase.

V SLC.   As the size and complexity of software systems increase and the need for more reliable software grows, a V SLC that emphasizes testing has become more popular. The left side of the V in Figure 4.6 is made up of the Analysis, Feasibility, System Design, and Unit Design phases. The point of the V is the Coding phase. Then the right of the V is the Unit Test, System Test, **Feature** Test, and Operation & Maintenance phases.

During the Unit Test phase, you verify that each branch of a program is completely tested. You pretend that the computer is a glass box where you can peer into each unit to verify that each software unit is properly verified according to the unit design. Next you integrate the individual software units into a system and verify that the entire system is operating properly according to a predefined α test. Then the **Feature** Test (or β Test) phase begins. The **Feature** Test phase treats the computer system as a black box. The **Feature** Test phase validates **Feature**s to see that you receive an appropriate output response for a given input. During this phase, you do not care what happens within the computer system. You should run coverage tests to see that every program static branch is exercised, regression tests to see that **Feature**s that were working are still working, and configuration tests to see that the software operates with each expected type of configuration. The testing phases are over when you complete the final acceptance test and the **SoftwareProduct** is released for the Operation & Maintenance phase.

Prototype SLC.   When you design hardware, often you may develop an engineering prototype before you develop the final version that you plan to manufacture. This was one of the concepts recommended by Royce [Royce70]. The engineering prototype is used to see that you have a proper design and to assure that the hardware operates properly before you create a final version that you plan to manufacture. You can do the same when creating a **SoftwareProduct**. You may develop the prototype using a high-level application generator and then develop the final version of the **SoftwareProduct** using an efficient programming high-level language. This process is called rapid prototyping.

Incremental SLC.   After the Feasibility phase of the Waterfall SLC model, you should know all of the customer requirements for which you plan to build **Feature**s of the **SoftwareProduct**. Seldom does the customer or the software developer know all customer requirements. Jones says that customer requirements typically grow at 1% per month [Jones92] during development. This means that, over the life

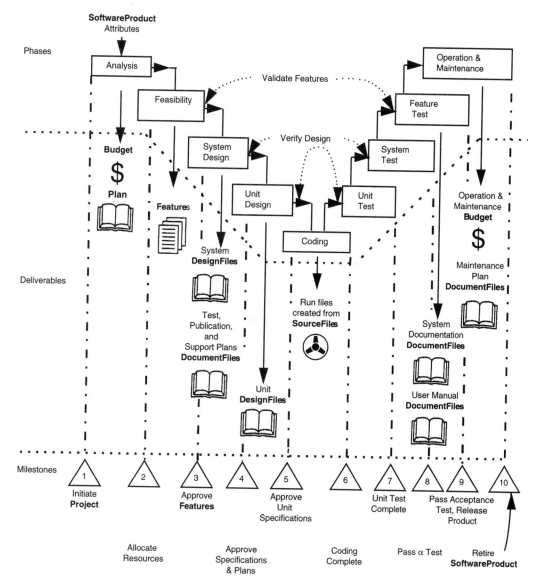

Figure 4.6 V SLC

of a 3-year **Project,** requirements will grow 36%. He also says that user requirements grow 5% to 7% per year during deployment.

One approach to reducing the effect of the ever changing customer requirements is to incrementally develop a system. Mills introduced incremental development as a method of developing large systems [Mills71]. He believed that the system should first be made to run by stubbing out many of the subroutines. Then, bit by bit it is fleshed out, with the subprograms in turn being developed into actions or calls to empty stubs in the levels below.

Brooks strongly recommends incrementally growing systems instead of trying to build a single working version [Brooks87]. He has found that teams can grow much more complex entities in a given amount of time than they can build. At every stage of incremental development, you have a running system. You can start user testing earlier, and you can adopt a build-to-budget strategy that protects absolutely against schedule or budget overruns. You can avoid these overruns by trading **Features** for costs and schedule.

In Chapter 2 we mentioned that the United States started introducing continuous quality improvement methodology to improve both quality and productivity for both manufacturing and service industries. The methodology used to develop large systems during the Black Box SLC period could no doubt be improved. In about 1985, the U.S. software industry began to seriously apply process improvement techniques to the software industry.

PROCESS SLC (1985 TO THE PRESENT)

The process-based SLC period began when Watts Humphrey suggested applying the process-based philosophy to programming. In 1985, Watts Humphrey, a director of programming quality and process at IBM, wrote that an orderly and structured process addresses programming quality by providing an environment that fosters predictable results and eliminates mistakes [Humphrey85]. He said that process discipline reduces such waste, permits more orderly learning, and allows the professionals to build on the experiences of others. He felt that process discipline also provides the essential foundation for increased mechanization of the programming job itself. In Chapter 2 we described the Software Engineering Institute's capabilities maturity model for assessment and evaluation, which was developed by Humphrey. We also discussed the Malcolm Baldrige National Quality Award criteria, ISO 9000 standards for quality systems, and the methodologies used by the IBM Santa Teresa Laboratory in their software quality improvement program. In the following we will examine two flexible SLC models that can be adapted for process improvement. We will now investigate the Spiral SLC and the Natural Milestone SLC.

Spiral SLC

Boehm proposed a Spiral SLC that contains many characteristics of the Waterfall, Prototype, and Incremental SLCs. The Spiral SLC shown in Figure 4.7 is based directly on the Spiral SLC model developed by Boehm [Boehm87b,87c,88]. The radial dimension in Figure 4.7 represents the cumulative cost incurred in accomplish-

Determine objectives,
alternatives, and constraints

Evaluate alternatives,
identify risks, and
resolve risks

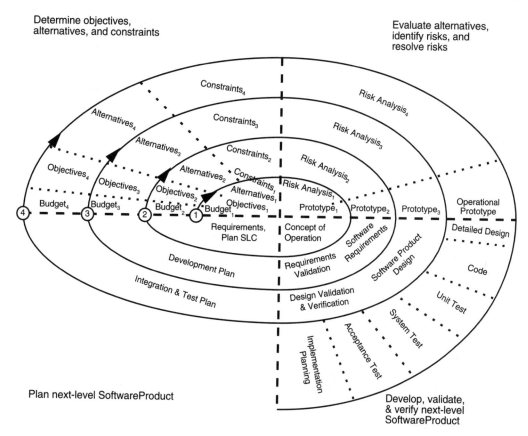

Figure 4.7 Spiral SLC

ing the phases to date; the angular dimension represents progress made in completing each cycle of the spiral. One cycle through the spiral is similar to one pass through a Waterfall SLC. Different objectives are accomplished with each pass through the spiral.

We will now examine passes through the spiral. The number of cycles through the spiral depends on what one is trying to accomplish with the software development **Project.** The Spiral SLC in the example shown in Figure 4.7 has four cycles through the spiral. Cycle 1 of the spiral is initiated by allocation of a budget to the **Project.** Then you must determine the cycle 1

- objectives of the **SoftwareProduct** (**Feature**s, performance, and so on),
- alternatives [create a new system, use COTS (commercial off-the-shelf software), reuse software, and so on] and
- constraints imposed on the alternatives (resources, schedule, and so on).

Table 4.8 Spiral Results from Example in Figure 4.7

Cycle	Develop and Validate	Plan
1	Concept of operation	Requirements, SLC
2	Software requirements	Development
3	Design	Integration and test
4	Operational prototype	

The alternatives are evaluated with respect to the objectives and constraints. The output of the evaluation will be identification of areas of uncertainty associated with **Project** risks. The **Project** risks will then be analyzed to determine a cost-effective strategy for reducing the uncertainty associated with **Project** risks. You may use a prototype, simulation, benchmarks, analytic modeling, or combinations of these to resolve the risks. You would then validate the part of the **SoftwareProduct** related to the risks that had been resolved and plan for the next cycle. For Figure 4.7, the risks resolved for each cycle and the plan prepared for the next cycle are shown in Table 4.8.

The spiral model is very flexible and can be adapted to the needs of many different evolutionary development **Project**s. While Boehm is no longer at TRW, in 1987 when he described the Spiral SLC he said that the spiral model of the software process has been evolving at TRW for several years. He points out that the spiral model applies equally to development or enhancement efforts. You must start with the hypothesis that a product or process can be improved by applying the spiral model to a software **Project**. The spiral model then involves a test of this hypothesis: At any time, if the hypothesis fails the test, the spiral is terminated. Otherwise, it terminates in installation of the **SoftwareProduct.** The use of the spiral model can be extended into the operation and maintenance phase of a **Project.** The hypothesis can continue to be tested as risks are continually assessed during the maintenance and modification cycles through the spiral in the operation phase.

Natural Milestone SLC

With the exception or the Spiral SLC, we have looked at SLCs that were meant to be fairly rigid frameworks around which to organize software **Project**s. What we would like is to manufacture software like an assembly line product where we could build to plans. We find that once we start a software **Project** the needs of the **Project** do not always meet the needs of predefined SLC frameworks.

McCarthy [McCarthy95] recently described 54 rules that he applies to software development at Microsoft Corporation to build successful **SoftwareProduct**s. We will use approximately half of his rules to describe a set of natural milestones to track the progress of a software development **Project**. In Figure 4.8, we show the

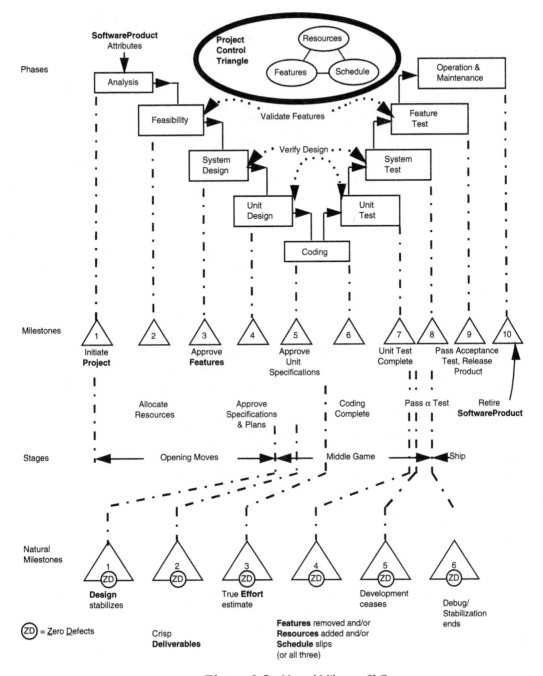

Figure 4.8 Natural Milestone SLC

Natural Milestone SLC drawn below the more conventional V SLC. Only the phases and milestones are shown for both SLCs. **Project** deliverables are very important and must be produced, but they are left out of Figure 4.8 to simplify the discussion. Before a **Project** starts, the initial plan will be to generally follow a V SLC. You then model the natural milestones around the stages of playing a game. The stages are Opening Moves, Middle Game, and Ship (instead of end game).

The Opening Moves stage starts with the initiation of a software **Project** and terminates when the design stabilizes. A software manager is assigned to be in charge of the **SoftwareProduct** development. The **SoftwareProduct** will be created by empowered teams. For this example, we will assume that we would like to create a **SoftwareProduct** that we will sell to customers. The development team is composed of members from quality assurance (QA), development, documentation, program management, marketing, and so on.

The **SoftwareProduct** requirements are described as **Features**. The **SoftwareProduct** is partitioned into packages of **Features**. You assign each package to a **Feature** team around a matrix organization (that is, the QA team member will have organizational ties to the **Feature** team and to QA, the marketing team member will have ties to the **Feature** team and to marketing, and so on). The team members are identified with the **Feature** team, empowered to contribute to the design of their **Feature** package, accountable for their actions, and participate in consensus decision making about the package. The distribution of team members in one of McCarthy's typical **Feature** teams at Microsoft is one program manager, six developers, two or three QA people, and two documentation people.

A multirelease technology plan must be created to guide the team. The technology plan is the output of empowered consensus where each team member provides input. This input is rigorously sought and each team member has a vote. The technology plan is the basis for all team behavior and the map to reaching your goal. For a commercial **SoftwareProduct,** you must have a multirelease strategy to assure that your product will have a long life. To stay competitive, the releases should be frequent, based on a rapid cycling through the development cycle.

The Middle Game stage starts when the design stabilizes and terminates during final testing. It is about expectations, uncertainty, and struggle. The middle game is full of nasty surprises and unexpected failures. You use the natural milestones to guide you through this stage. You control the development process through control of **Features**, resources, and schedule. You can reduce your schedule by adding resources or removing **Features**, you can increase your **Features** by increasing your resources and schedule, you can reduce your costs by reducing **Features** or decreasing resources, and so on. The **Features**, resources, and schedule **Project** control triangle is shown at the top of Figure 4.8 to represent the mechanism for controlling a software development **Project.**

The Natural Milestone SLC is based on the Incremental SLC philosophy. You should build a version of the product as soon as possible and as often as possible.

During the early builds, your main goal should be to create a working version that exists in a known state. Once you have achieved the known state, then you should try to stay there.

We track progress of a **Project** by determining when milestones are reached. For each milestone, you establish understandable goals that allow you to precisely and accurately determine when the milestone has been met. For all members of the team, specific contracts for each goal should be established. At Microsoft, they use Zero Defect (ZD) milestones to precisely determine when a milestone has been achieved. At a ZD milestone, the team achieves the quality level set for the milestone, in the time allotted to meet it, and the product is tested to that effect. At a ZD milestone, bugs may still exist in the system and there may be missing functionality. The ZD milestone only means that you have successfully met all the goals set for the milestone. A 1-year product cycle at Microsoft typically has three or four ZD milestones in the product cycle. In his book, McCarthy describes a typical large **Project** that has six ZD milestones, which are shown in Figure 4.8.

Each milestone should reflect goals that occur naturally as part of a software development **Project.** In addition to the goals, a simple one- or two-line story should be associated with the milestone to summarize the goals of the milestone. The story lines for the six milestones in the Figure 4.8 example are (1) **Design** stabilizes; (2) Crisp **Deliverables;** (3) True **Effort** estimate; (4) **Feature**s removed and/or **Resources** added and/or **Schedule** slips (or all three); (5) **Development** ceases; (6) **Debug/Stabilization** ends.

In most **Project**s, rapid change occurs to the original design specifications. When development starts, typically numerous unknowns remain in a design. As unknowns are eliminated, changes occur to a design. All unknowns are eliminated only at the end of development, not at the beginning. Thus, the first natural milestone is when the design stabilizes, not when all unknowns are eliminated. Design stabilization is communicated throughout the team by some combination of electronic mail, specifications, prototypes, hallway conversations, whiteboarding, and implementation. A manager assesses status by drilling down into some aspect of the design and evaluating whether all members of the team are aware of it.

The second natural milestone is when the deliverables become crisp. Crisp deliverables are clear, simple, and credible. After design stabilization and all levels of the **Project** understand the full extent of what is being created, everyone realizes the true characteristics of the deliverables. Then negotiations are reopened and detail is sketched into the schedule.

The third natural milestone may actually occur many times. Often this occurs after a major slip in schedule. At this point, leadership meets to chart a course of action that results in the development of a consensual plan of action.

The fourth natural milestone occurs when the **SoftwareProduct** is evolving into its final form. Final resolution of conflicts in **SoftwareProduct**s must be resolved. Conflicts are resolved by applying the **Project** control triangle in Figure 4.8.

As conflicts are resolved, **Feature**s are adjusted or eliminated, resources may or may not be added, and the schedule may have to be adjusted again.

The fifth natural milestone occurs when all development ceases. All coding stops and the **SoftwareProduct** is **Feature** complete. This is the point where no more adjustments to the design can be made and all that is left is the final stabilization of the **SoftwareProduct.**

The sixth natural milestone occurs when the **SoftwareProduct** is debugged and stabilized. This is similar to the passing of an internal α test process, and a **SoftwareProduct** transitions into the rigorous final β test.

The Ship stage starts when final testing begins and terminates with the delivery of the **SoftwareProduct**. The **SoftwareProduct** should be tested to ensure that it works as expected in as many configurations as possible. The **SoftwareProduct** is often shared with friendly customers to determine that it works properly in the customer environment. This is not the time to seek customer input on design or new **Feature**s.

We have examined the evolution of SLCs. During this era of process improvement, the concept of SLC is expanded to treat software development as a process made up of numerous subprocesses and activities that all must work together to produce high-quality, cost-effective **SoftwareProduct**s that are usable by customers. In the next section we will look at a portrayal of the software life cycle process.

SOFTWARE LIFE CYCLE PROCESS

In Chapter 2 we described the criteria and standards for quality improvement. When we improve quality, productivity improvement often follows. We described the DoD Software Assessment and Evaluation programs. DoD is evolving away from developing software in conformance to rigorous military standards. In the past when you developed software according to a rigorous Waterfall SLC-based standard, you had to obtain waivers if you did not want to perform to every milestone review and to produce every deliverable. Today, DoD encourages agencies to buy COTS software instead of producing software using military standards. When DoD contractors develop software, they are encouraged to improve their software development process methodology and then evaluate it according to the CMM framework described in Chapter 2.

We have found that software can be developed for both government and industry that costs less, has higher quality, and is more usable by improving the software process. In this section, we will first look at how we define process in the context of quality improvement methodology. Then we, will examine a software process model based on the IEEE Standard Life Cycle Processes [IEEE91]. After that we will explore how to approach continuous process improvement.

Process

The software development process is mainly a people process. The main cost of software development is the people cost. We are very interested in the processes and activities performed by people. A process is a system of inputs, activities, work flows, information flows, and other interdependencies that produces a specific set of outputs and results. A process receives inputs from other processes called supplier processes in Figure 4.9. Outputs are supplied as inputs to other processes called customer processes. There must be close working relationships between supplier, process, and customer. These relationships are represented by the forward flows and then the feedback relationships in Figure 4.9. While there are suppliers to a software **Project** and there are customers that use a **SoftwareProduct,** each internal process is a supplier of inputs to other processes and a customer of outputs from other processes.

A process is composed of activities or activities and other processes. Process improvement is based on identification, empowerment, accountability, and consensus. Each process must be identified and a process owner identified. The people engaged in process activities must be empowered to make suggestions about process improvement. Decisions should be made with an emphasis on consensus among individuals involved in the process.

IEEE SLC Process Model

The IEEE SLC Process Model Standard includes activities that are grouped into processes that may be included as processes within a higher-level process. The IEEE SLC Process Model acts as a skeleton framework on which to map activities to produce a SLC to serve as a sequenced map of activities for a specific **Project** [IEEE91]. The standard also defines 17 processes as functions that must be performed in the SLC. A process is composed of activities. We have modified the standard model to include three processes for validation, verification, and evaluation, instead of a single verification and validation process. Each activity within a process has inputs from

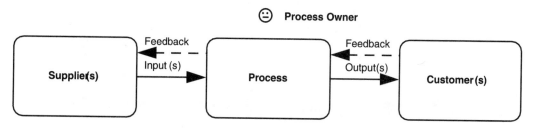

Figure 4.9 Customer/Supplier Process Improvement Model

source (supplier) activities and outputs to destination (customer) activities. The processes then can be mapped into phases to describe **Project**-oriented SLCs. In the following we will look at a version of the SLC processes and not try to map them into phased SLCs. The SLC Process Model partitions processes into Development processes, **Project** Management processes, and Integral processes.

The Development processes are shown in Figure 4.10. The Development processes are grouped into those that occur predevelopment, during development, and postdevelopment. The processes that occur predevelopment are Concept Exploration and System Allocation. Those that occur during development are Requirements, Design, and Implementation. Those that occur after development are Instal-

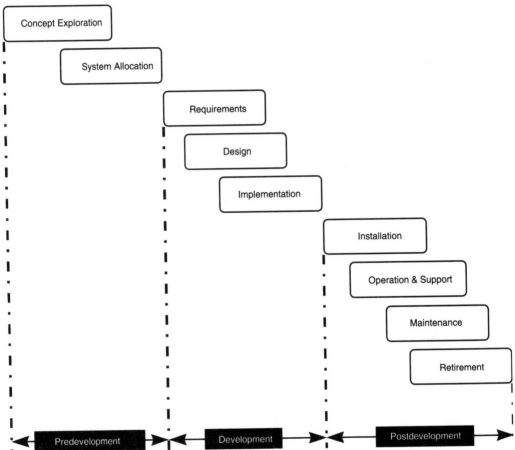

Figure 4.10 Development Processes

lation, Operation & Support, Maintenance, and Retirement. Each of the processes have many activities that occur. Each activity has an owner responsible for the activity. The actual standard provides detail about activities that make up each process. We will describe the activities in an example process to show typical activities that you should include as part of a process.

We will use as an example the activities within the Implementation process. The Implementation activities list is as follows:

1. Create test data.
2. Create source.
3. Generate object code.
4. Create operating documentation.
5. Plan integration.
6. Perform integration.

Each of these can be described by another level of activities with inputs, activities, outputs, and so on.

For each of the development processes, the output of one process is used as input to other processes. Figure 4.11 shows how a **Project** can continuously cycle through each of the processes until a **SoftwareProduct** is ready for retirement. The cycling process is represented by Incremental and Spiral SLCs. The cycling ceases when a **SoftwareProduct** is retired from use.

The **Project** Management processes shown in Figure 4.12 are **Project** Initiation, **Project** Monitoring & Control, and Software Quality Management. The two main people involved in large software development **Projects** are the lead manager and the lead designer. If either of these two people lacks appropriate skills and abilities, he or she can be the cause of **Project** failure. The top **Project** manager controls the **Project** Management processes. The relationships of the Management processes with the Development processes of the SLC are shown in Figure 4.13.

The **Project** Initiation process contains activities that create the framework for the **Project.** The SLC is created and plans for managing the **Project** are established. Policies, methodologies, and tools needed to manage and execute the **Project** are identified and a plan prepared that contains initial schedules and resource allocation.

The **Project** Monitoring & Control process tracks, reports, and manages costs, schedules, problems and performance throughout the SLC. This process is pervasive and interacts with most of the other SLC processes.

The Software Quality Management process is where the software QA program is planned, initiated, administered and reviewed. This process is responsible for understanding and improving the quality throughout the SLC. Here is where metrics are defined to monitor software quality. The responsibilities, functions, obligations,

Software Life Cycle Processes

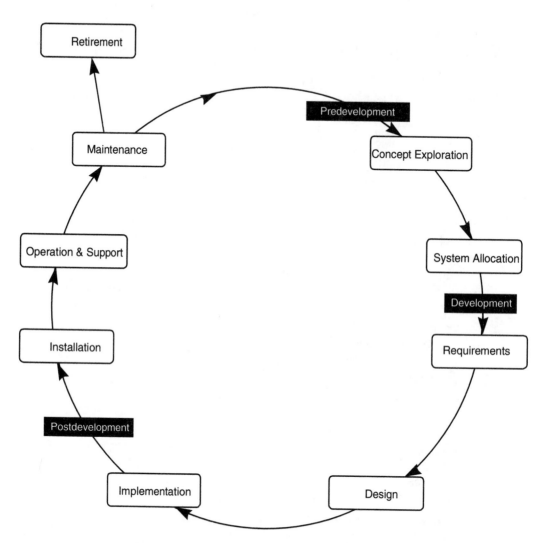

Figure 4.11   SLC Process Model with the Development Processes

and duties of QA are interspersed into all SLC activities. The activities of this process span the entire SLC.

The Integral processes shown in Figure 4.14 are Software Configuration Management, **Feature** Validation & Tracking, Design Verification & Tracking, Usability Evaluation & Tracking, Documentation Development, and Training. These

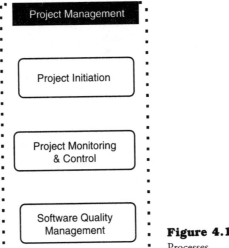

Figure 4.12 **Project** Management Processes

processes are needed to successfully complete other SLC activities. These processes are used to ensure the completion and quality of **Project Features**. The IEEE Standard for Developing Software Life Cycle Processes has a single Verification & Validation process. We have expanded that single process into three processes: **Feature** Validation & Tracking, Design Verification & Tracking, and Usability Evaluation & Tracking. The creation and tracking of **Feature**s supports a multirelease incremental design philosophy. All desired **Feature**s should be tracked and validated that they perform properly.

The verification and tracking of the design places additional emphasis on the tracking of anomalies during testing and the resultant determination and resolution of defects. The evaluation and tracking of usability places emphasis on the **SoftwareProduct**s that match customer desires and needs. The relationship of the Integral processes to the Development and Management processes of the SLC are shown in Figure 4.15.

The Software Configuration Management process identifies the items in a software development **Project** and provides both for control of the items and for the gathering of measurements for management visibility and accountability throughout the SLC. Examples considered for inclusion are user requirements, design specifications, source files, documentation, plans, and others.

Feature Validation & Tracking process activities include validation planning, execution of validation activities, test planning and execution, data collection and analysis, and tracking of all defects to the source. We validate a **SoftwareProduct** to ensure that we have created correct **Feature**s and that the system operates to customer expectations. When **Feature** anomalies are determined to be **Defect**s, you

Software Life Cycle

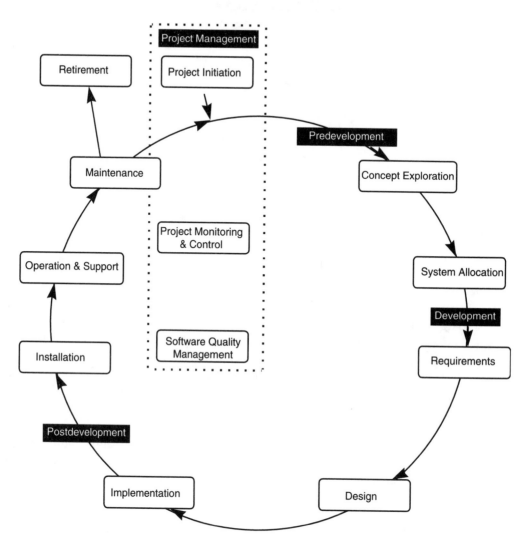

Figure 4.13   SLC Process Model with Development and Management Processes

should track the **Defect**s to the root cause and try to prevent similar **Defect**s in the future.

Design Verification & Tracking process activities include verification planning, execution of verification activities, test planning and execution, data collection and analysis, and tracking of all defects to the source. We verify a **SoftwareProduct** to

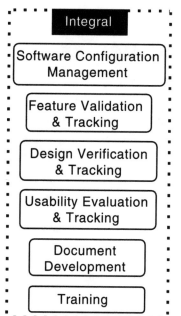

Figure 4.14 Integral Processes

ensure that the product operates in conformance with the design. When design anomalies are determined to be **Defect**s, you should track the **Defect** to the root cause and try to prevent similar **Defect**s in the future.

Usability Evaluation & Tracking process activities include usability evaluation planning, execution of usability evaluation activities, usability test planning and execution, data collection and analysis, and tracking of all usability problems to the source. We evaluate a **SoftwareProduct** to ensure that the product operates in conformance with established usability criteria and with customer expectations. When usability anomalies are determined not to be within expectations, you should track the usability problem to the root cause and try to prevent similar problems in the future.

The Document Development process is the set of activities that plans, designs, implements, edits, produces, distributes, and maintains those documents needed by developers and customers. These activities occur concurrently with the Management and Development processes. The purpose of the Documentation Development process is to provide timely documentation to those who need it, based on input from the invoking processes. This process covers both product- and procedure-oriented documentation for internal and external users. Examples of internal users include those who plan, design, implement, or test software. External users may include those who install, operate, apply, or maintain the software.

Software Life Cycle

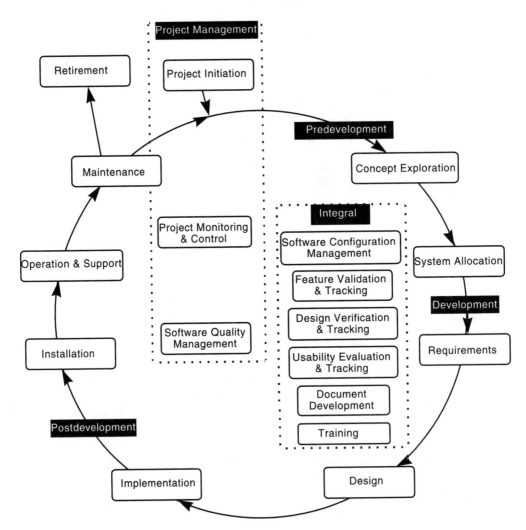

Figure 4.15 SLC Process Model with Development, Management, and Integral Processes

Training process activities include planning, development of training materials, validating the training program, and implementing the training program. A successful **Project** depends on knowledgeable and skilled technical and support staff that is properly trained. Customer personnel may also have to be trained to install, operate, and maintain the **SoftwareProduct**. Training planning and material must be completed early in the SLC prior to the time when personnel are expected to apply the required expertise to the **Project**.

Continuous Process Improvement

In this book we are interested in improving the quality, productivity, and usability of software systems. We can do this through continuous process improvement. You may have one of the best software development processes, but if you do not focus on improvement, then you will lose out to competitors that do. In Figure 4.16 we portray a continuous process improvement cycle that consists of the following steps:

1. Define process.
2. Establish ownership.
3. Identify customer requirements.
4. Measure.
5. Access conformance to customer requirements.

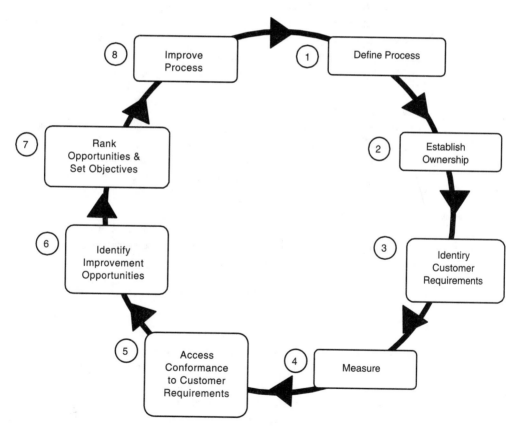

Figure 4.16 Continuous Process Improvement

6. Identify improvement opportunities.

7. Rank opportunities and set objectives.

8. Improve process.

To initiate software process improvement, you must first define how the software process works. We have defined a version of SLC processes based on the IEEE Standard for Developing SLC processes. You may define your software processes based on the IEEE model or on your own process model.

The next step is to establish ownership of the overall software process and each of the processes and activities that make up the software process. Each activity should be assigned a single owner. An owner is a single point of contact and is identified by organizational position. Ownership is assumed by the person currently filling that position. Each owner has the responsibility and authority to control and complete the activity within the planned schedule and budget. In addition, each owner is accountable for the quality of the activity outputs. If activities are to be performed by multiple organizations, the owning organization and position of the owner should be identified. In the case of multiple instances of an activity, an owner for each instance should be identified.

Customer requirements should be identified next. The customer is the user of process output. For a commercial **SoftwareProduct,** the customer is the buyer of the product. For a process internal to the Development process, the customer is another process. For example, in Figure 4.15 a customer of the Design process is the implementation process. In the case of the **SoftwareProduct,** the customer requirements must be identified and implemented as **Features** in the product.

Once you know the customer requirements, you gather measurements of software metrics. The metrics represent attributes of the process, product, personnel, conformance to plans, and the like. Measurements are critical to understanding the software process and to gaining insight into how to improve the process.

You next access conformance to customer requirements. For the software produced by the SLC process, you access how the product **Features** conform to the requirements of the **SoftwareProduct** customer. For the Implementation process, you gather measures and analyze them to see how the outputs of the Design process conform to the requirements of the Implementation process.

You next identify opportunities for improvement. Typically, you use many of the statistical and charting tools to select activities that can be improved.

Next you rank opportunities for improvement that you have identified. Pareto diagrams can be used for rank ordering opportunities from the most to least significant. The Pareto diagram is based on the Pareto principle, which states that just a few of the causes often account for most of the effect. You select the problems that you would like to solve; then you set your objectives for process improvement to solve the problem.

Finally, you make the necessary changes to improve the process. Notice that the process does not cease. You continually cycle through the process improvement cycle. In an ideal sense, improvement is everyone's job. You should continually strive to improve your process, which will result in an improved product, a more satisfied customer, and a larger market share for your product.

Managers have difficulty understanding and visualizing software systems. A documentation-driven approach with numerous milestones was applied during the Black Box SLC period to assist managers in visualizing what was happening with a software **Project.** We know that, instead of clarifying what is happening, these costly deliverables and milestone reviews often obscure the actual status and give managers a false sense of progress when actually a **Project** may be in trouble. A metric-based management approach [Simmons92] along with continuous process improvement can be used to reduce the number of deliverables and milestones required.

In this book we will show how metrics can be unobtrusively gathered by computers and retained for archival and planning purposes. We will show how computerized reporting to managers allows them to accurately track the progress of a software development **Project** and assist them in dynamically modifying their plans. Computer-based intelligent agents can be created to assist managers in planning, organizing, staffing, scheduling, measurement, visualization, and control of **Project**s [Simmons93]. We will show how testing tools and test selection agents can help to reduce the cost and time of testing. We will also show how metrics combined with planning agents can analyze and report the actual usability of a **SoftwareProduct** under development.

SUMMARY

We have reviewed the different SLCs. We then described software processes that can be mapped into the SLCs. Software processes are the foundation for process improvement. Once we define and understand the software process that we are using, we can gather measurements related to the process activities. The measurements will be used to determine the progress that we are making toward improving the software processes.

In Chapter 5 we will describe a system of objects for a software **Project.** The objects will be easily understandable to management, customers, and developers. Once we have an object structure, you can gather software metrics that describe the attributes of **Project** objects. In later chapters we will describe software metrics.

REFERENCES

[Agresti86]   Agresti, W. W., *Tutorial: New Paradigms for Software Development.* IEEE Computer Society Press, Washington, DC, 1986.

[Alberts76]   Alberts, D. S., "The Economics of Software Quality Assurance," *Proceedings of the 1976 National Computer Conference*, UFOs, 1976, pp. 433–441.

[Albrecht79]   Albrecht, A. J., "Measuring Application-Development Productivity," *Proceedings Joint Share/Guide/IBM Application-Development Symposium*, Share, Chicago, 1979, pp. 83–92.

[Aron70]   Aron, J. D., "Estimating Resources for Large Programming Systems," *Software Engineering Techniques*, Report on a Conference sponsored by the NATO Science Committee, Rome, Italy, October 27–31, 1969, Button, J. N., and Rankled, B. (eds.), April 1970, pp. 68–84.

[Aron71]   Aron, J. D., "In Estimating Systems Costs," Fourth Annual Regional Seminar of Tennessee State Chapter of Association for Systems Management, February 13, 1971.

[Banker89]   Banker, R. D., and Kemerer, C. F., "Scale Economies in New Software Development," *IEEE Transactions on Software Engineering*, Vol. 15, No. 10, October 1989, pp. 1199–1205.

[Boehm76]   Boehm, B. W., "Software Engineering," *IEEE Transactions on Computers*, Vol. C-25, No. 12, December 1976, pp. 1226–1241.

[Boehm81]   Boehm, B. W., *Software Engineering Economics*, Prentice Hall, Upper Saddle River, NJ, 1981.

[Boehm87a]   Boehm, B. W., "Industrial Software Metrics Top 10 List," *IEEE Software*, September 1987, pp. 84–85.

[Boehm87b]   Boehm, B. W., "A Spiral Model of Software Development and Enhancement," *Tutorial: Software Engineering Project Management*, Thayer, R. H. (ed.), IEEE Computer Society Press, Washington, DC, 1987, pp. 128–142.

[Boehm87c]   Boehm, B. W., "A Spiral Model of Software Development and Enhancement," IEEE, EH0263-4/87/0000/0128, 1987.

[Boehm88]   Boehm, B. W., "A Spiral Model of Software Development and Enhancement," *Computer*, Vol. 21, No. 5, May 1988, pp. 61–72.

[Brooks75]   Brooks, Jr., F. P., *The Mythical Man-Month: Essays on Software Engineering*, Addison–Wesley Publishing Co., Reading, MA, 1975.

[Brooks87]   Brooks, F. P., "No Silver Bullet: Essence and Accidents of Software Engineering," *IEEE Computer Magazine*, April 1987, pp. 10–19.

[Buxton69]   Buxton, J. N., and Randell, B., *Software Engineering Techniques*, Kynoch Press, Birmingham, England, Report on a conference sponsored by the NATO Science Committee, Rome, Italy, October 27–31, 1969.

[Canning56]   Canning, R. G., *Electronic Data Processing for Business and Industry*, John Wiley & Sons, New York, 1956.

[Dorfman90]   Dorfman, M., and Thayer, R. H., *Standards, Guidelines, and Examples of System and Software Requirements Engineering*, IEEE Computer Society Press, Los Alamitos, CA, 1990.

[Gates95]   Gates, B., *The Road Ahead*, Viking Press, New York, p. 136.

[Gholson73]   Gholson, R. K., "Managing Programming Productivity," presented at the Diebold Research Program Thirtieth Plenary Meeting, Colorado Springs, CO, October 1973.

[Gunther78]   Gunther, R. C., *Management Methodology for Software Product Engineering*, John Wiley & Sons, New York, 1978.

[Hester81]   Hester, S. D., Parnas, D. L., and Utter, D. F., "Using Documentation as a Software Design Medium," *Bell System Technical Journal*, Vol. 60, No. 8, October 1981, pp. 1941–1977.

[Humphrey85]   Humphrey, Watts S., "The IBM Large-systems Software Development Process: Objectives and Direction," *IBM Systems Journal*, Vol. 24, No. 2, 1985, pp. 76–78.

[IEEE91]   IEEE Developing Software Life Cycle Processes Working Group, *Standard for Developing Software Life Cycle Processes*, IEEE, P1074, January 1, 1991, p. 121.

[Jensen79]   Jensen, R. W., and Tonies, C. C., *Software Engineering*, Prentice Hall, Upper Saddle River, NJ, 1979.

[Jones77]   Jones, C., *Program Quality and Programmer Productivity*, IBM Technical Report TR 02.764, January 1977, pp. i, 42–78.

[Jones86]   *Programming Productivity*, McGraw-Hill Book Co., New York, 1986.

[Jones92]   Jones, Capers, "CASE's Missing Elements," *IEEE Spectrum*, June 1992, pp. 38–41.

[Kustanowitz77]   Kustanowitz, A. L., "System Life Cycle Estimation (SLICE): A New Approach to Estimating Resources for Application Program Development," *Proceedings of COMPSAC 77*, IEEE, New York, 1977, pp. 226–232.

[Laden63]   Landen, H. N., and Gildersleeve, T. R., *System Design for Computer Applications*, John Wiley & Sons, New York, 1963.

[McCarthy95]   McCarthy, J., *Dynamics of Software Development*, Microsoft Press, Redmond, WA, 1995.

[McHenry78]   McHenry, R. C., and Walston, C. E., "Software Life Cycle Management: Weapons Process Developer," *IEEE Transactions on Software Engineering*, Vol. SE-4, No. 4, July 1978, pp. 334–344.

[Mills71]   Mills, H. D., "Top-down Programming in Large Systems," *Debugging Techniques in Large Systems*, R. Rustin (ed.), Prentice Hall, Upper Saddle River, NJ, 1971.

[Nelson78]   Nelson, R., *Software Data Collection and Analysis at RADC*, Rome Air Development Center, Rome, NY, 1978.

[Parnas86]   Parnas, D. L., and Clements, P. C., "A Rational Design Process: How and Why to Fake It," *IEEE Transactions on Software Engineering*, Vol. SE-12, No. 2, February 1986, pp. 251–257.

[Patrick76]   Patrick, R. L., "Software Engineering and Life Cycle Planning," *Datamation*, December 1976, pp. 79–80.

[Pietrasanta70]   Pietrasanta, A. M., "Resource Analysis of Computer Program System Development," *On the Management of Computers*, Weinwurm, G. F. (ed.), Auerbach Publishers, Princeton, NJ, 1970, pp. 67–87.

[Royce70]   Royce, W. W., "Managing the Development of Large Software Systems," *Proceedings of IEEE WESCON*, 1970, pp. 1–9.

[Shere88]   Shere, K. D., *Software Engineering and Management,* Prentice Hall, Upper Saddle River, NJ, 1988.

[Simmons82]   Simmons, D. B., Marchbanks, M. P., Quick, M. J., Sheppard, S. V., and Brenner, B. C., "Complexity and Productivity Monitoring of Very Large Software Development Projects," *Proceedings of International Computer Symposium 1982,* Taiwan, 1982, pp. 439–446.

[Simmons92]   Simmons, D. B., "A Win–Win Metric Based Software Management Approach," *IEEE Transactions on Engineering Management,* Vol. 39, No. 1, February 1992, pp. 32–41.

[Simmons93]   Simmons, D. B., Ellis, N. C., and Escamilla, T. D., "Manager Associate," *IEEE Transactions on Knowledge and Data Engineering,* Vol. 5, No. 3, June 1993, pp. 426–438.

[Walston77]   Walston, C. E., and Felix, C. P., "A Method of Programming Measurement and Estimation," *IBM Systems Journal,* Vol. 10, No. 1, 1977, pp. 10–29.

[Wolverton74]   Wolverton, R. W., "The Cost of Developing Large-scale Software," *IEEE Transactions on Computers,* June 1974, pp. 282–303.

5
Project *Object* *Classes*

Does your company measure everything it does in the software arena? Does it measure the process of software development as well as the final product? Does it have a separate software metrics group? Are its metrics of project size, defects, and effort available for all to see? Are the metrics used in a positive way, so that everyone in the organization can see how they can improve?

Edward Yourdon
[Yourdon92]

INTRODUCTION

The key to successful process improvement is measurement of existing processes and predicting the effect that will result from modifying the activities within a process. We decide on the software metrics needed before we initiate the software process improvement cycle. Software metrics are standard measurements of a software **Project**. An example of a size metric is **Volume** measured in source lines of code (SLOC). **Volume** is an object containing size attributes of a **RequirementsFile**, **DesignFile**, **DocumentFile**, or a **Chunk** object. **Chunk** and other size metrics are explained in Chapter 6. We assign values to metrics by

- prediction,
- setting (or initializing),
- inference,
- measurement (or gathering), and
- calculation.

$Effort_{Predict}$ in person-months required to produce a **SoftwareProduct** is an example of an attribute defined within an object. At the start of a **Project**, if you know the size of a **SoftwareProduct** that you plan to produce, you can predict the effort required to produce the product using $Effort_{Predict}$ equations. Notice that we use a special font, italics, and a subscript to show that the attribute was predicted instead of measured directly. $Effort_{Predict}$ will be explained in detail in Chapter 7. From effort prediction equations and your past experience, you can set a planned value for $Effort_{Set}$. Once a software **Project** has begun, you can infer $Effort_{Infer}$ using intelligent agents. At any time during a software **Project**, you can calculate the $Effort_{Calculate}$ required to date to produce the **SoftwareProduct** and see how close the $Effort_{Calculate}$ is to the predicted $Effort_{Predict}$, planned $Effort_{Set}$, and inferred $Effort_{Infer}$. In Chapters 8, 9, 11, and 13 we explain Productivity, Schedule (development time), Reliability, and Usability attribute prediction models.

We will use objects to represent entities that make up a software **Project**. An example of a **Project** object class is the **SourceFile** object class that reflects the source code produced by software developers. A specific named object of object class **SourceFile** we will call an instance of the object class. Metrics that we gather will be represented as attributes of an object. For example, attributes of a **SourceFile** are **Volume** attribute $SLOC_{Calculate}$, **Structure** attribute $NestingDepth_{Calculate}$, and **Rework** attribute $Turmoil_{Calculate}$ expressed as a function of Adds, Deletes, and Changes.

In this chapter we will first explain a notation that will be used to portray the relationships between object classes. Then we will describe the object classes that can be used to portray a software **Project**. Notice that these objects have the same names as the **Project** items described in Chapter 3 and the **Project** SLCs described in Chapter 4. You can view the object attributes to see exactly what is happening in a software development **Project**. All activities of SLC processes can be made visible to you. Detailed descriptions of all **Project** objects, attributes, and relationships are presented in Appendix A.

NOTATION

We will now look at the object classes that contain information about a software **Project**. An example of an object class is **Individual,** which represents any individual person that is associated with a **Project**. Associated with each **Individual** is the **Assignment** class, which contains attributes describing assignments. Also associated with each **Individual** is the **Salary** class, which contains an **Individual's Salary** history, and the **Activity** class, which describes activities performed by **Individuals**. In Figure 5.1(a) we represent a class by a rectangle, with the class name enclosed within the rectangle. We will use a graphical notation based on the notation developed by Rumbaugh et al. [Rumbaugh91]. In Figure 5.1(b) we show an object represented by

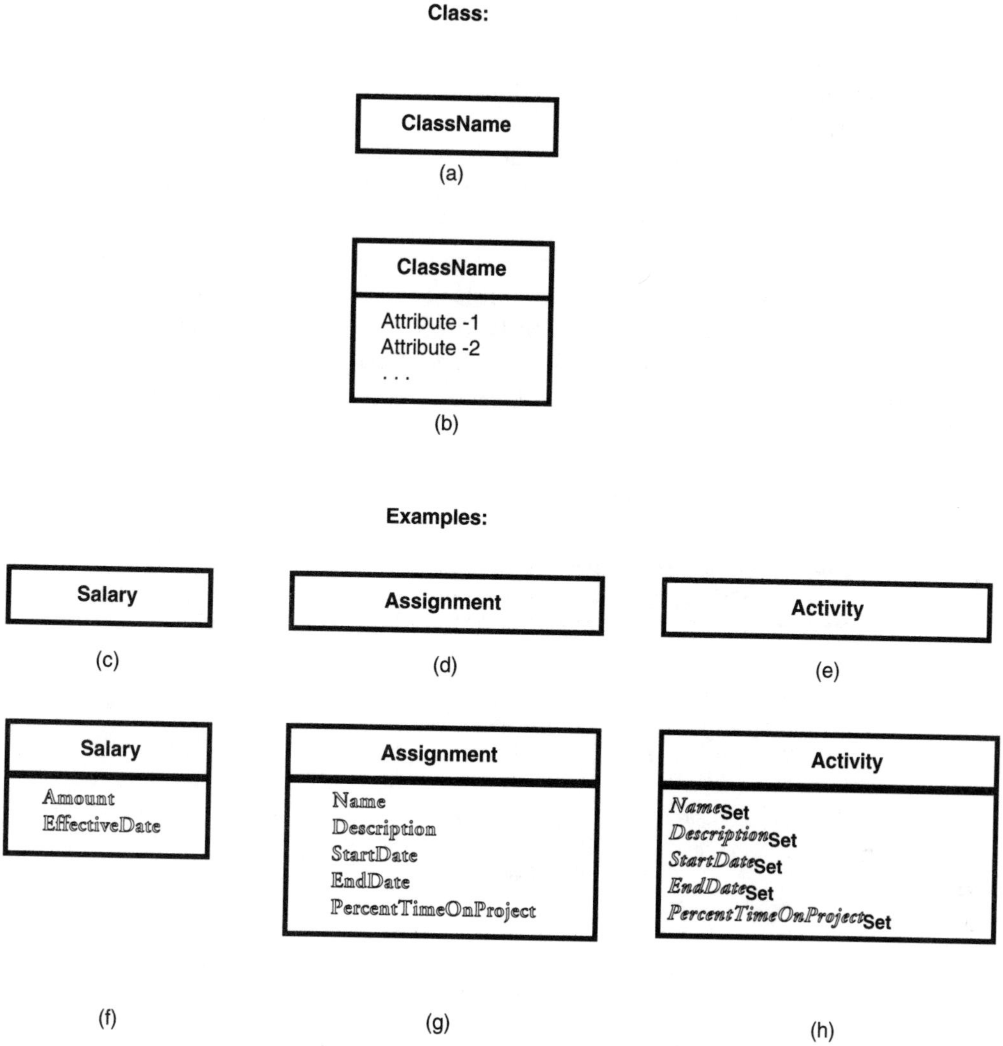

Class:

ClassName

(a)

ClassName

Attribute -1
Attribute -2
. . .

(b)

Examples:

| Salary | | Assignment | | Activity |

(c)　　　　　　　　　(d)　　　　　　　　　(e)

Salary

Amount
EffectiveDate

Assignment

Name
Description
StartDate
EndDate
PercentTimeOnProject

Activity

Name$_{Set}$
Description$_{Set}$
StartDate$_{Set}$
EndDate$_{Set}$
PercentTimeOnProject$_{Set}$

(f)　　　　　　　　　(g)　　　　　　　　　(h)

Figure 5.1 Object Class Notation

a named rectangle, with the object attributes in an attached rectangle immediately below the class name. For example, in Figure 5.1(c), (d), and (e) we show **Salary**, **Assignment**, and **Activity** object classes. In Figure 5.1(f) we show object class **Salary** with attributes Amount and EffectiveDate, and in Figure 5.1(g) we show the object class **Assignment** with attributes Name, Description, StartDate, EndDate, and PercentTimeOnProject. We use a special outline type font to represent attributes that are transparent to software process personnel and that can be nonobtrusively gathered from computerized personnel and payroll information systems of an **Organization**. The **Activity** attributes $Name_{Set}$, $Description_{Set}$, $Start$-$Date_{Set}$, $EndDate_{Set}$, and $PercentTimeOnActivity_{Set}$ are shown as being set by **Project** members interested in process improvement.

You can associate an object class with other object classes. In Figure 5.2(a), exactly one **Class-2** is associated with **Class-1**. In Figure 5.2(b), many (zero or more) **Class-2**s are associated with **Class-1**. The small black circle on the line connecting the two object classes indicates that zero or more **Class-2** instances are associated with each **Class-1** instance. Examples of association are shown in Figure 5.2(c) and (d). The first example shows that each instance of a **UsabilityTest** object is associated with exactly one instance of a **Usability** attributes object. The other example shows that an **Individual** can have from zero to many **Assignment**s. An instance of an **Individual** object can be associated with many instances of **Assignment** object. This

Association:

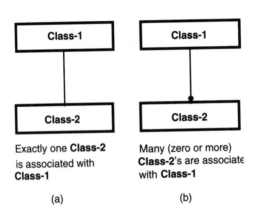

Examples:

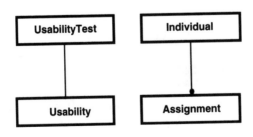

(c)　　　　　　　(d)　　　　**Figure 5.2** Association Notation

means that a person can be assigned to more than one **Project** with a different percentage of time on each **Assignment**.

A detailed textual description of each object class can be found in Appendix A. The description of the **Assignment** class follows:

Assignment

Relationships

Assignments are related to an **Individual**

Attributes

Name
Description
StartDate
EndDate
PercentTimeOnProject ($0 \le \times \le 1$)

This class definition shows the relationship between **Assignment**s and an **Individual** and lists the attributes of the **Assignment** object class. Notice that the PercentTimeOnProject has an added property listed stating that its value should be between zero and one.

We will now introduce aggregation notation as a special form of association. Aggregation adds semantic connotations in certain cases. In Figure 5.3(a), Part-1-Class is shown to be tightly bound by a part–whole relationship, which we call aggregation. The diamond on the line below the **Assembly Class** indicates aggregation. If the two objects are usually considered as independent, even though they may often be linked, it is an association.

Aggregation is a strong form of association in which an aggregate object is *made of* components. Components are *part of* the aggregate. The aggregate is semantically an extended object that is treated as a unit in many operations, although physically it is made of several lesser objects. The example in Figure 5.3(b) shows that a software **Project** is an aggregation of **Supplier**s, **Organization**s of people, a **SoftwareProduct**, and **Customers**. Notice that we use a bold line to interconnect components of an aggregate.

An **Individual** can have more than one association. In Figure 5.4(a) we see that Class-1 is associated with Class-2, but there is an additional association between Class-2 and Class-1. The second association can be distinguished from the first by attaching an *Association Name* to the second association. Figure 5.4(b) is an example of a named association. An **Individual** *manages* a **Group**, a different **Individual** *manages* an **Area** made up of **Group**s, and so on. The label *manages* is the *Association Name*. Also in Figure 5.4(b) we see that an **Individual** *works for* a **Group**, **Area**, or **Organization**, and an **Activity** is *performed by* an **Individual**, **Group**, **Area**, or **Organization**.

Aggregation:

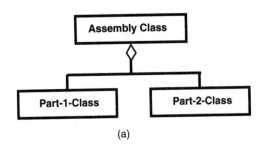

(a)

Example:

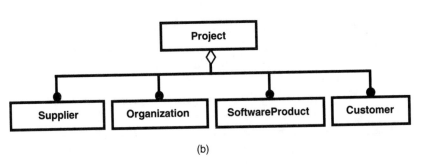

(b)

Figure 5.3   Aggregation Notation

PROJECT

We will define a software **Project** as a planned undertaking to develop a **Software-Product**. Resources are provided by **Suppliers**, **Customers** use the **SoftwareProduct**, and an **Organization** of people create the **SoftwareProduct**. We will now examine, from an object class point of view, the **Supplier**, **Customer**, **Organization**, and **SoftwareProduct**.

Supplier

SoftwareProducts are created by people using computers. Over time the cost of computers relative to the cost of people has continued to decline. When you cost out a **Project**, you first look at the **Salary** of **Project Individual**s and multiply the salary cost by an overhead factor that takes into account the cost of fringe benefits, administrative staff, buildings, utilities, laboratory equipment, and so on. While the cost of

Named Association:

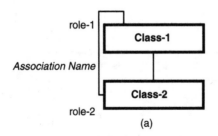

(a)

Example:

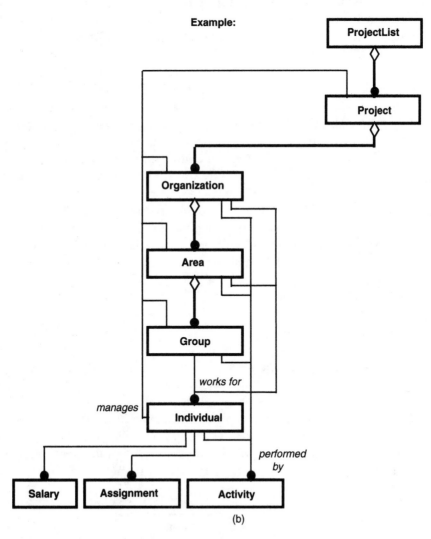

(b)

Figure 5.4   Named Association

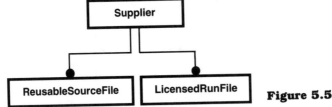

Figure 5.5   Supplier Object Class

computers could be directly added to the cost of a **Project**, we recommend that the computers be included in the **Project** overhead factor. Thus, the main resources supplied to a software **Project** are pieces of software that will be used as part of the **SoftwareProduct**. Figure 5.5 shows **Supplier** object class hierarchy.

The **Supplier** object class is made up of reusable **SourceFile**s (**ReusableSourceFile**s) and commercial off-the-shelf (COTS) software (**LicensedRunFile**s). Reusable software normally has to be modified before it can be used by a software **Project**. You may want to reuse software from one of your previous **Project**s or from a software library. Typically, the cost of reusing software is between 5% to 60% of the cost of writing code from scratch. As the cost of modifying software exceeds 60%, you should consider writing the entire software unit from scratch.

You purchase COTS software from your suppliers. Whenever possible, buy software instead of building it. If you decide to build a software system from scratch, use as much COTS software as possible in creating your **SoftwareProduct**. Frequently, you only receive a run time file and do not receive a **SourceFile**. You know the size and cost of the COTS software and the hardware and software environment necessary for the COTS software to operate. You expect to use COTS operating systems, database management systems, language compilers, and the like, when you develop a **SoftwareProduct**.

Customer

The object class **Customer**s is represented as a single class, as shown in Figure 5.6. We are very interested in **Customer** attributes and how they like our **SoftwareProduct**. Measurements of **Customer** satisfaction is normally accomplished by questionnaires that are voluntarily completed by **Customer**s. In this book, we will concentrate on measurements that can be gathered from the software **Project** as part of the SLC. We assume that you will be very aware of the **Customer** needs and how you can improve a **SoftwareProduct** to increase **Customer** satisfaction.

Customer

Figure 5.6   Customer Object Class

To predict **Customer** satisfaction before a product is released to **Customer**s, you can run usability tests by paying test subjects to act as typical **Customer**s. Extensive measurements of these subjects can be gathered and analyzed to improve the usability of software before it is released to **Customer**s.

Organization

The main cost in creating a **SoftwareProduct** is the people cost. While you should set a goal to computerize as many SLC process **Activit(y)**ies as possible, you will find the single major cost in software development continues to be the cost of people. When you measure and analyze **Activit(y)**ies within an SLC process, most of the **Activit(y)**ies will be performed by people. You can have **Individual**, team (or **Group**), department (or **Area**), or company (or **Organization**) **Activit(y)**ies. In Figure 5.4 we show an object class hierarchy that can gather metrics from four-level **Organization**s. Four levels is an arbitrary limit. As many levels as are necessary can be added to the hierarchy.

Software Product

We create software by composing and debugging source code. The producing of the source code is what is normally called programming. Source code is stored in a **SourceFile**. You can gather measurements from **SourceFile**s to create the **SourceFile** object class shown in Figure 5.7. A **SourceFile** object instance along with its attributes reflects the true status and attributes of the actual source file. We have created a program to nonobtrusively gather measurements from the source file and save them as object attributes. Attribute classes of interest are **Rework**, **Chunk**, **Volume**, and **Structure**.

Rework metrics (portrayed as **Rework** attributes) reflect Adds, Deletes, and Changes that occur between successive builds using the **SourceFiles** of a **SoftwareProduct**. These metrics reflect the *Turmoil*$_{\textbf{Calculate}}$ that is taking place in a file. Files with a large amount of *Turmoil*$_{\textbf{Calculate}}$ usually contain many **Defects** and are not ready for delivery. You can calculate *Turmoil*$_{\textbf{Calculate}}$ to predict the status of **SourceFile**s, software **Subsystem**s, and **SoftwareProduct** **Version**s. *Turmoil*$_{\textbf{Calculate}}$ should grow incrementally smaller as a **SoftwareProduct** is debugged.

A **SourceFile** is composed of **Chunk**s (portrayed as **Chunk** objects) of code. Examples of code **Chunk**s are functions, subroutines, scripts, macros, procedures, modules, objects, methods, worksheets, and so on. In creating **SoftwareProduct**s, **Chunk**s are used to match the human cognitive skills to the proper programming language level.

Chunk attributes are grouped into **Volume** attributes and **Structure** attributes. The **Volume** attributes measure the size or bulk of a **Chunk**. The **SourceFile Vol-**

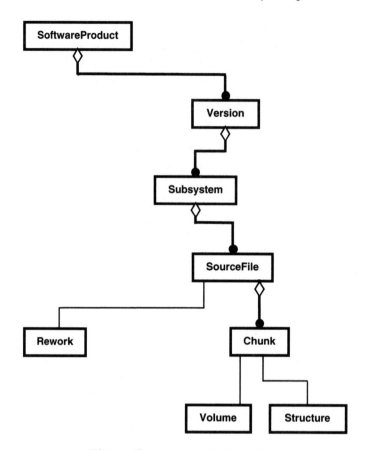

Figure 5.7 SoftwareProduct Software

ume attribute $SLOC_{\textbf{Calculate}}$ is the sum of the **Chunk Volume** $SLOC$ attributes. Similarly, the **Structure** attributes are used to indicate **Chunk** complexity. The **SourceFile** complexity can be determined from the **Chunk** complexity.

A software **Subsystem** is an aggregation of **SourceFiles**. A **Version** of a **SoftwareProduct** is an aggregation of **Subsystems**. Each time **Features** are added to a **SoftwareProduct**, a new **Version** is created. Over time, many **Versions** of **SoftwareProducts** can evolve. In this book, we consider each of these **Versions** to be part of the **SoftwareProduct**.

We know that in the process of developing software there are many other activities than creating source code. You must ensure that the software has the correct **Features**, is properly tested, is **Defect** free, and is usable. Figure 5.8 shows object classes that have been added to portray **SoftwareProduct Features**, **Defects**, verification and validation (V&V) tests (**VAndVTest** objects), and usability tests (**Usabil-**

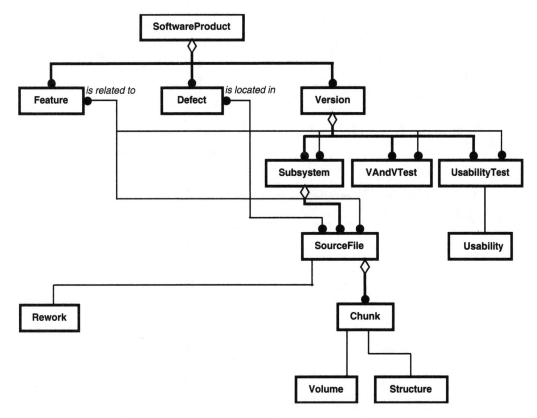

Figure 5.8 SoftwareProduct Feature, Defect, VAndVTest, and UsabilityTest Objects

ity Test objects and **Usability** attributes objects). Notice that there is a relationship (the *is located in* relationship) between **Defect**s and their location in **Source-File**s and between **Feature**s (the *is related to* relationship) and **Subsystem**s, **VAndV-Test**s, **UsabilityTest**s, and **SourceFile**s.

Many types of documents may be created as part of the software development process. We can keep track of these documents and measure their growth and turmoil. Figure 5.9 shows documents that have been added to reflect user requirements (**RequirementsFile** objects), design specifications (**DesignFile** objects), and all other documents, such as user manuals and test plans (**DocumentFile** objects). Notice the relationships between **Feature** and **Defect** object classes and the file object classes in Figure 5.9.

Individual people produce **SoftwareProduct**s. The cost of people involved in the **SoftwareProduct** development normally dominates all other costs. We must know the relationship between all activities in the SLC processes and the **Individual**s

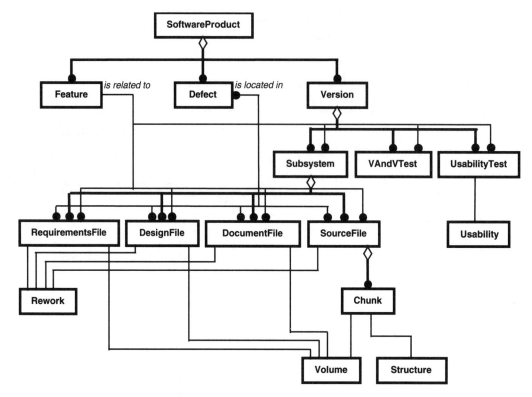

Figure 5.9   SoftwareProduct **RequirementsFile**, **DesignFile**, and **DocumentFile** Object Classes

that participate in the processes. In Figure 5.10 we show the relationships an **Individual** can have to **SoftwareProduct** objects. We show that an **Individual** *owns*, *runs*, or *authors* objects.

The *owns* relationship is key to process improvement. Process improvement is accomplished by empowering **Individual**s to affect a process and making them accountable for their actions. This is accomplished by assigning **Individual** ownership to processes and activities of SLC processes. Ownership of an **Activity** implies responsibility of the output from the **Activity**. **Individual**s must be assigned ownership to the **SoftwareProduct**, **Feature**s, **Defect**s, **Version**s, **Subsystem**s, **VAndVTest**s, **UsabilityTest**s, **Product** requirements (**RequirementsFile**s), design specifications (**DesignFile**s), all output documents (**DocumentFile**s), **SourceFile**s, and so on.

The *runs* relationship describes the **Individual** that actually runs tests. In Figure 5.10, we see that an **Individual** *runs* **VAndVTest**s to validate and verify a **SoftwareProduct** and **UsabilityTest**s to determine how usable the product is by the **Customer**.

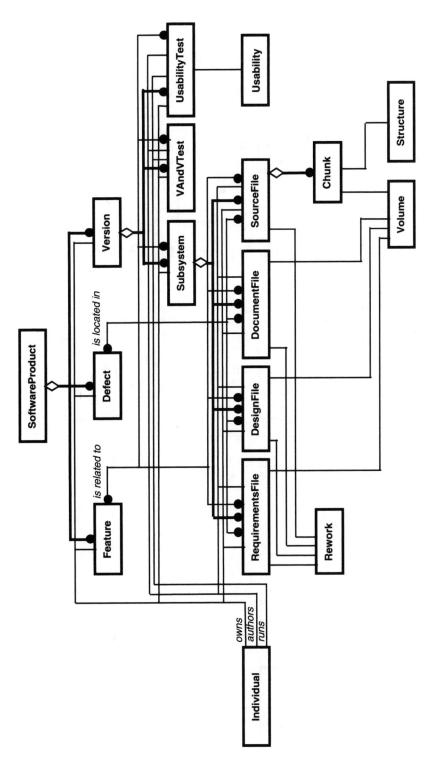

Figure 5.10 Relationships of an **Individual** to **SoftwareProduct** Objects

117

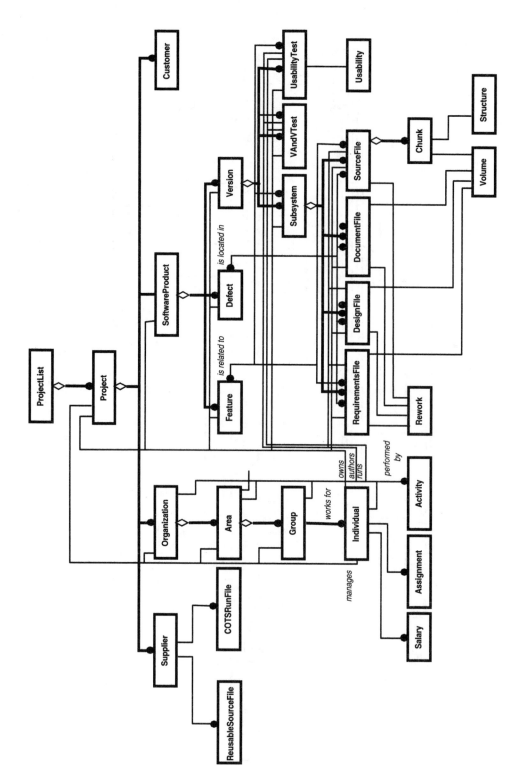

Figure 5.11 Project Object Classes

The *authors* relationship describes the **Individuals** that actually create output. **Individuals** *author* source code (**Sourcefiles**), **Subsystems**, product requirements (**RequirementsFile**), design specifications (**DesignFiles**), all output documents (**DocumentFiles**), **VAndVTests**, and **UsabilityTests**.

The object classes and the relationships among classes are shown in Figure 5.11. The **ProjectList** is an aggregation of **Projects**. A detailed description of the object classes, attributes, and relationships are given in Appendix A.

SUMMARY

In this chapter we have explored the software objects and object attributes that represent a software **Project**. There are a number of **Project** attributes that you will want to understand and predict. In the following chapters, size (**Volume**, **Structure**, and **Rework**), Effort, Schedules, Productivity, quality, **VandVTests**, Reliability, and Usability will be explained and prediction models will be explored. In Chapter 15 we will describe the Project Attribute Monitoring and Prediction Associate (PAMPA) tool to help you to gather **Project** information from a software development environment, save it as objects/attributes/relationships/properties, and visualize all aspects of a software **Project**.

REFERENCES

[Bailey81]   Bailey, J. W., and Basili, V. R., "A Meta-model for Software Development Resource Expenditures," *Proceedings of the Fifth International Conference on Software Engineering*, 1981, pp. 107–116.

[Rumbaugh91]   Rumbaugh, J., Blaha, M., Premerlani, W., Eddy, F., and Lorensen, W., *Object-Oriented Modeling and Design*, Prentice Hall, Upper Saddle River, NJ, 1991.

[Yourdon92]   Yourdon, E., *Decline & Fall of the American Programmer*, Yourdon Press, Englewood Cliffs, NJ, 1992, p. 19.

Part Two

MODELS
AND METRICS

6

Size

I must admit that I have frequently asked myself whether these systems require many people because they are large, or whether they are large because they have many people.

Jules I. Schwartz
[Schwartz69]

INTRODUCTION

Size attributes are used to describe physical magnitude, extent, or bulk. A size attribute can represent relative or proportionate dimensions. We will classify software size attributes as **Volume, Structure,** and **Rework.** You can use **Volume** attributes to predict the amount of effort required to produce a **SoftwareProduct, Defect**s remaining in a **SoftwareProduct,** and time required to create a **SoftwareProduct. Structure** attributes indicate software complexity. Complex software is harder to understand and create than simple software. Examples of **Structure** attributes are number of unconditional branches, depth of control loop nesting, and module fan-in and/or fan-out. **Rework** attributes describe the size of adds, deletes, and changes that are made to a **SoftwareProduct** between **Version**s. When **Rework** attributes are combined, they measure the amount of turmoil in a file.

Attributes that can be unobtrusively measured by a data gatherer program will be represented by a True Type Colonna MT font. This is a standard type font distributed with Microsoft **SoftwareProduct**s. For example, we will represent the **Volume** of a file in bytes by the attribute label Bytes. Attributes that can be calculated from gathered metrics will be represented by italic font with the subscript **Calculate**. For example, we will represent the turmoil of a file by the attribute label *Turmoil*_{Calculate}, since we determine the size of turmoil of a file from the Adds, Deletes, and Changes that are made to the file. Attributes that must be initialized and cannot be unobtrusively gathered will be represented by italic font with the subscript **Set**. For example, we may want to logically group **SourceFile**s into arbitrary groups called **Feature**s. We would have to store the **Feature** name under attribute label *Name*_{Set}. Attributes that can be predicted from other attributes will be represented by italic font with the subscript **Predict**. For example, we will represent equivalent **Volume** of new code predicted from new and reused code by the attribute label *EquivalentVolume1*_{Predict}. In the following sections, we will describe **Volume**, **Structure**, and **Rework** attributes. After we describe an attribute, we will give an example of how to determine the attribute value.

VOLUME

Each metric will be enclosed in a box on the left-hand side of the page. Then the metric will be defined and an example of the metric will be explained. We will first examine **SoftwareProduct Volume** bulk attributes by starting with the finest grain measurement bytes (Bytes), the number of 8-bit characters used to represent software. We then will look at **Volume** attributes in the following order of increasing granularity: software science mental comparisons required to generate a program (*VolumeSoftSci*_{Calculate}), source lines of code (SLOC), logical source statements (*SS*_{Calulate}(**SourceFile**s), SS (**RequirementsFile**s, **DesignFile**s, and **DocumentFile**s), **Chunk**s, function points (*FunctionPoints*_{Predict}), and object points (*ObjectPoints*_{Predict}).

   We will next explain how you can measure the **Volume** of unique software in your environment. You can measure the amount of unique software on a single computer or in a system of distributed networked computers. By eliminating all duplicate SLOCs, we can determine the amount of unique code in a computing environment. To determine the magnitude of effort required to reengineer a **SoftwareProduct** or to convert to a new hardware/software environment, you should measure the amount of unique software in your environment.

   Volume is a major cost driver used to predict the Effort_{Predict} in person-months to produce a **SoftwareProduct**. We know that less effort is required when we recycle software from previous development projects. The last part of the **Volume** section will explain models for predicting the equivalent **Volume** (*Volume*_{equivalent}) of new code based on actual **Volume** of new code produced (*Volume*_{new}) and the **Volume** of code adapted from existing software (*Volume*_{recycled}).

Volume **Bulk Attributes**

To predict the amount of effort required to produce a **SoftwareProduct**, you must know how large it is. We now look at the size metrics, starting with the finest-grain metric first.

Bytes   The **SoftwareProduct** is stored in files on a mass storage device. The **Volume** of each file can be measured in bytes. We will define **Chunks** as subunits of a **SourceFile** that partition the **SourceFile** into cognitively simpler subunits. A **Chunk** can be a function, subroutine, script, macro, procedure, module, object, method, worksheet, and so on. We will measure the number of bytes in a **Chunk** as attribute Bytes. The **Volume** of a **SourceFile** is the sum of the **Volume**s of the **Chunk**s within the file. The **Volume** of **RequirementsFile**s, **DesignFile**s, and **DocumentFile**s can be measured directly without summing the **Volume** of subunits.

EXAMPLE 6.1

Consider the **SourceFile** shown in Figure 6.1. A byte measure of its two **Chunk**s would yield:

$$Bytes(PlaceNode) = 327 \text{ bytes}$$
$$Bytes(PrintTree) = 216 \text{ bytes}$$
$$Bytes(\textbf{SourceFile}) = 543 \text{ bytes}$$

---

*VolumeSoftSci*Calculate   Halstead [Halstead77] originated software science as a field of natural science concerned initially with algorithms and their implementation as computer programs. As an experimental science, it deals only with those properties of algorithms that can be measured, either directly or indirectly, statistically or dynamically, and with the relationships among those properties that remain invariant under translation from one language to another. The original properties that he measured were number of operators and operands that make up an implementation of an algorithm (or computer program).

The properties that he counted were

η_1 = UniqueOperators = number of unique operators

η_2 = UniqueOperands = number of unique operands

N_1 = Operators = total number of operators in a computer program

N_2 = Operands = total number of operands in a computer program

```
 1  #include <stdio.h>
 2
 3  int PlaceNode(struct tree_node *spTree, struct tree_node *spTemp)
 4  {
 5      if(spTree == NULL)
 6      {
 7          spTree=spTemp;
 8          return 0;
 9      }
10      else
11      {
12          if (spTree->iNumber > spTemp->iNumber)
13              PlaceNode(spTree->spLeft_Child, spTemp);
14          else
15              PlaceNode(spTree->spRight_Child, spTemp);
16      }
17  }
18
19  int PrintTree(struct tree_node *spTree)
20  {
21      if(spTree == NULL)
22          return;
23      else
24      {
25          PrintTree(spTree->spLeft_Child);
26          printf("%d\n", spTree->iNumber);
27          PrintTree(spTree->spRight_Child);
28      }
29  }
```

Figure 6.1   Tree Manipulation Program

He defined the size of the vocabulary as

$$\eta = \eta_1 + \eta_2 = Vocabulary_{\textbf{Calculate}} \tag{6.1}$$

and the length of an algorithm implementation (computer program) as

$$N = N_1 + N_2 = Length_{\textbf{Calculate}} \tag{6.2}$$

and the computer program volume V as

$$V = N \log_2 \eta = VolumeSoftSci_{\textbf{Calculate}} \tag{6.3}$$

where the **Volume** is a count of the number of mental comparisons required to generate a program.

There can be many different implementations of an algorithm in a computer program. He defined the volume V^* to be the most succinct expression possible of an algorithm. He defined the program level L to be the ratio

$$L = \frac{V^*}{V} \tag{6.4}$$

EXAMPLE 6.2

Measuring the **Chunk** `PlaceNode()` in Figure 6.1, the following software science metrics can be gathered:

$$\eta_1 = 7$$
$$\eta_2 = 8$$
$$N_1 = 17$$
$$N_2 = 19$$
$$\eta = \eta_1 + \eta_2 = 15$$
$$N = N_1 + N_2 = 36$$
$$VolumeSoftSci_{\textbf{Calculate}} = N \log_2 \eta = 140.65$$

$\boxed{\text{SLOC}}$ A source line of code (SLOC) is any line of source program text regardless of the number of statements or fragments of statements on the line. Comments and blank lines are included in this definition. This definition specifically includes all Comments (CommentSLOC) and all noncomment ($NCSLOC_{\textbf{Calculate}}$) lines containing headers, declarations, and executable and nonexecutable statements. A source line of code is equivalent to a line printed on an output device. Thus, a SLOC is

$$\text{SLOC} = NCSLOC_{\textbf{Calculate}} + \text{CommentSLOC} \tag{6.5}$$

EXAMPLE 6.3

Consider the **Chunk** `SortArray` shown in Figure 6.2. The following line measures can be taken:

$$\text{SLOC} = 35$$

$$NCSLOC_{\textbf{Calculate}} = \text{Lines } (1, 2, 7\text{--}11, 16, 17, 19\text{--}22, 25\text{--}35) = 24$$

$$\text{CommentSLOC} = \text{Lines } (3\text{--}6, 12\text{--}15, 18, 23, 24) = 11$$

```
 1 int SortArray(int List[], int NumberOfElements)
 2 {
 3 /*
 4  * The following algorithm is an implementation of the insertion
 5  * sort.
 6  */
 7
 8 int k,j;
 9 int Done;
10 int Temp;
11
12 /* Insertion sort works on the same principle as how a person
sorts
13    cards when they are being dealt one at a time. If a person has
14    N sorted cards in his hand, then when he receives the N+1st
card,
15    it is immediately placed in the correct place. */
16    for(k=1;k<NumberOfElements;k++)
17 {
18    /* Initialize algorithm variables for this pass of the loop
*/
19    j=k;
20    Done=0;
21    while(j >= 1 && !Done)
22    {
23        /* Starting at the kth card, move it backward until it is
24            in the correct place */
25        if(List[j] < List[j-1])
26        {
27            Temp=List[j];
28            List[j]=List[j-1];
29            List[j-1]=Temp;
30        }
31        else
32            Done=1;
```

Figure 6.2 Insertion Sort **Chunk**

$SS_{\text{Calculate}}$(**SourceFiles**)   We will refer to logical source statements as source statements ($SS_{\text{Calculate}}$). A logical source statement is composed of the characters that are contained between source statement delimiters. The **Volume** of source statements for a **Chunk** is equal to the sum of the noncomment source statements ($NCSS_{\text{Calculate}}$), comment source statements ($CommentSS$), and blank source statements ($BlankSS$) or

$$SS_{\text{Calculate}} = NCSS_{\text{Calculate}} + CommentSS + BlankSS \qquad (6.6)$$

The source statements contained in a **SourceFile** are equal to the sum of the source statements in the **Chunk**s that make up the file.

To calculate $SS_{Calculate}$ for **SourceFile**s, we must first determine $NCSS_{Calculate}$. The number of noncomment source statements ($NCSS_{Calculate}$) is equal to the sum of the compiler directive source statements (CompilerDirectiveSS), data declaration source statements (DataDeclarationSS), and executable source statements (*ESS* or ExecutableSS), or

$$NCSS_{Calculate} = CompilerDirectiveSS + DataDeclarationSS + ExecutableSS \quad (6.7)$$

EXAMPLE 6.4

Consider the **Chunk** BubbleSort() in Figure 6.3:

$$ComplierDirectiveSS = Lines(6\text{--}10) = 5$$
$$DataDelcarationSS = Lines(3, 4) = 2$$
$$ExecutableSS = Lines(12, 14, 18, 19, 20, 27, 28) = 7$$
$$NCSS_{Calculate} = 14$$

Once we know **Chunk** information, we can calculate $SS_{Calculate}$ for **Source-File**s.

EXAMPLE 6.5

Refer to the **SourceFile** shown in Figure 6.4. We know that SLOC for this file is 36. However, for $SS_{Calculate}$ we need to consider the measure for each **Chunk**:

For main ():
$$NCSS_{Calculate} = Lines(5, 6, 12, 13, 18, 20) = 6$$
$$CommentSS = Lines(8\text{--}10, 15\text{--}17) \text{ Each counts as 1 block} = 2$$
$$BlankSS = Lines(7, 11, 14, 19) = 4$$
$$SS_{Calculate} = 12$$

For WhichIsBigger ():
$$NCSS_{Calculate} = Lines(30\text{--}35) = 6$$
$$CommentSS = Lines(26\text{--}28) = 1$$
$$BlankSS = Lines(29) = 1$$
$$SS_{Calculate} = 8$$

For the **SourceFile**:
$$SS_{Calculate} = 20$$

```
 1 void BubbleSort(int List[], int NumberOfElements)
 2 {
 3 int j,k;
 4 int TempElement;
 5
 6 #ifdef _DEBUG_
 7     #define CHECK 1
 8 #else
 9     #define CHECK 0
10 #endif
11
12 for(j=0;j<NumberOfElements-1;j++)
13 {
14     for(k=j+1;k<NumberOfElements;k++)
15     {
16         if(List[j] > List[k])
17         {
18             Temp=List[j];
19             List[j]=List[k];
20             List[k]=Temp;
21         }
22     }
23 }
24
25 if(CHECK)
26 {
27     for(j=0;j<NumberOfElements;j++)
28         printf("%d\n", List[j]);
29     }
30 }
```

Figure 6.3 BubbleSort **Chunk**

$\boxed{\text{SS (\textbf{RequirementsFile}s, \textbf{DesignFile}s, and \textbf{DocumentFile}s)}}$ We will assume that the requirements, design specifications, and documents are composed of text files and graphic objects. A logical source statement (SS) will be a sentence ending in a period, a line of a table, a figure, or a graphic object.

EXAMPLE 6.6

Consider the previous paragraph describing SS. In this example

$$SS = 2$$

```
 1 /* Example Source File */
 2
 3 void main()
 4 {
 5     int Number1, Number2;
 6     int ReturnVal;
 7
 8     /*
 9     * Fill the two dummy numbers of values.
10     */
11
12     Number1 = 15;
13     Number2 = 27;
14
15     /*
16     * Determine which number is bigger.
17     */
18     ReturnVal = WhichIsBigger(Number1, Number2);
19
20     printf("Number%d is bigger.\n", ReturnVal);
21 }
22
23
24 int WhichIsBigger(int Num1, int Num2)
25 {
26     /*
27     * Determine which is bigger.
28     */
29
30     if (Num1 > Num2)
31         return 1;
32     else if (Num2 > Num1)
33         return 2;
34     else
35         return 0;
36 }
```

Figure 6.4   Number Comparison **SourceFile**

Chunks**Calculate**   Early software developers created software using machine language. Very quickly they learned that productivity could be improved by reusing software **Chunk**s by adding macro and subroutine capabilities to the early software assembler utilities used by programmers to create **SoftwareProduct**s. As software production methodology continued to advance, new ways of reusing **Chunk**s of software evolved. Today, scripts, objects, worksheets, graphic user interface (GUI) tool kits, and loosely bound distributed components [Orfali96] are examples of different types of cognitive **Chunk**s that help the software developer to produce a **Software-Product**. The **Volume** of a **Chunk** can be measured in terms of Bytes, *VolumeSoftSci*_{**Calculate**}, SLOC, and *SS*_{**Calculate**}. The **Volume** of a **SourceFile** can be measured as *Chunks*_{**Calculate**}, which is determined by summing the number of **Chunk**s in a **SourceFile**.

EXAMPLE 6.7

We will assume that the tree manipulation program described in Figure 6.1 is stored as a **SourceFile**. The **Volume** attributes for **Chunk** `PlaceNode()` are

$$Bytes = 327$$
$$VolumeSoftSci_{\textbf{Calculate}} = 141$$
$$SLOC = 15$$
$$SS_{\textbf{Calculate}} = 8$$

The **Volume** of **Chunk**s in the **SourceFile** described in Figure 6.1 is

$$Chunks_{\textbf{Calculate}} = 2$$

$\boxed{FunctionPoints_{\textbf{Predict}}}$ Albrecht [Albrecht79] has developed a methodology to predict effort based on information that is known during phases of a software development **Project**. At the time that Albrecht developed his function point model, he was a manager at IBM's DP (Data Processing) Services **Organization**. He analyzed data gathered from 22 completed IBM DP Services application development **Project**s. The **Project**s ranged in size from a 3 person-month **Project** to a 700 person-month **Project**. He found that the basic value of the application function was consistently proportional to a weighted count of the number of external user inputs, outputs, inquires, and master files. The weights were determined by debate and trial. The resulting **Volume** of a **SoftwareProduct** in function points is

$$Volume_{FPs} = 4 \times Size_{inputs} + 5 \times Size_{outputs} + 4 \times Size_{inquiries} + 10 \times Size_{master\_files}$$

$$= FunctionPoints_{\textbf{Predict}} \tag{6.8}$$

where $Volume_{FPs}$ = **SoftwareProduct Volume** in a dimensionless number defined as function points

$Size_{inputs}$ = number of inputs to the product = *Inputs*_{**Set**}
$Size_{outputs}$ = number of outputs produced by the product = *Outputs*_{**Set**}
$Size_{master\_files}$ = number of master files used by the product = *MasterFiles*_{**Set**}
$Size_{inquiries}$ = number of types of inquires that can be made to the product = *Inquiries*_{**Set**}

The items counted are designed to reflect the **SoftwareProduct** functions to the **Customer** and to be determined during the early stages of **SoftwareProduct** requirements specification.

EXAMPLE 6.8

Consider the BubbleRead() **Chunk** shown in Figure 6.5:

$$Inputs_{\textbf{Set}} = 1$$
$$Outputs_{\textbf{Set}} = 1$$
$$MasterFiles_{\textbf{Set}} = 1$$
$$Inquires_{\textbf{Set}} = 0$$

$$FunctionPoints_{\textbf{Predict}} = 19$$

The function point analysis (FPA) has become increasingly more popular since first developed by Albrecht in 1979. Many refinements have been made to Albrecht's original FPA. Refinements in 1983 and 1984 addressed the structure of FPA [Albrecht 83][IBM 84]. By 1986 there were enough users of FPA that the International Function

```
int BubbleRead(int List[])
    {
        int j,k;
        int NumberOfElements;
        int TempElement;
        char sBuffer[256];
        FILE *InputFile;

        NumberOfElements=0;
        InputFile = fopen("Numbers.txt","r");
        while(fgets(sBuffer, InputFile, 256))
           List[NumberOfElements++]=atoi(sBuffer);

        for(j=0;j<NumberOfElements-1;j++)
        {
            for(k=j+1;k<NumberOfElements;k++)
            {
               if(List[j] > List[k])
               {
                   Temp=List[j];
                   List[j]=List[k];
                   List[k]=Temp;
               }
            }
        }
    }
```

Figure 6.5   Modified Bubble Sort

Point Users Group (IFPUG) [Jones97] was formed. Since FPA is a subjective methodology for determining the number of function points, IFPUG has tried to reduce the inaccuracy inherent in complex subjective metrics. IFPUG has created four versions (IFPUG 86, IFPUG 88, IFPUG 90, IFPUG 94) providing clarification of the rules and counting guidelines [Abran96]. A study in 1994 by Quality Assurance Institute and IFPUG found that counting variance between trained counters was 22% [Hotle96].

A Mk II FPA version was created by Symons in the United Kingdom [Symons91]. The Mk II function point construction involves adding weighted counts. There is no problem with the individual counts, but the additive model causes problems. There are no standard conversion factors to equate inputs, outputs, and entity accesses. Industry-average weights do not solve the problem. Questions are raised as to the inherent variability of the averages, how representative systems contributing to the average are, and how stable the averages are over time [Kitchenham97]. Even with these problems, there is a general feeling that FPA is useful when applied on a local basis.

$\boxed{\textit{ObjectPoints}\textbf{Predict}}$ Boehm, Horwitz, Selby, and Westland use object points as a high-level **Volume** estimator for the Application Composition Model of their new COCOMO 2.0 [Boehm95]. This model addresses applications that are too diversified to be created quickly in a domain-specific tool such as a spread sheet, yet are well known enough to be composed from interoperable components. Examples of these are window tool builders, database systems, and domain-specific components such as financial packages. The second **SoftwareProduct Volume** predictor model is

$$Volume_{OP_s} = \sum_{i=1}^{m} w_i + \sum_{j=1}^{n} x_j + \sum_{k=1}^{p} y_k = \textit{Object Points}\textbf{Predict} \qquad (6.9)$$

where **Volume** is in object points, w_i is the object point weight of the ith screen, x_j is the object point weight of the jth report, and y_k is the object point weight of the kth 3GL component. You can determine the complexity of a screen from Table 6.1 and

Table 6.1 Screen Complexity

Number of Views Contained in Screen	Number of Data Tables < 4 Source: Less than 2 Server, Less than 3 Client	Number of Data Tables < 8 Source: 2 or 3 Server, 3 to 5 Clients	Number of Data Tables ≥ 8 Source: Greater Than 3 Server, Greater Than 5 Client
Less than 3	Simple	Simple	Medium
3 to 7	Simple	Medium	Difficult
Greater than 8	Medium	Difficult	Difficult

Table 6.2 Report Complexity

Number of Sections Contained in Report	Number of Data Tables < 4 Source: Less than 2 Server, Less than 3 Client	Number of Data Tables < 8 Source: 2 or 3 Server, 3 to 5 Clients	Number of Data Tables ≥ 8 Source: Greater Than 3 Server, Greater Than 5 Client
0 or 1	Simple	Simple	Medium
2 or 3	Simple	Medium	Difficult
4 or more	Medium	Difficult	Difficult

the complexity of a report from Table 6.2. The object point weight can be determined from Table 6.3.

Equivalent Volume

When we develop software, most of the time we reuse software from previous **Projects**. Grady and Caswell call reused software the software that is used intact from a different **SoftwareProduct** or another part of the **SoftwareProduct** [Grady87]. They define recycled software as the software that is incorporated into a **Software-Product** that was either used intact or highly leveraged from a different **Software-Product** or another part of the same **SoftwareProduct**. When you estimate the effort to create a **SoftwareProduct**, most estimation techniques assume that you will develop all new software. When you use recycled software, effort to create a **SoftwareProduct** is reduced in comparison to a product of all new software. We will define equivalent volume (*Volume_{equivalent}*) of a proposed **SoftwareProduct** to be a function of newly written statements *Volume_{new}* and statements adapted from existing or reused software *Volume_{recycled}*. A study conducted at IBM's Santa Teresa Laboratory found that 77% of all program code is written in order to add new **Features** to existing **SoftwareProduct**s [Paulsen83]. To date, there is no consensus about how to compute equivalent volume. Methods have been proposed by Boehm, Bailey and Basili, and Thebaut.

Table 6.3 Object Point Weight

Object Type	Complexity		
	Simple	Medium	Difficult
Screen	1	2	3
Report	2	5	8
3GL component			10

OBSERVATIONS

There is no perfect **Volume** metric. There is no single **Volume** attribute that should be applied by itself to measure the bulk of a **SoftwareProduct**. They should be used in combination to assist you in your various information requirements related to controlling software **Project**s and improving the software development process. Consider the following:

1. When you purchase hardware on which to run your software, you use the *Bytes* attribute to size the computer memory.

2. While originally very popular, the *VolumeSoftSci*_{Calculate} is not any better than the other volume metrics and is more difficult to measure.

3. The $\mathbb{SLOC}$ Volume attribute is probably still the most widely used attribute because it is
   - relatively easy to define and discuss unambiguously,
   - easy to objectively measure,
   - conceptually familiar to software developers,
   - used directly or indirectly by most cost estimation models and rules of thumb for productivity estimation, and
   - is available directly from many organization's project databases.

   Problems with the $\mathbb{SLOC}$ attribute are [Jones97] the following:
   - It does not accurately support cross-language comparisons for productivity or quality for the more than 500 programming languages in current use.
   - There is no national or international standard for a source line of code.
   - Paradoxically, as the level of language gets higher, the most powerful and advanced languages appear to be less productive than the lower-level languages.

   Even with these deficiencies, $\mathbb{SLOC}$ is still gathered by most metric programs.

4. The **Chunk** metric is introduced in this book. The intent is to measure software at the cognitive level at which software is developed. **Chunk**s can be applied to objects, scripts, spreadsheets, graphic icons, application generators, and the like.

5. *FunctionPoints*_{Predict} are based on functional requirements and can be estimated and counted much earlier than lines of code. Function points let organizations normalize data such as cost, effort, duration, and defects [Furey97]. The Gartner Group [Hotle96] claims that "Function points will provide the primary means for measuring application size, reaching a penetration of approximately 50 of development organizations by the year 2000." Even though function points are a popular measure, they do have problems:
   - They are based on a subjective measure, which has resulted in a 30% variance within an organization and more than 30% across organizations [Kitchenham97].
   - Function points behave well when used within a specific organization, but they do not work well for cross-company benchmarking.

6. *ObjectPoints*_{Predict} are similar to *FunctionPoints*_{Predict}. They have the same advantages and disadvantages, but can be estimated and counted earlier than *FunctionPoints*_{Predict}.

$\boxed{\mathcal{E}\textit{quivalentVolume1}_{\textbf{Predict}}}$ Boehm proposed the following equivalent volume function for his COCOMO model [Boehm81]:

$$Volume_{KNCSS,1} = Volume_{new} + \frac{a_1}{100} \; Volume_{recycled} = \mathcal{E}\textit{quivalentVolume1}_{\textbf{Predict}} \quad (6.10)$$

where a_1 $= 0.4(DM) + 0.3(CM) + 0.3(IM)$

DM = percentage of total effort to design modified code = $\mathcal{D}\textit{esign-}$ $\mathcal{M}\textit{odifiedCode}_{\textbf{Set}}$

CM = percentage of total effort to code modified code = $\mathcal{C}\textit{ode-}$ $\mathcal{M}\textit{odifiedCode}_{\textbf{Set}}$

IM = percentage of total effort to integrate modified code = $\mathcal{I}\textit{nte-}$ $\textit{grationModifiedCode}_{\textbf{Set}}$

$Volume_{new}$ = estimated **Volume** of new source statements

$Volume_{recycled}$ = estimated **Volume** of recycled source statements

The maximum value of adjustment factor a_1 is 100, which corresponds to the case in which it is as difficult to adapt recycled code as to rewrite it completely.

$\boxed{\mathcal{E}\textit{quivalentVolume2}_{\textbf{Predict}}}$ Bailey and Basili [Bailey81] proposed the following equivalent volume model based on a study of **Project**s:

$$Volume_{KNCSS,2} = Volume_{new} + k_1 Volume_{recycled} = \mathcal{E}\textit{quivalentVolume2}_{\textbf{Predict}}$$

$$(6.11)$$

where k_1 = a constant derived from a study of **Project**s = $k1_{\textbf{Set}}$. For the **Project**s studied by Bailey and Basili, a value of $k_1 = 0.2$ was found. The value of k_1 would vary depending on the software development **Organization.**

$\boxed{\mathcal{E}\textit{quivalentVolume3}_{\textbf{Predict}}}$ Thebaut [Thebaut83] proposed a model where the contribution of recycled code is nonlinear:

$$Volume_{KNCSS,3} = Volume_{new} + Volume_{recycled}^{k_2} = \mathcal{E}\textit{quivalentVolume3}_{\textbf{Predict}}$$

$$(6.12)$$

where $k_2 = 0.857$ for values of $Volume_{recycled}$ up to 98,000 for the **Projects** studied by Thebaut = $k2_{\textbf{Set}}$.

$\boxed{\mathcal{E}\textit{quivalentVolume4}_{\textbf{Predict}}}$ Boehm, Horwitz, Selby, and Westland are principals in a program to update the COCOMO model to a new version that they call COCOMO 2.0 [Boehm95]. A modified equivalent volume in NCSS for the COCOMO 2.0 Post-Architecture Model has been developed based on the original COCOMO model and on work of Selby. In 1988, Selby at the NASA Software Engineering Laboratory gathered reuse data on 2,954 modules [Selby88,91]. He found that modules that are reused but not modified still cost about 5% of the cost of producing a new module. This is due to the effort required to assess, select, and assimilate the reusable module. Also, small modifications generate disproportionately large costs. He found that even though only 10% of a module is modified, the costs may be as high as 55% of producing a new module. This is due to the effort required to understand the software being modified and check all the intermodule interfaces.

The COCOMO 2.0 also introduces a breakage percentage that reflects the requirements volatility in a **Project** and an automatic translation percentage for code that is reengineered by automatic translation. Boehm gives an example of a **Project** that delivers 100,000 instructions but discards the equivalent of an additional 20,000 instructions having a breakage percentage of 20. The resulting COCOMO 2.0 equivalent volume model for reused software that includes factors for (1) assessment and assimilation, (2) software understanding, (3) breakage, and (4) automatic translation is

$$Volume_{KNCSS,4} = \left(Volume_{equivalent1} + Volume_{recycled} \times \frac{AA + SU - AT}{100} \right) \times \frac{100 + BRAK}{100}$$

$$= EquivalentVolume4_{\textbf{Predict}} \qquad (6.13)$$

where $AA = AssessmentAssimilation_{\textbf{Set}}$ = the degree of assessment and assimilation needed to determine whether a fully reused software module is appropriate to the application and to integrate its description into the overall product description. The value of AA varies from 0 to 8 depending on the amount of test, evaluation, and documentation required.

$SU = SoftwareUnderstanding_{\textbf{Set}}$ = the software understanding increment based on *structure, application clarity*, and *self-descriptiveness*. *SU* varies from a value of 50 for a module that has *structure* with very low cohesion, high coupling, spaghetti code, *application clarity* that has no match between program and application world views, and *self-descriptiveness* with obscure code and documentation missing, obscure or obsolete to a value of 10 for a module that has *structure* with strong modularity, information hiding in data/control structures, *application clarity* that demonstrates a clear match between program and application world views, and *self-descriptiveness* with self-descriptive code and documentation up to date, well organized, with design rationale.

$AT = Automatic\ Translated_{\textbf{Set}}$ = percentage of the code that is reengineered by automatic translation.

$BRAK = Breakage_{\textbf{Set}}$ = amount of code thrown away divided by the amount of code delivered multiplied by 100.

$\boxed{\textit{EquivalentVolume5}_{\textbf{Predict}}}$ A modified equivalent volume in object points for the COCOMO 2.0 Application Composition Model has been developed [Boehm95]. If you reuse screens, reports, or 3GL components, then the equivalent product volume would be smaller.

$$Volume_{OP_5,5} = Volume_{OP_5} \times \frac{100 - REUSED}{100} = \textit{EquivalentVolume5}_{\textbf{Predict}} \qquad (6.14)$$

where *REUSED* is the percent of components that is reused.

$\boxed{\textit{EquivalentVolume6}_{\textbf{Predict}}}$ For completeness, we will define the following estimator model that consists of an estimate made by an experienced computer professional:

$$Volume_{a,6} = Volume_a = \textit{EquivalentVolume6}_{\textbf{Predict}} \qquad (6.15)$$

where *a* are the units of volume for the **SoftwareProduct** that will be developed. For the rest of the book, we will use $Volume_{a,6}$ and $Volume_a$ interchangeably.

Unique Volume

When you create a new **Chunk** of software, usually between 75% to 90% of the lines of code are unique. The unique lines in your **Chunk** are mostly different from the unique lines in someone else's **Chunk** even though you are implementing a **Chunk** of software to perform the same function. A **Volume** attribute that measures unique source lines of code indicates whether software is a new **Chunk** or if it is a copy of code from elsewhere in an environment. If software is copied from elsewhere in your reference environment, there will be no unique lines when compared against a reference vector. You can create a reference vector of unique lines of code from your environment. Then, if a **Chunk** of code is copied from elsewhere, there will be no unique lines of code when compared against the reference vector. In a distributed network environment of clients and servers, you can use a reference vector to determine the amount of new code in either client or server files.

$\boxed{\text{UniqueSLOC}}$ We can determine the number of unique source lines of code (UniqueSLOC) by first eliminating leading blank characters on each line, sorting the source lines of code, eliminating duplicates, and then counting the remaining lines.

The **Volume** of UniqueSLOC for a **SourceFile** cannot be summed from the **Volume Chunk**s UniqueSLOCs.

$\boxed{\text{UniqueReferenceSLOC}}$ You can measure reuse of software by comparing new software with existing software. Existing software can be represented by a reference

EXAMPLE 6.9

```
 1
 2 * sort.
 3 * The following algorithm is an implementation of the insertion
 4 */
 5 /*
 6 /* Initialize algorithm variables for this pass of the loop */
 7 /* Insertion sort works on the same principle as how a person
     sorts
 8 /* Starting at the kth card, move it backward until it is in
 9 {
10 }
11 cards when they are being dealt one at a time. If a person has
12 Done=0;
13 Done=1;
14 else
15 for(k=1;k<NumberOfElements;k++)
16 if(List[j] < List[j-1])
17 int Done;
18 int k,j;
19 int SortArray(int List[], int NumberOfElements)
20 int Temp;
21 it is immediately placed in the correct place. */
22 j=k;
23 List[j-1]=Temp;
24 List[j]=List[j-1];
25 N sorted cards in his hand, then when he receives the N+1st
     card,
26 Temp=List[j];
27 the correct place */
28 while(j >= 1 && !Done)
```

The **Chunk** SortArray() from Figure 6.2 is shown above sorted with duplicates removed. It has the following unique measure:

$$\text{UniqueSLOC} = 28$$

vector of unique source lines of code from your environment. If you use a program from the reference library, then the number of unique source lines of code (UniqueReferenceSLOC) compared to reference library source lines of code would be zero. If you reuse a program but make changes to approximately 5% of the program, then the unique reference source lines of code would be less than or equal to 5% of unique source lines of code.

EXAMPLE 6.10

Refer to the **SourceFile** example in Figure 6.4 that is composed of two **Chunk**s main() and WhichIsBigger().

For main():

$$UniqueSLOC = 14$$

For WhichIsBigger()

$$UniqueSLOC = 13$$

The sum of UniqueSLOC for main() and WhichIsBigger() is 27. For the **SourceFile** example in Figure 6.4

$$UniqueSLOC = 23$$

EXAMPLE 6.11

Think of the **SourceFile** in Figure 6.1 as a library file. Consider the case when the user implements the function PlaceNode as

```
int PlaceNode(struct tree_node *spTree, struct tree_node *spTemp)
{
/* This program orders a list of people's names and their addresses */
    if(spTree == NULL)
    {
        spTree=spTemp;
        return 0;
    }
    else
    {
        if (spTree->sName > spTemp->sName)
            PlaceNode(spTree->spLeft_Child, spTemp);
        else
            PlaceNode(spTree->spRight_Child, spTemp);
    }
}
```

Only one line was changed and one comment was added, so

$$UniqueReferenceSLOC = 2$$

UniqueNCSLOC   We can determine the number of unique noncomment source lines of code (UniqueNCSLOC) in a **Chunk** by first sorting the source lines of code, eliminating duplicates, and then counting the remaining lines of code.

EXAMPLE 6.12

Sorting the **Chunk** `BubbleSort()` in Figure 6.3 and then removing duplicates, we have

$$NCSLOC = 30$$
$$UniqueNCSLOC = 20$$

UniqueReferenceNCSLOC   You can determine the **Volume** of unique reference noncomment source lines of code (UniqueReferenceNCSLOC) in same way that you determine unique reference source lines of code. Instead of using all source lines of code for comparison, you only use the noncomment source lines of code for comparison against the reference.

EXAMPLE 6.13

Consider the implementation of the `PlaceNode` function in Example 6.11. Since comments are ignored, this program has only one change from the reference file. So we have

$$UniqueReferenceNCSLOC = 1$$

STRUCTURE

Large **SoftwareProduct**s are usually harder to understand than small **SoftwareProduct**s. We can read and understand a small product of a few hundred lines of source code with relative ease. As the **Volume** of a product grows, so does complexity. We have a hard time keeping track of all aspects of the variables, functions, and control structures of large programs. As the **Volume** of a **SoftwareProduct** grows, we can reduce complexity by creating structures that are easy to read and understand. The architecture of a **SoftwareProduct** should be matched to the human cognitive process. A well-structured program is much easier to understand than one that is poorly structured.

Our ability to understand software is restricted by limitations of the human mind. Billions of memory cells make up our brain, which weighs approximately 3 pounds. While we do not know exactly how the brain is constructed or works, we know that it is composed of an ability to process information and store information in memory. We will portray the human brain as a computer composed of a processor and memory.

The cycle time of the processor is 40 milliseconds and the access time from peripherals is 50 milliseconds. About 80% of the processing time is normally spent doing I/O-related activities and only 10% number crunching. The unique feature of this system is word size. Since processing is mostly symbolic in nature, the word size is conceptually infinite. Information can be chunked together and a symbolic name given to represent this cluster of information or chunk. Chunks consists of functions, subroutines, scripts, macros, objects, methods, and the like. Overhead is reduced by utilizing the symbolic name for processing purposes. Our memory system consists of three levels: sensory memory, short-term memory and long-term memory.

Our sensory memory has buffers for sensory information. The buffers hold the information for only short periods of time, from about 0.25 to 8 seconds depending on the sensory channel, and then the information rapidly decays. Aside from channel capacity, the contents of sensory memory are largely controlled by two processes known as sensory gating and attention. When information from two or more sensors arrives simultaneously, sensory gating determines priority for processing by enhancing one and diminishing the others. The amount of attention given to the contents of sensory memory controls the type and amount of information provided to short- and long-term memory.

Our conscious state draws heavily from short- and long-term memory. Short-term memory is also referred to as working memory. Short-term memory is used to perform momentary, familiar, repetitive tasks. When we drive to work over a familiar route, we are under the influence of short-term memory. Information from the environment is received and only stored for the few seconds it takes to complete a momentary task, and then it is replaced by information associated with short-term memory for the next task. This process is repeated many times during the drive to work. Often, when we are asked to describe the drive, we have difficulty distinguishing that drive from many other past drives.

Short-term memory with its limits in terms of duration (20 to 45 seconds) and the number of simple stimuli that can be processed ($n = 7 \pm 2$) is smaller than long-term memory. Chunking single stimuli into larger structures coupled with learning serves to compensate for the limitation on number. Limits in duration are considered benefits. The limits serve to protect the human brain from being overloaded with the millions of pieces of information that are good only for momentary tasks. Depending on stimulus intensity, we can recognize changes that occur in the environment at the rate of about 5 to 60 cycles per second. For example, the rate that frames change in a moving picture or television is about 20 to 60 frames per second, and we do not recognize that they are separate events.

Long-term memory appears to have no limits on size or duration. The down side of long-term memory is retrieval. Retrieval is highly dependent on frequency of use and recency of use. Time to retrieve information from long-term memory is shorter if the information has been used recently or has been frequently used in the past. Therefore, information in some cases can be recovered in a few seconds, and other times the retrieval process can take minutes or longer. While the long-term memory is a nondestructive read-out, sometimes the retrieval path to the stored information is lost and must be reestablished. The error rate or processing confusion increases when similar sounding pieces of information are manipulated.

SoftwareProducts should be structured to fit the capabilities of the human mind. Large, complex programs can be structured to make them understandable to teams of software developers. A form of hierarchical decomposition should be used to break a large **SoftwareProduct** into understandable **Chunk**s. The interaction of data items and control should be encapsulated into a few **Chunk**s that can be conceptualized at one time. Over time, we have learned a number of software attributes that we can measure to determine if a **SoftwareProduct** is well-structured and can be easily understood by the human mind. A well-structured **Chunk** should have the following characteristics:

- *Cohesive.* **Chunk** should perform a single function.
- *Loosely coupled.* **Chunk**s should be loosely versus tightly coupled.
- *Structured.* A structured program is made up of structured control constructs each of which have a single input and a single output. An example of control constructs are (1) statements sequenced one after another, (2) IF . . . . THEN . . . . ELSE . . . . ENDIF statements, and (3) DO_WHILE or DO_ UNTIL loops.
- *Properly scoped.* The scope of effect of a **Chunk** should be a subset of the scope of control of the **Chunk**.
- *Nonpathological.* A pathological connection is a communication link that does not follow the hierarchical software structure. A program that transfers into or out of a loop is one that has pathological connections.
- *Shallow.* A shallow program has shallow depth of control loops or object class inheritance [Zolnowski81].
- *Small in live variables.* Live variables are those that are actually used during execution of a program.
- *Small in spans.* Spans are a count of statements that reference a variable.
- *Small in chunk-global variable usage pairs.* A chunk-global variable usage pair occurs when a global variable is read or set by a **Chunk**.

- *Small in chunk-global variable usage triples.* A chunk-global variable usage triple occurs when a global variable is set by one **Chunk** and read by another **Chunk**.
- *Small in information flow.* Information flow metrics are related to the product of information that flows into and out of a **Chunk**.

We will now examine a number of the **Structure** attributes.

$\boxed{\text{Decisions}}$ The number of decisions in a **Chunk** is the count of direct conditional statements or conditional statements that are found as part of loop statements.

EXAMPLE 6.14

Consider the `PlaceNode()` **Chunk** in Figure 6.1:

$$\text{Decisions} = 2$$

$\boxed{CyclomaticNumber_{\textbf{Calculate}}}$ The number of decision statements in a program is directly related to the number of branches that must be tested. McCabe [McCabe76] named the number of branches in a program the cyclomatic number. For a single **Chunk**, the cyclomatic number is

$$CyclomaticNumber_{\textbf{Calculate}} = \text{Decisions} \qquad (6.16)$$

A **SourceFile** may contain many **Chunk**s. The cyclomatic number of a **SourceFile** is

$$CyclomaticNumber_{\textbf{Calculate}} = \sum_{i=1}^{n} CyclomaticNumber_{\textbf{Calculate}_i} + n \qquad (6.17)$$

where n = number of **Chunk**s in the **SourceFile**.

EXAMPLE 6.15

Now consider the entire **SourceFile** shown in Figure 6.1:

For `PlaceNode()`:

$$CyclomaticNumber_{\textbf{Calculate}} = 2$$

For `PrintNode()`

$$CyclomaticNumber_{\textbf{Calculate}} = 1$$

So for the **SourceFile**,

$$CyclomaticNumber_{\textbf{Calculate}} = 5$$

$\boxed{\text{EssentialComplexity}}$ Dijkstra pointed out that go-to statements are harmful [Dijkstra68] and that they can be avoided by using structured programming. Structured programming is a form of go-to-less programming where each control construct has a single input and a single output. Code is easy to follow and easy to understand because each section of code follows the previous section in a read forward sequential manner. Structured programming is highly cohesive, and the scope of effect is included in the scope of control. When global variables are avoided, then the structured programs are loosely coupled.

A structured program contains three type statements: (1) sequence nontransfer statements, (2) single input/output conditional transfer statements of the form IF ... THEN ... ELSE ... ENDIF, and (3) single input/output DOWHILE or DOUNTIL loop statements.

A program can be examined to determine how well structured it is. We recommend that you examine software at the **SourceFile** level. An iterative procedure can be used to reduce a program to one that only contains nonstructured control constructs. A program is reduced by replacing each series of sequential statements by a single statement. Then, each IF ... THEN ... ELSE ... ENDIF, DOWHILE, or DOUNTIL statement that contains no other conditional statements is reduced to a single statement. This iterative procedure continues until no additional statements can be reduced. Essential complexity (EssentialComplexity) is the cyclomatic number of a reduced **SourceFile**. If the software is structured, then the essential complexity is equal to 1. If software is completely not structured, then the essential complexity will be equal to the cyclomatic complexity of the nonreduced program. Most software is somewhere in between.

$\boxed{\text{NestingDepth}}$ The structure of the nesting depth of loops can lead to complex software [Zolnowski81]. A simple statement in the sequential part of a **Chunk** may be executed only once. A similar statement can be executed many times if it is within an inner loop. The higher the nesting depth (NestingDepth), the more difficult it is to assess the entrance conditions for a certain statement.

$\boxed{\text{InheritanceDepth}}$ Objects are **Chunk** types that contain class hierarchies. Methods (or operations) and attributes values can be inherited from higher levels in the class hierarchy. Inheritance depth (InheritanceDepth) measures the number of levels through which values must be remembered. As inheritance depth increases, the complexity increases.

$\boxed{\textit{SourceLiveVariables}_{\textbf{Calculate}}}$ A live variable is based on the hypothesis that the more data items that a programmer must keep track of when constructing a statement, the more difficult it is to construct [Conte86]. Conte et al. give three defini-

EXAMPLE 6.16

PlaceNode in Figure 6.1 can be reduced to the following **Chunk**:

```
PlaceNode()
{
    If-Then-Else Construct
}
```

So, EssentialComplexity = 1.

However, the following **Chunk**:

```
int PlaceNode(struct tree_node *spTree, struct tree_node *spTemp)
{
    if(spTemp->iNumber < 0)
        return 0

    if(spTree == NULL)
    {
        spTree=spTemp;
        return 0;
    }
    else
    {
        if (spTree->iNumber > spTemp->iNumber)
            PlaceNode(spTree->spLeft_Child, spTemp);
        else
            PlaceNode(spTree->spRight_Child, spTemp);
    }
}
```

can be reduced to

```
PlaceNode()
{
    If Construct
    If-Then-Else Construct
}
```

So, EssentialComplexity = 2.

EXAMPLE 6.17

Consider the following code segment:

```
for(j=0;j<NumberOfElements-1;j++)
{
    for(k=j+1;k<NumberOfElements;k++)
    {
        if(List[j] > List[k])
        {
            Temp=List[j];
            List[j]=List[k];
            List[k]=Temp;
        }
    }
}
```

NestingDepth = 2.

---

tions of live variables: (1) source live variables are those from the beginning of a **Chunk** to the end of the **Chunk**, (2) threshold live variables are those at a particular statement only if it is referenced a certain threshold number of statements before or after that statement, and (3) span live variables that are live from their first to last reference within a **Chunk**. Assume that Variables live variables are active somewhere in a **Chunk**. Then the number of live variables in a **Chunk** is equal to the number of ex-

---

EXAMPLE 6.18

Consider the following three class definitions:

```
class LinkedList
{ /* some code */ }

class Queue : public LinkedList
{ /* some code */

class Stack : public Queue
{ /* some code */
```

InheritanceDepth = 2.

ecutable source statements ExecutableSS times Variables. Thus, the number of source live variables in a **Chunk** is

$$LV_1 = \text{ExecutableSS} \times \text{Variables} = SourceLiveVariables_{\text{Calculate}} \qquad (6.18)$$

EXAMPLE 6.19

Consider the chunk shown in Figure 6.6:

$$\text{ExecutableSS} = 6$$
$$\text{Variables} = 5$$
$$SourceLiveVariables_{\text{Calculate}} = 30$$

ThresholdLiveVariables   To calculate the threshold live variables, we will define the number of variables that are referenced by threshold number n_1 executable logical statements before or after an executable logical source statement within a **Chunk**. We can compute threshold live variables using

$$LV_2(n_1) = \sum_{i=1}^{n} x_i = \text{ThresholdLiveVariables} \qquad (6.19)$$

where x_i is the number of variables that are live $n_1(n1_{\text{Set}})$ statements before or after statement i for a **Chunk** of n statements.

```
 1 void BubbleSort(int List[], int NumberOfElements)
 2 {
 3      int j,k;
 4      int Temp
 5
 6      for(j=0;j<NumberOfElements-1;j++)
 7      {
 8          for(k=j+1;k<NumberOfElements;k++)
 9          {
10              if(List[j] > List[k])
11              {
12                  Temp=List[j];
13                  List[j]=List[k];
14                  List[k]=Temp;
15              }
16          }
17      }
18 }
```

Figure 6.6 Simple Bubble Sort

EXAMPLE 6.20

Refer to the **Chunk** in Figure 6.6

Line Number	Live Variables ($n_1 = 3$)
1	Skip
2	Skip
3	Skip
4	Skip
5	Skip
6	5
7	Skip
8	5
9	Skip
10	5
11	Skip
12	5
13	5
14	4
15	Skip
16	Skip
17	Skip
18	Skip

TresholdLiveVariables = 29

SpanLiveVariables   Span live variables are the maximum number of variables that are active for any individual statement within a **Chunk**. A variable is active between the first reference to the variable until the last reference to a variable within a **Chunk**. For a **Chunk** of n statements,

$$LV_3 = \sum_{i=1}^{n} x_i = \text{SpanLiveVariables} \qquad (6.20)$$

where x_i is the number of variables that are live at statement i.

SourceLiveVariablesPerExecutableSS   The more live variables that a software developer must track for each statement, the harder it is to follow a program. For a **Chunk**, the average number of source live variables per executable source statement is

$$\text{SourceLiveVariablesPerExecutableSS} = \text{Variables} \qquad (6.21)$$

EXAMPLE 6.21

Refer to the **Chunk** in Figure 6.6

Line Number	Variables	Live Variables
1	Start List, NumberOfElements	2
2		2
3	Start j, k	4
4	Start Temp	5
5		5
6		5
7		5
8	End Number of Elements	5
9		4
10		4
11		4
12		4
13	End j	4
14	End List,k,Temp	3
15		0
16		0
17		0
18		0

$$SpanLiveVariables = 56$$

EXAMPLE 6.22

Refer to Example 6.19.

$$Variables = 5$$

So

$$SourceLiveVariablesPerExecutableSS = 5$$

$\boxed{\textit{ThresholdLiveVariablesPerExecutableSS}_{\textbf{Calculate}}}$ The average number of threshold live variables per executable source statement in a **Chunk** is

$$\textit{ThresholdLiveVariablesPerExecutableSS}_{\textbf{Calculate}} = \text{ThresholdLiveVariables} \div \text{ExecutableSS} \tag{6.22}$$

EXAMPLE 6.23

Refer to Example 6.20.

$$\text{ThresholdLiveVariables} = 29$$
$$\text{ExecutableSS} = 6$$

So

$$\textit{ThresholdLiveVariablesPerExecutableSS}_{\textbf{Calculate}} \approx 5$$

$\boxed{\textit{SpanLiveVariablesPerExecutableSS}_{\textbf{Calculate}}}$ The average number of source live variables per executable source statement in a **Chunk** is

$$\textit{SpanLiveVariablesPerExecutableSS}_{\textbf{Calculate}} = \text{SpanLiveVariables} \div \text{ExecutableSS} \tag{6.23}$$

EXAMPLE 6.24

Refer to Example 6.21.

$$\text{SpanLiveVariables} = 21$$
$$\text{ExecutableSS} = 6$$

So

$$\textit{SpanLiveVariablesPerExecutableSS}_{\textbf{Calculate}} \approx 3.5$$

$\boxed{\text{Spans}}$ Conte et al. [Conte86] say that a metric that captures some of the essence of how often a variable is used in a **Chunk** is called the span (*SP*). For a given variable, the span metric is the number of statements that use that variable between two successive references to that same variable [Elshoff76]. The span is related to, but not the same as, the definition of span live variables. For a **Chunk** that references a variable in n statements, there are $n - 1$ spans for that variable. Notice that statements that do not reference the variable are not spans. If there are m variables v_i in a **Chunk**, then the number of spans for that **Chunk** would be

$$SPs = \sum_{i=1}^{m} v_i = \mathbb{Spans} \tag{6.24}$$

EXAMPLE 6.25

Refer to the Bubble Sort Code in Figure 6.6.

Variable	Number of Reference Lines
NumberOfElements	3
List	5
j	6
k	5
Temp	3

$$\mathbb{Spans} = 17$$

[Knots] Whenever possible, pathological connections should be avoided. A pathological connection is a communication or control link not following the hierarchical software structure. Examples of pathological connections are global variables and knots. Global variables and knots are a type of communication outside the hierarchical software structure. A global is one that is available to any and all **Chunk**s in a

---

EXAMPLE 6.26

Consider the following code segment:

```
1   printf("%d\n", j);
2   j=j+1;
3   if(j < 10)
4       goto 1;
5   end
```

We have the following pairs:

$$(1,2) \quad (2,3) \quad (3,4) \quad (3,5) \quad (4,1)$$

And

$$\min(4,1) < \min(3,5) < \max(4,1) \text{ AND } \max(3,5) > \max(4,1)$$

$$\mathbb{Knots} = 1$$

program. Knots (Knots) occur when transfer lines cross that are drawn in the margin of a program listing [Woodward79]. To measure knots in a program, assume that the lines in a program are numbered sequentially. Let an ordered pair of integers (a, b) indicate that there is a direct transfer from line a to line b. Given two pairs (a, b) and (c, d), there is a knot if one of the following two cases is true:

1. $\min(a,b) < \min(c,d) < \max(a,b)$ and $\max(c,d) > \max(a,b)$
2. $\min(a,b) < \max(c,d) < \max(a,b)$ and $\min(c,d) < \min(a,b)$

Programs with lower knot counts are believed to be better designed.

Pairs   A chunk-global variable usage pair is ($Chunk_{SET\ or\ READ}$, $GlobalVariable$), where the $GlobalVariable$ is either set or read by $Chunk_{SET\ or\ READ}$. The number of

---

EXAMPLE 6.27

Consider the following **SourceFile**:

```
#include <stdio.h>

int NumberOfNodes;

main()
{
    int UserSelection;
    << some code >>
    NumberOfNodes = UserSelection
    AnalyzeNodes();
    << some code >>
}

void AnalyzeNodes()
{
    int I;

    for(I=0;I<NumberOfNodes;I++)
    {
        <<look at each node and analyze it >>
    }
    /* Now we'll add a new node to the end */
```

```
    << Add a node >>
    NumberOfNodes++;
}
```

The `main` **Chunk** has one pair while the `AnalyzeNodes` **Chunk** has two pairs:

(main$_{SET}$, NumberOfNodes)
(NumberOfNodes, AnalyzeNodes$_{READ}$)
(AnalyzeNodes$_{SET}$, NumberOfNodes)

$$\text{Pairs} = 3$$

such pairs in a **Chunk** is represented by Pairs. For a given **Chunk** or **SourceFile**, the number of pairs should be kept as small as possible.

$\boxed{\text{RelativePercentageUsagePairs}}$ In a programming language that allows the definition of individual scopes for global variables, a module can access a global variable, but it can make neither set nor read operations. Thus, the metric can be normalized by dividing the count of potential pairs into the actual count. The metric is called the $\text{RelativePercentageUsagePairs}$.

EXAMPLE 6.28

Refer to the code in Example 6.27:
The maximum number of pairs is equal to the number of global variables $\times$ 2. So for each **Chunk** in this **SourceFile**, there are possibly 20 pairs.
For the AnalyzeMode function, there are 2 pairs. So,

$$\text{RelativePercentageUsagePairs} = 2/2 = 100\%$$

$\boxed{\text{Triples}}$ The usage pair metric can be further refined to represent the binding of data between two **Chunk**s in a **SourceFile**. ($Chunk_{SET}$, $GlobalVariable$, $Chunk_{READ}$) infers that global variable ($GlobalVariable$) is set by **Chunk** ($Chunk_{SET}$) and read by **Chunk** ($Chunk_{READ}$). The existence of ($Chunk_{SET}$, $GlobalVariable$, $Chunk_{READ}$) requires the existence of pairs ($Chunk_{SET}$, $GlobalVariable$) and ($Chunk_{READ}$, $GlobalVariable$). These triples are used to describe how information flows through a **SourceFile** or an entire **SoftwareProduct**. The number of such triples for a **SourceFile** or program is a metric Triples that indicates the sharing of data among **Chunk**s.

EXAMPLE 6.29

Once again refer to Example 6.27. However, this time the main function looks like

```
main()
{
    int UserSelection;
    << some code >>
    NumberOfNodes = UserSelection
    AnalyzeNodes();
    << some code >>
    PrintNodes();
}

void PrintNodes()
{
    int j;

    for(j=0;j<NumberOfNodes;j++)
    {
        << Print out node information >>
    }
}
```

So now we have the following pairs:
$(\text{main}_{SET},\ \text{NumberOfNodes})$
$(\text{NumberOfNodes},\ \text{AnalyzeNodes}_{READ})$
$(\text{AnalyzeNodes}_{SET},\ \text{NumberOfNodes})$
$(\text{NumberOfNodes}, \text{PrintNodes}_{READ})$

These can be divided into the following triples:
$(\text{main}_{SET},\ \text{NumberOfNodes},\ \text{AnalyzeNodes}_{READ})$
$(\text{AnalyzeNodes}_{SET},\ \text{NumberOfNodes},\ \text{PrintNodes}_{READ})$

So

$$\text{Triples} = 2$$

RelativePercentageUsageTriples   The count of triples can also be normalized by dividing the count of potential triples into the actual count to obtain RelativePercentageUsageTriples.

EXAMPLE 6.30

Refering to Example 6.29 we have the following triples:

(main*SET*, NumberOfNodes, AnalyzeNodes*READ*)
(AnalyzeNodes*SET*, NumberOfNodes, PrintNodes*READ*)

The maximum number of triples is equal to the number of chunks × number of global variables × number of chunks −1. So in this case, the max = 6.

Thus,

$$RelativePercentageUsageTriples = 2/6 = 33\%$$

$\boxed{InformationFlow1\textbf{Calculate}}$ Information flow metrics will be defined in terms of fan-in and fan-out. Fan-in (FanIn) for a **SourceFile** is the number of **Chunk**s that pass data into the **Chunk** either directly or indirectly. Fan-in of a **Chunk** Q is the number of unique **Chunk**s P in **SourceFile** for which at least one of the following conditions holds: (1) there exists a global variable R for which the triple (P, R, Q) is a valid data binding triple, or (2) there exists a **Chunk** T and variables R, S, so that the triples (P, R, T) and (T, S, Q) are valid data binding triples. The fan-in definition is based on a one by Henry and Kafura [Henry81].

Fan-out can be defined in a similar manner. Fan-out (FanOut) for a **Source-File** is the number of **Chunk**s to which data are passed either directly or indirectly. Fan-out of a **Chunk** P is the number of unique **Chunk**s Q in **SourceFile** so that at least one of the following conditions holds: (1) there exists a global variable R so that the triple (P, R, Q) is a valid data binding triple, or (2) there exists a **Chunk** T and variables R, S, so that the triples (P, R, T) and (T, S, Q) are valid data binding triples. The fan-out definition is based on a one by Henry and Kafura [Henry81]. The first definition of information flow for a **SourceFile** or group of **SourceFiles** is

$$InformationFlow1\textbf{Calculate} = FanIn \times FanOut \qquad (6.25)$$

EXAMPLE 6.31

Refer to Figure 6.7 which has the following triples:

(main*SET*, ListOfNumbers, SortNumbers*READ*)
(main*SET*, NumberOfElements, SortNumbers*READ*)
(SortNumbers*SET*, ListOfNumbers, PrintNumbers*READ*)
(main*SET*, NumberOfElements, PrintNumbers*READ*)

Chunk	Fan In	Fan Out
main()	0	3
SortNumbers()	1	1
PrintNumbers()	2	0

$$InformationFlow1_{\textbf{Calculate}} = 3 * 4 = 12$$

$\boxed{InformationFlow2_{\textbf{Calculate}}}$ The second definition of information flow is

$$InformationFlow2_{\textbf{Calculate}} = (FanIn \times FanOut)^2 \qquad (6.26)$$

EXAMPLE 6.32

Refer to Example 6.31 and Figure 6.7:

$$InformationFlow2_{\textbf{Calculate}} = (3 * 4)^2 = 144$$

$\boxed{InformationFlow3_{\textbf{Calculate}}}$ The third definition of information flow is

$$InformationFlow3_{\textbf{Calculate}} = NCSS_{\textbf{Calculate}} \times (FanIn \times FanOut)^2 \qquad (6.27)$$

EXAMPLE 6.33

Refer to Example 6.31 and Figure 6.7:

$$InformationFlow3_{\textbf{Calculate}} = 23 * (3 * 4)^2 = 3312$$

REWORK

One measure of software quality is **Defect**s per KSLOC (thousand source lines of code). Throughout a development **Project**, the **Volume** of **Defect**s should be kept as small as possible through organized code walk-throughs and both formal and informal testing. When **Defect**s are prevented, quality improves and **Rework** is reduced. When **Rework** is reduced, productivity improves.

```
int *ListOfNumbers;
int NumberElements;

main()
{
    int j;
    int returncode;

    /* Create the array */
    NumberOfElements=100;
    ListOfNumbers=malloc(sizeof(int)*NumberElements);

    if(ListOfNumbers == NULL)
        exit(1);

    /* Fill an array with the numbers NumberElements..1.*/
    for(j=0;j<NumberElements;j++)
        ListOfNumbers[j]=NumberElements-j;

    returncode = SortNumbers();

    if(returncode)
        PrintNumbers();
}

int SortNumbers()
{
    int j,k;
    int TempElement;

    for(j=0;j<NumberElements-1;j++)
    {
        for(k=j+1;k<NumberElements;k++)
        {
            if(ListOfNumbers[j] > ListOfNumbers[k])
            {
                Temp=ListOfNumbers[j];
                ListOfNumbers[j]=ListOfNumbers[k];
                ListOfNumbers[k]=Temp;
            }
        }
    }
    return 1;
}
void PrintNumbers()
{
    int k;

    for(k=0;k<NumberElements;k++)
        printf("%d\n", ListOfNumbers[k]);
}
```

Figure 6.7 Number Sorting **SourceFile**

In a **SoftwareProduct**, **Rework** occurs when source statements are added to, deleted from, or changed in a **RequirementsFile**, **DesignFile**, **DocumentFile**, or **SourceFile**. We will measure **Rework** by a turmoil attribute.

$\boxed{Turmoil_{\textbf{Calculate}}}$ We will define turmoil as the amount of change activity that occurs in a file between successive **Version**s of that file. Change activity occurs when statement additions (Adds) are made to a file, deletions (Deletes) are made from a file, or changes (Changes) are made within a file. Instead of changing a statement, the old one can be deleted and a new one added to reflect a change. Thus, we will assume that a change to a statement is equivalent to a statement being deleted and then a new statement being added. Turmoil represented by change activity can be determined as follows:

$$Turmoil_{\textbf{Calculate}} = \text{Adds} + 2 \times \text{Changes} + \text{Deletes} \tag{6.28}$$

SUMMARY

SoftwareProduct size attributes are the main information gathered to aid in visualizing software. The **Volume** size attributes help us to determine product bulk, the **Structure** size attributes indicate cognitive complexity, and the turmoil size metrics help us to visualize how fast a product is stabilizing. By collecting the size metrics, we can determine the characteristics of the software product at all levels of the software product hierarchy and can then relate the effort of **Individual**s, teams (**Group**s), and **Organization**s to the **SoftwareProduct** being produced.

REFERENCES

[Abran96]   Abran, A., "Function Points Analysis: An Empirical Study of Its Measurement Processes," *IEEE Transactions on Software Engineering*, Vol. 22, No. 12, December 1996, pp. 895–910.

[Albrecht79]   Albrecht, A. J., "Measuring Application Development Productivity," *Proceedings of the Joint SHARE/GUIDE/IBM Application Development Symposium*, October 1979, pp. 83–92.

[Albrecht83]   Albrecht, A. F., and Gaffney, J. E., "Software Functions, Source Lines of Code, and Development Effort Prediction: A Software Science Validation," *IEEE Transactions on Software Engineering*, Vol. 9, No. 6, November 1983, pp. 639–648.

[Bailey81]   Bailey, J.W., and Basili, V.R., "A Meta-model for Software Development Resource Expenditures," *Proceedings of the Fifth International Conference on Software Engineering*, 1981, pp. 107–116.

[Boehm81]   Boehm, B. W., *Software Engineering Economics*, Prentice Hall, Upper Saddle River, NJ, 1981, 767 p.

[Boehm95]   Boehm, B., Horowitz, E., Selby, R., and Westland, J. C., *COCOMO 2.0 User's Manual*, Version 1.1, copyrighted by University of Southern California, received in April 1995.

[Conte86]   Conte, S. D., Dunsmore, H. E., and Shen, V. Y., *Software Engineering Metrics and Models*, Benjamin/Cummings Publishing Co., Inc., Menlo Park, CA, 1986, 396 p.

[Dijkstra68]   Dijkstra, E. W., "Go to Statements Considered Harmful," *Communications of the ACM*, Vol. 11, No. 3, March 1968, pp. 147–148.

[Elshoff76]   Elshoff, J. L., "An Analysis of Some Commercial PL/1 Programs," *IEEE Transactions on Software Engineering*, Vol. SE-2, No. 2, June 1976, pp. 113–120.

[Furey97]   Furey, S., "Point: Why We Should Use Function Points," *IEEE Software*, March/April 1997, pp. 28, 30.

[Grady87]   Grady, R. B., and Caswell, D. L., *Software Metrics: Establishing a Company-wide Program*, Prentice Hall, Upper Saddle River, NJ, 1987.

[Halstead77]   Halstead, M. H., *Elements of Software Science,* Elsevier North-Holland, New York, 1977.

[Henry81]   Henry, S., and Kafura, D., "Software Structure Metrics Based on Information Flow," *IEEE Transactions on Software Engineering*, Vol. SE-7, No. 5, September 1981, pp. 510–518.

[Hotle96]   Hotle, M., "Understanding and Improving the AD Estimating Process," *Application Development and Management System Strategies*, Gartner Group, Stamford, CN, November 1996, p. 25.

[IBM84]   IBM CISGuidelines 313, *AD/M Productivity Measurement and Estimate Validation,* November 1984.

[Jones97]   Jones, C., *Applied Software Measurement*, McGraw-Hill, New York, 1997.

[Kitchenham97]   Kitchenham, B., "Counterpoint: The Problem with Function Points," *IEEE Software*, March/April 1997.

[McCabe76]   McCabe, T.J., "A Complexity Measure," *IEEE Transactions on Software Engineering*, Vol. SE-2, No. 4, December 1976, pp. 308–320.

[Orfali96]   Orfali, R., Harkey, D., and Edwards, J., *The Essential Distributed Objects Survival Guide*, John Wiley & Sons, Inc., 605 Third Avenue, New York, 1996, 604 p.

[Paulsen83]   Paulsen, L.R., Fitsos, G.P., and Shen, V.Y., "A Metric for the Identification of Error-prone Software Modules," *TR-03.228*, IBM Santa Teresa Laboratory, San Jose, CA, June 1983.

[Schwartz69]   Schwartz, Julies I., *Software Engineering Techniques*, Report on a Conference Sponsored by the NATO Science Committee, Rome, Italy, October 27–31, 1969, p. 41.

[Selby88]   Selby, R., "Empirically Analyzing Software Reuse in a Production Environment," in *Software Reuse: Emerging Technology*, W. Tracz, IEEE Computer Society Press, New York, 1988, pp. 176–189.

[Selby91]   Selby, R., Porter, A., Schmidt, D., and Berney, J., "Metric-driven Analysis and Feedback Systems for Enabling Empirically Guided Software Development," *Proceedings of the Thirteenth International Conference on Software Engineering (ICSE 13)*, Austin, TX, May 13–16, 1991, pp. 288–298.

[Symons91]   Symons, C. R., *Software Sizing and Estimating, Mk II FPA (Function Point Analysis)*, John Wiley & Sons, New York, 1991.

[Thebaut83]   Thebaut, S.M., "The Saturation Effect in Large-scale Software Development: Its Impact and Control," Ph.D. Thesis, Department of Computer Science, Purdue University, West Lafayette, IN, May 1983.

[Woodward79]   Woodward, M.R., Hennell, M.A., and Hedley, D., "A Measure of Control Flow Complexity in Program Text," *IEEE Transactions on Software Engineering*, Vol. SE-1, No. 1, January 1979, pp. 45–50.

[Zolnowski81]   Zolnowski, J. C., and Simmons, D. B., "Taking the Measure of Program Complexity," *Proceedings of the National Computer Conference*, 1981, pp. 329–336.

7
Effort

Many organizations responsible for the evolution of software systems seem to operate constantly in a reactive mode, fighting the flames of the most recent fire. Behind this visible sense of urgency, though, managers appear to emphasize one of three primary strategies:

- *maximize customer satisfaction,*
- *minimize engineering effort and schedule, and*
- *minimize defects.*

Robert B. Grady
[Grady92]

INTRODUCTION

We are interested in software life cycle process productivity, quality, and **Usability** improvement. Productivity is improved when we reduce the effort to produce a product. In this chapter, we will focus on process attributes called cost drivers that affect the effort required to develop software.

The effort required to produce a product is inversely related to productivity. When effort decreases, productivity improves. When effort increases, productivity worsens. In this chapter we will study effort prediction models and what causes effort to vary. These models range from simple effort prediction models based on a single cost driver to complex composite models based on many cost drivers.

As the number of effort model cost drivers that can be varied increases, accuracy may or may not improve. As the number of variables increases, the chance of them all being independent of each other declines. Ideally, we should select a model based on independent variables. Also, we should select significant variables that have a major effect on the output of the model. For example, the size or **Volume** of a software system has a major effect on the effort required to produce it. Therefore, all the effort models will have at least one variable directly related to size.

Martin [Martin82] and Jones [Jones78, 86] have studied techniques for improving productivity. They stated that any single step toward use of inspections, structured techniques, and the like, can improve productivity by up to 25%. Use of these techniques in combination can yield improvements of between 25% and 50%. They declared that the only single technique that by itself can improve the productivity level by more than 50% is a change in programming language. Gains of between 50% and 75% can be achieved by single high achievers or teams of high achievers. Gains of 100% or more can be achieved by database user languages, application generators, and software reuse [Factor88]. Object-oriented techniques emphasize reuse.

Techniques for worsening productivity also exist. For example, a **Project** with ineffective, incompetent management will fail. Even though the effectiveness of management is very important, this factor is normally not a variable in an effort prediction model. Bad management can be a dominator of other attributes. When we improve the quality of a product, there are fewer **Defect**s in the product. When quality is designed and built into the product, the cost of **Rework** and maintenance is reduced. When costs are reduced, productivity improves. The **SoftwareProduct** quality will be addressed in later chapters.

Our goal is to produce software to **Customer** satisfaction that is on time and within budget. Kemerer and Patrick [Kemerer93] provided ample anecdotal evidence that in general these goals are not being met. They quoted a 1984 report by Jenkins, Naumann, and Wetherbe [Jenkins84] that of 72 medium-scale software **Project**s in 23 major US corporations the **Project**s had an average budget overrun of 36%, with only 9% of the **Project**s completed within budget. They quoted a 1988 University of Arizona study of 827 **Project**s that found an average budget overrun of 33%, with only 16% of the respondents who stated that they "rarely" or "never" experienced cost overruns [Phan88]. Also, Kemerer and Patrick quoted a DeMarco and Lister 1987 survey [DeMarco87] of 500 software **Project**s where 15% of all **Project**s were so late that they were canceled and a full 25% of the large **Project**s were canceled. To improve the software development process, you must know which factors affect productivity.

Simmons [Simmons 91] defines a dominator as a single factor that can reduce software **Group** productivity by an order of magnitude (that is, 10 to 1). Dominators may or may not appear as variables in an effort model. We will first discuss effort dominators and then we will discuss effort models.

DOMINATORS

Dominators are **Project** attributes that cause effort (and productivity) to vary by an order of magnitude. Therefore, they are major cost drivers. Dominators may or may not appear as variables in effort models. For example, we often assume that all **Project**s are properly managed, even though they may not be. The result can be a failed

Project dominated by poor management. Dominators like management often do not have a 10:1 effect on reducing effort, but they definitely can have over a 10:1 effect on increasing effort. The amount of effort spent on a **Project** is limited by resource constraints. Instead of increasing the resources by an order of magnitude, the **Project** often fails.

Dominators are not independent of each other. For example, a poor **Customer** interface and volatile requirements can result in excessive communications. An infrastructure-heavy **Project** life cycle process can result in need for excessive documentation. We will examine each dominator on its own merits without considering all the possible dependency relationships.

Many factors external to a **Project** can have a direct effect on a **Project**. Social, economic, political, and legal factors can affect a **Project**, but in this book we will only consider dominators that are internal to a **Project**.

Dominators exist as attributes of the overall **Project**, **SoftwareProduct**, **Organization**, **Supplier**s, and **Customer**s. For each of these, the dominators are as follows:

Overall **Project**	Development schedule constraints
	Project life cycle process
SoftwareProduct	**Size**
	Amount of documentation
	Programming language
	Complexity
	Type of application
	Work breakdown structure
Organization	Management quality
	Lead designer
	Individual developers
	Personnel turnover
	Communications
	Number of people
Suppliers	Software reuse
Customers	**Customer** interface complexity
	Requirements volatility

We will now look at effort dominators.

Development Schedule Constraints. Pietrasanta [Pietrasanta70] describes an allowable elapsed time constraint. He says that the effort-time trade-off function can be divided into four regions: minimum cost, inefficient, crash **Project**, and impossible. As scheduled time decreases, effort increases through the four regions. Costs begin to increase exponentially when a **Project** transitions from the inefficient region to the impossible region. The boundary between the crash **Project** region and the impossible region is a minimum possible schedule boundary. An infinite amount of effort can be expended, and a **Project** cannot be completed in less time than that minimum schedule boundary. We will examine **Project** development schedule predictor models in Chapter 8.

Project *Life Cycle Process.* A complex **Project** life cycle process requires an enormous amount of effort. For example, Simmons [Simmons92] points out that government **Project**s require extensive bureaucratic red tape in the form of standard deliverables and formal reviews at milestone points. He describes a Jet Propulsion Laboratory [Dorfman90] **Project** that had 10 phases, 38 separate documents as deliverables and as many as 13 major milestone reviews. Shere [Shere88] points out that government **Project** milestone reviews can last up to a week and can cost as much as $580,000. The multiple deliverables, milestone reviews, and **Project** infrastructures result in costly, inefficient large government software **Project**s. Most software can be developed by a simple **Project** life cycle process. When the wrong **Project** life cycle is chosen, a huge amount of unnecessary effort can be expended, and **Project** life cycle costs can dominate.

Size. Product size is the main cost driver in all effort models. We look at three types of size metrics: **Volume**, **Structure**, and **Rework**. **Volume** is the size cost driver that we find in effort prediction models. It can be expressed in many ways, including source lines of code, noncomment source statements, function points, object points, mental comparisons required to generate a program, and so on. We all agree that large products require greater effort than small products. When you select an effort model, you usually have to decide which cost drivers other than product **Volume** are relevant to your **Project**.

Amount of Documentation. Documentation can be both a help and a burden. Documentation of **Customer** requirements can be a major help to software developers [Scott74]. The effort to produce the 38 separate documents required by some government agencies can be a major burden [Simmons91]. Major variations exist in the amount of effort required to develop products with different documentation requirements.

Programming Language. Product **Volume** is a major cost driver. Software written in higher-level languages has fewer source statements (SS) and requires less effort. If we assume that the effort required to create a computer program is approximated by the number of noncomment SS (NCSS) written, then we can compute effort based on language level. Language level of a high-level language is the assembler language program **Volume** in NCSS required to implement a function divided by the high-level language **Volume** in NCSS to implement the same function. The list of language levels in Figure 7.1 is based on the work of Jones [Jones86,91]. Language level only applies to the amount of effort required to code and unit test a program. When you consider the other phases of the product life cycle, the effect of language level will be reduced.

Complexity. Product complexity is a major cost driver. The effort required to create a program for an ultrareliable computer embedded space probe is much greater than the effort to code and test a simple program to generate a report. Brooks [Brooks87] states that software entities are more complex for their size than perhaps any other human construct. He says that many development and management prob-

Language	Language Level	NCSS per Function Point
Assembler	1	320
Macro Assembler	1.5	213
C	2.5	128
COBOL	3	107
FORTRAN	3	107
JOVIAL	3	107
Pascal	3.5	91
RPG	4	80
PL/1	4	80
Ada	4.5	71
PROLOG	5	64
LISP	5	64
BASIC	5	64
Fourth-generation database	8	40
APL	10	32
C++	11	29
SMALLTALK	15	21
Query languages	24.6	13
Spread-sheet languages	53	6
Graphic Icons	80	4

Figure 7.1 Language Level Measured as (1) Ratio of Assembler Language **Volume**$_{NCSS}$ to High-level Language **Volume**$_{NCSS}$ and (2) NCSS per Function Point

lems derive from complexity and its nonlinear increase with size. Many of the effort models use some form of complexity as a cost driver.

Type of Application. Product application type is used as a cost driver by many effort models. There is a direct overlap between complexity and type of application. Effort models often use either complexity or type of application as cost drivers, but not both.

Work Breakdown Structure. For more than one member of a team to work in parallel on a software task, the task must be broken down into a structure that can be worked on in parallel. Brooks [Brooks75] points out that a programming task is hard to break into completely independent tasks because of the sequential nature of debugging. Simmons [Simmons91] shows that **Group** efficiency declines rapidly when even a few tasks are developed in sequence with other tasks.

Management Quality. Boehm [Boehm81] says that poor management can increase software costs more rapidly than any other factor. Boehm, like most other model developers, assumes that a **Project** is well managed. Poor management often leads to excessive consumption of effort and **Project** failure.

Lead Designer. Brooks [Brooks87] believes that the central question in how to improve the software art centers on people. He proclaims that great designers are as important to the success of a **Project** as quality managers. He says that study after study shows that the very best designers produce structures that are faster, smaller, simpler, cleaner, and produced with less effort. He says that the difference between a great designer and the average approaches an order of magnitude.

Individual Developers. Boehm [Boehm87] states that variations between people account for the biggest differences in software productivity. He says that studies of **Individual** programmers have shown productivity ranges of up to 26:1 [Sackman68]. Boehm says that you should do everything you can to get the best people working on your **Project**.

Personnel Turnover. Simmons [Simmons72] points out that personnel turnover is a factor that we must cope with when developing large systems. Boehm [Boehm81] believes that as long as you have an average amount of personnel turnover, there is no reason to treat it as a special cost driver. Only when you have turnover of key people or excessive turnover of other people does turnover become a dominator. Both of these cases are impossible to predict in advance.

Communications.   Scott and Simmons [Scott75] showed that there is an upper limit to the number of programmers that can effectively add to the total **Group** productivity, and the potential of highly productive people can be neutralized by assigning them to positions with high communications requirements. Communications are useful only if they are effective and related to the **Project**. Simmons [Simmons91] shows that productivity can be a dominator.

Number of People.   Conte, Dunsmore, and Shen [Conte86] say that estimates based on size alone cannot be expected to produce good predictions. They include number of people as a cost driver in the COPMO model that they recommend. When people are added to a late **Project**, they often make it later [Brooks75]. The additional people added to a late **Project** actually worsen the **Project** status instead of improving it. Small **Group**s of experienced and productive software developers can create large systems. Pyburn Systems [Carlyle89] looks for the best analytical thinkers, who love to create order from chaos, love to work long hours, and are driven to succeed. They work in small teams of never more than five members to produce large successful systems. Simmons [Simmons91] shows that people can be added to **Project**s without productivity gain. If fact, a large number of personnel working on a software **Project** can have a dominate negative effect on the **Project**.

Software Reuse.   Jones [Jones78] states that for programs over 500K SLOC a number of theorists claim that the only viable technology for economical large-system development is that of reusable code. Biggerstaff and Perlis [Biggerstaff89] believe that very large scale reuse is necessary to fully realize the benefit of reuse to reduce the effort required to produce a software system. Brooks [Brooks87] observes that the most radical possible solution for constructing software is not to construct it at all. In other words, total reuse eliminates the need to expend any effort on development. When reuse is applied, it can dominate the development costs.

Customer Interface Complexity.   Walston and Felix [Walston77] worked for IBM Federal Systems Division when they collected data on 60 completed software development **Project**s. For the **Project**s in their database, **Volume** ranged from 4,000 to 467,000 SLOC and effort from 12 to 11,758 person-months. They selected a set of 68 variables from their database and analyzed them to determine which were significantly related to productivity. Twenty-nine of the variables showed a significantly high correlation to productivity. In the current context, we would call the 29 significant variables cost drivers.

The most significant cost driver of their study was **Customer** interface complexity. Those that said the **Customer** interface complexity was less than normal had a mean productivity of 500 SLOC per person-month, normal had a mean productivity of 295 SLOC per person-month, and less than normal had a mean productivity of 124 SLOC per person-month. The ratio of the largest to the smallest mean productivity is 4.03. The absolute productivity ratios should classify **Customer** interface complexity as a dominator.

Requirements Volatility.   Boehm feels that requirements volatility is clearly a significant factor affecting the cost of software. In fact, in his book [Boehm81] he cited an example of a highly ambitious radar software application where software costs escalated by a factor of 4 because of changes in requirements. When estimating effort, he feels that requirements volatility is a highly subjective, imprecisely defined parameter whose value is not known until the completion of a **Project**. We agree with Boehm that requirements volatility is a significant cost driver and can, for highly volatile requirements, dominate cost.

We will find that the above dominators can help us to determine **Area**s where we can improve productivity. Many of them are used as cost drivers in effort prediction models. Some of them cannot be estimated during the early stages of a **Project** and thus are not used in prediction models. For example, management quality, personnel turnover, and requirements volatility are usually not known until a **Project** is complete. Dominators that cause expenses to rise rapidly and for **Project**s to terminate before completion are usually not considered as cost drivers for effort predictor models. The reason is that effort models are usually derived from **Project**s that are successfully completed. Knowledge that can be gained from failed **Project**s is usually lost because the data are incomplete and often not considered useful in deriving effort prediction models.

EFFORT PREDICTION MODELS

The cost of personnel is the main cost in a software development **Project**. For a specific **Project**, the average **Salary** per person-month is usually known. Once the total effort is known in person-months, then the total **Salary** expense can be computed. People cost is usually the main expense for a software development **Project**. The cost of workstations, travel, supplies, benefits, administration, and so on, is a function of the number of people that work on a **Project** and can be expressed as *Overhead*. The total cost of a **Project** is

$$Cost_{total} = Cost_{to\_date} + Effort_i \times Salary \times Overhead \qquad (7.1)$$

where $Cost_{to\_date}$ is total computed cost from the start of a **Project** to the current date; $Effort_i$ is effort computed using one of the i effort predictor equations; *Salary* is the average monthly **Salary** for **Project** personnel; and *Overhead* is the **Project** overhead adjustment multiplier, where $1 \leq Overhead \leq 3.0$.

The effort required to produce a **SoftwareProduct** is a function of the product **Volume**. We can measure product **Volume** using source lines of code, noncomment source statements, operators and operands, modules, **Chunk**s, function points, and so on. Software system **Volume** is a major cost driver used in effort equations. Many other cost drivers can have a major effect on effort. We will now examine specific effort models and explore the role of the cost drivers.

Conte, Dunsmore, and Shen classified effort models into four categories [Conte86]: historical/experimental, statistical, theoretical, and composite.

HISTORICAL/EXPERIMENTAL MODELS

One of the crudest forms of estimation is the experimental model. An expert who is skilled in cost estimation expresses his experience and ideas in model form. The model is then used to predict effort. Historical information is gathered and compared with the model's prediction. Then the model is modified to conform to the collected data. We will describe three historical/experimental models in this section:

1. TRW Wolverton model
2. Brooks model
3. IBM Albrecht function point model

TRW Wolverton model

The historical/experimental-based effort model used by Wolverton [Wolverton74] at TRW, Inc., is

$$Effort_1[Volume_{SLOC}(k), i(k), j(k)] = Volume_{SLOC}(k) \times m_{i(k), j(k)} \times K_{Effort_1} \quad (7.2)$$

where $Effort_1(k)$ is the effort in person-months of the kth module of a **SoftwareProduct**; $Volume_{SLOC}(k)$ is the kth program module **Volume** in SLOC (source lines of code); $m_{i(k), j(k)}$ is an adjustment multiplier for module k selected by one cost driver from the ith row and by a second cost driver from the jth column of a software effort matrix; and K_{Effort_1} is the effort in person-months to produce a minimum effort line of code. The total effort required to produce a system of k modules is

$$Effort_{1\_Total} = \sum_{m=1}^{k} Effort_1(m) \quad (7.3)$$

This is a common model used by Wolverton and many other experienced managers.

The TRW Wolverton model [Wolverton74] is an early historically based model. The model has been updated to use a ratio of the cost for each module type

Table 7.1   TRW Wolverton Effort Adjustment Multiplier $m_{i(k), j(k)}$ Matrix

i	Type	j	Complexity: Old–Easy 1	Old–Medium 2	Old–Hard 3	New–Easy 4	New–Medium 5	New–Hard 6
1	Control		1.40	1.80	2.00	2.20	2.67	3.27
2	I/O		1.13	1.60	1.80	1.87	2.33	2.87
3	Pre/Postprocessor		1.07	1.53	1.73	1.87	2.27	2.80
4	Algorithm		1.00	1.33	1.47	1.67	2.00	2.33
5	Data management		1.60	2.07	2.33	2.47	3.07	3.80
6	Time critical		5.00	5.00	5.00	5.00	5.00	5.00

divided by the minimum cost module type. Wolverton decided that when determining effort at TRW there were three main cost drivers: (1) **Volume** in source lines of code, (2) type of program module, and (3) complexity. From experience, you may determine that other cost drivers are more effective in your software development environment. Table 7.1 contains a modified example of their effort adjustment multiplier matrix where a software module is classified by type and complexity. The six program types used at TRW were (1) control, (2) input/output, (3) pre/postprocessor, (4) algorithm, (5) data management, and (6) time critical. The complexity scale proposed by Wolverton was old–easy, old–medium, old–hard, new–easy, new–medium, and new–hard. To use the TRW Wolverton model, we first compute an effort for each module k in a **SoftwareProduct** using equation 7.2. Then we compute the total system effort using equation 7.3.

Brooks Model

Brooks served as **Project** manager for the IBM System/360 and for OS/360, its operating system. He observed that industrial teams spend more average effort per **Individual** in creating a program than an **Individual** programmer working alone in a nonindustrial environment [Brooks75]. He attributed the difference to what is produced. An **Individual** working alone produces a *program*. An industrial team that produces software for sale produces a *programming system product*. The difference between what is produced is shown in Table 7.2.

Table 7.2 Brooks Effort Adjustment Multiplier $m_{i(k), j(k)}$ Matrix

i	Type	j	Complexity: Single-Use Program 1	Product 2
1	Single program		1	3
2	System of programs		3	9

The effort to produce a *programming product* (see $i = 1, j = 2$ in Table 7.2) is at least three times as much as the effort to produce a program. A programming product is a program that can be run, tested, repaired, and extended by anyone. It runs in many operating environments, for many data sets, and on many different hardware configurations. It must accept a wide range and variety of inputs. The product must be extensively tested before it is released to a **Customer,** and **Defect**s must be tracked after release to continually improve the product.

The effort to produce a *programming system* (see $i = 2, j = 1$ in Table 7.2) is also at least three times as much as the effort to produce a program. A programming system is a collection of interacting programs, coordinated in function and disciplined in format, so that the assemblage constitutes an entire facility for large tasks. Its input and output must conform in syntax and semantics with precisely defined interfaces. Testing of a system must be extensive, and the number of necessary test cases grows combinatorially. Locating subtle bugs can be both time consuming and difficult.

The effort to produce a *programming system product* (see $i = 2, j = 2$ in Table 7.2) is at least nine times as much as the effort to produce a program. It has attributes of both the programming product and the programming system. A programming system product is a truly useful object and the intended result of most industrial software development **Project**s.

Notice that the Wolverton effort adjustment multiplier has a range of 5, while the Brooks adjustment multiplier has a range of 9. The Wolverton adjustment multiplier matrix was developed at TRW by software developers that use TRW's development standards to develop software for the defense industry. The Brook's matrix compared the work of an **Individual** programmer in a nonindustrial setting to that of an industrial team producing a **SoftwareProduct**. You will find both matrices useful under the appropriate circumstances. From your own experience and past historical data of you company, you can develop your own effort adjustment multiplier matrix.

IBM Albrecht Function Point Model

Effort in person-months can be determined by the Albrecht function point model [Albrecht79]:

$$Effort_2[Volume_{FPs}, m(X), m_{Language}] = Volume_{FPs} \times K_{Effort} \times m(X) \times m_{Language} \qquad (7.4)$$

where $Volume_{FPs}$ is **Volume** in function points, K_{Effort} is a constant reflecting the person-months required to produce a function point, $m(X)$ is an effort adjustment multiplier, and $m_{Language}$ is a language adjustment multiplier.

The cost drivers that make $m(X)$ up are 1.05 for extra-complicated inputs, outputs, or files; 1.05 for complex internal processing; and so on. Albrecht allows $m(X)$ to vary ±25% or $0.75 \leq m(X) \leq 1.25$.

The languages for the 22 **Project**s analyzed by Albrecht were COBOL, PL/1, and DMS/VS. If we let $m_{COBOL} = 1$, then his results show that the other language adjustment multipliers would be $m_{PL/1} = 0.80$ and $m_{DMS/VS} = 0.77$. If you are interested in using function points to estimate effort, Jones has written two excellent books on the relationships between function points and languages and between cost drivers and productivity [Jones86, 91].

STATISTICALLY BASED MODELS

Regression analysis is often used to determine the relationship between effort and cost drivers. A large number of models, both linear and nonlinear, have been proposed for effort estimation. We will give examples of some of these models beginning with a linear model.

Linear Statistical Models

A general linear model will have the form

$$Effort_3(x_0, \ldots, x_n) = \sum_{i=0}^{n} c_i x_i \qquad (7.5)$$

where the x_i are cost drivers believed to affect effort. We will describe three linear statistical models in this section that use equation 7.5:

1. Nelson 1966 model
2. Nelson 1970 model
3. Farr and Zagorski model

Nelson 1966 Model

The values of the coefficients and cost driver definitions for a 1966 cost driver model [Nelson66] developed by Nelson at System Development Corporation (SDC) are listed in Table 7.3. In developing the model, 104 attributes were identified initially. Using a database of 169 **Project**s, he tried different combinations of attributes, eventually resulting in a regression model based on 14 of the most significant cost drivers. The only cost driver related to **Volume** is number of subroutines.

Nelson stated that his model serves to identify cost drivers that have statistically significant impact on expenditures and hence can direct management attention to those that can be controlled. He also pointed out that a disadvantage arises when the results of cost research are published in the form of equations, as in equation 7.5 and

Table 7.3   Coefficients and Cost Drivers in the Nelson 1966 SDC Study

c_i	Value		Cost Driver	Value
c_0	−33.63	x_0	Y axis intercept	1
c_1	9.15	x_1	Lack of requirements	0–2
c_2	10.73	x_2	Stability of design	0–3
c_3	0.51	x_3	Percent math instructions	Actual percent
c_4	0.46	x_4	Percent I/O instructions	Actual percent
c_5	0.40	x_5	Number of subprograms	Actual number
c_6	7.28	x_6	Programming language	0–1
c_7	−21.45	x_7	Business application	0–1
c_8	13.5	x_8	Stand-alone program	0–1
c_9	12.35	x_9	First program on computer	0–1
c_{10}	58.82	x_{10}	Concurrent hardware development	0–1
c_{11}	30.61	x_{11}	Random-access device used	0–1
c_{12}	29.55	x_{12}	Different host, target hardware	0–1
c_{13}	0.54	x_{13}	Number of personnel trips	Actual number
c_{14}	−25.20	x_{14}	Developed by military **Organization**	0–1

the corresponding Tables 7.3, 7.4, and 7.5. Such equations, with their coefficients and cost drivers, are frequently interpreted by the user as demonstrating a specific causative relationship. This is not the case. Equations developed by multiple regression techniques do reveal important cost drivers and may represent the relationships that provide the most statistically significant manner of describing the character of the sample. However, they do not necessarily represent natural laws, as do many of the equations used by the engineer or physicist. Also, they must be used in their entirety or not at all. If the value for any one of the cost drivers in Tables 7.3, 7.4, or 7.5 is not available, then the equation could not be used as it stands, since repeating the multiple regression analysis without the missing cost driver would result in a reassignment of weights to all the remaining cost drivers and the Y axis intercept.

Nelson 1970 Model

In 1970, Nelson [Nelson70] published a **Version** of his model that he applied to the 106 largest software **Project**s of the 169 **Project**s that he had in his database. The coefficients and cost drivers for his 1970 model are shown in Table 7.4. Notice that the only cost driver related to **Volume** is pages of external documentation for the **Customer**.

Table 7.4 Coefficients and Cost Drivers in the Nelson 1970 SDC Study

c_i	Value		Cost Driver	Value
c_0	0.049	x_0	Y axis intercept of the equation	1
c_1	15.2	x_1	Complexity of program system interface	0–2
c_2	−0.236	x_2	Percent clerical instructions	Actual percent
c_3	0.528	x_3	Percent information storage and retrieval functions	Actual percent
c_4	4.50	x_4	Frequency of operation	0–5
c_5	0.091	x_5	External documentation	Number of pages
c_6	−17.5	x_6	Business application	0–1
c_7	25.1	x_7	First program on computer	0–1
c_8	22.0	x_8	Special display equipment	0–1
c_9	26.0	x_9	Random-access device used	0–1
c_{10}	−0.251	x_{10}	Percent programmers participating in design	Actual percent
c_{11}	−14.9	x_{11}	Personnel continuity	Totals Instantaneous
c_{12}	10.4	x_{12}	Number of locations for program data point development	Actual number

Farr and Zagorski Model

Farr and Zagorski [Farr65] derived coefficients and cost drivers depending on a priori complexity classifications. One set of their coefficients and cost drivers is given in Table 7.5. The large negative c_0 will almost surely result in negative effort estimates for small- or medium-**Volume Project**s. Also, the c_4 coefficient will certainly lead to effort underestimates when used with programmers with a lot (10 years or more) of

Table 7.5 Coefficients and Cost Drivers in the Farr–Zagorski Study

c_i	Value		Cost Driver	Value
c_0	−188	x_0	Y axis intercept of the equation	1
c_1	2.68	x_1	Number of instructions	Number in thousands
c_2	2.3	x_2	Number of miles traveled	Number in thousands
c_3	33	x_3	Number of document types delivered	Actual number
c_4	−17	x_4	System programmer experience	Number in years
c_5	10	x_5	Number of display consoles	Actual number
c_6	1	x_6	Percentage of new instructions	Decimal equivalent

experience. These are natural consequences of regression and examples of why **Individual** coefficients should not be interpreted independently of the other terms in equation 7.5.

Conte, Dunsmore, and Shen [Conte86] stated that, in general, linear models have not proved to be satisfactory for effort estimation. One possible explanation for this is that effort is a highly nonlinear function of a large number of variables, and this nonlinearity cannot be adequately captured in a linear model. They also emphasized that the application of a regression model to **Project**s outside of the range of data from which it was derived is ill advised.

Nonlinear Statistical Models

Conte, Dunsmore, and Shen [Conte86] observed that most of the nonlinear models that have been studied can be expressed in the form

$$Effort_4[Volume_d^c, a, b, m(X)] = (a + b \times Volume_d^c) \times m(X) \qquad (7.6)$$

where a, b, and c are constants usually derived from regression analysis; **Volume** is the estimated **Volume** of the **Project** measured in unites of d; d is the units of **Volume,** such as KSLOC (thousands of source lines of code) or KNCSS (thousands of noncomment source statements); and $m(X)$ is an adjustment multiplier that depends on one or more cost drivers denoted by the vector X. Since $m(X)$ can be a complicated nonlinear function of several variables, equation 7.6 is too complex to derive using standard regression analysis techniques. To simplify the derivation, you can use least-squares techniques to derive a base-line or nominal estimator of the form

$$Effort_5[Volume_d^c, a, b, m(X) = 1] = a + b \times Volume_d^c \qquad (7.7)$$

You can then adjust this nominal effort $Effort_5$ with the adjustment factor $m(X)$. Typical coefficients for the $Effort_5$ nominal effort model are listed in Table 7.6.

The exponent c in Table 7.6 signifies the rate at which productivity increases or decreases with **SoftwareProduct Volume**. When $c < 1$, productivity increases with **Volume**. Notice that this happens for the Walston and Felix models as well as the Nelson model. Both of these models were developed based on government **Project**s that require numerous deliverables, milestone reviews, and control procedures. These may be necessary for large **Project**s, but are overkill for smaller **Project**s.

Most model builders find a diseconomy of scale with **SoftwareProduct Volume**. When $c > 1$, productivity decreases with **Volume**. Notice that in Table 7.6 most of the models confirm that productivity decreases with **Volume**. The range of c's for models that are based on empirical data from actual **Project**s is $1 \leq c \leq 1.3$. The models where $c > 1.3$ were based more on theory than on empirical data validation. Thus, when estimating effort for actual **Project**s, you should use a c of slightly

Table 7.6   Nominal Effort Model Equation Coefficients

a	b	c	d		Reference
0	5.2	0.91	KSLOC	[Walston77]	
0	4.9	0.98	KNCSS	[Nelson78]	
5.5	0.73	1.16	KNCSS	[Bailey81][a]	
0	3.0	1.01	KNCSS	[Boehm95]	COCOMO 2.0, min scale factors
0	2.4	1.05	KNCSS	[Boehm81]	Basic: organic mode
0	5.3	1.06	KNCSS	[Herd77]	
0	3.0	1.12	KNCSS	[Boehm81]	Basic: semidetached mode
0	2.43	1.18	KNCSS	[Frederic74]	
0	3.6	1.20	KNCSS	[Boehm81]	Basic: embedded mode
0	3.0	1.26	KNCSS	[Boehm95]	COCOMO 2.0, max scale factors
0	0.99	1.275	KNCSS	[Phister79]	
0	1.0	1.40	KNCSS	[Jones77]	
0	1.12	1.43	KSLOC	[Walston77a]	
0	5.288	1.047	KNCSS	[Herd77]	
0	0.70	1.50	KNCSS	[Halstead77]	

[a]For the Bailey and Basili model, **Volume**$_{KNCSS}$ is defined as new code plus 20% of all old code.

greater than 1 for small, simple **Project**s and a *c* that is closer to the 1.3 for larger, more complex **Project**s. You should calibrate the *a*, *b*, *c*, and *d* parameters to your development environment. When you improve your software quality and productivity through continual process improvement, you will notice that the parameters must be changed to reflect the improvement.

We will treat models that have a complex adjustment multiplier *m(X)* as composite models, instead of nonlinear statistical models, because the adjustment multiplier in usually determined using a combination of analytic methods, statistical data fitting, and expert judgment.

THEORETICALLY BASED MODELS

A number of models have been developed on theories of how humans communicate and how the human mind communicates during the programming process and on the mathematical laws that the programming process is thought to follow. Conte, Dunsmore, and Shen [Conte86] call these *theoretically based models*. We will describe four such effort models in this section:

1. Brooks work partition model
2. Simmons communications model
3. Halstead software science model
4. Putnam resource allocation model

Brooks Work Partition Model

In his book *The Mythical Man-Month* [Brooks75], Brooks says that a fallacious thought mode is practiced when the person-month is used as the basic unit for estimating effort and schedules. He says that the person-month as a unit for measuring the effort required on a job is a dangerous and deceptive myth. The implication of the myth is that software development team members and months are interchangeable.

People and months are interchangeable only when a work breakdown structure results in a perfect partitioning of a task into parts that can be worked on in parallel without communication required among team members. We can express Brooks idea by examining the ratio of the time required for a team of n members to complete a programming task to the time required for a single programmer to complete a task as

$$Ratio_{T(n)/T(1)}(n, f_s) = \frac{T(n)}{T(1)} = \frac{1 - f_s}{n} + f_s \qquad (7.8)$$

where $Ratio_{T(n)/T(1)}$ is the ratio of the task completion time, $T(n)$, of an n-member team to the task completion time, $T(1)$, of a single-member team; f_S is the ratio of time spent on a sequential task to total time; and n = is the number of members in a team.

For a perfectly partitionable task, $f_S = 0$, the task could be partitioned among the members of a team with no need to communicate. When you add people to a team, the total time for the **Project** becomes smaller. This works for manual labor like digging a ditch, but this does not work for software development. For $f_S = 0$, the time to complete the task is

$$Ratio_{T(n)/T(1)} = \frac{1 - 0}{n} + 0 = \frac{1}{n} \qquad (7.9)$$

A plot $Ratio_{T(n)/T(1)}$ is given in Figure 7.2. The effort to complete the task is

$$Effort_6(n, f_s) = n \times T(n) = n \times Ratio_{T(n)/T(1)}(n, f_s) \times T(1) = n \times \left(\frac{1 - f_s}{n} + f_s \right) \times T(1)$$

$$(7.10)$$

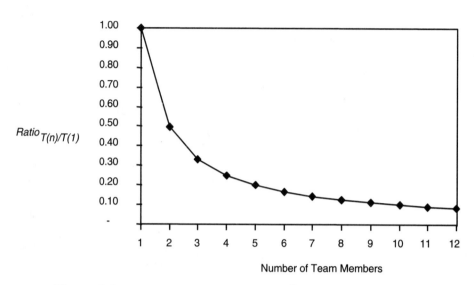

Figure 7.2   *Ratio*$_{T(n)/T(1)}$ versus Number of Team Members for a Perfectly Partitionable Task (that is, $f_S = 0$)

For the case where $f_S = 0$, effort is

$$Effort_6 = n \times \left(\frac{1}{n}\right) \times T(1) \qquad (7.11)$$
$$= T(1)$$

What this means is that for a perfectly partionable task with no need to communicate, the effort in person-months remains constant, and as the number of team members increases, the total time to complete a task becomes smaller. As the number of team members becomes very large, the completion time would approach zero.

This does not happen for programming tasks. When a task cannot be partitioned because of sequential constraints, the application of more effort has no effect on schedule. If a task cannot be partitioned, then $f_S = 1$, and as shown in Figure 7.3.

$$Ratio_{T(n)/T(1)} = \frac{1-1}{n} + 1 = 1 \qquad (7.12)$$

The amount of effort becomes

$$Effort_6 = n \times Ratio_{T(n)/T(1)} T(1) \qquad (7.13)$$
$$= n \times (1) \times T(1)$$
$$= n \times T(1)$$

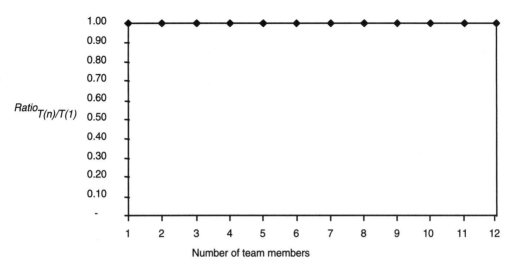

Figure 7.3 *Ratio*$_{T(n)/T(1)}$ versus Number of Team Members for an Unpartitionable Task (that is, $f_S = 1$)

Brooks points out that bearing a child takes nine months, no matter how many women are assigned to the task. For this case, the effort is anything but constant. As n increases, the time to complete the task remains constant, even though the effort increases.

Software development falls somewhere between these two extremes. Many software development tasks are sequential in nature. Software debugging is a task that is sequential in nature. A developer is often delayed while a team member debugs and eliminates a software fault. Often, tests are performed sequentially, causing additional delays. Delays occur while waiting for computers, new **Version**s of the system under development, and conference rooms. For a well-run **Project**, the resulting sequential characteristic of a software development **Project** results in a typical $f_S = 0.3$, as shown in Figure 7.4, for

$$Ratio_{T(n)/T(1)} = \frac{1-0.3}{n} + 0.3 = \frac{0.7}{n} + 0.3 \tag{7.14}$$

The effort to complete the task is

$$Effort_6 = n \times \left(\frac{0.7}{n} + 0.3\right) \times T(1) \tag{7.15}$$
$$= (0.7 + 0.3 \times n) \times T(1)$$

Notice that, as n becomes very large, effort becomes very large. But as n grows, $T(n)$ approaches the constant $0.3 \times T(1)$.

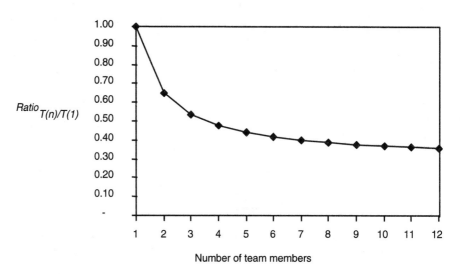

Figure 7.4   *Ratio*$_{T(n)/T(1)}$ versus Number of Team Members for a Partitionable Task with $f_S = 0.3$ and One Requiring No Communication

Brooks [Brooks75] observed essentially the same phenomenon. He observed that, when milestones are missed and new team members are added to help accomplish tasks, existing members are involved in training and repartitioning tasks. Both of these activities have a negative effect on system testing. Brooks states that without a doubt the regenerative disaster will yield a poorer product, later, than would rescheduling with the original team members, unaugmented. He then states his thoughts as Brooks's law.

OBSERVATIONS

1. Even with an infinite amount of effort, the minimum time to complete a task cannot be reduced to less than f_S multiplied by the amount of time required for a single software developer to complete the task.

2. Implicitly, f_S for a product is set during requirements and the design phases. Once these two phases are complete and programming tasks have been assigned, f_S increases when additional members are added to teams late in the development life cycle. When members are added to a team and f_S increases, then the average productivity per team member decreases.

> **Brooks's Law:** *Adding people to a late software* **Project** *makes it later.*

Simmons Communications Model

In software development, effective communications is absolutely necessary. Unnecessary communications can lead to avoidable loss in productivity. Organizational structures in the United States before the 1980s were characterized by multilevel infrastructures of administration. This concept was noted by the pioneering nineteenth-century organizational researcher Graicunias [Jones78,86], whose work on military **Organization** introduced squads and platoons into the U.S. Army. He noticed that, as the number of workers who had to communicate increased arithmetically, the number of communication channels increased geometrically. According to Graicunias, the upper limit of effective staff size for cooperative **Project**s is about eight. Jones mentioned that this is the origin of the industrial and commercial dogma that departments sizes should be limited to about eight workers per manager for professional tasks [Jones78,86]. Simmons combined the work partition model to develop the communications model [Simmons91].

$$T(n) = \frac{1 + f_s \times (n-1) + n \times (n-1) \times f_c}{n} \times T(1) \tag{7.16}$$

Effort can be computed by the following equation:

$$Effort_7(n, f_s, f_c) = [1 + f_s \times (n-1) + n \times (n-1) \times f_c] \times T(1) \tag{7.17}$$

For a perfectly partitioned task, where $f_s = 0$, the ratio of $T(n)$ to $T(1)$ is

$$Ratio_{T(n)/T(1)} = \frac{1 + n \times (n-1) \times f_c}{n} \tag{7.18}$$

where communications factor f_C is the ratio defined by the average time each team member spends communicating to each of the other team members divided by total time. The effect of communications on time to complete a perfectly partitioned task with a team of n members is shown in Figure 7.5. For $f_C = 0$, the completion time continues to decrease when team members are added to a team. Notice that for $f_C \geq$ 1% the improvement in completion time begins to level off. When f_C becomes 2% and larger, the completion time can actually increase when team members are added to a team of five or more members.

The effort for a perfectly partitioned task where each member communicates with every other member becomes

$$Effort_7 = [1 + n \times (n-1) \times f_c] \times T(1) \tag{7.19}$$

Effort increases geometrically with n as f_C increases above 1%.

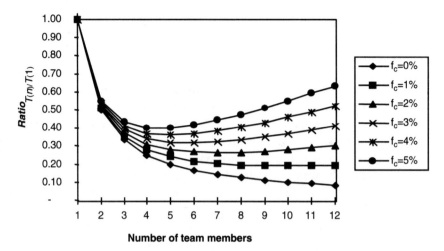

Figure 7.5 $Ratio_{T(n)/T(1)}$ versus Number of Team Members for a Perfectly Partitionable Task $(f_s = 0)$ for $f_C = 0$ through $f_C = 5\%$

Effective communication among team members is absolutely necessary for a successful **Project**. Team members must communicate in relation to **Customer** requirements, design specifications, test status and procedures, and so on. But excessive communication can lead to avoidable costs. When a software developer is communicating, no product is actually being produced.

OBSERVATIONS

1. Software development team members must communicate among themselves.

2. Communication can lead to lost productivity.

3. A software development team size should be from five to eight members unless extraordinary precautions are made to create an environment for effective communication.

4. Everything possible should be done to assure effective communications. Some suggestions are to:
   - Transform **Customer** requirements into a form easily understood by developers and testers.
   - Create a design where the work breakdown structure reduces the need to communicate (i. e. $f_S = 0$). The design should be clear and easily understood by everyone.
   - Use electronic mail to reduce interruptions and communication time.
   - Use voice mail to leave messages and reduce telephone tag.
   - Organize meetings with a moderator and a note taker to assure that the goals of a meeting are accomplished and that the results are recorded.
   - Use electronic aids to increase the effectiveness of meetings.

Software developers have many duties that occupy their typical workday. Scott and Simmons point out that a highly productive developer spends 51% to 79% of a day productively working on software development [Scott75]. If we assume for a typical team member that 65% of the workday is actually spent in productive activities, then 5 out of 8 hours of the workday would be spent on productive activities.

When a team member communicates directly with you, he interrupts you. When the number of team members increases, the number of interruptions increases. We can represent the time consumed by interruptions as an increased f_C. Esterling [Esterling80] determined that the average duration of a work interruption was 5 minutes for a typical programmer. The average time to regain a train of thought after an interruption was 2 minutes. Thus, an average interruption consumes about 7 minutes. When we assume 5 productive hours per day, a single interruption consumes about 2.3% of the productive time. Ten interruptions would assume about 23% of the productive time, and 20 interruptions would consume about 46%. While we know that 20 interruptions per day is excessive, we also know that interruptions result in lost time and increased costs.

Halstead Software Science Model

Halstead defines effort $Effort_8$ as the total number of elementary mental discriminations required to generate a program, where

$$Effort_8(V,L) = \frac{V}{L} = \frac{V^2}{V^*} \qquad (7.20)$$

Halstead Observation [Halstead77]. The mental effort required to implement any algorithm with a given potential **Volume** should vary with the square of its **Volume** in any language, rather than linearly. Since the square of the sum is greater than the sum of the squares, properly designed modularization can definitely reduce programming effort for partitionable programs.

Putnam Resource Allocation Model

This model assumes that effort during program development follows a Rayleigh-type curve [Putnam78]. The number of **Project** members per unit of time modeled by the Rayleigh curve equation is

$$\frac{dy(t)}{dt} = 2 \times K \times a \times t \times e^{-at^2} \qquad (7.21)$$

where $dy(t)/dt$ is the personnel utilization rate in persons per months; K is the total life cycle effort from the start of a **Project** through maintenance; a is a parameter that affects the shape of the curve; and t is elapsed time.

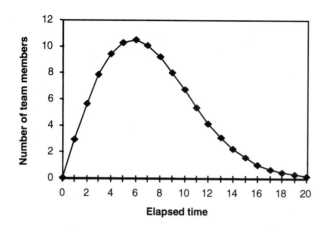

Figure 7.6   Rayleigh Curve Showing Number of Team Members versus Elapsed Time

A plot of the above Rayleigh curve is shown in Figure 7.6. Notice that the peak number of people assigned to the **Project** is 10. The **Area** under the curve in Figure 7.6 is total effort for the **Project**. The **Area** under the curve is equal to

$$y(t) = \int_0^t \frac{dy(t)}{dt} = K \times (1 - e^{-at^2}) \tag{7.22}$$

The cumulative effort $y(t)$ as a function of elapsed time t is plotted in Figure 7.7. For $y(\infty)$, the total life cycle effort is equal to K. A **Project** life cycle is normally divided into phases, each of which can be modeled using a Rayleigh curve. The overall life cycle K results from a composite sum of the **Individual** curves.

The point in Figure 7.6 where $dy(t)/dt$ is a maximum is at

$$a = \frac{1}{2 \times T_{Dev}^2} \tag{7.23}$$

where T_{Dev} is the amount of time spent on development. The effort at the end of development is

$$Effort_9(K) = y(T_{Dev}) = K \times \left(1 - e^{-1/2}\right) = 0.3935 \times K \cong 0.4 \times K \tag{7.24}$$

The K and T_{Dev} for a **Project** are selected from charts based on data gathered from past U.S. Army development **Project**s. The equation derived from empirical data states that

$$Size_{NCSS} = C \times K^{1/3} \times T_{Dev}^{4/3} \tag{7.25}$$

where C is a constant called a technology factor by Putnam. It reflects the effect of numerous cost drivers, such as hardware constraints, program complexity, personnel experience levels, and the programming environment. He has proposed using a discrete spectrum of 20 values of C ranging from 610 to 57,314. Putnam has incorpo-

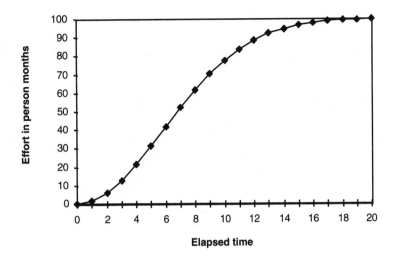

Figure 7.7 Effort in Person-months versus Elapsed Time

rated his methodology into a **SoftwareProduct** called SLIM (Software Life Cycle Methodology). The Putnam model was validated using a U.S. Army **Project** database. As would be expected, Conte, Dunsmore, and Shen [Conte86] found that the model works well on very large systems, but overestimates effort on medium- or small-**Volume** systems. The model relies heavily on **Volume** and development schedule attributes while downplaying all other cost drivers. The constant C is used to reflect all other attributes, including complexity, use of modern programming practices, personnel attributes, and others.

COMPOSITE MODELS

Composite models incorporate a combination of analytic equations, statistical data fitting and expert judgment. We will examine the following three composite models:

1. Boehm COCOMO and COCOMO 2.0 models
2. Jensen model
3. COPMO model

Boehm COCOMO and COCOMO 2.0 Models

The best known of all composite models is COCOMO (COnstructive COst MOdel) [Boehm81]. It is the most complete and thoroughly documented of all models for effort estimation. We will look at two versions: COCOMO and CO-

COMO 2.0. The initial version was created by Boehm while he was at TRW during the early 1980s. COCOMO 2.0 is currently under development by Boehm and his colleagues at the University of Southern California [Boehm95]. We will now examine both COCOMO and COCOMO 2.0.

COCOMO.   COCOMO has three modes of software development process: organic, semidetached, and embedded. In the organic mode, relatively small software teams develop software in a highly familiar, in-house environment. Most people connected with the **Project** have extensive experience in working with related systems within the **Organization** and have a thorough understanding of how the system under development will contribute to the **Organization**'s objectives.

The semidetached mode represents an intermediate stage between the organic and embedded modes. Intermediate here means one of two things: an intermediate level of the **Project** characteristics or a mixture of the organic and embedded mode characteristics.

The embedded mode software **Project** operates within tight constraints. The product must operate within (is embedded in) a strongly coupled complex of hardware, software, regulations, and operational procedures, such as an electronic funds transfer system or an air traffic control system. In general, the costs of changing the other parts of this complex are so high that their characteristics are considered essentially unchangeable, and the software is expected both to conform to their specifications and to take up the slack for any unforeseen difficulties encountered or changes required within the other parts of the complex.

The effort required to produce a **SoftwareProduct** can be determined using a simple overall basic-level model, a more detailed intermediate-level model, or a detailed-level model. All the models use the following form of equation 7.6:

$$Effort_{10}[Volume_{KNCSS}, b, c, m(X)] = b \times Volume_{KNCSS}^{c} \times m(X) \qquad (7.26)$$

where $a = 0$; the values of b and c are as listed in Table 7.7; d is *KNCSS*; and the range of values of $x_1 \ldots x_{15}$ for X in the adjustment multiplier $m(X)$ are given in Table 7.8.

The basic-level effort model has two cost drivers: process mode and KNCSS (that is, thousands of NCSS). The adjustment multiplier $m(X) = 1$. Boehm found that with respect to the COCOMO database the basic model estimates were within a factor of 1.3 of the actuals only 29% of the time, and within a factor of 2 of the actuals only 60% of the time. Thus, you should only use the basic-level model during early product definition to make gross overall effort estimates.

The intermediate-level effort model allows a more accurate estimate once more information about a **Project** is known. The intermediate model has a total of 17 cost drivers: process mode, **Volume**$_{KNCSS}$, and 15 additional cost drivers as part of the adjustment multiplier. The adjustment multiplier is

Table 7.7 COCOMO Model Parameters

Level:	Basic		Intermediate		Detailed	
Mode	*b*	*c*	*b*	*c*	*b*	*c*
Organic	2.4	1.05	3.2	1.05	3.2	1.05
Semidetached	3.0	1.12	3.0	1.12	3.0	1.12
Embedded	3.6	1.20	2.8	1.20	2.8	1.20

$$m_1(X) = \prod_{i=1}^{n} x_i \tag{7.27}$$

where $X = x_i, \ldots, x_n$; x_i is a measure of the ith cost drivers; and $n = 15$ for the intermediate level COCOMO. Boehm tries to select COCOMO adjustment multiplier cost drivers that are independent of each other. COCOMO cost driver ranges are listed in Table 7.8. Notice that the range of the product cost drivers is 5.43, computer cost drivers is 5.09, personnel cost drivers is 10.56, and the **Project** cost drivers is 2.77. The overall adjustment multiplier range is over 800, or almost three orders of magnitude.

In actual practice, you will find that a **Project** that is successfully completed does not normally cost over 10 times as much as another **Project** that produces a similar **SoftwareProduct**. Once the costs become excessive, a **Project** fails and is terminated by management.

You can apply the intermediate model to make overall product-level estimates or component-level estimates. It can be used to make accurate predictions after the product is defined and personnel are being assigned to product development. Boehm found that the intermediate model is within 20% of the **Project** actuals 68% of the time.

The detailed level model allows a finer grain estimate than the intermediate-level model. Ideally, when you apply more detail to prepare a cost estimate, your resulting estimate should be more accurate. The detailed model applies a three-level hierarchical decomposition of a **SoftwareProduct**. Three levels are module, **Subsystem**, and system.

The module is described by the NCSS in a module and by those cost drivers that tend to vary at the module level. The module-level cost drivers are

1. product complexity,
2. programmer capability,
3. virtual machine experience, and
4. language experience.

Table 7.8 COCOMO Cost Driver Ranges

Attributes	Cost Driver	Range
Product	Required reliability	1.87
	Database **Volume**	1.23
	Product complexity	2.36
	Product attributes range = 5.43	
Computer	Timing constraint	1.66
	Storage constraint	1.56
	Virtual machine volatility	1.49
	Turnaround time	1.32
	Computer attributes range = 5.09	
Personnel	Analyst capability	2.06
	Programmer capability	2.03
	Applications experience	1.57
	Virtual machine experience	1.34
	Language experience	1.20
	Personnel attributes range = 10.56	
Project	Modern programming practices	1.51
	Software tools	1.49
	Schedule constraint	1.23
	Project attributes range = 2.77	
Adjustment multiplier range = 808		

A **Subsystem** is a grouping of modules. The **Subsystem** level of the Detailed module uses cost drivers that tend to vary from **Subsystem** to **Subsystem**, but that tend to be the same for all the modules within a **Subsystem**. The **Subsystem** level cost drivers are

1. required reliability,
2. database **Volume**,
3. timing constraint,
4. storage constraint,
5. virtual machine volatility,
6. turnaround time,
7. analyst capability,
8. applications experience,
9. modern programming practices,
10. software tools, and
11. schedule constraint.

The Detailed model has a set of tables that shows the effect of each cost driver during each development phase [Boehm81].

The system level is used to apply nominal **Project** effort and schedule breakdown by phase and major relations to the overall **Project**.

In summary, COCOMO is a widely used model for prediction effort. You can use the basic-level model to make gross overall predictions during the early phases of the product life cycle. Then you can use the intermediate-level model to make detailed predictions during the design phase of a product. Finally, you can use the detailed level to make phase-dependent predictions during the later phases of the **SoftwareProduct** life cycle.

COCOMO 2.0. The three modes of the software development process defined in COCOMO have been replaced by a scaling exponent approach in CO-COMO 2.0. The exponent c in equation 7.26 accounts for the economies or diseconomies of scale encountered in different size development **Project**s. If $c < 0$, then the **Project** exhibits economies of scale. This means that as the size of a **Project** increases the productivity improves. Economies of scale usually occur when the software life cycle process is optimized for high-overhead, large **Project**s. If $c = 0$, then economies and diseconomies of scale are in balance. This means that productivity is linear with product **Volume**. If $c > 0$, the **Project** exhibits diseconomies of scale. Diseconomies of scale are due to interpersonal communications overhead and a poorly partitioned **Project**. When the software life cycle process is optimized for low-overhead, small **Project**s, the productivity decreases as the size of **Project**s grow. The COCOMO 2.0 model assumes that $1.26 \geq c \geq 1.01$, which assumes diseconomies of scale. The exponent model is defined as

$$c = 1.01 + 0.01 \times \sum_{i=1}^{5} x_i \qquad (7.28)$$

where x_i are scaling drivers that vary from 0 through 5. The five scale driver categories are as follows:

1. *Precedentedness.* Maps scale drivers onto a scale where the top score is for thorough organizational understanding of product objectives, extensive experience in working with related software systems, some concurrent development of associated new hardware and operational procedures, and minimal need for innovative data-processing architectures and algorithms.

2. *Flexibility.* Maps scale drivers onto a scale where the top score is for basic need for software conformance and prestablished requirements, basic need for software conformance with external interface specifications, and low premium on early completion.

3. *Architecture/risk resolution.* Maps scale drivers onto a scale where the top score is for a risk management plan that identifies all critical risk items; establishes milestones for resolving them by PDR; schedule, budget, and internal milestones through PDR that is compatible with the risk management plan; at least 40% of development schedule that is devoted to establishing architecture after general product objectives are given; 100% of required top software architects are available to **Project**; tool support that is fully available for resolving risk items and developing and verifying architectural specifications; very low level of uncertainty in key architecture drivers: mission, user interface, COTS (commercial off-the-shelf software), hardware, technology, and performance.

4. *Team cohesion.* Maps scale drivers onto a scale where the top score is for full consistency of stakeholder objectives and cultures; full ability and willingness of stakeholders to accommodate other stakeholders' objectives; extensive experience of stakeholders in operating as a team; and extensive stakeholder team building to achieve shared vision and commitments.

5. *Process maturity.* Organized around the 18 key process **Area**s in the SEI Capability Maturity Model. The goal-based level of compliance is determined by a judgment-based averaging across the goals for each key process **Area**.

Another difference between the COCOMO and COCOMO 2.0 models is that for the COCOMO model there were three levels of detail (Basic, Intermediate, and Detailed) of a model that was driven by estimates based on **Volume** in NCSS. The COCOMO 2.0 has three models for three different levels of granularity: object points, function points, and NCSS.

The stage 1 Application Composition model uses an object point sizing approach. This model is applied to applications that are too diversified to be created quickly in a domain-specific tool, but are able to be composed from components. Examples of these systems are graphic interface tools, relational database systems, hypermedia handlers, and others. Effort can be estimated using the model

$$Effort_{11}(Volume_{OPs}, PROD_{OPs}) = \frac{Volume_{OPs}}{PROD_{OPs}} \qquad (7.29)$$

where $PROD_{OPs}$ = *ObjectPointProductivity*_**Set** = productivity in object points per person-month. The value of $PROD_{OPs}$ varies from a low of 4, to a nominal value of 13, to a high of 50 depending on the experience and capability of the developers.

The stage 2 Early Design model sizes **Project**s using product **Volume** in function points (**Volume**$_{FPs}$). To determine effort, first you must convert the estimated product volume in function points to $Volume_{KNCSS}$ for language *m*:

$$Volume_{KNCSS,m} = \frac{Volume_{FPs}}{PROD_{FPs,m}} \qquad (7.30)$$

where $PROD_{FPs,m} = FunctionPointProductivity_{Set}$ = productivity in function points per KSLOC for language m. The value of $PROD_{FPS,m}$ can be determined by dividing 1,000 by the value NCSS per function point for the language m in Figure 7.1. Effort in person-months is computed using equation 7.26 for $Effort_{10}$, where $b = 3.0$, c is computed using equation 7.28, and the adjustment multiplier $m(X)$ uses values for the seven stage 2 attributes listed in Table 7.9. The range of values for the cost driver attributes should be calibrated to the local environment. Once experience is gained using COCOMO 2.0, value ranges for the seven cost driver attributes for stage 2 will be made available. The COCOMO 2.0 **Project** suggests making additional adjustments for any software that is reengineered with the aid of an automatic translator.

The stage 3 Post-Architecture model sizes **Project**s using product **Volume** in KNCSS (**Volume**$_{KNCSS}$). Effort in person-months is computed using equation 7.26

Table 7.9 COCOMO and COCOMO 2.0 Cost Driver Attributes

Attribute Class	Cost Driver Attribute	COCOMO	COCOMO 2.0 Stage 1	Stage 2	Stage 3
Product	Product reliability and complexity			RCPX	
	Required reliability	RELY			RELY
	Database **Volume**	DATA			DATA
	Product complexity	CPLX			CPLX
	Documentation to match SLC needs				DOCU
	Required reuse			RUSE	RUSE
Computer	Platform difficulty			PDIF	
	Time constraint	TIME			TIME
	Storage constraint	STOR			STOR
	Virtual machine volatility (platform volatility)	VIRT			PVOL
	Turnaround time	TURN			
Personnel	Personnel capability			PERS	
	Analyst capability	ACAP			ACAP
	Programmer capability	PCAP			PCAP
	Personnel continuity				PCON
	Personnel experience			PREX	
	Applications experience	AEXP			AEXP
	Platform experience				PEXP
	Language and tool experience				LTEX
	Virtual machine experience	VEXP			
	Language experience	LEXP			
Project	Facilities			FCIL	
	Software tools	TOOL			TOOL
	Multisite development				SITE
	Schedule constraint	SCED		SCED	SCED

for $Effort_{10}$, where $b = 3.0$, c is computed using equation 7.28, and the adjustment multiplier $m(X)$ uses values for the 3 stage 17 attributes listed in Table 7.9. You should calibrate the range of values for the 17 cost driver attributes to your local environment. Boehm and co-workers include terms to account for code breakage (code thrown away due to requirements volatility) and automatically translated code.

Jensen Model

Jensen [Jensen84] proposed a model similar to the Putnam model. Jensen proposed the **Project Volume** equation:

$$Volume_{NCSS} = C_{te}T_{Dev}K^{1/2} \tag{7.31}$$

where C_{te} is called the effective technology constant and is computed by

$$C_{te} = C_{tb}m(X) \tag{7.32}$$

where C_{tb} is the basic technology constant and the cost driver adjustment multiplier $m(X)$ is defined in equation 7.27. The cost drivers defined in X take into account the product, personnel, and resource attributes that affect effort. Conte, Dunsmore, and Shen [Conte86] tested the Jensen model against their **Project** database and found that the results were better than the Putnam model, but were still poor.

COPMO Model

Thebaut [Thebaut83] developed the following COPMO (Cooperative Programming Model) effort model that incorporates average team size n and $Volume_{KNCSS}$:

$$Effort_{12}(Volume_{KNCSS}, n) = a + b \times Volume_{KNCSS} + c \times n^d \tag{7.33}$$

where a and b can be derived from **Project**s, where $n \cong 1$. Then, by choosing an a and b, c and d can be determined using a least-squares fit. Conte, Dunsmore, and Shen [Conte86] applied the COPMO model to five different **Project** databases to determine the parameters a, b, c, and d for the following generalized COPMO model:

$$Effort_{13}(Volume_{KNCSS}, n) = a_i + b_i \times Volume_{KNCSS} + c_i \times n^{d_i} \tag{7.34}$$

where i is used to denote an effort complexity class. Their empirical results showed that a was usually small in relation to reported effort. Thus, they arbitrarily set $a_i = 0$ for all i. They also found the weighted average of d was 1.53. For simplicity, they arbitrarily set $d_i = 1.5$. With these assumptions, they were able to write the generalized equation as

**Table 7.10   Conte, Dunsmore, and Shen Partitions
of $m(X)$ into Seven Complexity Classes Using
the COCOMO Database**

Complexity Class i	$m(X)$ Range	b_i	c_i
1	$m > 3.75$	4.7	3.6
2	$2.75 < m \leq 3.75$	4.3	2.8
3	$1.70 < m \leq 2.75$	4.0	2.8
4	$1.25 < m \leq 1.70$	2.6	2.0
5	$0.75 < m \leq 1.25$	1.9	1.5
6	$0.50 < m \leq 0.75$	1.8	1.5
7	$0 < m \leq 0.50$	1.1	0.7

$$Effort_{14}(Volume_{KNCSS} i, n, a_i = 0, d_i = 1.5) = b_i \times Volume_{KNCSS} + c_i \times n^{1.5} \quad (7.35)$$

They tried a number version of complexity classes, but one that was easiest to apply was one based on the COCOMO adjustment multiplier $m(X)$ that was composed of 15 cost drivers. Their seven complexity classes partition version is given in Table 7.10. The partitioning in Table 7.10 is based on the range of $m(X)$ being from 0.25 to 5.50. They state that the COPMO model performed slightly better than the COCOMO intermediate model on the COCOMO **Project** database.

SUMMARY

In this chapter, we started out by looking at 17 major cost drivers, called dominators, that can cause effort to change by an order of magnitude. These dominators were categorized by the main parts of the software life cycle process: overall **Project**, product, personnel, resources, and **Customer**. By monitoring dominators, you can gain insight into ways of improving software productivity.

We then introduced a simple cost model based on effort models. From the numerous effort models that people have developed, we examined three historical/experimental models, three linear statistical models, thirteen nominal effort nonlinear statistical models, four theoretically based models, and four composite models. You can use many of these models to make effort predictions after you have calibrated them to your software development environment. After you create a **Project** database of successful completed **Project**s, you can improve your effort prediction accuracy by deriving your own equation coefficients.

REFERENCES

[Albrecht79]   Albrecht, A. J., "Measuring Application Development Productivity," *Proceedings of the Joint SHARE/GUIDE/IBM Application Development Symposium*, October 1979, pp. 83–92.

[Bailey81]   Bailey, J. W., and Basili, V. R., "A Meta-model for Software Development Resource Expenditures," *Proceedings of the Fifth International Conference on Software Engineering*, 1981, pp. 107–116.

[Biggerstaff89]   Biggerstaff, T. J., and Perlis, A. J., *Software Reusability*, Vol. I, Addison–Wesley Publishing Co., Reading, MA, 1989.

[Boehm81]   Boehm, B. W., *Software Engineering Economics*, Prentice Hall, Upper Saddle River, NJ, 1981.

[Boehm87]   Boehm, B. W., "Industrial software metrics top 10 list," *IEEE Software*, Sept. 1987, pp. 84–85.

[Boehm95]   Boehm, B., Horowitz, E., Selby, R., and Westland, J. C., *COCOMO 2.0 User's Manual*, Version 1.1, copyrighted by University of Southern California, received in April 1995.

[Brooks75]   Brooks, Jr., F. P., *The Mythical Man-Month Essays on Software Engineering*, Addison–Wesley Publishing Co., Reading, MA, 1975.

[Brooks87]   Brooks, Jr., F. P., "No Silver Bullet Essence and Accidents of Software Engineering," *IEEE Computer*, April 1987, pp. 10–19.

[Carlyle89]   Carlyle, R., "Leaping Ahead in Software Productivity," *Datamation*, December 1, 1989, pp. 2–32.

[Conte86]   Conte, S. D., Dunsmore, H. E., and Shen, V. Y., *Software Engineering Metrics and Models*, Benjamin/Cummings Publishing Co., Inc., Menlo Park, CA, 1986.

[DeMarco & Lister87]   DeMarco, T. and Lister, T., *Peopleware*, Dorset House, New York, 1987.

[Dorfman90]   Dorfman, M., and Thayer, R. H., *Standards, Guidelines, and Examples of System and Software Requirements Engineering*, IEEE Computer Society Press, Los Alamitos, CA, 1990.

[Esterling80]   Esterling, B., "Software Manpower Costs: A Model," *Datamation*, March 1980, pp. 164–170.

[Factor88]   Factor, R. M., and Smith, W. B., "A Discipline for Improving Software Productivity," *AT&T Technical Journal*, July/August 1988, pp. 2–9.

[Farr65]   Farr, L., and Zagorski, H. J., "Quantitative Analysis of Programming Cost Factors: A Progress Report," *ICC Symposium Proceedings on Economics of Automatic Data Processing*, edited by A. B. Frielind, North Holland, Amsterdam, 1965.

[Freburger79]   Freburger, K. and Basili, V. R., "The Software Engineering Laboratory: Relationship Equations," Report TR-764, University of Maryland, May 1979.

[Frederic74]   Frederic, B. C., "A Provisional Model for Estimating Computer Program Development Costs," Tecolote Research, Inc., December 1974.

[Grady92]   Grady, R. B., *Practical Software Metrics for Project Management and Process Improvement*, Prentice Hall, Upper Saddle River, NJ, 1992, p. 22.

[Halstead77]   Halstead, M. H., *Elements of Software Science*, Elsevier, New York, 1977.

[Herd77]   Herd, J. R., Postak, J. N., Russell, W. E., and Steward, K. R., "Software Cost Estimation Study—Study Results," Final Technical Report, *RADC-TR-77-220*, Doty Associates, Inc., Rockville, MD, June 1977.

[Jenkins84]   Jenkins, A. M., Naumann, J. D., and Wetherbe, J. C., "Empirical investigation of systems developed practices and results," *Information Management*, Volume 7, 1984, pp. 73–82.

[Jensen84]   Jensen, R. W., "A Comparison of the Jensen and COCOMO Schedule and Cost Estimation Models," *Proceedings of International Society of Parametric Analysis*, 1984, pp. 96–106.

[Jones77]   Jones, C., "Program Quality and Programmer Productivity," *IBM Technical Report TR 02.764*, January 1977, pp. i, 42–78.

[Jones78]   Jones, C., "Measuring Programming Quality and Productivity," *IBM Systems Journal*, Vol. 17, No. 1, 1978, pp. 39–63.

[Jones86]   Jones, C., *Programming Productivity*, McGraw-Hill Book Co., New York, 1986.

[Jones91]   Jones, C., *Applied Software Measurement*, McGraw-Hill, Inc., New York, 1991.

[Kemerer93]   Kemerer, C. F., and Patrick, M. W., "Staffing Factor in Software Cost Estimation Models," *Software Engineering Productivity Handbook,* edited by J. Keyes, Windcrest/McGraw-Hill, New York, NY, 1993, pp. 175–190.

[Martin82]   Martin, J., *Application Development without Programmers*, Prentice Hall, Upper Saddle River, NJ, 1982.

[Nelson66]   Nelson, E. A., "Management Handbook for the Estimation of Computer Programming Costs," *AD-A648750*, Systems Development Corporation, October 31, 1966.

[Nelson70]   Nelson, E. A., "Some Recent Contributions to Computer Programming Management," *On the Management of Computer Programming*, edited by G. F. Weinwurm, Auerbach Publishers, Inc., Princeton, NJ, 1970, pp. 159–184.

[Nelson78]   Nelson, R., *Software Data Collection and Analysis at RADC*, Rome Air Development Center, Rome, NY, 1978.

[Phan88]   Phan, D., Vogel, D., and Nunamaker, J., "The Search for Perfect Project Management," *Computerworld*, 1988, pp. 95–100.

[Phister79]   Phister, Jr., M., *Data Processing Technology and Economics,* Digital Press, Bedford, MA, 1979.

[Pietrasanta70]   Pietrasanta, A. M., "Resource Analysis of Computer Program System Development," *On the Management of Computer Programming*, edited by G. F. Weinwurm, Auerbach Publishers, Inc., Princeton, NJ, 1970.

[Putnam78]   Putnam, L. H. "A General Empirical Solution to the Macro Software Sizing and Estimating Problem," *IEEE Transactions on Software Engineering*, Vol. SE-4, July 1978, pp. 345–361.

[Sackman68]   Sackman, H., Erikson, W. J., and Grant, E. E., "Exploratory Experimental Studies Comparing Online and Offline Programming Performance," *Communications ACM*, Vol. 11, No. 1, January 1968, pp. 3–11.

[Scott74]   Scott, R. F., and Simmons, D. B., "Programmer Productivity and the Delphi Technique," *Datamation*, May 1974, pp. 71–73.

[Scott75]   Scott, R. F., and Simmons, D. B., "Predicting Programming Group Productivity—A Communications Model," *IEEE Transactions on Software Engineering*, Vol. SE-1, No. 4, 1975, pp. 411–414.

[Shere88]   Shere, K. D., *Software Engineering and Management*, Prentice Hall, Upper Saddle River, NJ, 1988.

[Simmons72]   Simmons, D. B., "The Art of Writing Large Programs," *Computer*, March/April 1972, pp. 43–49.

[Simmons91]   Simmons, D. B., "Communications: A Software Group Productivity Dominator," *IEEE Software Engineering Journal*, November 1991, pp. 454–462.

[Simmons92]   Simmons, D. B., "A Win–Win Metric Based Software Management Approach," *IEEE Transactions on Engineering Management*, Vol. 39, No. 1, February 1992, pp. 32–41.

[Thebaut83]   Thebaut, S. M., *The Saturation Effect in Large-scale Software Development: Its Impact and Control*, Ph.D. thesis, Department of Computer Science, Purdue University, West Lafayette, IN, May 1983.

[Walston77]   Walston, C. E., and C. P. Felix, "A Method of Programming Measurement and Estimation," *IBM Systems Journal*, Vol. 16, No. 1, 1977, pp. 54–73.

[Walston77a]   Walston, C. E., and C. P. Felix, "Authors' Response," *IBM Systems Journal*, Vol. 16, No. 4, 1977, pp. 54–73.

[Wolverton74]   Wolverton, R. W., "The Cost of Developing Large-scale Software," *IEEE Transactions on Computers*, June 1974, pp. 282–303.

8
Development Time

The maximum number of men depends upon the number of independent subtasks. From these two quantities one can derive schedules using fewer men and more months. (The only risk is product obsolescence.) One cannot, however, get workable schedules using more men and fewer months. More software projects have gone awry from lack of calendar time than for all other causes combined.

Frederick P. Brooks, Jr.
[Brooks75]

INTRODUCTION

Managers predict size of **Project**s, estimate costs, allocate resources, create all levels of plans, and establish schedules. In this chapter we will concentrate on estimating the development time schedule. Setting the development schedule is one of the primary methods that a manager has to control a **Project**. If a manager establishes a schedule that is unrealistically short, the **Project** may end as a disaster, even though very capable developers apply their maximum effort to the **Project**. If the schedule is too long, the **SoftwareProduct** may miss the marketing window of opportunity where it would be profitable.

In this chapter we will take a brief look at how development time is estimated under the software science model. Next we will examine development schedule prediction using well-known, empirically developed models. In this section we will examine the relationship between product size, effort, time, and staff required to produce the product. We will next look at how much you can compress the development schedule. We will look at compression from a team viewpoint and then

199

from the overall **Project** perspective. We will then examine models for tracking schedule slippage.

SOFTWARE SCIENCE DEVELOPMENT TIME

In developing the software science model, Halstead took a very simplistic approach to schedule prediction. He defined computer program **Volume** V to be the mental comparisons required to generate a program. The $Effort_8$ equation computes effort as the total number of elementary mental discriminations required to generate a program. Stroud, a psychologist, claimed that the human mind is capable of making between 5 and 20 elementary discriminations per second [Stroud67]. Based on Stroud's work, Halstead chose what he called the *Stroud number* β to be 18. He then predicted the program development time in seconds to be

$$Time_1 = \frac{Effort_8}{\beta}$$

$$(8.1)$$

Halstead's programming time prediction is a simplistic approach to development time prediction. He only considers the time it takes a programmer to make mental comparisons and ignores all other factors. His methodology is useful in a controlled laboratory environment where subjects convert known algorithms to computer programs. Software science methodology is not useful in predicting **SoftwareProduct** development time in the complex real world.

NOMINAL DEVELOPMENT SCHEDULE PREDICTION

Schedule estimation equations that are a function of effort in person-months have been developed by a number of authors. Once you have determined the effort required to develop a **SoftwareProduct**, you can estimate the time that you should schedule to complete the product development. The nominal form of the development time estimation equation is

$$Time_2 = a \times Effort_n^{b}$$

$$(8.2)$$

where a and b are constants and $n = 1$ to 7 and 9 to 11 for the effort equations in Chapter 7. The constant a is the size in KNCSS of a program that a person can produce in one month. Since very few interesting programs can be produced that take less than a person-month, $Effort_n \geq 1$ in equation 8.2. Thus, as the size of a program increases, the effort to produce the program increases and the resulting development time increases.

Table 8.1 Nominal Development Time Estimation Equation Coefficients

a	b	Reference	
2.50	0.32	[Boehm81]	Organic mode
2.15	0.333	[Putnam78]	Minimal schedule
2.50	0.35	[Boehm81]	Semidetached mode
2.47	0.35	[Walston77]	
3.04	0.36	[Nelson78]	
2.50	0.38	[Boehm81]	Embedded mode

Table 8.1 shows the values for *a* and *b* that have been determined empirically from actual **Project** data. The development time predicting models are surprisingly similar to each other. Notice that for the equation 8.2

$$0.38 \geq b \geq 0.32$$

and that for these same equations

$$3.04 \geq a \geq 2.15$$

Thus, the empirically derived *a* and *b* constants for *Time*$_2$ vary within a very narrow range when compared to the constants for the equations used to estimate effort.

To predict development time, you must first estimate the size of a **Software-Product**. We can then use equation 7.8 to compute effort. Figure 8.1 shows a plot of effort in person-years versus size. The **Project**s range in size from 10 KNCSS to

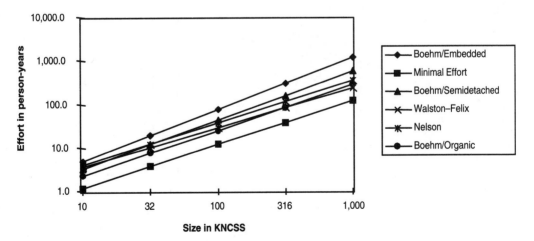

Figure 8.1　Effort in Person-years versus Size in KNCSS

1,000 KNCSS. **Project**s in this range are normally larger than those that would be developed by a single **Individual**. From the effort values in Figure 8.1, equation 8.2 can be used to determine the development time for a **SoftwareProduct** of a given size. Shown in Figure 8.2 is a plot of nominal development time **SoftwareProduct** size. Grady and Caswell [Grady87] at Hewlett–Packard said that one of their studies found that new code was produced at a rate of between 400 to 700 NCSS per person-month. We chose the 0.700 KNCSS per person month [that is, $b = 1/(0.700)$ = 1.43] to determine what we will call the minimal effort that is plotted in Figure 8.1. We also assume that effort increases linearly with size (that is, $c = 1.0$) and substitute b and c into equation 7.8 to determine minimal effort. In Chapter 9 we will examine the effect of the constants b and c on productivity.

We can use the effort determined from equation 7.8 to compute development time using equation 8.2. Figure 8.2 is a plot of development time versus **Software-Product** size in KNCSS. Boehm [Boehm81] used the Putnam minimum development time criteria [Putnam78] to determine for equation 8.2 that $a = 2.15$ and $b = 0.333$. Putnam and many other researchers have determined that software development time has a limit to the amount that it can be reduced. He empirically determined the minimum development time from data gathered by observing actual development **Project**s. Putnam has continued to study factors that affect development and has developed a computer program that estimates minimum development time based on an empirically determined productivity index, empirically determined personnel buildup index, and estimated **SoftwareProduct** size [Putnam and Myers92].

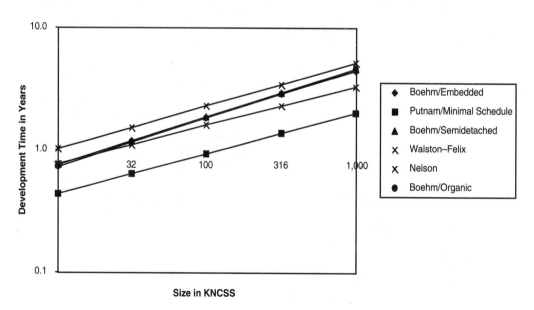

Figure 8.2   Development Time versus **SoftwareProduct** Size

After we have estimated a **SoftwareProduct** size, used an effort estimation model to predict nominal effort, and used a development time model to predict nominal development time, we can estimate the average number of software developers n by using the equation

$$n = \frac{Effort_n}{Time_2} \tag{8.3}$$

where $Effort_n$ is one of the effort estimating equations from Chapter 6 and $Time_2$ is equation 8.2. Using $Effort_n$ and $Time_2$ values from Table 8.1, we have plotted in Figure 8.3 the average number of software developers needed to produce a **Software-Product** of a given size.

We will estimate schedules for two different **Project**s: Example 1 is a simple 10 KNCSS business software system developed by a relatively small software team in a highly familiar, in-house environment, and Example 2 is a complex, embedded computer application where the application is a 200-KNCSS **SoftwareProduct** that operates within the tight constraints of a telecommunications system. For both estimates we will choose the Basic **Version** of Boehm's COCOMO model. For Example 1, we will choose the organic mode parameters from Table 7.7. Using equation 7.31 and parameter values $b = 2.4$, $c = 1.05$, and $Size_{KNCSS} = 10$, we estimate that approximately 27 person-months of effort will be required. Using parameters $a = 2.5$ and $b = 0.32$ for the COCOMO Organic mode in Table 8.1 and applying them to equation 8.2, we determine that the **Project** in Example 1 will take approximately 7.2 months

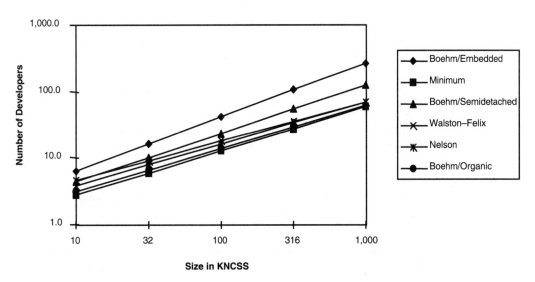

Figure 8.3 Number of Software Developers Required to Produce a Product of a Given Size

or a little over half a year. Using equation 8.3, we estimate that a four-member team will be required to develop the system.

In Example 2, the **SoftwareProduct** must operate within the strongly coupled complex of telecommunications hardware, software, regulations, and operational procedures. We will choose COCOMO embedded mode parameters from Table 7.7. Again using equation 7.31 and parameter values $b = 3.6$, $c = 1.20$, and $Size_{KNCSS}$ = 200, we estimate that 1,847 person-months of effort will be required. Using parameters $a = 2.5$ and $b = 0.38$ for the COCOMO embedded mode in Table 8.1 and applying them to equation 8.2, we determine that the **Project** in Example 2 will take approximately 28 months or a little over two years. Using equation 8.3, we estimate that a 66-member **Organization** will be required to develop the telecommunications product. The **Organization** will most likely be composed of multiple teams of developers. The **Project** in Example 2 is larger and more complex than the **Project** in Example 1 and will require more time and effort to complete.

We made the above development time estimates using models based on historical **Project** data. Decision makers for **Organization**s often have competitive pressures that cause them to want a **SoftwareProduct** developed as soon as possible. By adding more people to a **Project**, a **SoftwareProduct** can be developed faster. We will now examine how much we can compress a software development schedule that is based on the normal development time from past **Project**s.

DEVELOPMENT SCHEDULE COMPRESSION

We will now examine how much we can compress the development schedule for a software development **Project**. Many researchers agree that no matter how many people are added to a software development **Project** there is a limit to the amount that the development schedule can be reduced. The chart in Figure 8.4 shows what happens when you try to compress the software development schedule for the telecommunications **Project** in Example 2 above. The **Project** was to develop a telecommunications product of 200 KNCSS, use about 1,847 person-months of effort, and employee an average of 66 software developers. By adding additional staff at the start of a **Project**, the **Project** can be completed in less than normal time at an increased cost. Figure 8.4 has scheduled development time divided into five ranges. The longest allowable schedule is the *Excessive Staff* range. When an **Organization** is allowed more time than necessary to develop a system, the cost increases with time unless the staff is reduced to offset the extra time. When the number, qualifications, and skills of staff are matched to the requirements of a system under development, the allowable schedule is in the *Minimum Cost* range. Pietrasanta [Pietrasanta70] reported that a change in elapsed time in this range does not significantly affect total **Project** cost. This is only true if the number of software developers is significantly re-

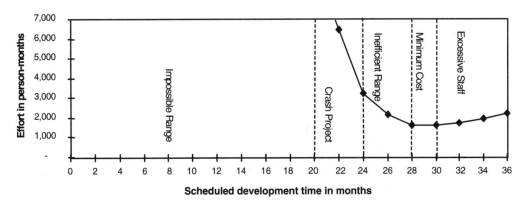

Figure 8.4   Effort Required to Compress a Development Schedule

duced as the scheduled development time is increased. Otherwise, the total effort increases with time past the point of minimum cost. The number of software developers can be increased to reduce the development time, but the effort (and cost) must be increased beyond the minimum cost range. When effort is slightly increased to improve the schedule, this is the *Inefficient Range*. When maximum effort is applied to reduce development time, the schedule is in the *Crash* range. For a given software life cycle process, there is a minimum time past which development time cannot be reduced. The range below the minimum range we will refer to as the *Impossible Range*. No matter how much effort is applied to a **Project**, it is impossible to reduce development time below the minimum time.

MINIMUM DEVELOPMENT TIME

There is no reason to try to reduce development time to less that the minimum. We will next examine factors that affect minimum development time for a team of software developers, and then we will look at the minimum development time for an entire **Project**.

Team Minimum Development Time

The minimum development time $Time_{Minimum}$ depends on many factors, including the dominators and cost drivers that we discussed in Chapter 7. In the early stages of a **SoftwareProduct** software life cycle, management has control over the f_s and f_c parameters that were introduced in Chapter 7. The value of f_s results from the design and resulting work breakdown **Structure**. Early design decisions determine how many software tasks can be developed in parallel. Once a design is finalized, a given design has an f_s, which is the ratio of time spent on tasks that are developed in sequence to the sum of time than is spent on tasks that are developed in sequence or parallel. The range of f_s is

$$1 \geq f_s \geq 0$$

For an effective design, f_s approaches zero. For an ineffective design, f_s is greater than zero.

Effective communications are absolutely essential to successful completion of any software development **Project**. Ineffective communications can result in a failed **Project**. The value of f_c reflects the amount of time spent communicating divided by the total work time. The range is

$$1 \geq f_c \geq 0$$

For the ideal case, where all time is spent developing software and no time is spent communicating with others, f_c is 0. Some communication is absolutely essential; thus, for actual software development **Project**s, $f_c > 0$. But we should try to keep its value as close to zero as possible.

Using equation 7.17, we can determine minimum development times for a team of programmers. First, we look at the case of ideal communications, where $f_c = 0$ and $n \to \infty$. As n becomes very large, $T(\infty) = Time_{Minimum}$.

$$Time_{Minimum}(f_s > 0, f_c = 0, n \to \infty) = f_s \times T(1) \tag{8.4}$$

For example, as shown in Chapter 7, if $f_s = 0.3$, then the most you can reduce the schedule over a single programmer working alone is $0.3 \times T(1)$.

Also, management decisions determine f_c, which results from personnel **Organization Structure,** physical communication facilities, and effectiveness of the design. If we assume a perfect design where all activities can be performed in parallel (that is, $f_s = 0$), but a considerable amount of communication is required (that is, $f_c > 0$), then the development time based on equation 7.19 would be

$$T(n) = \frac{1 + n \times (n-1) \times f_c}{n} \times T(1) \tag{8.5}$$

The minimum development time for a given f_c would be

$$\frac{dT(n)}{dn} = \frac{d}{dn}\left[\frac{1 + n \times (n-1) \times f_c}{n} \times T(1) \right] = -\frac{1}{n^2} + f_c = 0 \tag{8.6}$$

By solving the above equation for n, we can find the $n_{Maximum}(f_c)$, where the minimum development time occurs, which is

$$n_{Maximum}(f_c) = \sqrt{\frac{1}{f_c}} \tag{8.7}$$

When more than $n_{Maximum}(f_c)$ members are added to a team, instead of decreasing the development time, it actually increases. For $f_s = 0$ and $f_c > 0$, the minimum development time becomes

$$Time_{Minimum}(f_s = 0, f_c > 0) = \left(2 \times \sqrt{f_c} - f_c\right) \times T(1) \qquad (8.8)$$

Table 8.2 shows the relationship among amount of communications f_c and minimum development time $Time_{Minimum}(f_s = 0, f_c > 0)$ and number of team members n. For example, if each member communicates 1% of the time with each other team member, then by using 10 programmers you can reduce development time to 19% of the time that it would take a single programmer to program the task. This assumes that the task can be broken down into at least 10 tasks and that all programmers produce software at an equal rate. If each member communicates 5% of the time with each other team member, you could only reduce the development time to 40% of the time it would take a single programmer to program the task. Also, if you used five or more programmers as members of the team, then the development time would increase above minimum. From the above you can see why you should try to minimize unnecessary communications.

Communication by e-mail reduces untimely interruptions. Well-organized meetings with preplanned agendas and succinct, accurate minutes reduce time wasted in meetings. Well-organized video conference meetings also help to save time.

Project Minimum Development Time

Teams are organized into **Project**s to produce **SoftwareProduct**s. Once the software design specifications have been completed, the work breakdown **Structure** determined, and the **Project** members organized into teams, there is a minimum development time that cannot be reduced. When the same **Organization** develops similar **SoftwareProduct**s, the development time can be determined from past experience. A **Project** database should be retained that contains metrics for development time prediction.

Table 8.2 Minimum Development Time and Maximum Team Members

f_c	$Time_{Minimum}(f_s = 0, f_c > 0)$	Maximum Number n of Team Members for Minimum Time
0.01	$0.19 \times T(1)$	10.0
0.02	$0.26 \times T(1)$	7.1
0.03	$0.32 \times T(1)$	5.8
0.04	$0.36 \times T(1)$	5.0
0.05	$0.40 \times T(1)$	4.5

OBSERVATIONS

1. The work breakdown structure resulting from the design specifications should allow all team members to work on independent tasks. The f_s resulting from work breakdown structure determines a minimum development time that cannot be reduced.

2. The amount of communications among team members determines an f_c-based minimum development time. As the amount of communication increases, the minimum development time increases.

3. Unnecessary communications should be kept to a minimum.

4. Once team members have been selected and the communications pattern resulting in f_c has been established for a team, there is a maximum number of additional members that can be added to a team to help to reduce the development time.

A number of researchers have empirically determined the minimum development time for their development environment. Table 8.1 lists coefficients for a minimum development time from empirical data gathered by Putnam [Putnam78]. For the environments studied by Putnam, he has developed a computer program that estimates minimum development time based on **Project** size, a productivity index, and a personnel buildup index.

Boehm uses required development schedule (SCED) as one of the cost driver parameters for his Intermediate and Detailed COCOMO models that we discussed in Chapter 7. He states that the required development schedule should never be below 75% of the nominal development schedule estimated by equation 8.2 and the parameters chosen from Table 8.1. He says that his experience has shown that it is virtually impossible to compress the nominal schedule more than 25%, or

$$Time_{Minimum} \geq 0.75 \times Time_2 \tag{8.9}$$

where $Time_{Minimum}$ is minimum development time.

Conte, Dunsmore, and Shen used the COPMO model described in Chapter 7 to determine a relationship between minimum development time and the development schedule that should be chosen for a **Project** [Conte86]. They applied the COPMO model to five **Project** databases that contained information on 187 **Project**s. They concluded that a good choice of **Project** duration should be about 10% greater than $Time_{Minimum}$. By combining Boehm's results and Conte et al.'s results, we can conclude that we should choose a scheduled development time $Time_{Scheduled}$ of

$$0.85 \times Time_2 \leq Time_{Scheduled} \leq Time_2 \tag{8.10}$$

If you plan to develop a software application in a minimum amount of time, the cost will rise rapidly between $0.85 \times Time_2$ and $0.75 \times Time_2$.

We will now examine how development schedules are chosen.

SELECTION OF SOFTWARE DEVELOPMENT SCHEDULE

Jones [Jones91] states that in the United States more than half the large **Project**s are scheduled in an irrational manner. Predetermined end dates are forced on **Project**s by arbitrary decree. When the scheduled end date exceeds staff capabilities by more than 25%, a disaster often results. The disaster results in a late **Project** that is catastrophically over budget that is delivered to a very unsatisfied **Customer**.

Even top computer companies often do not use effective schedule estimating methodology. Grady and Caswell [Grady87] report that a member of the HP Software Metrics Council decided to analyze past **Project** data of his division. The records did not contain much data that related to metrics of software development, but they did report **Project** schedule estimates and actual results. He discovered what he called a software estimating wall. In many years of data, there were virtually no **Project**s that estimated completion more than 2 years from the point of estimation. The actual completion dates were spread mostly after the 2-year mark. **Project** completion schedules were determined more by budget cycles than realistic estimating methodology.

SCHEDULE SLIPPAGE

When Brooks [Brooks75] is asked the question "How does a **Project** get to be a year late?" his reply is "One day at a time." Disastrous schedule slippage in a **Project** frequently does not result from major calamities. Major schedule slippage results from the hard to recognize day by day slippage. These slippages are even harder to prevent or make up. They come from unplanned everyday interruptions such as jury duty, family problems, sickness, and late equipment. We will define the schedule slip metric as

$$ScheduleSlip = \frac{Time_{Completion}}{Time_{Schedule}} \tag{8.11}$$

where $Time_{Completion}$ = either current schedule or final schedule if **Project** has been completed

$Time_{Schedule}$ = original **Project** schedule

If a task is on schedule, then *ScheduleSlip* = 1.0; 10% behind schedule, then *ScheduleSlip* = 1.1; and 10% ahead of schedule, then *ScheduleSlip* is 0.9.

Grady [Grady92] suggests measurements that can help managers to improve schedule accuracy while at the same time reducing schedule slippage. He described a Hewlett–Packard Laboratory that created products that were integrated with products from several other laboratories. This laboratory had a poor reputation for meeting its schedules. The laboratory members tracked average months of progress per month for n **Project**s as

$$AverageProgress_n = 1 - \frac{\sum_{i=1}^{n} \frac{\left(1 - \frac{1}{ScheduleSlip_i}\right) \times 100}{PercentComplete_i}}{n} \tag{8.12}$$

The **Project** percentage complete is

$$PercentComplete = \frac{Time_{Elapsed}}{Time_{Completion}} \times 100 \tag{8.13}$$

where $Time_{Elasped}$ is the time that has elapsed since the start of a **Project**. For example, if a laboratory was involved in four **Project**s and all were on schedule, then $AverageProgress_4$ would be 1.0. If each of the **Project**s was scheduled to be a 24-month **Project**, 12 months had elapsed for each **Project**, and each had slipped 3 months, the $AverageProgress_4$ would be 0.75 average months of progress per month. Tracking the $AverageProgress_n$ on a monthly basis allows an **Organization** to reduce slippage and to improve its schedule estimates.

OBSERVATIONS

1. All the dominators and cost drivers explained in Chapter 7 either directly or indirectly have an effect on development time.
2. The most effective way to reduce development time is to create a design specification and work breakdown structure that allows the maximum number of tasks to be developed in parallel while requiring minimal communication.
3. Once a nominal development schedule has been established based on design, **Organization**s policies, standards, and past **Project** history, it is very difficult to reduce the minimum development time by more than 25%.
4. Costs rise very rapidly when you try to reduce development time by more than 15%.
5. Once the design is finalized and implementation has begun, you might increase both delivery time and costs when you add people to a **Project**.
6. Brooks's law: Adding people to a late **Project** only makes it later [Brooks75].

Brooks recommends status review meetings [Brooks75] where an atmosphere of openness and honest appraisal is encouraged. Both scheduled and estimated dates should be listed in the milestone report. The estimated dates should be the property of the lowest-level manager who has responsibility for the work in question. The **Project** manager should not try to intimidate the lower-level manager and should emphasize accurate, unbiased estimates, rather than self-protective conservative ones. In fact, estimated task completion dates can best be left to a computerized manager associate [Simmons92,93].

SUMMARY

In this chapter we started out by examining the Halstead software science method for predicting development time, which was based on the number of human mind elementary discriminations per second. We found this method simple but not robust. We then examined well-known, empirically based nominal development time prediction models. From examining development teams, we concluded that the development time is affected by work breakdown **Structure** and the communications practices of the team. Also, when you add people to a **Project**, you can compress the development schedule up to a point, but then additional people might actually cause the development time to increase. If fact, adding people to a late **Project** only makes it later.

REFERENCES

[Boehm81] Boehm, B. W., *Software Engineering Economics*, Prentice Hall, Upper Saddle River, NJ, 1981.

[Brooks75] Brooks, Jr., F. P., *The Mythical Man-Month Essays on Software Engineering*, Addison–Wesley Publishing Co., Reading, MA, 1975.

[Conte86] Conte, S. D., Dunsmore, H. E., and Shen, V. Y., *Software Engineering Metrics and Models*, Benjamin/Cummings Publishing Co., Inc., Menlo Park, CA, 1986.

[Grady87] Grady, R. B., and Caswell, D. L., *Software Metrics: Establishing Company-wide Program*, Prentice Hall, Upper Saddle River, NJ, 1987.

[Grady92] Grady, R. B., *Practical Software Metrics for Project Management and Process Improvement*, Prentice Hall, Upper Saddle River, NJ, 1992.

[Jones91] Jones, C., *Applied Software Measurement*, McGraw-Hill, Inc., New York, 1991.

[Nelson78] Nelson, R., *Software Data Collection and Analysis at RADC*, Rome Air Development Center, Rome, NY, 1978.

[Pietrasanta70] Pietrasanta, A. M., "Resource Analysis of Computer Program System Development," *On the Management of Computer Programming*, edited by G. F. Weinwurm, Auerbach Publishers, Inc., Princeton, NJ, 1970, pp. 67–88.

[Putnam78]   Putnam, L. H. "A General Empirical Solution to the Macro Software Sizing and Estimating Problem," *IEEE Transactions on Software Engineering*, Vol. SE-4, July 1978, pp. 345–361.

[Putnam92]   Putnam, L. H., and Myers, W., *Measures for Excellence—Reliable Software on Time, within Budget*, Yourdon Press, Prentice Hall, Upper Saddle River, NJ, 1992.

[Simmons92]   Simmons, D. B., "A Win–Win Metric Based Software Management Approach," *IEEE Transactions on Engineering Management*, Vol. 39, No. 1, February 1992, pp. 32–41.

[Simmons93]   Simmons, D. B., Ellis, N. C., and Escamilla, T. D., "Manager Associate," *IEEE Transactions on Knowledge and Data Engineering*, Vol. 5, No. 3, June 1993, pp. 426–438.

[Stroud67]   Stroud, J. M., "The Fine Structure of Psychological Time," *Annals of New York Academy of Science*, Vol. 138, No. 2, 1967, pp. 623–631.

[Walston77]   Walston, C. E., and Felix, C. P. "A Method of Programming Measurement and Estimation," *IBM System Journal*, Vol. 16, No. 1, 1977, pp. 54–73.

9

Productivity

In this scientific world, productivity is only productivity if it is measurable.

James R. Johnson
[Johnson77]

INTRODUCTION

In past chapters, we have examined the software life cycle process. We have also looked at how to measure the size of a **SoftwareProduct** in terms of **Volume**, **Structure**, and **Rework**. We then looked at how to predict effort and time required to produce a **SoftwareProduct** of a known size. We will now explore how to improve the process by which we create the **SoftwareProduct**.

When we improve the quality of a **SoftwareProduct**, there are fewer **Defect**s in the **SoftwareProduct**. When quality is designed and built into the **SoftwareProduct**, the cost of **Rework** and maintenance is reduced. When costs are reduced, productivity improves. The **SoftwareProduct** quality will be addressed in later chapters.

Our goal is to produce software to customer satisfaction that is on time and within budget. Kemerer and Patrick [Kemerer93] provided ample anecdotal evidence that in general these goals are not being met. They quoted a 1984 report by Jenkins, Naumann, and Wetherbe [Jenkins84] that of 72 medium-scale software **Project**s in 23 major U.S. corporations the **Project**s had an average budget overrun of 36%, with only 9% of the **Project**s completed within budget. They quoted a 1988 University of Arizona study of 827 **Project**s that found an average budget overrun of 33%, with only 16% of the respondents who stated that they "rarely" or "never" experienced cost overruns [Phan88]. Also, Kemerer and Patrick quoted a DeMarco and Lister 1987 survey [DeMarco87] of 500 software **Project**s where 15% of all **Project**s were so late that they were canceled, and a full 25% of the large **Project**s were canceled.

Projects overrun budgets because productivity is inaccurately estimated for a specific **Project**. In this chapter we will define productivity. We will then show how to estimate productivity based on **Volume** and effort models. Then we will explore how cost driver attributes affect productivity and how each of the cost drivers can contribute to a budget overrun.

PRODUCTIVITY MEASUREMENT

The IEEE standard definition of software productivity is the ratio of the output product to the input effort that made it [IEEE89]. In the context of this book, the overall output product is **SoftwareProduct**. For computation purposes, we are interested in the **Volume** of the output product at the **SoftwareProduct** level or at a lower level. The **SoftwareProduct** levels are

```
SoftwareProduct
    Features
    Defects
    Versions
        Subsystems
            RequirementsFiles
                Rework(RequirementsFile)
                Volume(RequirementsFile)
            DesignFiles
                Rework(DesignFile)
                Volume(DesignFile)
            DocumentFiles
                Rework(DocumentFile)
                Volume(DocumentFile)
            SourceFiles
                Chunks
                    Volume(Chunk)
                    Structure
                Rework(SourceFile)
        VAndVTests
        UsabilityTests
            Usability
```

The **SoftwareProduct** is composed of **Defect**s and **Version**s. While **Defect**s are not a positive concept, for the purpose of process improvement, we are definitely interested in the rate that **Individual**s, teams, and so on, produce and correct **Defect**s. On the positive side, we would like to produce **Defect**-free **Version**s of the **SoftwareProduct**.

Version SoftwareProduct level is composed of **Feature**s, **Test**s, and **UsabilityTest**s. **Test**s require effort, but are not part of the **SoftwareProduct** that is delivered to the customer. They are the results of the testing process. **UsabilityTest** is a special type of test to assure that a **SoftwareProduct** is usable by a typical customer. A **Feature** is composed of files used to design and create a **Version** of a **SoftwareProduct**.

Feature SoftwareProduct level is composed of **RequirementsFile**s, **DesignFile**s, **DocumentFile**s, and **SourceFile**s. **RequirementsFile**s, **DesignFile**s, and **DocumentFile**s require effort, but are not part of the **SoftwareProduct** that is delivered to the customer. The **SourceFile**s are compiled and linked with other compiled files to form the object code that is delivered to a customer. **SourceFile**s are composed of **Chunk**s and **Rework**. The **Chunk**s contain source code that is compiled and delivered to the customer. The **Rework** object describes the code adds, deletes, and changes to the **SourceFile**. As part of process improvement, when **Rework** declines, quality and productivity improve.

Chunk SoftwareProduct level has **Volume** and **Structure** attributes. The **Structure** attributes are used to describe software complexity. The **Volume** attributes are used to describe the bulk of what is delivered.

Input effort of an **Organization** is the person–months required to produce a specific **Volume** of a **SoftwareProduct**. **Organization** levels are

> **Organization**
>> **Area**s
>>> **Group**s
>>>> **Individual**s
>>>>> **Salar(y)**ies
>>>>> **Assignment**s
>>>>> **Activit(y)ies**

We can calculate person-months from the **Assignment** attribute of the **Individual** object. The **Individual** is the lowest **Organization** level. Effort of **Individual**s can be combined to determine effort at the **Group Organization** level. Effort of **Group**s can be combined to determine effort at the **Area Organization** level. Effort of **Area**s can be combined to determine effort at the **Organization** level. **Organization** is the highest level and reflects productivity of the overall **Project**.

We will now define productivity as

$$Productivity_{Organization\_Level} = \frac{Volume_a(Product\_Level)}{Effort_{Organization\_Level}} \tag{9.1}$$

where *a* is a **Volume** attribute. In Chapter 6 we defined the following **Volume** attributes:

Bytes	Bytes of eight physical bits
*Chunks***Calculate**	Number of **Chunks**
*FunctionPoints***Calculate**	**Volume** expressed in function points of a **Software-Product**
*NCSS***Calculate**	Noncomment logical source statements
*ObjectPoints***Calculate**	**Volume** expressed in object points of a **Software-Product**
SLOC	Source lines of code
SS (**RequirementsFile**s, **DesignFile**s, and **DocumentFile**s)	Text statements measured directly from a **RequirementsFile,** design specification file, or **DocumentFile** of a **Version**
*SS***Calculate** (**SourceFile**s)	Logical source statements contained in a **Software-Product Chunk, SourceFile, Feature,** or a **Version**
UniqueNCSS	Unique noncomment logical source statements
UniqueReferenceNCSS	Unique noncomment logical source statements that do not exist in a reference file of source statements
UniqueReferenceSS	Unique logical source statements that do not exist in a reference file of source statements
UniqueSLOC	Unique source lines of code
UniqueSS	Unique logical source statements in a **Chunk**
*FunctionPoints***Calculate**	**Volume** expressed in function points of a **Software-Product**
*VolumeSoftSci***Calculate**	Mental comparisons required to generate a program

These attributes used to directly measure productivity for a **Project** where we have gathered measurement data. Often we would like to predict future productivity. To predict future productivity, we have to predict both **SoftwareProduct Volume** and the effort required to produce a **SoftwareProduct** of that **Volume**.

PRODUCTIVITY PREDICTION

We presented a number of models for estimating **Volume** in Chapter 6 and a number of models for estimating effort in Chapter 7. Using these models, we will define the following productivity predicting model:

$$Productivity_{m,n} = \frac{Volume_{a,m}}{Effort_n} \qquad (9.2)$$

where a is the units of **Volume**, m is the number of the **Volume** estimating model from Chapter 6, and n is the number of the effort estimating model from Chapter 7. Productivity is expressed in a per person-month. For example, if a = KNCSS, then the units of productivity would be KNCSS per person-month.

The **Volume** estimating models from Chapter 6 are as follows:

$Volume_{KNCSS,1}$	Equivalent **Volume** of new KNCSSs as defined by Boehm [Boehm81]
$Volume_{KNCSS,2}$	Equivalent **Volume** of new KNCSSs as defined by Bailey and Basili [Bailey81]
$Volume_{KNCSS,3}$	Equivalent **Volume** of new KNCSSs as defined by Thebaut [Thebaut83]
$Volume_{KNCSS,4}$	Equivalent **Volume** of new KNCSSs as defined by Boehm, Horwitz, Selby, and Westland [Boehm95] for the COCOMO 2.0 Post-Architecture Model
$Volume_{KNCSS,5}$	Equivalent **Volume** of new object points as defined by Boehm, Horwitz, Selby, and Westland [Boehm95] for the COCOMO 2.0 Application Composition Model
$Volume_{KNCSS,6}$	**Volume** of new source statements estimated by an experienced computer professional expressed in KNCSS

The following effort predicting models were defined in Chapter 7:

Historical/experimental models (TRW Wolverton and Brooks models)

$Effort_1 [Volume_{SLOC}(k), i(k), j(k)]$	Person-months to produce the kth module of a **SoftwareProduct**
$Effort_{1\_Total}$	Person-months required to produce a software system of k modules

IBM Albrecht function point model

$Effort_2 [Volume_{FP}, m(X), m_{Language}]$	Person-months to produce a **Software-Product** that has $Volume_{FP}$ function points,

an effort adjustment multiplier of $m(X)$,
and a language multiplier of $m_{Language}$

Linear statistical models ([Nelson66,70] and [Farr and Zagorski65] models)

$Effort_3\,(x_0, \ldots, x_n)$ — Person-months required to produce a **SoftwareProduct** with effort cost drivers $x_0, \ldots, x_n$

Nonlinear statistical models [Bailey81], [Boehm81: COCOMO; Boehm95: COCOMO 2.0], [Frederic74], [Halstead77], [Herd77], [Jones 77], [Nelson78], [Phister79], [Walston77a], and [Walston77]

$Effort_4\,[Volume^c_d, a,b,m(X)]$ — Person–months required to produce a **SoftwareProduct** of **Volume** $Volume^c_d$, where d is the units of **Volume**, a, b, and c are constants derived from regression analysis, and $m(X)$ is the effort adjustment multiplier

$Effort_5\,[Volume^c_d, a,b,m(X) = 1]$ — Nominal person–months required to produce a **SoftwareProduct** of **Volume** $Volume^c_d$, where d is the units of **Volume**, a, b, and c are constants derived from regression analysis, and the effort adjustment multiplier $m(X)$ equals 1

Theoretically based models

$Effort_6(n, f_s)$ — Brooks work partition model expresses person months it would take n people to produce a **SoftwareProduct** with a sequential work breakdown structure factor f_s

$Effort_7(n, f_s, f_c)$ — Simmons communications model expresses person-months it would take n people to produce a **SoftwareProduct** with a sequential work breakdown structure factor f_s and a communications factor f_c

$Effort_8(V, L)$ — Halstead software science model expresses mental discriminations required to generate a **SoftwareProduct** written at a program level L

$Effort_9(K)$ — Putnam resource allocation model expresses person-months expended during the life cycle of a software **Project,** where K is a constant selected from charts based on data gathered from past U.S. Army development **Project**s

Composite models

$Effort_{10}[Volume_{KNCSS}, b, c, m(X)]$

Boehm COCOMO effort model and COCOMO 2.0 Early Design and Post-Architecture stages effort model expresses person-months required to produce a **SoftwareProduct** of **Volume** $Volume^c_{KNCSS}$, where b and c are constants derived from regression analysis and $m(X)$ is the effort adjustment multiplier

$Effort_{11}(Volume_{OPs}, PROD_{OPs})$

Boehm COCOMO 2.0 Application Composition stage effort model expresses person-months required to produce a **SoftwareProduct** of **Volume** $Volume_{OPs}$ in object points and $PROD_{OPs}$ in object points per person-month

$Effort_{12}(Volume_{KNCSS}, \bar{n})$

Thebaut COPMO effort model expresses person-months required to produce a **SoftwareProduct** of **Volume** $Volume_{KNCSS}$ by a team of average size n

$Effort_{13}(Volume_{KNCSS}, \bar{n}, i)$

Conte, Dunsmore, and Shen **Version** of COPMO effort model expresses person-months required to produce an i effort complexity class **SoftwareProduct** of **Volume** $Volume_{KNCSS}$ by a team of average size n

$Effort_{14}(Volume_{KNCSS}, \bar{n}, i, a_i = 0, d_i = 1.5)$

Conte, Dunsmore, and Shen **Version** of COPMO effort model expresses person-months required to produce an i effort complexity class (where model constants a_i is assumed to equal 0 and exponent of $\bar{n}$ is assumed to equal 1.5) **SoftwareProduct** of **Volume** $Volume_{KNCSS}$ by a team of average size n

We can measure productivity at all **Organization** and **SoftwareProduct** levels to determine the productivity of an **Organization**. Also, we can use the productivity prediction model to estimate how process changes will affect an **Organization**'s productivity. We can now use measurement and prediction models to improve productivity.

In the next section, we will describe productivity cost drivers and explore their effect on productivity.

PRODUCTIVITY COST DRIVERS

We will first look at the relationship between productivity and effort. Ideally, we would like productivity to be as high as possible. As productivity increases, the effort required to produce a given **Volume** decreases. Thus, effort is inversely proportional to productivity and can be expressed as

$$Effort = \frac{Volume_a}{Productivity} \tag{9.3}$$

Whenever productivity increases, effort is reduced, which results in reduced costs of producing a **SoftwareProduct**. In Chapter 7 we defined dominators as **Project** attributes that cause effort (and productivity) to vary by an order of magnitude. Dominators are also process cost drivers. To the list of dominators, we have added **Salary** as a cost driver. Within the United States, the **Salar(y)**ies are comparable for similarly experienced staff. When you compare software development in the United States with software development in other countries, the **Salar(y)**ies frequently can vary as much as 5 to 1 for software developers. In extreme cases, **Salar(y)**ies can vary by 10 to 1 or more.

Process cost driver attributes can be categorized into the same categories as dominators. The cost drivers that we will discuss are the following:

Overall **Project**   **Salary**
                             Development schedule constraints
                             Project life cycle process
Organization   Management quality
                             Lead designer
                             Individual developers
                             Number of people
                             Personnel turnover
                             Communications
SoftwareProduct   **Volume**
                             Amount of documentation
                             Programming language
                             Complexity

Type of application (includes required reliability)
Work breakdown structure

Suppliers   Software reuse

Customers   Interface
Requirements volatility

We will now examine the affect of process cost driver attributes on productivity.

OVERALL Project ATTRIBUTES

In this section, we will examine the effect of **Salar(y)**ies, development schedule constraints, and the **Project** life cycle process on productivity.

Salary

If all personnel are paid comparable **Salar(y)**ies, then **Salar(y)**ies are not a factor in determining productivity. But, if we can find a way to receive more output for the same money, then productivity is increased. **Salary** costs for the same work can be reduced by the three following techniques: (1) low **Salar(y)**ies, (2) unpaid overtime, and (3) contract labor.

Today we live in a world economy where inexpensive computers are available everywhere. Software can be developed anywhere that developers have access to computers. **Salar(y)**ies between the United States and other countries may vary as much as 3 to 1, 5 to 1, or in extreme cases 10 to 1. There are excellent software firms in countries like India where very low **Salar(y)**ies are paid. Many major industrial firms are contracting out their software development to **Area**s of the world that pay much lower **Salar(y)**ies. There are even firms in low-cost labor **Area**s like Lagos, Nigeria, that would like to compete for software development. Labor costs can be held to a minimum by sending software development **Project**s to **Area**s that have low labor costs.

The second way to hold **Salary** costs down is to have employees work extra hours for the same pay. Many computer professionals are classified as exempt from overtime. When they work a 60-hour week but are paid for a 40-hour week, the cost of labor can be reduced by a third. When **Project** schedules begin to fall behind, extra hours are frequently worked to meet the original schedule. This method is effective as long as employees are not expected to work long hours for extended periods. Employees who continually work long hours are susceptible to burnout.

A third common way to hold **Salary** costs down is to hire contract labor. When you use contract labor, you have more flexibility than when you hire permanent employees. You only pay contract labor while a software development **Project** is active. When the **Project** ends, you have no more responsibility for them. In addition, the cost of benefits is much lower for contract labor than for permanent employees.

When cost of input effort is reduced for producing the same output, productivity increases. When you have the opportunity to reduce **Salary** costs, you can realize major increases in productivity.

Development Schedule Constraints

In Chapter 8 we developed a number of development time models. Even with an infinite amount of resources, there is a minimum time that it will take to produce a **SoftwareProduct**. The software architecture and communication among team members directly affects the minimum time.

For a given architecture, there is an f_s defined as the ratio of time spent on sequential development to total sequential and parallel development. From equation 8.4, we know that even with an infinite number of programmers we cannot develop a software system in less than f_s times the time that a single programmer could develop the system.

Communications between team members affect the minimum development time. The communications factor f_c can be used to express the ratio of minimum team development time [$Time_{Minimum}(f_c)$] to one-member team development time [$T(1)$] (see equation 8.8) and the maximum number of team members for a given f_c (see equation 8.7). Table 9.1 shows minimum development time and maximum number of team members as a function of f_c. This table shows the minimum time that a team will take to create a **SoftwareProduct** over the time that a single programmer would take to produce the same **SoftwareProduct**. If each programmer communicates 5% of the time with each of the other programmers, then the minimum time is only 40% of that of a single programmer, no matter how many more programmers are added to the team. Any more than five programmers would actually reduce team productivity. If

Table 9.1   Minimum Development Time and Maximum Number of Team Members Versus f_c

f_c	$Time_{Minimum}(f_c)$ $T(1)$	$n_{Maximum}(f_c)$
0	0	∞
0.01	0.19	10
0.02	0.26	7.1
0.03	0.32	5.8
0.04	0.36	5.0
0.05	0.40	4.5

each programmer communicates 1% of the time with each of the other programmers, then the minimum time of a 10-programmer team is only 19% of the time it would take a single programmer to complete the task. More than 10 programmers on the team will cause team productivity to decline.

Assuming that we have a perfect design and there is no need to communicate between team members, we could have an infinite number of team members. This assumption is unrealistic. Team members have a need to communicate with each other. Table 9.1 shows that if team members communicate with each other 1% of the time then the maximum number of team members should be 10; 2% of the time, then the maximum number should be 7; 3% of the time, the maximum number should be 6, and so on. Simmons [Simmons91] has shown that a single interruption to communicate may take 2.33% of a programmer's productivity. Ten interruptions from team members would take 23.3% of the productive workday. Thus, a reasonable range for f_c expressed as a percent would be $4\% \geq f_c \geq 2\%$. The number of team members should be between five and seven. Productivity declines for larger team sizes. A system architecture should partition a software development **Project** into team work tasks that minimize the need to communicate between teams.

Large **Project**s require more than one team. Using empirically validated predictor equations like those described in Chapter 8, we can predict the nominal development time that a large software development **Project** should take to finish. For numerous reasons, often we would like to complete a **Project** in less than the nominal time. As we compress a schedule to complete a **Project** in less time, costs rise at a rapid rate, resulting in a loss in productivity. There is a minimum time required to complete a software **Project**. Boehm [Boehm81] stated that you cannot compress a schedule more than 25% below the nominal development time. Conte, Dunsmore, and Shen [Conte86] believe that costs rise rapidly, with a resulting decline in productivity, when you try to compress a schedule more than 15% of the nominal development time.

Project Life Cycle Process

As mentioned in Chapter 7, most software can be developed using a simple life cycle process. But many **Project**s require teams of programmers. Figure 9.1 displays the effect of software process life cycle on productivity. Three different software process life cycles are portrayed in Figure 9.1. The first life cycle is for developing small, simple programs where the customer knows the developer. The optimum **Software-Product Volume** for this life cycle is approximately 3.2 KNCSS, where productivity is over 5 KNCSS per person-year. Notice that as the **SoftwareProduct Volume** increases the productivity falls. The simple life cycle process is no longer effective for **SoftwareProduct**s larger than 10 KNCSS.

The second example is for a **SoftwareProduct** of medium complexity developed by a team of programmers. Because of fixed costs associated with this life cycle,

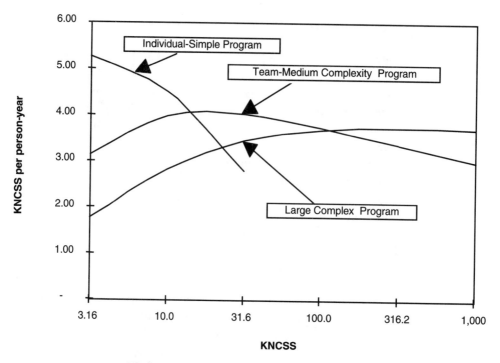

Figure 9.1   Software Process Life Cycle Comparison

it is costly when used with small programs. Figure 9.1 shows that the example life cycle for medium-complexity programs is optimum for development of 32-KNCSS **SoftwareProduct**s, where productivity is approximately 4 KNCSS per person-year.

The third example is a life-cycle for large, complex **Project**s that are usually developed by more than one team. Notice that the life cycle process for large, complex **SoftwareProduct**s is not effective for small- or medium-sized **Project**s. To optimize productivity, you should select the correct life cycle process for the **SoftwareProduct** that you plan to develop.

Organization **ATTRIBUTES**

At the beginning of a **Project** when we are in the hiring mode we have the most control over personnel selection. The success or failure of a **Project** often rests on the personnel that have been selected to work on the **Project**. In this section we will look at the effect on productivity of managers, designers, developers, and number of employees. We will then consider the effect on productivity of employee turnover and communications among team members.

Management Quality

When **Project** costs increase, productivity declines. Software management is an intangible but important factor that affects productivity. Boehm [Boehm81] says that poor management is the main factor that causes **Project** costs to increase. In fact, **Project** failure of large, complex **Project**s often can be traced to poor management. Poor management allows internal politics and power struggles to negatively affect **Project**s. Jones [Jones86] hypothesizes that 10% to 15% of the really catastrophic **Project** failures are at least partly caused by personal human dislikes and political or territorial disputes. Reifer [Reifer81], in his 18 principles of software management, states a principle that is too often used to select software managers:

> **Reifer's Peter Principle of Software Management:** Managers rise to their level of incompetence and then are transferred to head a software development **Project**.

Management quality is very difficult to measure. In selecting managers, those who have been successful in the past will probably be successful in the future. To be successful, a large software **Project** should be lead by a top experienced manager. Otherwise, productivity may decline and the **Project** might fail.

Lead Designer

The lead designer of a large, complex **Project** is another intangible but important factor that affects productivity. The lead designer makes the architectural decisions related to a **Project**. His decisions determine the work breakdown structure that results in **Assignment**s to **Individual**s. A great designer should be able to produce faster, smaller, simpler, and cleaner structures that can be produced in less time, resulting in higher productivity [Brooks87]. A great design should result in low f_s and f_c. Once a designer has proved himself or herself to be a great designer, they will probably succeed in the future. The best way to assure a great design is to select a lead designer who has created great designs in the past.

Individual Developers

All software development starts with the **Individual** developer. How much software can a single developer produce? What is the typical software productivity for an **Individual**? How much does productivity change between developers? We will now answer these questions.

Average Individual Productivity. The average productivity of **Individual**s working on **Project**s varies a great deal. In a speech to Hewlett–Packard software engineers in July 1983, Don McNamara of General Electric stated that the typical U.S. rate of software production is 100 to 500 NCSS per person-month (1.2 to 6.0 KNCSS per person-year) [McNamara83]. Four years later in 1987, Grady and Caswell reported results of a study of 75 **Project**s at Hewlett–Packard [Grady87]. They found the probability of producing a **SoftwareProduct** at a productivity rate between 300 and 500 NCSS per person-month (3.6 and 6.0 KNCSS per person-year) is 30% and between 250 and 600 NCSS per person-month (3.0 and 7.2 KNCSS per person-year) is 55%. They cautioned managers that few **Project**s achieved greater than 900 NCSS per person-month (10.8 KNCSS per person-year).

We can obtain a nominal rate from the effort equations described in Chapter 7. The highest nominal productivity rates for the 1981 COCOMO model are [Boehm81]

Basic: organic mode	5.0 KNCSS per person-year
Basic: semidetached mode	4.0 KNCSS per person-year
Basic: embedded mode	3.33 KNCSS per person-year

The highest nominal productivity rate for the 1995 COCOMO 2.0 model is [Boehm95]

COCOMO 2.0	4.0 KNCSS per person-year

These nominal rates fall within 55% of the 75 **Project**s evaluated by Grady and Caswell at Hewlett–Packard in 1987.

Individual Productivity Variations. We will now examine productivity range for **Individual** programmers. Corbato at the Massachusetts Institute of Technology developed a number of the early operating systems. In 1968, he claimed that the source lines of code (SLOC) produced per programmer during development of the CTSS system in assembler language was approximately the same as that produced by programmers during development of the MULTICS system using a high-level language [Corbato68]. From the work of Corbato and others, we can assume that for software of similar complexity, quality, and the like, the average rate of production of NCSS per person-month is approximately constant. Researchers have found that programmers have a limit to the rate that they can produce code, and the only way for an **Individual** to produce functions (or **SoftwareProduct Feature**s) at a higher rate is to program with a higher-level source language. Thus, the amount of software functions (and/or **Feature**s) produced depends on the source language used.

We will now examine the productivity variations among **Individual** programmers. Many of the statements on range of productivity variations are based on System Development Corporation (SDC) questionnaire data collected on 169 **Project**s that started as early as 1959. The SDC data were published as early as 1963 in an SDC handbook. From 1967 to 1970, while working in the Technology Directorate of SDC, Sackman conducted research on user problems in time-shared computing facilities [Sackman70]. His studies featured a large-scale experimental comparison of time sharing and batch in teaching computer science at the Air Force Academy and other experimental comparisons of student and programmer performance under on-line and off-line conditions. His work on range of computer programmer productivity variation has been quoted by software productivity researchers as 28:1, 26:1, 10:1, and 5:1.

In 1973, Boehm [Boehm73] stated that studies by Sackman and others [Sackman68] showed variations between **Individual**s account for differences in productivity of factors up to 26:1. Based on the Sackman studies, Mills stated in 1983 that there is an undisputed differential among practicing programmers of 10 to 1 [Mills83]. Conte, Dunsmore, and Shen [Conte86] state that the effect of **Individual** capability on productivity can be as large as 26:1, based on the work by Sackman [Sackman68]. In 1987, Boehm [Boehm87] stated that the moral of the Sackman studies is "Do everything you can to get the best people working on your **Project**."

Kemerer and Patrick [Kemerer93] point out that the software productivity by Sackman, Erikson, and Grant [Sackman68] measured **Individual** engineers solving the same problem with on-line terminals and off-line batch submissions. To the surprise of Sackman and his colleagues, they noticed a 28:1 difference in the time between the fastest and slowest solution to the problem. Kemerer and Patrick state that the 28:1 ratio is widely and inaccurately cited as the range of **Individual** programmer performance capability. They justify their statement by a 1981 clarification by Dickey [Dickey81], who said that the 28:1 (and we also assume the 26:1) arose by comparing one subject's 170-hour assembly language batch mode solution to an algebra problem to another subject's 6-hour high-level language time-sharing mode solution to the same problem. The large difference was obviously due more to the use of a time-inefficient language used in a time-inefficient manner. When the same language and system were used, the Sackman **Individual** productivity range difference was only 5:1.

Number of People

Large **SoftwareProduct**s are created by teams of developers. As we transition from an **Individual** software developer to a team of n developers, we expect the output **SoftwareProduct Volume** of a **Group** to continue to increase, while average productivity of a **Group** member decreases. The average productivity per person-year as a function of **Project** member size based on the 187-**Project** database of Conte et al. [Conte86] is

$$Productivity_{Conte}(n) = 9.32 \times n^{-0.5} \tag{9.4}$$

We can derive similar equations for the 63 **Project**s used to validate the COCOMO basic organic mode and embedded mode models, which are

$$Productivity_{COCOMO\_Basic\_Organic}(n) = 4.86 \times n^{-0.0768} \tag{9.5}$$

$$Productivity_{COCOMO\_Basic\_Embedded}(n) = 3.30 \times n^{-0.245} \tag{9.6}$$

A chart showing how nominal productivity varies as a function of n for these three cases is given in Figure 9.2. Notice that for single **Individual Project**s, the Conte data reflect a productivity of about 9.3 KNCSS per person-year. The Boehm COCOMO models reflects an **Individual** productivity of 4.9 KNCSS per person-year for organic mode **Project**s and 3.3 KNCSS per person-year for embedded mode **Project**s. For **Project**s that have between five and eight members per **Project**, the nominal productivity ranges from 2.0 to 4.2 KNCSS per person-year for all three models.

We will examine the effect of number of team members on the average productivity by using effort equation *Effort₇* to derive efficiency defined by Simmons [Simmons91]. He defines efficiency as

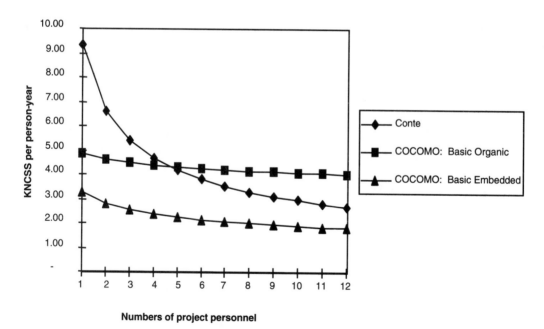

Numbers of project personnel

Figure 9.2   Productivity in KNCSS per Person-year versus Number of **Project** Personnel for the Conte et al. 187-**Project** Database and the COCOMO 63-**Project** Database

$$Efficiency_{6,7}(n, f_s, f_c) = \frac{Productivity_{6,7}(n, f_s, f_c)}{Productivity_{6,7}(1, f_s, f_c)}$$

$$= \frac{\dfrac{Volume_{a,6}}{Effort_7(n, f_s, f_c)}}{\dfrac{Volume_{a,6}}{Effort_7(1, f_s, f_c)}} \qquad (9.7)$$

$$= \frac{1}{1 + f_s \times (n-1) + n \times (n-1) \times f_c}$$

We assume that the highest productivity is when an **Individual** works alone on a single task and is not interrupted by others. Also, a single **Individual** does not have to worry about dividing a programming task into subtasks that can be worked on by more than one person. A team of two or more members is less efficient than an **Individual** working alone due to time lost interacting with other team members (that is, $f_c > 0$), and the programming task may not be divided into subtasks that can be worked on in parallel (that is, $f_s > 0$). For example, let's assume that we are working on a software development **Project** where $f_s = 0.1$ and $f_c = 0.015$. This means that each member of the team can work in parallel 90% with other team members without being delayed by other team members. Also, they are only interrupted about 1.5% of the time by each of the other team members. Figure 9.3 shows that for a one-member team the team is 100% efficient (that is, for a one-member team, f_s and f_c are irrelevant). For a two-member team, the team is 88% efficient. The decline in efficiency continues as members are added to the team. For a team of six members, the team is only 48% efficient.

We will now compare the efficiency of the Conte model, COCOMO basic organic mode model, and the COCOMO basic embedded mode model to the Simmons model. We will assume that software is developed by a single team of from 1 to 12 members. The efficiency of each of these models is charted in Figure 9.4 as a function of team size. Two different cases of the Simmons model are charted: One case assumes a perfect design partition with a communications factor of 0.0111 ($f_s = 0$, $f_c = 0.0111$), and the other case assumes a design partition with a sequential factor of 0.0974 and no communications ($f_s = 0.0974$, $f_c = 0$). The chart shows that, if communications burden is the main cause of declining productivity, then for the Conte model and Boehm COCOMO models, too much communication burden is applied to small teams and not enough communication burden is applied to large teams. If sequential factor is the primary cause of productivity decline, then a Simmons model curve with an appropriate sequential factor would approximately fit the other models.

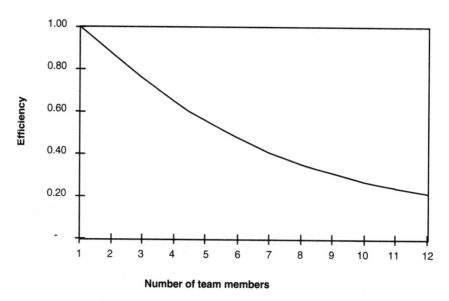

Figure 9.3   Team Efficiency versus Number of Team Members for $f_s = 0.1$ and $f_c = 0.015$

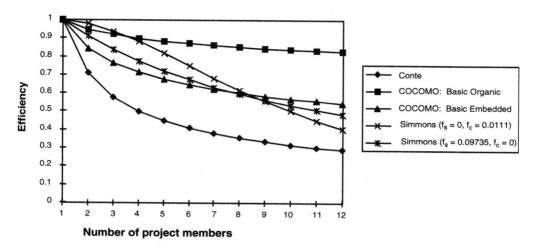

Figure 9.4   Efficiency versus Number of **Project** Members for Teams up to 12 Members

A concept closely related to efficiency is speedup. Simmons [Simmons91] defines speedup as

$$Speedup(n, f_s, f_c) = n \times Efficiency(n, f_s, f_c)$$

$$= \frac{n}{1 + f_s \times (n-1) + n \times (n-1) \times f_c} \qquad (9.8)$$

For the case where $f_s = 0$ and $f_c = 0$, $Speedup(n, f_s = 0, f_c = 0) = n$. This would mean that a six-member team would produce six times as many source statements as a single **Individual**. For our example, where $f_s = 0.1$ and $f_c = 0.015$, the speedup is shown in Figure 9.5. For a two-member team, instead of a speedup of 2, only a speedup of 1.75 is realized. For a four-member team, only a speedup of 2.60 is realized. For this example, there is no reason to have a team of more than four members. In fact, for more than seven members, the speedup of the team actually declines.

We will now chart in Figure 9.6 speedup for the Conte model, Boehm CO-COMO models, and Simmons model. Notice for the Simmons model with a communications factor of 0.0111 ($f_s = 0$, $f_c = 0.0111$), the speedup peaks at about 10 members and then declines. This implies that team size should be kept small enough that the communication factor does not become a problem.

When you organize teams, you should try to minimize the values of f_s and f_c. Once you have done that and selected an appropriate team size, every effort should be made to not require excessive communications among teams. Unnecessary communications among teams will cause overall productivity to decline further.

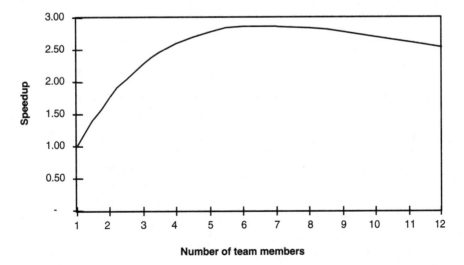

Figure 9.5 Speedup versus Numbers of Team Members for $f_s = 0.1$ and $f_c = 0.015$

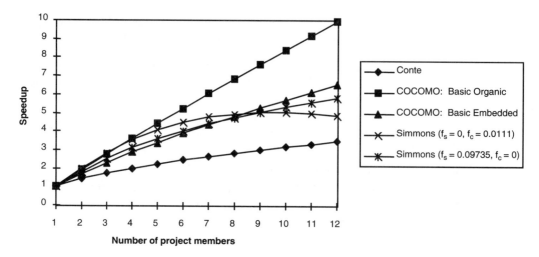

Figure 9.6   Speedup versus Number of **Project** Members for Teams up to 12 Members

Personnel Turnover

Costs related to turnover can cause productivity to decline and **Project**s to fail. Simmons observed that anyone who has been involved in writing large programs has observed personnel turnover problems [Simmons72]. Corbato said that when planning a long-term programming **Project** one should assume that there will be roughly a 20% per year personnel turnover [Corbato68]. Boehm had originally thought of including a turnover-related cost driver in the COCOMO model [Boehm81], but he decided not to because

- it is difficult to define precisely,
- critical personnel turnover problems are not easy to predict in advance, and
- a large majority of the COCOMO **Project** data points indicated an average level of personnel turnover, making it very difficult to ascertain the factor's influence on software cost.

Jones observed that the U.S. average programmer turnover rate in 1985 was 12% [Jones86]. He also observed a few **Individual** enterprises with attrition rates of 65% for staff sizes in excess of 100 technical employees. These rates, or course, are catastrophic.

In summary, even when a **Project** experiences low personnel turnover rates, the resignation of a few key personnel can cause major problems. On long-development **Project**s you can expect between 12% and 20% personnel turnover rates. If turnover begins to exceed 30%, a special effort should be made to see what is causing the turnover, and every effort should be made to reverse the trend.

Communications

In this section, we will examine the effect of communications expressed as f_c on productivity. We will assume that we have a prefect design ($f_s = 0$) and team members can work in parallel without the need to wait on another team member to complete a task. From equation 9.4 we can express productivity as

$$Productivity_{6,7}(n, f_s = 0, f_c) = Efficiency(n, f_s = 0, f_c) \times Productivity_{6,7}(n = 1) \quad (9.9)$$

We can see that productivity is directly proportional to efficiency. Thus, if we can improve efficiency, we can improve productivity. In the following we will examine the effect of f_c on efficiency.

The communications factor f_c is the ratio of time that a team member spends responding to interruptions for communications compared to the total time available for software development. We will first determine the amount of time during a typical workday that is available for software development.

All kinds of activities take time away from active software development. A team member may actually begin software development a few minutes after official work time begins in the morning and after lunch and may stop a few minutes before lunch and quitting time. During the day, coffee breaks and other types of breaks occur frequently. Also, there are meetings and training sessions that everyone must attend. Due to the many nonsoftware development tasks, a highly productive developer spends 51% to 79% of a day productively working on software development [Scott75]. We will assume that software developers spend 5 hours (300 minutes) of an 8-hour day or 62.5% as productive time. As the size of their work **Group** grows, they are interrupted more often by members of the **Group** for both work-related and nonwork-related reasons. Each interruption takes time away from the productive development time.

Esterling [Esterling80] found that the average duration of a work interruption was 5 minutes for a typical programmer. The average time to regain a train of thought after an interruption was 2 minutes. Thus, the average total time spent on a typical interruption of active development was approximately 7 minutes or 2.33% of the workday (or 0.107% of the work month). Ten interruptions of the productive time would take 23.3%, and 20 interruptions would take 46.6%. You can see that excessive interruptions can be catastrophic to a **Project.**

We will now determine f_c for typical team sizes. For an eight-member team where each member is interrupted by each other member once a month, f_c would be 0.015; twice a month, f_c would be 0.03; and three times a month, f_c would be 0.045.

Members of small teams would interrupt each other more often. For teams of three, four, and five, members that interrupt each other three times a month, the f_c would be 0.013, 0.019, and 0.026 respectively.

We will now determine efficiency as a function of f_c. Using equation 9.4, the equation for $f_s = 0$ becomes

$$Efficiency(n, f_s = 0, f_c) = \frac{1}{1 + n \times (n-1) \times f_c} \qquad (9.10)$$

A plot of efficiency versus number of team members for typical values of f_c is displayed in Figure 9.7. Notice that as the communication factor increases the efficiency declines rapidly. For the same communication factors, speedup versus number of team members is portrayed in Figure 9.8. For the case $f_c = 0$, where there is no need to communicate, a 12-member team would be 12 times as productive as a one-member team, which means that the speedup is 12. For a 12-member team with $f_c = 0.005$, the speedup would equal 7.23; with $f_c = 0.01$, the speedup would equal 5.17; and with $f_c = 0.02$, the speedup would equal 3.0. As the f_c increases, the speedup for a 12-member team declines.

By inspection of Figure 9.8, we see that for each value of f_c there is a maximum point where there is no need to add team members. We can use equation 8.7 to compute the maximum number of team members for which additional members do not cause productivity to decline. Table 9.2 shows the maximum $n_{Maximum}$ for each f_c. For a team where no communications takes place, productivity continues to increase

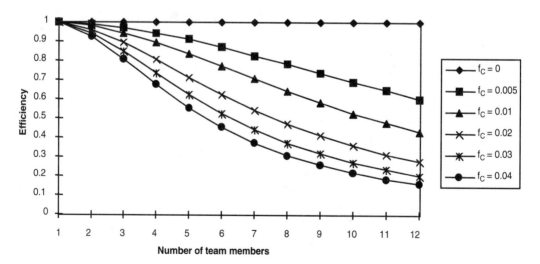

Figure 9.7 *Efficiency(n,f_s = 0,f_c)* versus Number of Team Members

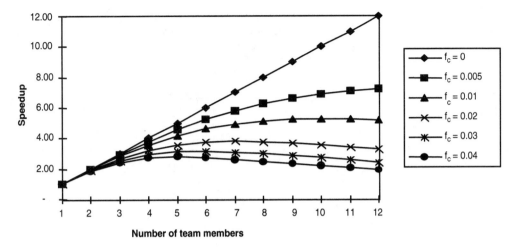

Figure 9.8 *Speedup(n, $f_s = 0$, f_c)* versus Number of Team Members

as long a members are added to the team. For a f_c of 0.005, team productivity peaks for a 14-member team; for f_c of 0.01, it peaks at 10 members; and for f_c of 0.02, it peaks at 7 members.

We can also solve for the maximum f_c for a given team size. Using equation 8.7, the equation for maximum f_c is

$$f_{c_{MAXIMUM}}(n) = \frac{1}{n^2} \tag{9.11}$$

Table 9.3 lists the $f_{cMAXIMUM}$ for team size 1 through 12. Notice that for a an eight-member team the $f_{c_{MAXIMUM}}$ is only 0.016. If the communications activity exceeds 0.016, the team would probably be more productive with fewer members. A communications factor of 0.015 is a typical value for a software development team. This

Table 9.2 Maximum Number of Team Members for a Given f_c

f_c	$n_{Maximum}(f_c)$
0	∞
0.005	14.14
0.01	10.0
0.02	7.07
0.03	5.77
0.04	5.0

**Table 9.3   Maximum
Communications Factor
as a Function of Number
of Team Members**

n	$f_{c_{MAXIMUM}}(n)$
1	1.0
2	0.25
3	0.11
4	0.625
5	0.04
6	0.023
7	0.02
8	0.016
9	0.012
10	0.01
11	0.008
12	0.007

would imply that team size should be held to eight or less members. As the value of the communications factor increases, the size of teams should be reduced to assure maximum productivity.

SoftwareProduct **ATTRIBUTES**

In this section we will examine the effect of **SoftwareProduct** attributes **Volume**, documentation, source language, complexity, type of application, and work breakdown structure on productivity.

Volume

For a number of years, researchers have maintained **Project** databases describing attributes of successful completed **Project**s. Using the data points in these **Project** databases, we can compute nominal effort and productivity. Coefficients for nominal productivity are the same as the nominal effort model equation coefficients that are listed in Table 7.6. The productivity model in productivity per person year for Table 7.6 coefficients is

$$Productivity_{6,5}[Volume_{KNCSS}, a, b, c, m(X) = 1] = \frac{Volume_{KNCSS,6}}{Effort_5} \times 12 \quad (9.12)$$

Representative models from Table 7.6 are plotted in Figure 9.9. These equations show how nominal productivity varies with **SoftwareProduct Volume.** We will examine the effect of equation 9.12 for the following three cases: $c < 1$, $c = 1$, and $c > 1$.

Case 1: c < 1. The Walston and Felix model shows what happens when $c < 1$. They validated their model equation using data gathered for 60 **Project**s by the software measurements program of the IBM Federal Systems Division. The IBM Federal Systems Division develops software for the federal government. This software has high start-up costs and high documentation costs for each program. They stated that the relationship between pages of documentation and **Volume** of delivered code was

$$Documentation = 49 \times Volume_{KNCSS}^{1.01} \qquad (9.13)$$

Since the exponent of *Volume* is approximately equal to 1.0, this means that the amount of documentation was independent of size. They required approximately 50 pages of document for every 1,000 lines of source code no matter how large the system. Because of their excessive overhead, their nominal productivity was optimum for large software development **Project**s. Their nominal productivity in KNCSS per person-year equation was

$$Productivity_{6.5}(Volume_{KNCSS}, a = 0, b = 5.2, c = .91) = 2.31 \times Volume_{NCSS}^{0.09} \qquad (9.14)$$

The positive exponent signifies that nominal productivity increases with size. The data used to validate the Walston and Felix model equation varies from a 25% quartile at 10 KNCSS to a 75% quartile at 59 KNCSS. The Walston and Felix equation

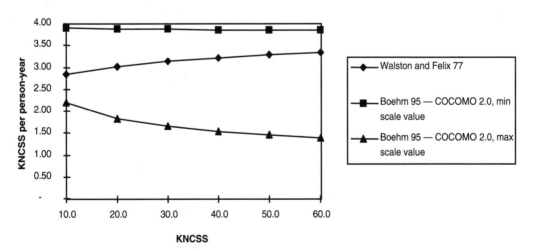

Figure 9.9 Nominal Productivity versus **SoftwareProduct Volume** for 10 KNCSS to 60 KNCSS Software **Project**s

is plotted from 10 KNCSS to 60 KNCSS in Figure 9.9. For the high-overhead government **Project**s developed by IBM Federal Systems Division, nominal productivity actually increases as **Project** grow.

Case 2: c = 1. Nominal productivity for well-run simple **Project**s with low overhead would not vary a lot as **SoftwareProduct Volume** increases. An example of this type of **Project** would be Boehm's COCOMO 2.0 model with minimal scale value for the exponent. These **Project**s are similar to the original COCOMO organic mode **Project**s, which were relatively small in size, requiring little innovation, having relaxed delivery requirements, and being developed in a stable in-house environment. The nominal productivity in person-years for case 2 is

$$Productivity_{6.5}(Volume_{KNCSS}, a=0, b=3.0, c=1.01) = 4.0 \times Volume_{KNCSS}^{-0.01} \quad (9.15)$$

The Boehm model for $c = 1.01$ is plotted in Figure 9.9. For the Boehm model, $c = 1.01 \approx 1.0$. If c were actually equal to zero, then the nominal productivity for Boehm's model would be

$$Productivity_{6.5}(Volume_{KNCSS}, a=0, b=3.0, c=1.0) = 4.0 \quad (9.16)$$

For this case the nominal productivity for Boehm's case would be constant at 4.0.

Case 3: c > 1. Most software development **Project**s follow this third case, where $c > 0$. Productivity is high and overhead is low for small **Project**s. As the **Volume** of **Project**s grows, the overhead increases and the effective productivity decreases. In Boehm's COCOMO 2.0 model, his scale factor for nominal productivity grows from 1.01 to a maximum of 1.26. These **Project**s, where $c = 1.26$, are similar to the original COCOMO embedded mode **Project**s, which were relatively large, needed to operate within tight constraints, had a high degree of hardware and **Customer** interface complexity, rigid requirements, and greater need for innovation. If we assume the worst case for nominal productivity recommended by Boehm, the nominal productivity equation would be

$$Productivity_{6.5}(Volume_{KNCSS}, a=0, b=3.0, c=1.26) = 4.0 \times Volume_{KNCSS}^{-0.26} \quad (9.17)$$

The Boehm model for the case where $c = 1.26$ is plotted in Figure 9.9. Notice that as the **Volume** of a **SoftwareProduct** increases from 10 KNCSS to 60 KNCSS the nominal productivity decreases from 2.2 KNCSS per person-year to 1.38 KNCSS per person-year. If we compared the nominal productivity for this case over the range of 1 to 1,000 KNCSS, we would find that the COCOMO 2.0 model nominal productivity can vary as much as 6 to 1.

We see that the three model equations in the range of 10 to 60 KNCSS shown in Figure 9.9 behave in a reasonable manner. The worst case and the best case for Boehm's model equations include the specific results found by Walston and Felix.

When we examine the productivity for small **Project**s, we find that they do not follow the same nominal productivity equations of larger **Project**s. Often there is a location-dependent fixed cost that should be associated with each of the **Project**s. Fixed costs bias productivity equations against small **Project**s. In fact, large companies that have high fixed costs often are not competitive with small **Organization**s with low fixed costs.

We can see the effect of fixed costs by examining the work of Bailey and Basili [Bailey81]. They used as a database a set of 18 **Project**s developed at NASA Goddard Space Flight Center. Their **Project**s were mainly scientific-type programs written in the FORTRAN language. Their coefficients for equation 7.7 are listed in Table 7.6. We can compute productivity in person years using equation 7.7 and the productivity definition equation 9.2:

$$Productivity_{6.5}(Volume_{KNCSS}, a, b, c) = \frac{Volume_{KNCSS}}{a + b \times Volume_{KNCSS}^{c}} \times 12$$

$$= \frac{1}{\dfrac{a}{Volume_{KNCSS}} + b \times Volume_{KNCSS}^{c-1}} \times 12$$

(9.18)

The **Volume** of the coefficients used by Bailey and Basili were based on 80% new code and 20% reused code. Also, their coefficients assumed that comments were included. Thus, we will adjust their coefficients to reflect KNCSS. We will divide the *a* and *b* coefficients by 0.8 to reflect all new code and by 0.75 to reflect no comments. Figure 9.10 shows the result of the fixed cost reflected in the Bailey and Basili model. Productivity declines due to the effect of the fixed costs on small **Project**s.

Case 1, where $c < 1.0$, used as an example the data gathered by Walston and Felix for high-overhead government **Project**s. Their model used a value of $c = 0.91$. We can apply a least-squares best fit of the Walston and Felix model to the Bailey and Basili model. If we assume that $c = 1.01$ and the fixed effort per **Project** is $a = 5.0$, then the best fit of the *b* coefficient would be $b = 2.58$. Figure 9.11 shows a comparison of the modified Walston and Felix model to the Bailey and Basili model. We feel that the modified version of the Walston and Felix model is a more realistic representation of the real-world situation.

Documentation

The life cycle process can require more effort to be spent on documentation than on the production and testing of code. For example, the Jet Propulsion Laboratory uses a software life cycle (SLC) of 10 phases that has 38 separate documents as deliverables [Shere88]. The 38 documents all cost money. Each document that is added to

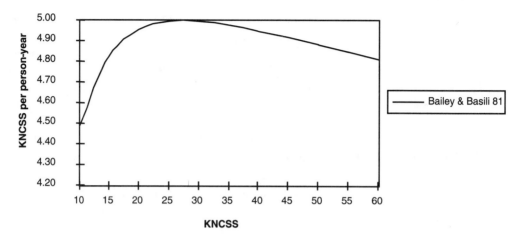

Figure 9.10   Productivity versus **Volume** Based on the Bailey and Basili Data from 18 **Project**s at NASA Goddard Space Flight Center

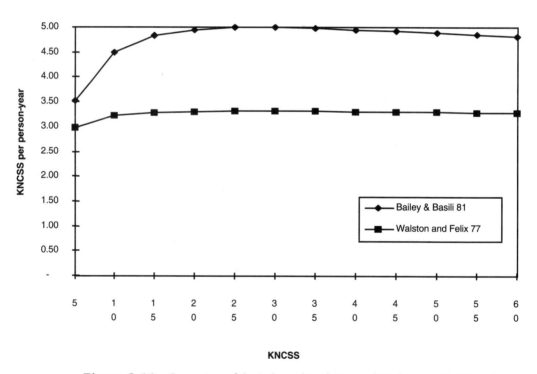

Figure 9.11   Comparison of the Bailey and Basili Nominal Productivity Model to the Modified Walston and Felix Model

a **Project** increases costs and reduces productivity. Productivity can be significantly improved by replacing many of the expensive person-intensive documents with inexpensive, nonintrusive metrics [Simmons92].

Source Language

The first computers were programmed directly in binary. Programmers very quickly started programming at the alphabetic character level and developed assemblers to translate their source-level programs into the binary objects code interpretable by computers. A third generation resulted when programmers developed higher-level languages that better matched the problem domain known to the computer users. Scientific high-level languages like FORTRAN and ALGOL were developed for the scientific domain, and COBOL was developed to solve business problems. There have been literally thousands of third-generation languages developed to better match the computer users problem domain to the computer language.

The rate at which a programmer produces source statements is independent of the language level. You are more productive when you use a higher-level language because you can produce more functions with fewer source statements. One way to measure software functionality is to determine the source statements required to produce a function point, which is a dimentionless metric defined by Albrecht [Albrecht79]. Figure 7.1 lists the number of NCSS per function point.

An assembler language program requires approximately 320 NCSS to produce a function point. If you use FORTRAN to produce a scientific program, you should be able to produce a function point with approximately 107 statements, which is a three-fold productivity improvement over coding scientific programs in assembler language. A developer using a forth-generation language can be up to 8 times as productive, an object language like Smalltalk 15 times as productive, a spread-sheet language 50 times as productive, and a graphic-icon-based language 80 times as productive.

When comparing productivity gains within language level, we can compare **Project**s directly using our standard definition of productivity that measures productivity in NCSS per person-month. When you compare productivity across different language levels, you will encounter one of the software measurement paradoxes described by Jones [Jones86].

> **Source statement measurement paradox:** Lines-of-code (source statements) measures penalize high-level languages and often move in the wrong direction as productivity improves.

We will use an example to explain the source statement measurement paradox. Assume that there is a software development **Project** to produce a system with requirements that can be measured as 300 function points. The requirements, design, documentation, and system test activities will require approximately 50 person-months. The coding phase will include unit test activities. Assume that during coding a programmer can produce 1,000 NCSS per person-month. Using Figure 7.1 to convert function points to NCSS, we can calculate the productivity. Table 9.4 shows the expected productivity for assembler, FORTRAN, and C++ languages.

Notice that the productivity for the entire software life cycle using assembler is 658 NCSS per person-month, FORTRAN is 391 NCSS per person-month, and C++ is 148 NCSS per person-month. This would imply that productivity declines as the level of the language increases. We know this is not true because the total person-months decline from 146 for assembler to 82.1 for FORTRAN and 58.7 for C++. Since all the **SoftwareProduct**s have the same functionality (that is, 300 function points), the total costs for the same functionality decrease as the language level increases. Notice that the productivity expressed in terms of function points increases with language level. Thus, to avoid the effects of the source language statement paradox, make sure that you only use productivity expressed in NCSS per person-month when comparing software **Project**s that use the same level of source language. When you compare productivity of **Project**s that use different levels of source languages, you should use a **Volume** metric like function points that measures the **Volume** of **Customer** requirements that are satisfied.

Complexity

When we refer to complex software, we mean that the software is either computationally complex or structurally complex. A **SoftwareProduct** is computationally complex if it takes an excessive amount of computer time to find a solution. A **SoftwareProduct** is structurally complex if it is difficult to understand and to follow. In this book we are interested in structural complexity that we can measure. We discussed in Chapter 6 that a well-structured **SoftwareProduct** should be cohesive, loosely coupled, structured, properly scoped, nonpathological, shallow, and small in live variables, spans, **Chunk**-global variable usage pairs, **Chunk**-global variable usage

Table 9.4   Productivity Comparison for Different Lanugage Levels

Source Lanugage	NCSS	NCSS per Person-month	Non-coding Person-months	Coding Person-months	Total Person-months	NCSS per Person-month	Function Points per Person-month
Assembler	96,000	1,000	50	96.0	146.0	658	2.1
FORTRAN	32,100	1,000	50	32.1	82.1	391	3.7
C++	8,700	1,000	50	8.7	58.7	148	5.1

triples, and information flow. Our productivity is higher when we produce simple software that is low in complexity.

We will now look at how much structural complexity affects productivity. Boehm [Boehm81] found that a complex **SoftwareProduct** can take 2.36 times as much effort to produce as a simple **SoftwareProduct**. We feel that a properly written, structurally complex **SoftwareProduct** can result in productivity variations as high as 10:1 over a simple **SoftwareProduct**. You can directly measure software structural complexity using the metrics described in Chapter 6 and keep it under control.

Type of Application (Includes Required Reliability)

A report is much simpler to produce than a highly reliable real-time system. Major telecommunication switching systems are designed to be down less that 2 hours in 40 years, which means that they can be out of service for only 0.00057% of the time and meet their design goals. Software in weapons of mass destruction have even higher constraints on all aspects of the software design and development. The type of allocation can cause the productivity to vary by more than 10 to 1.

Work Breakdown Structure

A large software development **Project** should be organized in a manner so that multiple teams and members of teams can work on the **Project** in parallel. The key designer/architect creates the work breakdown structure that defines tasks for **Individual** software developers. Very few **Project**s achieve perfect parallelization. Frequently, software developers have to wait on a work task of a colleague before they can complete their task. In Chapter 7 we defined sequential factor f_s as the ratio of time spent on sequential tasks to the total time spent on both sequential and parallel tasks, where $1.0 \geq f_s \geq 0$. Efficiency as a function of f_s is

$$Efficiency_{6,7}(n, f_s \geq 0, f_c = 0) = \frac{1}{1 + f_s \times (n-1)} \tag{9.19}$$

Efficiency for this case is plotted in Figure 9.12 for $0.3 \geq f_s \geq 0$. The highest efficiency occurs when $f_s = 0$. As the value of f_s increases, efficiency decreases.

Speedup as a function of f_s can be expressed as

$$Speedup_{6,7}(n, f_s \geq 0, f_c = 0) = \frac{n}{1 + f_s \times (n-1)} \tag{9.20}$$

Speedup for this case is plotted in Figure 9.13, where $0.3 \geq f_s \geq 0$. For a **Project** for which the design can be perfectly partitioned into n parts, the speedup is equal to n. In real life, these **Project**s do not exist. We can see by examining Figure 9.13 that for

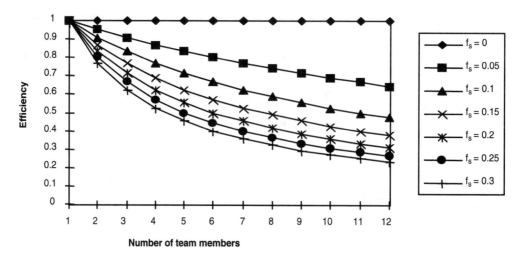

Figure 9.12   *Efficiency*$_{6,7}$($n, f_s \geq 0, f_c = 0$) versus Number of Team Members

a six-member team, where $f_s = 0.1$, the speedup would be 4, for $f_s = 0.2$ the speedup would be 3.0, and for $f_s = 0.3$ the speedup would be 2.4. The maximum speedup for a **Project** is

$$Speedup_{6,7}(n, f_s \rightarrow \infty, f_c = 0) = \frac{1}{f_s}$$ (9.21)

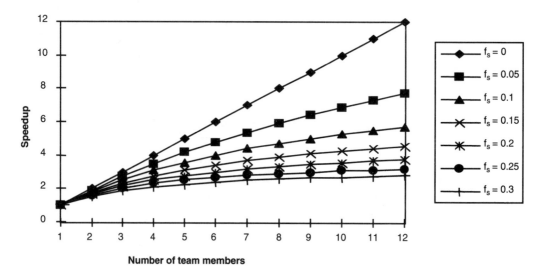

Figure 9.13   *Speedup*$_{6,7}$($n, f_s \geq 0, f_c = 0$) versus Number of Team Members

This says that, even with an infinite number of software developers, there is a known limit to the speedup achievable. For $f_s = 0.1$, the maximum speedup is 10, for $f_s = 0.2$ the maximum speedup is 5, and for $f_s = 0.3$ the maximum speedup is 3.3.

Supplier **ATTRIBUTES**

In this section we will examine the effect of the **Supplier** attribute reuse on software productivity.

Software Reuse

The highest level of productivity is when we decide not to produce a software system, but instead to reuse one that already exists. Software reuse is one of the only ways to remain competitive when producing large systems. Reusable **Chunk**s of code must be developed and creatively reused. Object-oriented methodology is used to encapsulate procedures and data into reusable **Chunk**s. As we program at higher and higher source language levels, in reality we are developing **SoftwareProduct**s with larger and larger **Chunk**s of reusable code. Reusable software is one of the major techniques for improving productivity.

Customer **ATTRIBUTES**

In this section we will examine the effect of **Customer** attributes **SoftwareProduct** interface and requirements volatility on software productivity.

Interface

The **Customer** interface can mean the person-to-person interface between the **Customer** and the developer or it can mean the interface between the **Customer** and the **SoftwareProduct**. A complex **Customer**-to-developer interface can lead to many misunderstandings and to high cost development with resulting low productivity. A complex **Customer** to **SoftwareProduct** interface can result in an unsatisfied **Customer**. An unsatisfied **Customer** can lead to a **SoftwareProduct** that is not used, which results in an unsuccessful **SoftwareProduct**. **Usability** metrics can help us predict **Customer** satisfaction with the interface and with the **Software-Product**.

Requirements Volatility

In any major software development **Project,** there will be requirements that change. Some requirements volatility should be expected on all **Project**s. Excessive volatility can lead to major cost overruns and eventually to failed **Project**s. You should do everything that you can to minimize requirements volatility. You should work closely with **Customer**s to determine their needs. After requirements have been developed, the **Customer** should be consulted to assure that the resulting **Software-Product** will satisfy his or her needs. During early design, prototypes should be used to give the **Customer** a feel for the finished **SoftwareProduct**. Once actual development begins, you should have **Customer** support for the requirements.

Even though you do everything that you can to prevent changes in requirements, things can happen that will still require major perturbations in the requirements. If this happens, there will be major cost increases, schedule slips, and the resulting negative effect on productivity.

SUMMARY

In this chapter we have shown how to measure productivity by measuring **Soft-wareProduct Volume** and the effort required to produce the **SoftwareProduct**. We then developed a productivity prediction model based on **Volume** and effort prediction models. Productivity prediction models use some form of a nominal value prediction model that applies an adjustment multiplier to the nominal value to find the effect that cost drivers have on the nominal value. We reviewed 18 cost driver attributes and explained how they affect productivity and cause the nominal values to change.

Many of the cost drivers were used in Chapter 7 as adjustment multipliers for the effort prediction equations. Some of the cost drivers, such as management quality and lead designer quality, have a major effect on large-**Project** productivity, but they are hard to measure and to predict. Others, such as requirements volatility, are easy to measure at the end of a **Project,** but hard to predict at the beginning of a **Project.** We added **Salary** as a productivity cost driver because, if we measure effort in total dollars spent on labor, anything that we can do to reduce the **Salary** cost of labor will improve productivity.

To accurately predict productivity for a specific **Project,** we must know the effect of each cost driver attribute on the **Project.** Many of the **Individual** cost drivers can dominate the productivity and can have a 10:1 negative impact on productivity. **Project**s that incorrectly estimate productivity result in budget overruns and often in a failed **Project.** When cost driver attributes begin to significantly vary from nominal values, action should be taken to bring them back into an acceptable range.

REFERENCES

[Albrecht79]   Albrecht, A. J., "Measuring Application Development Productivity," *Proceedings of the Joint SHARE/GUIDE/IBM Application Development Symposium,* October 1979, pp. 83–92.

[Bailey & Basili81]   Bailey, J. W., and Basili, V. R., "A meta-model for software development resource expenditures," *Proceedings of the Fifth International Conference on Software Engineering,* 1981, pp. 107–116.

[Boehm73]   Boehm, B. W., "Software and Its Impact: A Quantitative Assessment," *Datamation,* May 1973, pp. 48–59.

[Boehm81]   Boehm, B. W., *Software Engineering Economics,* Prentice-Hall, Inc., Upper Saddle River, NJ, 1981.

[Boehm87]   Boehm, B. W., "Industrial Software Metrics Top 10 List," *IEEE Software,* September 1987, pp. 84–85.

[Boehm95]   Boehm, B., Horowitz, E., Selby, R., and Westland, J. C., *COCOMO 2.0 User's Manual,* Version 1.1, Copyrighted by University of Southern California, Received in April, 1995.

[Brooks87]   Brooks, Jr., F. P., "No silver bullet essence and accidents of software engineering," *IEEE Computer,* April 1987, pp. 10–19.

[Conte86]   Conte, S. D., Dunsmore, H. E., and Shen, V. Y., *Software Engineering Metrics and Models,* Benjamin/Cummings Publishing Co., Inc., Menlo Park, CA, 1986.

[Corbato68]   Corbato, F. J., *Sensitive Issues in the Design of Multiuse Systems,* Massachusetts Institute of Technology, December, 12, 1968.

[DeMarco87]   DeMarco, T., and Lister, T., *Peopleware,* Dorset House, New York, 1987.

[Dickey81]   Dickey, T. E., "Programmer Variability," *Proceedings of the IEEE,* Vol. 69, No. 7, 1981, pp. 844–845.

[Esterling80]   Esterling, B., "Software manpower costs: a model," *Datamation,* March 1980, pp. 164–170.

[Farr & Zagorski65]   Farr, L., and Zagorski, H. J., "Quantitative analysis of programming cost factors: a progress report," *ICC Symposium Proceedings on Economics of Automatic Data Processing,* edited by A. B. Frielind, North Holland, Amsterdam, 1965.

[Frederic74]   Frederic, B. C., "A Provisional Model for Estimating Computer Program Development Costs," Tecolote Research, Inc., December 1974.

[Grady87]   Grady, R. B., and Caswell, D. L., *Software Metrics: Establishing a Company-wide Program,* Prentice Hall, Upper Saddle River, NJ, 1987.

[Halstead77]   Halstead, M. H., *Elements of Software Science,* Elsevier, New York, 1977.

[Herd, Postak, Russell, & Stewart77]   Herd, J. R., Postak, J. N., Russell, W. E., and Steward, K. R., "Software cost estimation study—study results," Final Technical Report, *RADC-TR-77-220,* Doty Associates, Inc., Rockville, MD, June 1977.

[IEEE89]   Software Productivity Metrics Working Group, "Standard for Software Productivity Metrics," IEEE, Standard P1045/D20. November 20, 1989.

[Jenkins84]   Jenkins, A. M., Naumann, J. D., and Wetherbe, J. C., "Empirical Investigation of Systems Developed Practices and Results," *Information Management*, Vol. 7, 1984, pp. 73–82.

[Johnson77]   Johnson, J. R., "In This Scientific World, Productivity Is Only Productivity If It Is Measurable," *Datamation*, February 1977.

[Jones77]   Jones, C., "Program Quality and Programmer Productivity," *IBM Technical Report TR 02.764,* January 1977, pp. i, 42–78.

[Jones86]   Jones, C., *Programming Productivity*, McGraw-Hill Book Co., New York, 1986.

[Kemerer93]   Kemerer, C. F., and Patrick, M. W., "Staffing Factor in Software Cost Estimation Models," *Software Engineering Productivity Handbook*, edited by J. Keyes, Windcrest/McGraw-Hill, New York, 1993, pp. 175–190.

[McNamara83]   McNamara, D., Presentation to Hewlett–Packard engineers, Cupertino, CA, July 1983.

[Mills83]   Mills, H. D., *Software Productivity*, Little, Brown and Company, Boston, 1983.

[Nelson66]   Nelson, E. A., "Management handbook for the estimation of computer programming costs," *AD-A648750,* Systems Development Corporation, October 31, 1966.

[Nelson70]   Nelson, E. A., "Some Recent Contributions to Computer Programming Management," *On the Management of Computer Programming,* edited by G. F. Weinwurm, Auerbach Publishers, Inc., 1970, pp. 159–184.

[Nelson78]   Nelson, R., *Software Data Collection and Analysis at RADC,* Rome Air Development Center, Rome, NY, 1978.

[Phan88]   Phan, D., Vogel, D., and Nunamaker, J., "The Search for Perfect Project Management," *Computerworld*, 1988, pp. 95–100.

[Phister79]   Phister, Jr., M., *Data Processing Technology and Economics,* Digital Press, Bedford, MA, 1979.

[Reifer81]   Reifer, D. J., "The Nature of Software Management: A Primer," *Tutorial: Software Management,* IEEE, New York, 1981, pp. 9–12.

[Sackman68]   Sackman, H., Erikson, W. J., and Grant, E. E., "Exploratory Experimental Studies Comparing On-line and Off-line Programming Performance," *Communications of the ACM*, Vol. 11, No. 1, pp. 3–11.

[Sackman70]   Sackman, H., *Man–Computer Problem Solving*, Auerbach Publishers, Inc., Princeton, NJ, 1970.

[Scott75]   Scott, R. F., and Simmons, D. B., "Predicting Programming Group Productivity—A Communications Model," *IEEE Transactions on Software Engineering*, Vol. SE-1, No. 4, 1975, pp. 411–414.

[Shere88]   Shere, K. D., *Software Engineering and Management*, Prentice Hall, Upper Saddle River, NJ, 1988.

[Simmons72]   Simmons, D. B., "The Art of Writing Large Programs," *Computer*, published by the IEEE, New York, March/April 1972, pp. 43–49.

[Simmons91]   Simmons, D. B., "Communications: a software group productivity dominator," *IEEE Software Engineering Journal,* November 1991, pp. 454–462.

[Simmons92] Simmons, D. B., "A Win–Win Metric Based Software Management Approach," *IEEE Transactions on Engineering Management*, Vol. 39, No. 1, February 1992, pp. 32–41.

[Thebaut83] Thebaut, S. M., *The Saturation Effect in Large-Scale Software Development: its Impact and Control*, Ph.D. Thesis, Department of Computer Science, Purdue University, West Lafayette, IN, May 1983.

[Walston & Felix77] Walston, C. E., and C. P. Felix, "A method of programming measurement and estimation," *IBM Systems Journal*, Vol. 16, No. 1, 1977, pp. 54–73.

[Walston & Felix77a] Walston, C. E., and C. P. Felix, "Authors' response," *IBM Systems Journal*, Vol. 16, No. 4, 1977, pp. 54–73.

10

Quality

There is a direct relationship between quality and sales, quality and productivity, quality and profit, quality and competitive position. Good quality will lead to good things, such as increased profits, improved productivity, lower cost, and loyal customers. Quality is the responsibility of management.

Charles H. Schmauch
[Schmauch94]

INTRODUCTION

The purpose of this chapter is to present software quality as an integrated concept that includes **Usability, Feature**s, and reliability. Figure 10.1 depicts the concept of software quality as three vertices of a triangle. This figure also shows the relationship between the quality triangle and the **Project** control triangle presented in Figure 3.11. On one vertex of the software quality triangle is **Usability**, on a second is conformance to **Feature**s, and on the third is reliability. Although it is possible for a **SoftwareProduct** to have one or even two without the other, software quality requires all three. To that end, Roche stresses that software quality is the degree to which software has the desired combination of attributes required of that system [Roche94].

Definition of Quality

Early definitions of quality include "fitness for use" and "conformance to requirements." More recently, Vallabhaneni defines software quality in terms of the **Feature**s the software must exhibit, including

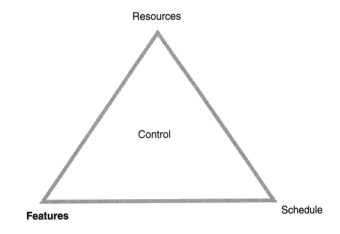

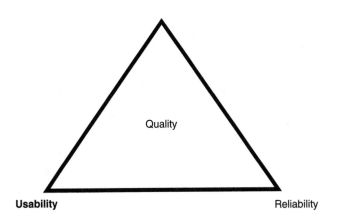

Figure 10.1 Software Quality Triangle

1. satisfy a broad spectrum of user requirements,
2. has few errors,
3. functions efficiently,
4. operates easily, and
5. has good user documentation [Vallabhaneni90].

From Vallabhaneni's point of view, software quality is the result of a complex combination of several **Feature**s, but in reality there is no conflict with the earlier definitions. On close examination it is apparent that some of the **Feature**s suggested by Vallabhaneni may be combined and thereby the total reduced to a smaller number of attributes, such as shown in Figure 10.1.

It is suggested that the quality of a product can be computed from a weighted function of the underlying attributes, where the weightings depend on user **Features**. However, Stockman et al. argued that in practice it is extremely difficult to justify a particular weighting scheme because of the large variability in quality needs that exist across different products and user populations [Stockman90]. They suggest instead that software quality be defined as a series of vector representations of the particular values of independent attributes, which together determine product quality at various stages of the life cycle. This approach requires a developer to classify quality attributes in terms of the relevant life cycle representations. Essentially, it consists of defining specific attributes and measures and investigating their interrelationships within the context of a well-defined life cycle. Meeting quality requirements at each stage is supposed to ensure quality of the end product.

Schneidewind emphasizes that "to achieve high software quality in a system, the software's attributes must be clearly defined; otherwise assessment of quality is left to intuition" [Schneidewind93]. To determine software quality, we must determine what variables underlie the quality attributes and the best metrics for their measurement. Obviously, the best metrics are those that provide assessment throughout the **SoftwareProduct** development cycle, ensure that the software quality attributes are being acquired, and predict the quality of the final **SoftwareProduct**.

Quality versus Productivity

The desire for increased productivity is the driver in the software development process that overrides many other considerations, and for many years even quality. Despite this past history, progressive software companies have discovered that both quality and productivity require consideration. Does such a discovery mean that the two are to be pitted against one another for programmer time and cost? No; the fact is that quality and productivity issues are fundamentally interlaced. From a survey of software managers, Keyes quotes TI managers:

> If you develop with quality in the first place, over time the maintenance burden will be lessened to the degree that will overshadow any productivity improvement you can get during the development process. . . . all the improvements made in technology in the last 20 years have averaged only a 4% to 7% annual productivity improvement. . . . Quality in the short term translates to productivity in the long term [Keyes91].

According to Glass, IBM employs their CUPRIMDSO program that monitors Capability, Usability, Performance, Reliability, Installability, Maintainability, Documentation, Service , and Overall, and at Hewlett–Packard the emphasis in on Functionality, Usability, Reliability, Performance, and Serviceability (FURPS) [Glass92]. Other software **Supplier**s have programs that focus on similar factors. The objective of these programs is increased productivity of quality software.

The interrelationship of quality and productivity suggests that similar approaches may be used to address both issues. Emphasis throughout this book is placed on four factors during the software development cycle: people, models, tools and metrics. Although each approach makes its own independent contribution to software quality, integration is the goal. According to the Gestalt principle, integration should lead to a contribution that is greater than the sum of the contributions of the parts. However, other than the following summary, no attempt will be made to rehash material that either has been or will be presented and documented elsewhere.

1. The Pareto principle (80/20 rule) must be remembered. That is, 80% of the trouble probably comes from 20% of the factors, and 20% of the people likely cause 80% of the problems. Implied is that there are only a few ways to do it right, but a large number of ways to do it wrong.

2. There is a differential between the best and worst programmers (20 to 1) and the best and worst teams (5 to 1).

3. Training improves competence, and teamwork improves quality.

4. Managing software development requires an integrated life cycle methodology that assists managers in visualizing the software development process and addresses problems while a system is being developed.

5. Software models including appropriate metrics may be used to measure and predict end product **Feature**s during a life cycle development.

6. There must be an early and continuous use of tools for estimation and planning.

DEVELOPING SOFTWARE QUALITY: USABILITY

One component of the quality triangle shown in Figure 10.1 is **Usability**. This is emphasized in the concept of quality as "fitness for use." This suggests that users must be considered to ensure quality. Guaspari also stresses the importance of this consideration:

> Your customers are in a perfect position to tell you about quality, because that's all they're really buying. They are not buying a product. They are buying your assurances that their expectations for that product will be met. . . . You haven't really got anything else to sell but quality [Guaspari85].

The quality of a **SoftwareProduct** is meeting the expectations of the **Customer**s who purchase the product and/or users who exercise that product. In some situations, **Customer**s and users are the same and in others they are not. To alleviate possible confusion, the terms **Customer**-purchaser and **Customer**-user are adopted throughout the balance of this chapter. Although both **Customer**-purchasers and **Customer**-users have wants and needs that combine to define each's expectations, distinctions between the two are important to understand.

Customer-purchasers' expectations pertain to receiving a product that is on schedule and within budget, full featured and **Defect** free, and reliable and usable. It may be concluded that if a product fails to meet these criteria a dissatisfied **Customer**-purchaser results. It is also a given that if most of these criteria are met, but the product is not usable, the **Customer**-purchaser will be dissatisfied. The alternative from the perspective of the **Customer**-user is not necessarily true. That is, meeting **Usability** criteria ensures **Customer**-user satisfaction regardless of whether a **Customer**-purchaser is satisfied. This underscores the importance of **Usability** to both parties.

Denning relates **Usability** to three basic outcomes: (1) all basic promises were fulfilled, (2) no negative consequences were produced, and (3) the user was delighted [Denning92]. A metric-based approach to predict these **Feature**s during design and development is important. Most of these outcomes are psychological and subjective in nature and therefore lend themselves to behavioral measurement only. This simply means measuring **Customer** subjective responses. Baecker, et al. recommend that, during design and development, subjective evaluations should be acquired from interviews and questionnaires using small but representative **Customer** focus **Group**s reacting to paper and pencil drawings, mock-ups, and prototypes [Baecker95]. The content of the interviews and questionnaires depends on the purpose of the **SoftwareProduct** (**Feature**s) and how it will used (**Usability**). Metrics include psychological scales such as ratings, pair comparisons, and Likert-type scales. An old but seminal reference for psychometric methods is Guilford [Guilford54].

In addition to psychological measurement, Nielson related **Usability** to performance-based factors such as learnability, relearnability, and efficiency [Nielson92]. Metrics for Nielson's performance-based factors include product or task learning time; product or task retention time; task completion time; percentages of users completing tasks; errors such as types, frequencies, and rates; and requests for help. Other metrics and variations are identified in Chapter 14. As the **SoftwareProduct** moves closer to the final product stage, **Usability** may be predicted employing one or more of these metrics. After the product is released, standard techniques for measuring user responses are beneficial. These include informal feedback, such as complaints and requests for help, and formal feedback from product **UsabilityTest**s and structured approaches, such as mail-out questionnaires and telephone interviews of samples of users representative of the user population. Whether the approach is psychological or performance based, it is important to predict user responses before the product reaches design freeze, as well as after the final product is released. Feedback based on measurement during the former improves the final product. Feedback based on measurement during the latter improves subsequent **Version**s of the product.

Card makes the additional point that **Customer**-purchasers and **Customer**-users of software **Supplier**s are very different from purchasers and users in commodity businesses [Card92]. In a commodity business, the target **Customer** is a large population, and it is safe to assume that current **Customer**s are representative samples. This suggests that the concerns of the sample are assumed to be shared by the larger target population. On the other hand, purchasers and users of **SoftwareProduct**s may be so few that it cannot be assumed that they are representative of a large number of potential **Customer**s. In such cases, **Customer** satisfaction cannot be treated the same for both commodity businesses and software **Supplier**s. The message is be careful not to be misled by the potential biases of small samples if they are unrepresentative of the target client and user populations.

Technical Assistance Research Programs, Inc., pointed to the need of a formal **Customer** feedback program The problem they define is that the average business only hears from 4% of its unhappy **Customer**s, and of the 96% who don't bother to complain, 25% have serious problems. To further acerbate the situation, an unhappy **Customer** with a problem will tell between 10 and 20 other people about it. The good news is that about 60% of the complainers will stay if their problem is resolved, and 95% of them will stay if they feel the problem was solved quickly. The point is that a successful feedback program keeps **Customer**s.

Glass and others offer a word of caution in regard to basing quality totally on a satisfaction **Feature** [Glass92]. Increasing overall satisfaction, as well as a simultaneous satisfaction of various quality attributes, is no easy task. The problem is that quality attributes are not always compatible with one another.

DEVELOPING SOFTWARE QUALITY: FEATURES

A second component of the quality triangle shown in Figure 10.1 is **Feature**s. **Feature** validation, in regard to quality, essentially implies no functional **Defect**s because the absence of a **Feature** or the presence of a functional **Defect** means that the **Feature** for a preferred function is not being provided. Jones found that at least 15% of all software **Defect**s are related to unmet **Feature**s [Jones92]. Evidently, a major problem in software development is errors in **Feature**s; therefore, it stands to reason that a design and development process that fails to address **Feature** validation produces inferior-quality software. With similar arguments, Palmer and Fields suggest that the greatest opportunity for developing software quality occurs when **Feature**s are collected objectively and unambiguously and that attention to **Feature**s is cost effective [Palmer92]. Although **Feature**s analysis accounts for only 5% of **Software-Product** costs, it provides 50% of the opportunity to influence quality.

The software-quality metric methodology IEEE Standard 1061 [IEEE92] provides a five-step systematic approach to establishing quality **Feature**s that spans the entire life cycle, including a process with associated software quality metrics for identification, analysis, validation, and implementation. Schneidewind summarizes the steps [Schneidewind93] as follows:

1. *Establish software-quality features.* A list of quality factors is selected, prioritized, and quantified at the outset of system development or system change. These **Feature**s guide and control system development and, on system delivery, assess whether quality **Feature**s are met.

2. *Identify software-quality metrics.* The software-quality metrics framework is applied in selecting relevant metrics.

3. *Implement software-quality metrics.* Tools are procured or developed. Data are collected and metrics are applied at each phase of the life cycle.

4. *Analyze the software-quality metrics results.* The results are used to help to control development and assess the final product.

5. *Validate software-quality metrics.* Predictive methods are compared with quality factors results to determine whether predictive metrics accurately measure their associative factors.

The product whose **Feature**s cannot be validated or that is delivered late or that has greater than a previously agreed on cost has quality problems. Stockman et al. suggest that establishing strong relationships between **Feature**s and the end product can be very difficult because the typical **Feature**s specification is closer to a statement of a problem than of a solution [Stockman90].

Although agreeing that **Feature** validation is a reasonable and practical approach to quality, Card called attention to the fact that the approach has its problems [Card92].

1. It assumes that stable and complete **Feature**s can be obtained.

2. It ignores the possible match or mismatch between **Feature**s and user needs.

3. It fails to validate services to other than the one who specified the requirements.

4. It fails to consider the economic consequences or the value of the delivered product.

In summary, **Feature** validation demands that **Feature**s be plainly established without misunderstanding and metrics for their measurement identified. Then, in the software development process, measurements can be made to predict and determine conformance. The degree of conformance is an estimator of quality. In this approach, the product whose **Feature**s are validated is by definition a quality product. Nonconformance can be considered as a **Defect**.

DEVELOPING SOFTWARE QUALITY: RELIABILITY

The last component in the quality triangle shown in Figure 10.1 is reliability. It is not unusual for some authors to relate software quality to reliability and make reliability a component of conformance to **Feature**s. For example, Glass suggests:

> In software, the narrowest sense of product quality is commonly recognized as lack of "bugs" in the product. It is also the most basic meaning of conformance to requirements, because if the software contains too many functional defects, the basic requirement of providing the desired function is not met. This definition is usually expressed in two ways: defect rate and reliability [Glass92].

Making software reliability one component of **Feature** conformance may be valid, but not necessarily practical. Because of the nature and complexity of software reliability, an independent coverage seems more reasonable. A summary coverage of software reliability related to software quality follows. A more thorough discussion of software reliability is given in Chapter 11.

Software reliability is defined in many ways. According to Jones, it is simply defined as **Defect** potential, **Defect** removal efficiency, and delivered **Defect**s [Jones93]. Using this definition, one approach to enhancing software quality is to catch **Defect**s during program testing. Reducing **Defect**s to the lowest possible number is of major interest to software developers. Binder and Poore indicate that the lack of **Defect**s is not only important from the standpoint of software quality, but also of cost [Binder90]. One question of importance is where **Defect**s are most likely to be found in testing. In a NASA-supported **Project** at MIT in the late 1960s and early 1970s, Margaret Hamilton, of Hamilton Technologies, found that 73% of software **Defect**s were interface **Defect**s, such as timing interface, data interface, and interface between two instructions. She subsequently developed a Case tool to ferret these interface **Defect**s out during the development cycle [Keyes91].

Another useful approach described in Chapter 11 defines software reliability as the probability that the software will be functioning without failure for a specified period of time in a specified environment. The overriding benefit of this definition is that it opens several avenues of approach. Time is a commonly used and understood metric, and the three kinds of time, execution, calendar, and clock, are available for use. For example, if a failure is caused by a software **Defect**, then it is reasonable to characterize occurrences of failure in terms of (1) time to failure, (2) time intervals between failures, (3) cumulative failures experienced up to a given time, and (4) failure experienced in a time interval.

Defining software reliability in terms of the probability of functioning in time without failure provides an additional advantage—the use of powerful software reliability models that can be employed not only to predict reliability during the development of software but also to predict reliability of the software end product. For example, the Software Quality Management System (SQMS) developed by the Software Quality Tools Corporation implements software reliability models by measuring the reliability of a product under development [Keyes91]. In one of the SQMS modules, data are collected either through problem logs or by code changes on a day to day basis. Data from the former are used to compute mean time to **Defect** repair, and the latter are used to calculate a volatility index. Software quality is calculated as the ratio of known and corrected **Defect**s to the predicted total number of **Defect**s. Another example is the approach suggested by Munson and Khoshgoftarr. Using data from previous **Project**s, they developed a model for identifying program modules that are prone to contain **Defect**s or require program modifications [Munson92]. Details of software reliability models can be found in Chapter 11.

Robinson indicated that, to resolve reliability problems efficiently, systematic methods for detecting problems must be used, and to eliminate the problems, performance must be tracked and consistently measured [Robinson93]. Total quality tools are available to a manager to handle these tasks.

Total Quality Tools

Several total quality tools exist for tracking a software development process. They serve the purpose of identifying, visualizing, and analyzing potential problems that lead to poor quality. Since details of these techniques may be found in other sources [Bennett96, Goetsch97, Summers97], only the more popular ones are briefly described here.

Flow Chart. Probably the most widely used total quality tool is the flow chart. It is a pictorial representation that identifies all steps of a process. Flow charts provide program documentation and are beneficial for examining the relationships among the steps, thereby documenting quality and/or identifying potential sources of poor quality. Figure 10.2 is a sample of a simple flow chart. A flow chart may used to identify the ideal path that a process follows in order to identify deviations.

Pareto Chart. A Pareto chart is a bar chart. Each bar represents some type of entity or activity, and the bars are arranged in descending order. The length of the bar is an indication of the importance of that item. Figure 10.3 is an example of a

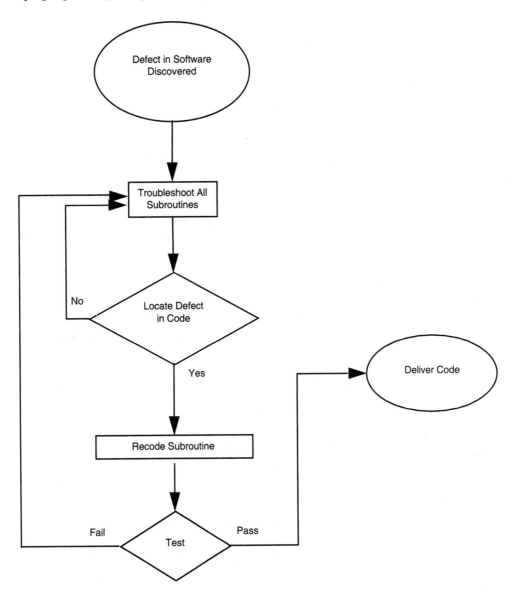

Figure 10.2 Simple Flow Chart

simple Pareto chart. The arrangement of the chart easily identifies for the manager those **Area**s where improvement would lead to the largest increases in quality.

Fishbone Diagram. A fishbone diagram (Figure 10.4) serves the purposes of identifying, exploring, and displaying possible causes of a problem in quality. It rep-

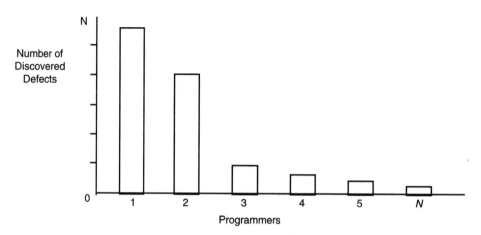

Figure 10.3   Simple Pareto Chart

resents the relationships between an effect, which serves as the head of a fish and all possible causes, which make up the bones of a fish body. The fishbone analogy fits well since every effect will likely have several major causes. In software development, for example, these may include policies, procedures, managers, programmers, requirements, methods, and hardware. The approach is (1) to identify all causes, (2) to push the causes back to sources by asking "why" for each cause, (3) to examine all possible sources, searching for deviations from normal patterns, and (4) to remedy the causes at the sources, not at the symptoms of the problem.

Scatter Diagram.   A scatter diagram is used to study possible relationships between two variables. It displays what happens to one variable when another variable changes. A scatter diagram uses the horizontal axis of an *X* and *Y* plot. The hori-

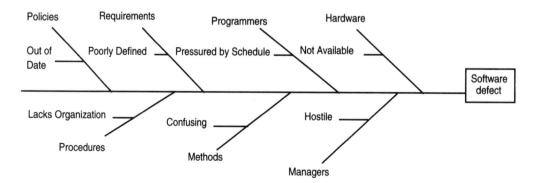

Figure 10.4   Simple Fishbone Diagram

zontal axis is used to represent measurements of one variable and the vertical axis to represent resulting measurements of a quality variable. The approach is to plot measurements of the two variables, which, in turn, will provide clues about (1) direction of the relationship, that is, positive or negative; (2) nature of the relationship, that is, linear, logarithmic, power, or exponential; and (3) strength of the relationship. Regression analysis assists the manager in determining the nature and strength of an existing relationship. Figure 10.5 shows examples of simple scatter diagrams.

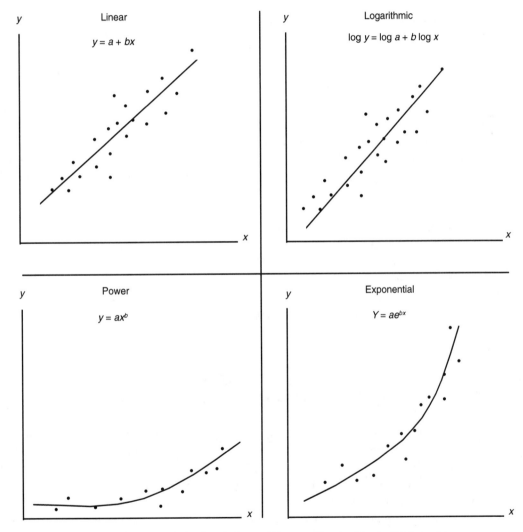

Figure 10.5   Simple Scatter Diagrams Showing Types of Relationships

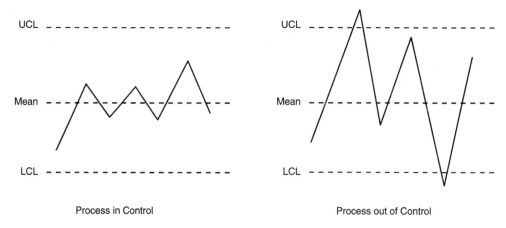

Figure 10.6   Simple Control Charts

Control Chart.   A control chart is a plot of measurements over a specified time period. It is a graphical technique for determining whether a process is or is not in a state of statistical control. The chart contains three **Feature**s of software quality: a process average and two statistically determined limits, an upper control limit (UCL) of quality and a lower control limit (LCL) of quality. These **Feature**s may be predicted using data from previous **Project**s. Measurements per the specified time period can then be plotted in the chart to determine whether any of the points fall within or outside the limits. Points falling within the limits result from required **Feature**s being built into the process. Points falling outside the limits indicate that the system is not operating normally or out of control. Sources of system abnormality are then examined and resolved. Figure 10.6 depicts examples of simple control charts.

AN ADDITIONAL NOTE ON DEVELOPING SOFTWARE QUALITY: TOTAL QUALITY MANAGEMENT

Total Quality Management (TQM) was introduced in Chapter 3. TQM uses a team-based methodology for continuous improvement for software development. In instances where problems in any or all of the components of the quality triangle shown in Figure 10.1 are discovered, Process Improvement Teams can be established. A through discussion of TQM is outside the purpose of this chapter. The book *Four Days with Dr. Deming* [Latzko95] is an excellent source for TQM principles and methods. The TQM principles associated with the human side of quality are briefly summarized as follows:

1. The problem is in the process; the solution is in the people.
2. People want to be involved and to do their jobs well.
3. Every person wants to feel like a value contributor.
4. The person doing the job is most knowledgeable about that job.

Process Improvement Teams is the methodology for applying TQM. The maxim that two heads are better than one is the foundation for the team process. Teams identify and study work processes in a structured environment that is designed to allow each member to contribute and think creatively. The characteristics of successful team activity include the following:

1. Clear goals and objectives
2. Effective leadership
3. Knowledge and application of statistical tools
4. Disciplined documentation
5. Consensus decision making
6. Frank discussion of all ideas
7. Recognition of **Individual** contributions

As teamwork progresses, ideas are explored, expanded, and made more workable and productive. The team enlarges the opportunity for better solutions through consensus. Members take more control of their progress and become better able to articulate the barriers that prevent them from doing their best work. Teams provide the vehicle for using TQM to involve software developers, address critical software process, and satisfy client and user expectations.

SUMMARY

The purpose of this chapter was to present software quality as an integrated concept that includes **Usability**, **Feature**s, and reliability. **Usability** pertains to the satisfaction of people who purchase and use software. Satisfaction may be measured in terms of psychological as well as performance-based metrics. Additional coverage of **Usability** may be found in Chapters 13 and 14.

Validation of **Feature**s essentially means no **Defect**s, because the reality of a **Defect** means that the preferred required **Feature** is not provided. The software-quality methodology IEEE 1061 [IEEE92] was described as providing a systematic approach to establishing quality **Feature**s that span the entire life cycle. The measurement and validation of **Feature**s and associated metrics are treated in more detail in Chapter 12.

Software reliability was defined as the probability that the software will be functioning without failure for a specified period of time in a specified environment. Time, as a commonly used and understood metric, opens an abundance of opportunities for exploration and use. The importance of software models to measure and predict reliability was stressed. The identification and application of software models and metrics are covered in Chapter 11.

The concept of Total Quality Management (TQM) was briefly presented to point out the importance of people in their roles as software developers. Among several TQM tenets, it was emphasized that most problems are in the process and most solutions are in the people. People solving problems improves both quality and productivity. The methodology for applying TQM involves Process Improvement Teams.

REFERENCES

[Baecker95]   Baecker, R. M., Grudin, J., Buxton, W. A. S., and Greenberg, S., *Human–Computer Interaction*, 2nd ed., Morgan Kaufman, San Francisco, CA, 1995.

[Bennett96]   Bennett, L. F., *The Management of Engineering*, John Wiley & Sons, New York, 1996.

[Binder90]   Binder, L. H., and Poore, J. H., "Field Experiments with Local Software Quality Metrics," *Software Practice and Experience*, Vol. 20, No. 7, 1990, pp. 631–647.

[Card92]   Card, D., "Beyond Quality to Customer Satisfaction," *IEEE Software*, March 1992, pp. 101–102.

[Denning92]   Denning, P. J., "What Is Software Quality?" *Communications of the ACM*, Vol. 35, No. 1, 1992, pp. 13–15.

[Glass92]   Glass, R. L., *Building Quality Software*, Prentice Hall, Upper Saddle River, NJ, 1992.

[Goetsch97]   Goetsch, D. L., and Davis, S. B., *Introduction to Total Quality*, 2nd ed., Prentice Hall, Upper Saddle River, NJ, 1997.

[Guaspari85]   Guaspari, J., *I Know It When I See It: A Modern Fable about Quality*, AMA, New York, 1985.

[Guilford54]   Guilford, J. P., *Psychometric Methods*, McGraw-Hill Book Co., New York, 1954.

[IEEE92]   IEEE Standard 1061, *Software-Quality Metrics Methodology*, IEEE Standards Office, Piscataway, NJ, 1992.

[Jones92]   Jones, C., *Critical Problems in Software Management*, Software Productivity Research, Burlington, MA, 1992.

[Jones93]   Jones, C., *Software Productivity and Quality Today: The Worldwide Perspective*, IS Management Group, Burlington, MA, 1993.

[Keyes91]   Keyes, J., "Peeling Back Layers of Quality Equation," *Software Magazine*, May 1991, pp. 42–55.

[Latzko95]   Latzko, W. J., and Saunders, D. M., *Four Days with Dr. Deming*, Addison–Wesley Publishing Co., Reading, MA, 1995.

[Munson92]   Munson, J., and Khoshgoftarr, T., "The Detection of Fault-prone Programs," *IEEE Transactions on Software Engineering*, Vol. 18, No. 5, 1992, pp. 423–433.

[Nielson92]   Nielson, J., "The Usability Engineering Life Cycle," *IEEE Computer*, Vol. 25, No. 3, 1992, pp. 12–23.

[Palmer92]   Palmer, J. D., and Fields, N. A., "An Integrated Environment for Requirements Engineering," *IEEE Software*, Vol. 9, 1992, pp. 83–85.

[Robinson93]   Robinson, J. A., "The Dark Side of Software Metrics," *Information Strategy: The Executives Journal*, Winter 1993, pp. 44–47.

[Roche94]   Roche, J. M., "Software Metrics and Measurement Principles," *Software Engineering Notes*, Vol. 9, No. 5, 1994, pp. 77–85.

[Schmauch94]   Schmauch, C. H., *ISO 9000 for Software Developers*, ASQC Quality Press, Milwaukee, WI, 1994.

[Schneidewind93]   Schneidewind, N. F., "New Software-Quality Metrics Methodology Standard Fills Measurement Need," *Computer*, Vol. 26, No. 4, 1993, pp. 105–106.

[Stockman90]   Stockman, S. G., Todd, A. R., and Robinson, G. A., "A Framework for Software Quality Measurement," *IEEE Journal on Selected Areas in Communications*, Vol. 8, No. 2, 1990, pp. 224–233.

[Summers97]   Summers, Donna C. S., *Quality*, Prentice Hall, Upper Saddle River, NJ, 1997.

[Vallabhaneni90]   Vallabhaneni, S., *Auditing Software Development*, Chapman & Hall, New York, 1990.

11
Reliability

Does your company care about software quality—does it care enough, for example, to delay putting a new system into production because its software reliability models indicate an unacceptable number of latent errors? Does it even have software reliability models?

Edward Yourdon
[Yourdon92]

INTRODUCTION

In the past 30 years, hundreds of papers have been published in the areas of software reliability modeling, models validation, and measurement [Kuo90]. Software has become an essential part of many industrial, military and commercial systems. In today's large systems, software life cycle cost (LCC) typically exceeds that of hardware, with 80%–90% of these costs going into software maintenance to fix, adapt, and expand the delivered program to meet the changing and growing needs of the users [Keene93]. Chapter 1 shows software costs were 15% of total cost in 1955, 50% in 1970, and 85% in 1985 and has continued to exponentially increase to past 90% in 1996. The investment in software increases even more dramatically for the military industry. The annual cost of computer software and services for the U.S. DoD increased from $4.6 billion in FY80 (fiscal year 1980) to $37.2 billion in FY90. If the cost of software continues to increase at this rate, computer software will consume the entire defense budget by the year 2015 [Hess88]. Both in microcomputers and supercomputers, we may find programs containing millions of lines of code.

The current system cost trend is approaching software domination rather than hardware domination [Hansen88]. Unfortunately, the relative frequency could be as high as 100:1 more software failures than hardware failures [Ferrara89]. This ratio may be higher for extremely complicated chips. In January 1986, the Reliability Plus Inc. measures show the mean time between failure (MTBF) for IBM central proces-

266

sors (3080 class machines) to be between 20,000 and 30,000 hours; in the fall of 1986, these same machines had demonstrated MTBFs of over 80,000 hours, a very substantial reliability growth (in hardware). However, newly developed software has an average of only 160 to 200 hours between faults, although the vast majority (more than 90%) of these software faults were not considered fatal [Koss88]. In 1994, a design flaw in Intel's Pentium processor forced the Intel Corporation to spend millions of dollars to replace the bad ones.

Although there have been many software reliability models suggested and studied, none of them is valid for all situations. The reason is probably due to the fact that the assumptions made for each model are only approximations or are correct for only some, but not all, situations. Analysts have to choose the models whose assumptions match their systems. This chapter presents a review of some well-known reliability models, both stochastic and nonstochastic (static) models, to pave the way for the future development and evaluation of highly reliable software and of systems involving software and hardware. Important issues like software safety and the necessity of documents are also addressed. We realize that software life cycle cost is a function of software reliability; therefore, modeling software reliability is an important task.

Because software reliability is an exciting and important research field, many new concepts have been introduced in the existing literature. Before specific models can be addressed, we need to first understand the basic terms and concepts of software reliability.

Failures, Faults, and Bugs

A system consisting of software and hardware may fail due to the incapability of the software executed by external instructions. Software may fail only if it is used and when it is used in an undesirable environment. A software failure is defined as a departure from the expected external result or the output of the program operation from the requirement, so the program has to be run for a failure to occur. A failure may be caused by a software fault or by other reasons.

Bugs are inherent **Defect**s created at the design stage. Therefore, an action taken to remove bugs from the software is commonly known as debugging. When an analyst, designer, or programmer makes an error, a fault is created. A fault is a **Defect** in the program that, when executed under particular conditions, causes a failure. A software is said to contain a fault if, for some input data, the output result is incorrect. It is very important to make the failure–fault distinction in the software reliability measurement.

Environment

The operational condition of software refers to the environment under which the software is designed to be used. Before we define software reliability, it is essential to become familiar with the term environment. For example, a spread sheet for a banking system or an academic institution would be used under different environments. An environment is defined under which a software runs.

Operational Profile

Operational profile is the frequency distribution of a set of run types that the program executes. It shows the relative frequency of occurrence as a function of different input states. A realistic operational profile will be a fuzzy function of possible input states. The software environment is usually described by the operational profile. We need to illustrate the concept of the operational profile with several terms: input variable, input state, and run type.

The input variable is a variable that exists external to the program and is used by the program in executing its function. Each program usually has a large quantity of input variables associated with it. Each set of values for different input variables characterizes an input state. Every individual input state identifies a particular run type of this program. Therefore, runs can always be classified by their input states. Each run type required of the program by the environment can be viewed as being randomly selected. Thus, we can define the operational profile as the set of run types that the program can execute along with the probabilities with which they will occur.

Software Reliability

The definition of software reliability used here is one that is widely accepted throughout the field. The definition of software reliability is also similar to the one for hardware reliability. Such a definition will make it possible to combine the software reliability and hardware reliability to achieve system reliability. It is the probability that the software will be functioning without failure for a specified period of time in a specified environment.

There are four general ways of characterizing failure occurrences in time:

1. Time of failure
2. Time interval between failures
3. Cumulative failures experienced up to a given time
4. Failures experienced in a time interval

From the definition, reliability quantities have usually been defined with respect to time, although it is possible to define them with respect to other variables, for example, number of failures in 100 printed pages or percent of transactions that fail. Three kinds of time are generally considered: execution time, calendar time, and clock time. The execution time for a program is the time that is actually spent by a processor in executing the instructions of the program. Although execution time is very important, calendar time is more meaningful to the engineers or managers.

Clock time represents the elapsed time from start to end of a program executed on a running computer. It includes the waiting time and the execution time of other programs. Given the usage information of personnel and computer, execution time, calendar time, and clock time are readily exchangeable.

Characteristics of Software

The hardware and software contributions to reliability are not independent [Ferrara89]. Changes in either the hardware or software can (and usually do) affect the other [Yates90]. In hardware testing, the statistical emphasis is often on estimating the failure rate of an item, whereas in software testing the main statistical emphasis is on estimating the number of errors (or **Defect**s or faults) remaining in the system [Kubat83]. Unlike software reliability models, for which it is recognized that no universally good ones have been found, hardware reliability models, especially the ones for electronic components and systems, are studied by many researchers, and many of them are generally accepted to describe the failure mechanisms of components; for example, the Weibull distribution is widely used for the failure behavior of many semiconductor components [for example, the integrated circuit (IC)] [Chien96]. The probability density function [pdf, $f(t)$], the cumulative distribution function [CDF, $F(t)$], and the failure rate function [$h(t)$] of the Weibull distribution with scale parameter λ and shape parameter β are (for $t \geq 0$)

$$f(t) = \lambda\beta(\lambda t)^{\beta-1} e^{-(\lambda t)^{\beta}}$$

$$F(t) = 1 - e^{-(\lambda t)^{\beta}}$$

$$h(t) = \lambda\beta(\lambda t)^{\beta-1}$$

Given an operational profile, software fails stochastically.

Software reliability and hardware reliability have distinct characteristics. Some major differences are outlined in Table 11.1 [Kuo90].

Some other characteristics of software are the following:

1. *No programmer is perfect.* When a **Defect** (or fault) is removed, new **Defect**s or (faults) can be introduced into the program [Lynch94] (imperfect debugging).

2. *Not all **Defect**s or (faults) are created equal.* Different **Defect**s (or faults) have different implications and thus need different handling [Lynch94]. And different faults (or **Defect**s) may differ greatly in contribution to the total failure rate [Xie87].

3. *Fast growing in complexity.* The basic problem in the software area is that the complexity of the tasks that software must perform has grown faster than the technology for designing, testing, and managing software development [Shooman84]. If fact, software complexity related to testing can be shown to be

Table 11.1 Differences between Hardware and Software Reliability

Category	Hardware Reliability	Software Reliability
Fundamental concept	Due to physical effects	Due to programmer errors [or Program **Defect**s (or faults)]
Life cycle causes		
Analysis	Incorrect **Customer** understanding	Incorrect **Customer** understanding
Feasibility	Incorrect user requirements	Incorrect user requirements
Design	Incorrect physical design	Incorrect program design
Development	Quality control problems	Incorrect program coding
Operation	Degradation and failure	Program errors (or remaining **Defect**s or faults)
Use effects	Hardware wears out and then fails	Software does not wear out but fails from unlocated **Defect**s (or faults)
Function of design	Physics of failure	Programmer skill
Domains	Time	Time and data
Time relationship	Bathtub curve	Decreasing function
Math models	Theory well established and accepted	Theory established but not well accepted
Time domain	$R = f(\lambda, t)$, λ = failure rate	$R = f\,[failures$ (or $defects$ or $faults$), $t]$
Functions	Exponential (constant λ) Weibull (increasing λ)	No agreement on the various time function models that have been proposed
Data domain	No meaning	Failures = f(data, tests)
Growth models	Several models exist	Several models exist
Metric	λ, MTBF (mean time between failures), MTTF (mean time to failure)	Failure rate, number of **Defect**s (or faults) detected or remaining
Growth application	Design, prediction	Prediction
Prediction techniques	Block diagram, fault trees	Path analysis (actual analysis of all paths is an unsolvable problem, i. e., the number of possible dynamic paths for even simple programs can be shown to be infinite), complexity, simulation
Test and Evaluation	Design and production acceptance	Design acceptance
Design	MIL-STD-781C (exponential) Other methods (nonexponential)	Path testing, simulation, error Seeding, Bayesian
Operation	MIL-STD-781C	None
Use of redundancy		
Parallel	Can improve reliability	Need to consider common cause
Standby	Automatic error detection and correction, automatic fault detection and switching	Automatic error detection and correction; automatic audit software and software reinitialization
Majority logic	m-out-of-n	Impractical

an intractable problem. Extensive testing of all dynamic paths in a software system cannot be carried out, even in infinite time and using infinite resources. In such cases, heuristic methods are our only resort.

4. *No universally applicable model.* It has been shown [Abdel-Ghaly86] that a good "model" is not sufficient to produce good predictions and that there is no universal "best buy" among the competing methods. Prediction systems perform with varying adequacy on different data sources. In other words, every software **Project** is different; the specific process models, tools, or even management techniques that have improved the reliability of one site will not necessarily have the same effect on all sites [Bukowski92]. Users need to be able to select, from a plethora of prediction systems, one (or more) that gives trustworthy predictions for the software being studied.

5. *Data aging.* It is not necessarily the case that all the failure data should be used to estimate model parameters and to predict failures [Schneidewind93]. The reason is that old data may not be as representative of the current and future failure processes as recent data; this can be called data aging.

6. *Fatal side effects might be expected from a hardware–software system.* It is understood that software is not intrinsically hazardous. However, when software is integrated with hardware, it has the potential for catastrophic effect [Hansen88].

7. *The earlier the tests are performed, the better.* The earlier in the development cycle that we can test, the earlier we can predict the operational reliability, and the more time we have to take action to improve the software in response to a gloomy prediction. However, the trade-off is that the earlier we go in the test cycle, the less realistic, the less documented, and the more scattered are the test results [Shooman84]. Throughout the software life cycle of a software **Project**, we should implement software configuration management, test management, and **Defect** tracking systems. Then even early software life cycle test results will be realistic, documented, and concentrated.

8. *Changeable and unpredictable users environments.* In general, software error detection during operation is different from that during testing [Ohtera90].

THE STOCHASTIC MODELS

To have good predictive results by using the reliability growth models, we have to make sure that the experimental environment is similar to the user's circumstances. Two commonly used stochastic models are the binomial-type and the Poisson-type models.

The basic assumptions for the binomial-type model are as follows:

1. The corresponding fault is removed immediately once a fault is found.
2. There are μ_0 inherent faults in the program.
3. Per fault hazard rate at time t, $Z_a(t)$, and the hazard rate for all faults are the same.

The assumption for the Poisson-type model is that the initial number of faults is a random variable:

$$(\text{r.v.}) \sim \text{Poisson}(\omega_0) = \frac{e^{-\omega_0}\omega_0^t}{\omega_0!}$$

where ω_0 is the number of faults inherent in the code.

A stochastic process is usually incorporated in the description of the failure phenomenon by the assumption that, given the process at a specific state, its future development does not depend on its past history and the transition probabilities among these states only depend on the present state. Stochastic models are very useful in studying software fault-removal processes, especially during the testing phase.

The state of the process at time t here is the number of remaining faults at that time. The fault-removal process can usually be described by a pure death process, since the number of remaining faults is a decreasing function of time provided, that no new fault(s) is (are) introduced. If we also consider the introduction of new faults due to incorrect debugging, the birth–death process can then be applied [Kuo83b]. Some Bayesian models deal mainly with the inference problems based on the failure data.

Selected stochastic models are discussed with their characteristics, merits, and shortcomings. The static models, such as the input-domain-based models, which do not take the failure process into consideration, are included in the next section.

Notation

The notation used in the stochastic models sections follow:

N	Number of faults present in the software at the beginning of the test phase
T	Time at which we want to estimate the software reliability after testing (observation time), assuming that the test begins at time 0
X_i	R.V. time between the $(i-1)$st and the ith failures, that is, the debugging interval; however, the time interval is used when data are collected with respect to constant time intervals, such as weeks or months
T_i	The ith software failure time; $T_0 = 0$ and $X_i = T_i - T_{i-1}$

m	Number of software failures observed; set $T = T_m$, if we terminate the test immediately after the mth failure and employ the software reliability model; otherwise, $T > T_m$
x_i	A realization of X_I
$R(t)$	Reliability at time t
t, t_i	A realization of T and T_i, respectively
m_i	Number of software faults removed during the ith debugging interval
R_t	Reliability at time t
n_i	Cumulative number of faults removed from the software during the first i debugging or time intervals; that is,

$$n_i = \sum_{j=1}^{j} m_j$$

n	Total number of faults removed from the software during $[0, \ T]$; that is, $n = n_m$
N_t	Number of faults remaining in the software at time t; $N_0 = N$ and $N_T = N - n$
λ_i	Hazard rate between the $(i-1)$st and the ith software failures
ϕ	The size of a fault

Jelinski–Moranda (JM) Model

The JM model [Jelinski71], one of the earliest software reliability models, assumes the following:

1. The number of initial software faults is an unknown but fixed constant.
2. A detected fault is removed immediately, and no new fault is introduced.
3. Times between failures are independent, exponentially distributed random variables; that is, T_1, T_2, . . . are independent r.v.'s with exponential pdfs.

$$\begin{cases} \Pr(t_i \mid \lambda_1) = \lambda_1 e^{-\lambda_1 1_i}, & t_i > 0 \\ \lambda_1 = (N - n_{i-1})\phi \end{cases} \tag{11.1}$$

4. All remaining software faults contribute the same amount to the software failure intensity.

The failure rate versus time diagram for the JM model is shown in Figure 11.1. The parameters of the JM model are N and ϕ, which can be estimated by the maxi-

Failure rate

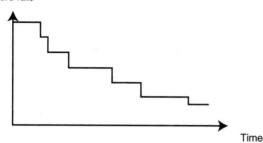

Time

Figure 11.1 Failure Rate of the JM Model

mum likelihood (ML) method given x_i, m, and m_i. The maximum likelihood estimators (MLEs) are solutions to the following simultaneous equations:

$$\begin{cases} \sum_{i=1}^{m} \frac{1}{N - n_{i-1}} - \sum_{i=1}^{m} \phi x_i = 0 \\ \frac{n}{\phi} - \sum_{i=1}^{m} (N - n_{i-1}) x_i = 0 \end{cases}$$

The JM model is easy to implement; however,

1. It assumes that all faults contribute equally to the unreliability of a program.
2. In certain cases, one might have $N = \infty$, $\phi = 0$ [Littlewood87].

Schick and Wolverton (SW) Model

Schick and Wolverton [Schick78] modified the JM model by assuming that

$$\lambda_i = \phi(N - n_{i-1}) x_i$$

The failure rate diagram for the S–W model is similar to that in Figure 11.1 except that the failure rate in each "stair" is dependent on x_i. This model differentiates the various faults regarding their contribution to the software failure.

Littlewood (L) Model

By assuming that the faults contribute different amounts to the unreliability of the software, Littlewood rewote the first equation in equation 11.1 [Littlewood81] as

$$\Pr(x_i | \Lambda_i = \lambda_i) = \lambda_i e^{-\lambda_i x_i}$$

where $\{\Lambda_i\}$ represents the successive current rate of occurrence of failures arising from the gradual elimination of faults. Here

$$\Lambda_i = \Phi_1,...,\Phi_{N-i+1}$$

where Φ_j represents the random rate associated with fault j. When the program is executed for a total time τ, the Bayesian theorem shows that the remaining rates are identically independently distributed (i.i.d) gamma (α, $\beta + \tau$) random variables. Furthermore, given $\Phi_i = \phi_i$, we have

$$\Pr(x_i | \Phi_i = \phi_i) = \phi_i e^{-\phi_i x_i} \tag{11.2}$$

If Φ_i has a gamma distribution with parameters α and β, the unconditioned probability of X_i (from equation 11.2) follows a Pareto distribution:

$$\Pr(X_i = x_i) = \frac{\alpha \beta^\alpha}{(\beta + x_i)^{\alpha+1}}$$

The ML method is applied for estimating the model parameters α, β, and N if m and $x_1, \ldots, x_{i-1}$ are known. The estimated current reliability based on data $x_1, \ldots, x_{i-1}$ is [Abdel-Ghaly86]

$$R_i(t) = \left(\frac{\beta + \tau}{\beta + \tau + t} \right)^{(N-i+1)q}$$

$$\tau = \sum_{j=1}^{i=1} x_j$$

The failure rate of the L model is shown in Figure 11.2.

Weibull Order Statistics (W) Model

The JM and the L models can be treated as special cases of a general class of stochastic processes based on order statistics [Abdel-Ghaly86]. These processes exhibit intervene times that are the spacing between order statistics from a random sample of

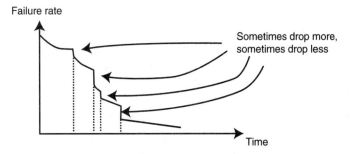

Figure 11.2   Failure Rate of the L Model

N observations with p.d.f. *f*(*x*) which is exponential and Pareto for JM and L, respectively. For the SW model, *f*(*x*) has the Weibull density. The parameters can also be obtained via the ML method.

Ross (R) Model

The objective here is to find a way to estimate the error rate of the revised software package. Some assumptions are [Ross85,89] as follows:

1. Initially, the interested package contains an unknown number, say *m*, of bugs.
2. Each of the bugs that is discovered would have been responsible for a certain number of errors.
3. Bug *i* will cause errors to occur in accordance with a Poisson process having an unknown rate λ_i, $i = 1, 2, \ldots, m$. If the system is operated for *s* units of time, then, on average, there will be $\lambda_i s$ errors resulted from bug *i*.
4. The errors caused by bugs are independent.
5. The test for this package will run for *t* time units.

Define the indicating function $\Psi_i(t)$ as

$$\Psi_i(t) = \begin{cases} 1 \text{ if bug } i \text{ has not caused an error by } t \\ 0 \text{ otherwise} \end{cases}$$

The quantity we wish to estimate is

$$\Lambda(t) = \sum_i \lambda_i \Psi_i(t)$$

which is the hazard rate of the revised final package. We can have

$$E[\Lambda(t)] = \sum_i \lambda_i E[\Psi_i(t)] = \sum_i \lambda_i e^{-\lambda_i t}$$

From assumption 2 above, we define $M_j(t)$ as the number of faults that were responsible for *j* errors; that is, $M_1(t)$ is the number of bugs that caused exactly one error, $M_2(t)$ the number of bugs that caused two errors, and so on. Therefore,

$$\sum_j j M_j(t)$$

will be the total number of errors that resulted. Further define

$$I_i(t) = \begin{cases} 1 \text{ if bug } i \text{ causes exactly one error} \\ 0 \text{ otherwise} \end{cases}$$

Then

$$M_1(t) = \sum_i I_i(t).$$

Taking expectation at both sides, we have

$$E[M_1(t)] = \sum_i E[I_i(t)] = \sum_i \lambda_i t e^{-\lambda_i t}$$

Since $E[\Lambda(t) - M_t(t)/t] = 0$, we can use $M_t(t)/t$ as an estimate of $\Lambda(t)$.

Bayesian JM Models (BJM)

For software systems, information is usually available about the software development. Useful information can also be obtained from similar **SoftwareProduct**s through, for example, some measurements of the software complexity (see Chapter 6), the fault-removal history during the design phase, and so on. The information can be used in combination with the collected test data to make a more accurate estimation and prediction of the software reliability. Bayesian analysis is a common technique for incorporating previous information. Attempts have been made at using Bayesian techniques to deal with the analysis of software failure data and previous information in the form of a so-called prior distribution of the unknown parameters.

The most important feature of a Bayesian model is that prior information can be incorporated into the estimation procedure. Bayesian methods are especially useful in reliability analysis because an increase in reliability is usually achieved by improving a similar **SoftwareProduct** previously developed. With an appropriate prior, Bayesian inference is quite accurate and gives much better results than other methods, such as the method of maximum likelihood or least squares. Also, Bayesian methods require fewer test data to achieve a high accuracy of estimation.

To avoid the use of MLE for making inference in the JM model; Littlewood and Sofer [Littlewood87] proposed a Bayesian approach (the BJM model; also refer to [Abdel-Ghaly86]) by assuming that λ and ϕ are described by gamma distributions [Littlewood87]. Thus,

$$\begin{cases} R_i(t) = \iint R_i(t \mid \lambda_i, \phi) f(\lambda_i, \phi \mid t_1, ..., t_{i-1}) d\lambda_i d\phi \\ R_i(t \mid \lambda_i, \phi) = e^{-(\lambda_i - (i-1)\phi)t} \end{cases}$$

from which we can obtain an analytical solution for software reliability.

The drawback of the JM and BJM models is that they treat debugging as a deterministic process: each fix is effective with certainty and all fixes have the same effect on the reliability, which will be solved by the Littlewood model [Littlewood81].

Goel–Okumoto (GO) Model

The Goel–Okumoto (GO) model is similar to the JM model except that N is treated as a Poisson random variable with mean y; Goel and Okumoto indicate that the differences from the JM model are in two respects [Goel79]:

1. The initial error content of a software system is treated as a r.v. in the GO model, while in the JM model it is an unknown, fixed constant.

2. In the JM model, the times between software failures are assumed to be s-independent of each other, while in the GO model the time between failure $k - 1$ and k depends on the time to failure $k - 1$.

NONHOMOGENEOUS POISSON PROCESS MODELS

A random process whose probability distribution varies with time is known as a non-homogeneous process. The class of nonhomogeneous Poisson process (NHPP) models is widely used, since most failure processes during tests fit this situation. The main characteristic of this type of model is that there is a mean value function, which is defined as the expected number of failures up to a given time. The failure intensity function is the rate of change of the mean value function or the number of failures per unit time.

The NHPP models have been widely applied by practitioners. The theory of NHPP is well developed and can be found in most of the established literature on stochastic processes. The calculation of the expected number of failures up to time t is very simple due to the existence of a mean value function. The estimates of the parameters are easily obtained by using either the method of maximum likelihood or the method of least squares. Also, NHPP models are useful in describing reliability growth. By using different mean value functions, we can fit software failure data to some satisfactory degree.

In this section, we select two models for presentation and application of the NHPP models: the basic execution time model and the logarithmic Poisson execution time model. These two models are chosen because each has certain advantages not possessed by the other. The reasons for selecting the basic execution time model are as follows:

1. It has a satisfactory record of prediction.
2. It is simple and easy to understand.
3. It is the model that is most thoroughly developed and has been reported to applications of actual **Project**s.
4. Its parameters have a clear physical interpretation and can be related to information existing prior to the program's execution. The information includes

characteristics of the software, such as size, and characteristics of the development environment.

5. It can handle evolving systems (systems that change in size) by adjusting the failure time to estimate results had all the code been present.

Musa's Basic Execution Time (Musa's Basic) Model

Musa's basic model [Musa90] assumes that failures occur as a nonhomogeneous Poisson process. The decrement in the failure intensity function remains constant for the basic execution time model whether it is the first failure that is being fixed or the last. The basic execution time model implies a uniform operational profile. Studies by Downs [Downs85] and Trachtenberg [Trachtenberg85], however, demonstrate that for a highly nonuniform operational profile, the logarithmic Poisson model may be a better choice.

Let μ denote the average number of failures experienced at a given point of time. Then the failure intensity λ as a function of μ is

$$\lambda(\mu) = \lambda_0 \left(1 - \frac{\mu}{v_0} \right)$$

where λ_0 is the initial failure intensity at the start of execution and v_0 is the total number of failures that would occur in an infinite amount of time. Let the execution time be denoted by τ. Then, for the basic model we have

$$\mu(\tau) = v_0 \left[1 - \exp\left(-\frac{\lambda_0}{v_0} \tau \right) \right] \tag{11.3}$$

and the failure intensity as a function of the execution time is

$$\lambda(\tau) = \lambda_0 \exp\left(-\frac{\lambda_0}{v_0} \tau \right)$$

Logarithmic Poisson (LP) Model

The logarithmic Poisson execution time model [Musa90] also assumes that failures occur as an NHPP. The decrement per failure in the failure intensity function becomes smaller with each failure experienced; that is, later fixes have less effect on program reliability than earlier ones. In fact, the decrement decreases exponentially.

With the same definitions for μ, λ_0, and τ as in the basic execution time model, the failure intensity λ as a function of μ is

$$\lambda(\mu) = \lambda_0 \exp(-\theta\mu)$$

where θ is called the failure intensity decay parameter. It represents the relative change of failure intensity per failure experienced. Similar to equation 11.3, we have

$$\mu(t) = \frac{1}{\theta}\ln(\lambda_0\theta\tau + 1)$$

Hence, the failure intensity as a function of the execution time is

$$\lambda(\tau) = \frac{\lambda_0}{\lambda_0\theta\tau + 1}$$

For the two models just described, we need the value of the initial failure intensity λ_0 in both models, the total failures experienced ν_0 for the basic execution time model, and the failure intensity decay parameter θ for the logarithmic Poisson model. Once enough failure data are gathered, we can estimate these parameters by the ML method, for example; the larger the failure sample size, the more accurate the estimates. It should be noted that the NHPP models are capable of coping with non-homogeneous testing and changing software, and hence they are very useful for software reliability measurements.

However, the logarithmic Poisson time model has a high predictive validity, which it attains early in the system test phase. So if the early predictive validity is very important or the operational profile is highly nonuniform, it has been suggested [Musa90] that the logarithmic Poisson execution time model is a better choice.

THE NONSTOCHASTIC SOFTWARE RELIABILITY MODELS

Software reliability models are presented here for which no dynamic assumption about the software failure process has been made. This class of models is mainly useful for the estimation of the number of software faults, and it is usually assumed that faults are not removed immediately after detection. Two models included here are the input-domain-based model and the fault-seeding model.

Input-domain-based Model

Nelson [Nelson73] proposes a method for estimating software reliability by taking representative samples from the input domain and looking at the resultant failure rate when the sample data are input to the system for execution. It is assumed that a number of test cases are chosen from the operational profile of the software.

Assume that the input space (which is also called the input domain) E is divided into M subsets; that is,

$$E = \{E_1, E_2, ..., E_M : M > 0\}$$

The reliability of a single execution of the software, R_1, is then equal to

$$R_1 = \sum_{i=1}^{M} p_i X_i$$

where p_i is the probability of choosing an input datum from E_i, and

$$X_i = \begin{cases} 1 \text{ if input } E_i \text{ leads to correct output} \\ 0 \text{ otherwise} \end{cases}$$

The quantity $\{p_i: i = 1, 2, \ldots, M\}$ is the operational profile of the software, which describes the user condition, and it is assumed to be known completely. If each test run consists of n executions of the software, then the reliability of the test run is

$$R(n) = \prod_{j=1}^{n} R_j$$

The weakness of the Nelson model and other input-domain-based models include [Ryerson89]

1. a large amount of testing is necessary in order to get a highly accurate estimate of the reliability,
2. the representative samples may not exist, and
3. there may be no correlation between results from one sample to another.

Fault-seeding Model

A known number of **Defect**s can be seeded into a software, which is then tested using a process that presumably has equal probability of finding a seeded or an indigenous **Defect**. The numbers of indigenous and seeded faults found are used to estimate the system reliability.

Ferrara [Ferrara89] uses fault injection: known faults are introduced purposely into the design. The best-known seeding model is the Mills model [Mills72] in which a statistical sampling technique called capture–recapture sampling is used to estimate software reliability. Let M denote the number of seeded faults. Suppose that during the testing k faults are detected and m of them are seeded faults. If both inherent faults and seeded faults are equally likely detected, then an estimate of the total number of inherent faults is

$$\hat{N} = \frac{M(k-m)}{m}$$

Let X_k be the number of seeded faults among the total number of k detected faults. And let p_i denote the probability of detecting i seeded faults, that is $p_i = P(X_k = i \mid M)$. Then X_i follows the hypergeometric distribution utilizing the results of capture–recapture sampling. It can be shown that the above estimate of inherent faults $\hat{N}$ is the ML estimate that maximizes p_m with respect to N.

It is a major assumption that the probability of detecting the seeded faults is the same as the probability of detecting the inherent faults. This is in practice impossible, since seeded faults can hardly be made representative of the inherent faults, and this will make the estimate biased and inaccurate. Some software captive–recaptive methods are also reported in [Vander Wiel93].

SOFTWARE LIFE CYCLE COSTS

Reliability Cost

Studies of software cost have concentrated on development cost. However, life cycle cost is the more appropriate one to be studied.

For hardware, the life cycle cost is usually studied from a buyer's standpoint. Life cycle costs can be divided into procurement, maintenance, and disposal costs. Since software development and maintenance are normally performed by the same **Organization**, the software life cycle cost is usually studied from the developer's point of view and is divided into costs of design and development and costs of operation and maintenance.

The software design and development process can be broken down into several phases [Chi90, Lin87]: requirement and specification, design, coding, and testing. Among these phases, testing (including unit tests, integration tests, and field tests) accounts for 40% or more of the development cost.

Operation and maintenance costs make up about 60% of software life cycle costs. Included in maintenance costs are such activities as preventive maintenance, corrective maintenance, adaptive maintenance, enhancement, and growth. Since testing is part of each of these operation and maintenance activities, it becomes a major factor in the cost of maintenance, as well as of design and development.

For common software **Project**s, the reliability cost is mainly incurred by testing. To produce highly reliable software, we incur additional reliability costs at every phase of the software life cycle. Indeed, a large portion of the software life cycle is devoted to achieving high reliability. Table 11.2 compares reliability costs incurred at each phase of the software life cycle for common and highly reliable software.

A number of time domain software reliability models have been proposed. A categorical limitation of the existing models is that they treat all software failures,

Table 11.2 Reliability Cost and Software Life Cycle Phases

Phase	Reliability Cost of Common Software	Additional Reliability Cost for Highly Reliable Software
Design and Development		
Requirements and specifications	Basic requirement and specification walkthrough	Parallel development of requirements and specifications and detailed validation
Design	Basic design walkthrough	Parallel design, fault-tolerant design, and detailed verification
Coding	Basic code walkthrough	Parallel coding of critical modules, fault-tolerance codes, and detailed code walkthrough
Testing	Basic testing	Extensive testing, stress test, and reliability assessment
Operational and Maintenance		
Preventive maintenance	Totally devoted to reliability	Higher frequency of preventive maintenance
Corrective maintenance	Totally devoted to reliability	Immediate correction and extra testing
Adaptive maintenance	Testing	Extra testing
Enhancement	Equivalent to a development subcycle	
Growth	Equivalent to a development subcycle	

equally, merely counting failures, and not taking into account the widely differing severities of these failures. What is needed is a software reliability modeling technique that enhances the existing models to take into account the penalty cost associated with each failure.

Reliability-related Software Cost Models

The program evolution model describes the dynamic nature of software. The software is subject to constant change after delivery. Correcting errors, adding new functions, deleting unnecessary functions, adapting to the new environment, and improving performance are among the major activities of the evolution process. As new functions and new codes are added, the reliability of the software decreases. Unless effort is devoted to keeping the reliability under control, further changes will make it even more costly to maintain the desired reliability. Resources can be devoted to growth (which tends to increase the failure rate), to error removal (which will decrease the failure rate), or to routine service (which does not affect the failure rate).

The ultimate purpose of the evolution model is to consider these conflicting factors under limited resources and to provide a guideline to management for setting up the optimum reliability level and the optimum release time.

The program evolution can be approached by an analytical or simulation model [Woodside80]. Reliability can be related to the size of the program (total number of modulars, number of modulars changed, number of modulars added), release number, system load, operational profile, and complexity measures. Unlike the cost estimation model and the resource allocation model, which are concerned with the amount of reliability cost, the program evolution model describes the interactions between reliability and other factors.

Software Reliability and Cost

The software reliability model measures and predicts the reliability of the software during testing and maintenance phases. Software reliability is defined as the probability of failure-free operation of a software program under the specified conditions for a specified period of time. Many software reliability models fall into the category of the "bug counting" model, which represents the number of remaining faults (or the number of failures experienced) at time t as a stochastic counting process.

The mean value function uses in various stochastic models previously [Lin87] can be incorporated into the software life cycle cost model to determine the optimal release time and the optimal reliability level. Total reliability cost, consisting of the reliability cost during testing and the reliability cost during maintenance, can be formulated on a per fault basis [Forman79, Koch83, Okumoto79, Shanthikumar83]. The reliability cost during testing is a function of the number of faults removed during testing and the length of testing time. The reliability cost during maintenance is also a function of the number of faults removed during operation and the length of operational time. Then, total reliability cost can be expressed as follows:

$$
\begin{aligned}
TC(t) &= C_1[M(0) - M(t)] + (C_2 + C_3)\,[M(t) - M(T)] \\
&\quad + C_4 t + C_5(T - t) \\
&= (C_2 + C_3 - C_1)M(t) + (C_4 - C_5)t \\
&\quad + C_1 M(0) - (C_2 + C_3)\,M(T) + C_5 T
\end{aligned}
$$

where C_1 = cost of correcting a fault during testing
C_2 = cost of correcting a fault during operation
C_3 = cost of damages or lost business per fault during operation
C_4 = cost of testing per unit of time
C_5 = cost of maintenance per unit of time
$M(t)$ = mean value function at time t, determined by one of the software stochastic models given in the previous section
TC = total reliability cost

VC = variable reliability cost with respect to time

t = optimal release time

T = useful life of the software

The minimum of the variable cost can be found by setting the derivative to zero.

The cost estimation model, the resource allocation model, and the program evolution models all deal with reliability—empirically, indirectly, subjectively, and respectively. However, these macro models point out different aspects of software reliability cost issues and pave the way for future development of reliability-related life cycle cost models. Software reliability models, based on rigorous reliability theory, provide a better way of reasoning. This chapter examines life cycle cost modeling with emphasis on reviewing reliability cost in the software life cycle. Once the software reliability costs are determined, the software life cycle cost can be readily obtained [Kuo90].

SUMMARY

In summary,

1. Embedding quality and reliability concepts into the software design process can decrease software life cycle costs.
2. Considering software reliability models as design tools, one should be able to evaluate reliability-related software cost from a system viewpoint.
3. An optimal software development should not only consider the software reliability but also the minimum life cycle cost, given a reliability level.

REFERENCES

[Abdel-Ghaly86] Abdel-Ghaly, A. A., Chan, P. Y., and Littlewood, B., "Evaluation of Competing Software Reliability Predictions," *IEEE Transactions on Software Engineering,* Vol. SE-12, 1986, pp. 950–967.

[Bukowski92] Bukowski, J. V., Johnson, D. A., and Goble, W. M., "Software-reliability Feedback: A Physics-of-Failure Approach," *Annual Reliability and Maintainability Symposium,* 1992, pp. 285–289.

[Chi90] Chi, D., and Kuo, W., "Optimal Design for Software Reliability and Development Cost," *IEEE Journal on Selected Areas in Communications,* Vol. 8, No. 2, February 1990, pp. 276–282.

[Chien96]   Chien, K., and Kuo, W., "A Nonparametric Approach to Estimate Burn-in Time," *IEEE Transactions on Semiconductor Manufacturing*, Vol. 9, No. 3, 1996, pp. 461–467.

[Downs85]   Downs, T., "An Approach to the Modeling of Software Testing with Some Applications," *IEEE Transactions on Software Engineering*, Vol. SE-11, No. 4, 1985, pp. 375–386.

[Ferrara89]   Ferrara, K. C., Keene, S. J., and Lane, C., "Software Reliability from a System Perspective," *Annual Reliability and Maintainability Symposium*, 1989, pp. 332–336.

[Forman79]   Forman, E. H., and Singpurwalla, N. D., "Optimal Time Intervals for Testing Hypothesis in Computer Software Errors," *IEEE Transactions on Reliability*, Vol. R-28, No. 3, 1979, pp. 250–253.

[Goel79]   Goel, A. L., and Okumoto, K., "Time-dependent Error-detection Rate Model for Software Reliability and Other Performance Measures," *IEEE Transactions on Reliability*, Vol. R-28, August 1979, pp. 206–211.

[Hansen88]   Hansen, M. D., "Software System Safety and Reliability," *Annual Reliability and Maintainability Symposium*, 1988, pp. 214–217.

[Hess88]   Hess, J. A., "Measuring Software for Its Reuse Potential," *Annual Reliability and Maintainability Symposium*, 1988, pp. 202–207.

[Jelinski71]   Jelinski, Z., and Moranda, P. B., "Software Reliability Research," McDonnell Douglas Astronautics paper ED 1808, presented at the *Conference on Statistical Methods for the Evaluation of Computer System Performance*, Brown University, Providence, RI, November 1971, pp. 465–484; also *Statistical Computer Performance Evaluation*, W. Freiberger, ed., Academic Press, New York, 1972.

[Keene93]   Keene, S. J., and Keene, K. C., "Reducing the Life Cycle Cost of Software through Concurrent Engineering," *Annual Reliability and Maintainability Symposium*, 1993, pp. 274–279.

[Koch83]   Koch, H. S., and Kubat, P., "Optimal Release Time of Computer Software," *IEEE Transactions on Software Engineering*, Vol. SE-9, No. 3, 1983, pp. 323–327.

[Koss88]   Koss, W. E., "Software-reliability Metrics for Military Systems," *Annual Reliability and Maintainability Symposium*, 1988, pp. 190–194.

[Kubat83]   Kubat, P., and Koch, H. S., "Pragmatic Testing Protocols to Measure Software Reliability," *IEEE Transactions on Reliability*, Vol. R-32, October 1983, pp. 338–341.

[Kuo83a]   Kuo, W., and Kuo, Y., "Facing the Headaches of ICs Early Failures: A State-of-the-art Review of Burn-in Decisions," *Proceedings IEEE*, Vol. 71, No. 11, November 1983, pp. 1257–1266.

[Kuo83b]   Kuo, W., "Software Reliability Estimation: A Realization of Computing Risk," *Microelectronics and Reliability*, Vol. 23, No. 2, May 1983, pp. 249–260.

[Kuo90]   Kuo, W., "Modeling and Management of Software Reliability: A Tutorial," in *Handbook of Software Reliability*, McGraw-Hill Book Co., New York, 1990.

[Lin87]   Lin, H. H., and Kuo, W., "Reliability Cost in Software Life-cycle Models," *Annual Reliability and Maintainability Symposium*, 1987, pp. 364–368.

[Littlewood81]   Littlewood, B., "Stochastic Reliability Growth: A Model for Fault Removal in Computer Programs and Hardware Designs," *IEEE Transactions on Reliability,* October 1981, pp. 313–320.

[Littlewood87]   Littlewood, B., and Sofer, A., "A Bayesian Modification to the Jelinski–Moranda Software Reliability Growth Model," *Software Engineering Journal,* March 1987, pp. 30–41.

[Lynch94]   Lynch, T., Pham, H., and Kuo, W., "Modeling Software Reliability with Multiple Failure Types and Imperfect Debugging," *Annual Reliability and Maintainability Symposium,* 1994, pp. 235–241.

[Mills72]   Mills, H. D., "On the Statistical Validation of Computer Programs," IBM Federal Systems Division, Report FSC-72-6015, Gaithersburg, MD, 1972.

[Musa90]   Musa, J. D., Iannino, A., and Okumoto, K., *Software Reliability,* McGraw-Hill Book Co., New York, 1990.

[Nelson73]   Nelson, E. C., "A Statistical Basis for Software Reliability Assessment," TRW Software Series, TRW-SS-73-03, Redondo Beach, CA, 1973.

[Norden63]   Norden, P. V., "Useful Tools for Project Management," in *Operations Research and Development,* John Wiley & Sons, New York, 1963.

[Ohtera90]   Ohtera, H., and Yamada, S., "Optimal Allocation and Control Problems for Software Testing Resources," *IEEE Transactions on Reliability,* Vol. 39, June 1990, pp. 171–176.

[Okumoto79]   Okumoto, K., and Goel, A. L., "Optimal Release Time for Software Systems," *Proceedings, COMPSAC,* 1979, pp. 500–503.

[Ryerson89]   Ryerson, C. M., and Ryerson, C., "Thought Provoking Gems from My Reliability Experience," *Annual Reliability and Maintainability Symposium,* 1989, pp. 234–238.

[Schick78]   Schick, G. J., and Wolverton, R. W., "An Analysis of Competing Software Reliability Models," *IEEE Transactions on Software Engineering,* Vol. SE-4, March 1978, pp. 104–120.

[Schneidewind93]   Schneidewind, N. F., "Software Reliability Model with Optimal Selection of Failure Data," *IEEE Transactions on Software Engineering,* Vol. 19, November 1993, pp. 1095–1104.

[Shanthikumar83]   Shanthikumar, J. G., and Tufekci, S., "Application of a Software Reliability Model to Decide Software Release Time," *Microelectronics and Reliability,* Vol. 23, No. 1, 1983, pp. 41–59.

[Shooman84]   Shooman, M. L., "Software Reliability: A Historical Perspective," *IEEE Transactions on Reliability,* Vol. R-33, April 1984, pp. 48–55.

[Trachtenberg85]   Trachtenberg, M., "The Linear Software Reliability Model and Uniform Testing," *IEEE Transactions on Reliability,* Vol. R-34, April 1985, pp. 8–16.

[Vander Wiel93]   Vander Wiel, S. A., Lawrence, G., and Votta, L. G., "Assessing Software Design Using Capture–Recapture Methods," *IEEE Transactions on Software Engineering,* Vol. 19, No. 11, November 1993, pp. 1045–1054.

[Woodside80]   Woodside, C. M., "A Mathematical Model for the Evolution of Software," *Journal of Systems and Software,* 1980, pp. 337–345.

[Xie87]   Xie, M., "A Shock Model for Software Failures," *Microelectronics and Reliability,* Vol. 27, No. 4, 1987, pp. 717–724.

[Yates90]   Yates III, W. D., and Shaller, D. A., "Reliability Engineering as Applied to Software," *Annual Reliability and Maintainability Symposium,* 1990, pp. 425–429.

[Yourdon92]   Edward, Y., *Decline and Fall of the American Programmer,* Yourdon Press, Englewood Cliffs, NJ, 1992, p. 19.

12
Verification and Validation Testing

Obviously, it doesn't do much good to write lots and lots of software if it doesn't work, or if it can't be trusted, or if it can't be easily modified and maintained.

Edward Yourdon
[Yourdon92]

INTRODUCTION

The software process can be mapped to various kinds of software life cycle models as explained in Chapter 4. No matter what software life cycle model you use, testing is an important and indispensable activity. The testing phases are often called the V&V (validation and verification) phases. Testing is performed to validate **Feature**s and/or verify design. Even if we take the validation activity only as an example, the cost for the activity runs from 25% to 40% of the entire process [Boehm76]. Therefore, it will be significantly beneficial to know the methodology of conducting effective and efficient testing and to understand testing tools. The keys to successful testing are (1) well-designed and timely test planning and strategy, (2) development of effective test cases, and (3) efficient and effective management of test activities.

Test planning and strategy describe the type of testing activity that should be performed during each phase of a software life cycle. When effective test cases are developed and used, the effectiveness of the testing process will be significantly increased. Also, all testing activities should be logged and used for the next **Project**; otherwise, you would repeat the same processes including the mistakes.

In this chapter we will discuss the above three points from various perspectives. In modern industry, obtaining high-quality software in a limited time is a must requirement. To achieve this goal, we should view the development and testing stages as parallel activities. Another required mental shift is that testing is just as important as development, if not more so. In many companies, testing responsibility is frequently given to junior engineers and viewed as a less important task. However, complex modern software requires a systematic and integrated testing approach. Another common misconception is that testing is an activity performed at the end of development phase. Such a testing activity is just one kind of testing, and there are many other tests that need to be performed at earlier stages of software development life cycle. The concept of orderly testing is important to be successful in testing activities, and a discussion of this is found later in this chapter.

Perry [Perry95] quoted the following statement made by an information services manager: "Too little testing is a crime—too much testing is a sin." In reality, however, you often do not have unlimited time for testing even if you want to commit the sin. Therefore, one of the important issues becomes how effectively we can test with as little resources as possible. Often you do not have the luxury of complete **Feature** or design specifications. Your **SoftwareProduct Feature**s may change after most of the implementation is completed. Thus, the objective of this chapter is not to explain rigid test techniques or methodologies, but rather to describe key testing activities.

TEST PLANNING AND STRATEGY

One factor that influences test planning and strategy is the size of the program being developed and tested. Programs used in industry are becoming larger and more complex, and the demand for developing complex and large software has been increasing as more things that were controlled at the hardware level are now controlled by software. In high-tech industries, software must be more flexible and practical in order to keep up with rapid technology advancement and market requirements.

The V SLC (see Figure 4.6) discussed in Chapter 4 is a model that emphasizes V&V and ties the V&V activities closely to development activities. Variations of V SLC are used in most test plans.

White-box Testing versus Black-box Testing

Testing is an activity to find **Defect**s in a program by executing the program. Two things drive a testing activity: logic and data. If the test strategy is driven by logic, it is called white-box testing, and if by data, black-box testing.

White-box Testing.   To execute white-box testing, the tester must know the internal structure of the program. That is, the tester should know exactly what input should be used to cover which path and what output should be produced by the execution of a particular part of a program. One may think that a program can be completely tested when every statement of the program is executed at least once. However, the reality is that even if all branches in a program are executed the program is still not completely tested. This is because each control flow may contain an exponentially large number of unique logic paths. In fact, the program size we deal with in industry is becoming larger and larger, and it is impossible to execute all possible logical paths in a program to attain complete testing.

Let's take a moment to think about successful or effective testing. Effective testing is to find as many **Defect**s as possible in a limited time. An effective test case is one that finds **Defect**s in the program or successfully identifies program failures. Effective use of white-box testing is not to exhaust all unique logic paths of the program, but to identify obvious logic or design **Defect**s in coding. One way to accomplish effective white-box testing is to prepare a set of the input data that produces a correct output and another set of input data that produces an incorrect output. Both sets of input data must be well controlled, which means that the output value is precisely known [Copi68]. Since white-box testing requires knowledge of the internal structure of the program, it is the programmer who should design and execute test cases.

It is often said that programmers should not test their own programs. Programmers may unconsciously avoid finding errors [Myers76]. We know it is difficult for programmers to find design errors in their own programs due to their misunderstanding of specifications. The reason we recommend that the programmer design test cases for white-box testing and even execute testing is because the programmer can take advantage of knowledge of the internal structure of the program.

Black-box Testing.   The tester does not know how the program internally behaves during black-box testing. Thus, the tester views the program as a black box in which internal operations cannot be seen. The tester makes sure that a program produces expected output and behaves to meet its specification. Since the tester does not care how and where data flow through software, black-box testing is often referred as data-driven testing.

How can we carry out effective black-box testing? The input data used for black-box testing should be prepared totally dependent on the specification. This may imply that every possible input data must be used to attain full coverage. However, this approach is impractical in most cases.

Instead of trying to produce exhaustive input, you should consider only the input data that cover most, if not all, functionality of the program. It may still seem like a large number of test cases; however, there would be a lot fewer than for exhaustive testing. And, in fact, it would be much more effective and practical. The tester does not need to know why and how the program produces the output; the tester only needs to know what outputs should be produced based on the input data. A combination of black-box and white-box testing can be very effective.

ORDERLY TESTING PROCESSES

The following sections discuss testing processes at different stages of the software life cycle. A key to success in testing software is to use a test process that corresponds to a development process. Figure 12.1 outlines the relationships between the testing phases and earlier activities of development phases. An important thing to understand here is that matching a test phase to a development phase helps to focus on the type of **Defect**s that the test phase intends to find.

Unit Test and System Test

Unit test activity tests the individual **Chunk**s, which are composed of objects, functions, procedures, subroutines, or any small building blocks of a **SoftwareProduct**. The unit test should be performed along with the development of each unit. Unit testing is generally white-box oriented. That is, testing needs to be performed with knowledge of the unit's internal behavior.

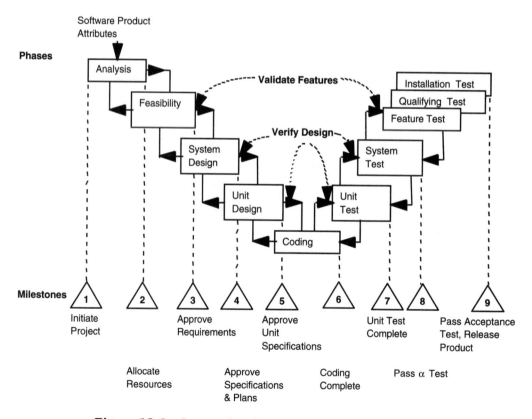

Figure 12.1   Correspondence between Testing Process and Development Activity

The idea is to test each building component of a program before combining them into a whole. The benefits of unit testing include the following:

1. Unit testing leads to an overall efficient software life cycle as multiple units can be tested simultaneously and the testing activities can proceed in parallel with development activities.

2. Since unit testing is focused on functionality and internal behavior, finding and correcting **Defect**s is easier.

3. Building an entire system with **Defect**-free units contributes to higher-quality software in less time. This concept is true not only in developing software, but also in other assembly processes. For example, if you are assembling a car, you would like to have high-quality parts so that your assembly process will be smooth and the final car will have fewer **Defect**s.

Unit Test Strategy. How can effective unit testing be accomplished? To execute unit testing, we must have source code and specifications for the unit. As discussed above, one of the objectives of unit testing is to determine if the unit produces the expected output. In other words, the functionality is correctly implemented in the unit. In order to verify the unit's functionality, typically input and output parameters specified in the unit's specification are used.

Procedures and techniques for designing test cases are well documented elsewhere in the literature and will not be repeated here. As mentioned before, unit testing is mainly white-box testing. That is, we first recommend designing test cases with input to exercise the logic of the unit. This is typical white-box testing, which could imply execution of all paths in the unit. However, since it is impossible to always execute every path in a program, it is best to first cover only the paths outlined in the specification. Then add randomly selected subsets from all possible input values to test the unit's outputs as in black-box testing.

System Test. System testing begins after the integration of all tested units. System testing is sometimes called integration testing. The beginning of system test can be viewed as the end of unit testing. If unit testing is properly performed, system testing is easier and less painful. To make system testing efficient, thorough unit testing should be emphasized. As shown in Figure 12.1, the objective of system testing is to determine if the integrated units work together as designed. An α test is normally required to assure that a system is properly integrated and is ready for the more comprehensive β testing process.

Feature Test

The objective of a **Feature** test is to validate that the **SoftwareProduct** operates correctly according to proposed **Feature**s. Instead of how does the system work, the question now becomes what does the system do? **Feature** test is, in general, black-box oriented. The testers do not care how the program behaves internally, but they check to see if the program behaves according to the required **Feature**s. What test engineers do at this stage is to profile general users. We mentioned that developers should normally perform unit and system testing. **Feature** testing, however, should be performed by people other than developers. This is simply because the knowledge of internal structure may prevent testers from running certain test cases, unconsciously or consciously, where failures could be suspected. **Feature** tests are often automated by running scripts, which is called scenario-based testing.

In order to perform an effective **Feature** test, a complete and detailed **Feature** specification must be available. The specification has to be well understood and analyzed so that a thorough test suite can be developed. In short, **Feature** testing should have test cases that validate that all the specified **Feature**s are included and correctly functioning.

Qualification Test

The purpose of a qualification test is to determine if the **SoftwareProduct** is acceptable for release to the market. The scope of the test is generally larger than other testing phases and may include testing to see if the software is backward compatible with the company's previous **SoftwareProduct** lines or if the software is acceptable for use in a restricted environment.

Qualification tests are important in the commercial environment. Even if previous test phases, such as unit, system and **Feature** testing, are completed successfully, the software should not be released if qualification test results are not satisfactory. Several aspects can be used to determine if the system is acceptable. Qualification test results are not simply pass or fail. Rather, they must be compared and analyzed based on the company's accepted policies and practices. For example, tests that are frequently used to qualify **SoftwareProduct**s are

- Durability
- Stress
- Performance
- **Usability**
- Compatibility

Durability.   During durability testing, the system is heavily exercised. For example, if an operating system or firmware is being tested, the system may be continuously run for several nights. Or if the program is a database system, large amounts of data may be entered to see if the system is durable. A high volume of data exchange and extensively long concentrated usage of a system are examples of intensive environments that can be used for durability testing.

Some software is tightly related to the performance of hardware; firmware is one example. Firmware is between software and hardware. It is software stored in read-only memory. Thus, testing firmware actually involves the durability of circuitry. Durability testing is particularly important when the software is a commercial **SoftwareProduct** where users may operate the system beyond its normal limits.

Stress. A stress test tries to hit the broader line of system capability. Executing a program with just above the required memory size is an example of a stress test. Users may not always have as much memory as the developers have, and the program could behave differently under the limited environment. Although hardware cost is declining and hardware resources such as memory and disk space may not be issues in the future, we still need to extend our testing to cover the environment, which may not be ample, or any other environment attribute that developers may take for granted.

Performance. Performance frequently becomes a trade-off with resources (or cost). A specified level of performance has to be obtained to release a **SoftwareProduct**. When developers are more concerned about internal behavior or resource limitations, performance sometimes degrades without being noticed. Thus, performance testing has to be included as a part of qualification tests so that internal changes do not affect performance.

Usability. Detailed discussion on **Usability** testing is found in Chapters 13 and 14. **Usability** testing is a process defined separately from V&V testing. However, confirming **Usability** of a program or software should not be overlooked. When software is released as a **SoftwareProduct**, **Usability** is very important.

Compatibility. Compatibility testing determines if software is compatible with a company's previous **SoftwareProduct**s or similar **SoftwareProduct**s of targeted competitors. From a business prospective, it is important to confirm that the software does not stand alone or cannot cope with other software that is commonly used with the **SoftwareProduct**. Failing to confirm compatibility could result in loss of sales.

Installation Test

The installation test is the last validation step for a commercial **SoftwareProduct**. To distribute a **SoftwareProduct**, you must select some type of secondary storage for the software, such as disks, CDs, or tapes. Whatever you select, you must verify that the system works properly in the new environment.

It is apparent that if the installation process does not work properly, users cannot access the software; thus, every effort spent for the software development and testing will become meaningless.

Regression Test

Utilizing regression testing is sensible and cost effective in real-life situations if it is used properly. Even after system testing has performed, making changes in the code is almost inevitable. When a change is made to a part of the code, we would like to assure that the change did not cause a problem or introduce new **Defect**s in the other part of code. Thus, regression testing should be performed whenever code is modified.

The objective of regression testing is to determine if the local change in the program has regressed other aspects of the program. By running an entire test suite, we can achieve the objective if time and cost are not an issue. However, the reality is that we always need to evaluate cost/benefit and time constraints very carefully. Thus, usually a subset of test cases is run to exercise the changed **Area** and the **Area** that could be affected by the changes.

Regression testing is necessary because any changes made in a program can introduce additional **Defect**s. As Figure 12.1 shows, testing and **Defect** fixing are iterative processes. However, if you have to run an entire system test or **Feature** test every time any part of a program is changed, the **SoftwareProduct** may never be released. The regression test rationale is to focus on the changes made and to test only the **Area** of changes, rather than the entire program. The three components of a successful regression test are (1) identification of the **Area** of code where changes are made, (2) exercise this **Area** and the related **Area**, and (3) identifying and selecting test cases that can articulately execute the said **Area**s.

As we discuss later in this chapter, the test data management tool is a useful tool for many testing activities. In particular, with the test data management tool that allows testers to select test cases that meet a specific criteria, regression testing can be executed effectively and efficiently.

In the following section, we will discuss the importance of test case development. If you understand which test case exercises what **Feature** or which part of a unit, you should be able to pinpoint test execution and regression testing.

SOFTWARE TESTING INTEGRATED ENVIRONMENT

Computer-aided software engineering (CASE) tools help developers analyze approaches to problem solving, develop requirements, create design specifications, and generate code. Similarly, many tools are being developed to assist in the conduct and management of testing activities. Current trends of the computer-aided software testing (CAST) tool market are in the direction of an integrated test environment. Testing is not an isolated activity that you can do in an ad hoc manner. Testing that is systematic and integrated with all development phases is the key to producing a successful **SoftwareProduct**.

As **SoftwareProduct**s become larger and more complex, demand to reduce time and cost increases. Thus, software tools should be used to obtain optimal results with minimum resources in order to deliver high-quality **SoftwareProduct**s within a limited time.

We look at the integrated test environment with CAST tools from three aspects: (1) test case development and test data management, (2) computer-based test execution, and (3) test process management. Only a sample of the tools currently available will be discussed.

Test Case Development

Suitable test cases are necessary for a successful test process. If your test cases are not developed properly, extensive amounts of testing may end in vain. Effective testing has two parts: (1) test execution and (2) test configuration, including required test data. Test cases contain what is to be executed. If test cases are not effective, the whole testing effort may be meaningless.

Let's now discuss effective test cases. We may say that a good collection of effective test cases gives you confidence that you have thoroughly exercised your code and can find most of the **Defect**s that reside in the code. Test cases must be clearly understood. We need to understand which test cases are testing what **Feature**s or what units. When each test case is clearly understood, a combined set of test cases can be defined to cover the program. In an industrial environment, you always want to obtain a maximum (or optimal) result with a minimum investment.

Test Case Development Tools

Since test execution is repeatedly performed, the time and effort required to develop test cases will be well spent. Many tools are commercially available to assist in developing test cases.

Test Design Tools. Test design tools help you to organize test plans and develop test cases from the set of software **Feature**s and design specifications. Some tools require that the design specifications be written in a tool-dependent language. Test design tools are sometimes included as a part of CASE environments. Using compatible tools provided in a CASE environment avoids compatibility problems. The drawback of using a CASE tool may be the rigid requirement that design specifications must be defined in a CASE tool language.

Profiling Tools.   Profiling tools allow testers (or developers) to understand the behavior and objective of a program. A memory profiling tool has been developed for use within Hewlett–Packard. As software tends to be bigger and more memory intensive, profiling memory is useful to both developers and testers. Understanding how a program uses memory allows engineers to determine if a failure is a **Defect** or not. As discussed in the first section of this chapter, a failure is not necessarily a **Defect**. If computer memory is smaller than what the program requires, the anomaly may not be a **Defect** but rather expected behavior. Understanding how a program is being executed and monitoring internal resource usage helps to create effective test cases.

Code Coverage Tool.   A code coverage tool provides information regarding how much of the code has been executed (or activated) by the test cases running against the code. Generally, coverage tools are used for a white-box-oriented environment. They monitor the program during execution, providing statistics on code statement and decision statement coverage. Coverage tools insert coverage data generation code into the program being tested.

A variety of code coverage tools are available from simple code coverage analyzers to sophisticated tools that measure line, branch, and data flow coverage. Some even give a graphical view of coverage. Some tools run during a single test case, whereas others can run against a series of test cases.

Code coverage tools have been used mainly to ensure full coverage of code by test cases. However, in addition to recording coverage information, a tool can also be used to enhance test cases. After running prepared test cases, new test cases can be added to exercise the parts of code that were not exercised before or remove test cases that had been exercised with other test cases. One of the drawbacks of using code coverage tools is overhead. Coverage tools require instrumentation, slow down test execution, and impose a heavy overhead. We found a code coverage tool is more useful for refining and improving test cases than for use during actual test execution.

Test Data Management Tool

Test cases may be reused for several **SoftwareProduct**s. It is useful to keep track of test cases and their results. Thus, a test data management tool should have access to a database of test cases. Commercial tools are available that can link test cases to **SoftwareProduct Feature**s, execution results, or a **Defect** tracking system. Items that the database should have for your reference are

- Test case number
- Test case name
- Description

- Type of test
- Location of test case
- Developed date
- Modified date
- Test case developer's name
- Functionality that is tested
- Requirements to run the test case
- **Project** names that use the test case
- User-defined execution result
- Execution history of the test case
- **Defect** tracking reference
- Requirements document reference
- Test design document reference

The test database is useful for managing test activity, selecting test cases (particularly for regression testing), and enhancing test cases for future test activities.

Managing Test Activity. Each test case, after execution, should result in a pass or fail. The result should be directly linked to the test case itself so that test developers can have a history of how the test case has performed. If a test case finds no **Defect**s in past **SoftwareProduct**s and it is redundant with other test cases based on its behavior profile, the test case may be removed from the test case database.

Test information from the test database can be produced as a report or retrieved by a query. Test execution status reports are available from the database. Management can see exactly how many test cases were executed and how many of them failed. Information available from the database is important for a test manager to understand **SoftwareProduct** quality and test activity status and progress.

Selecting Test Cases for Regression Test. Regression testing is described in the previous section. Since regression testing is performed against an **Area** (or **Area**s) of change, we can run more effective regression testing if we know exactly which test case is testing what **Area** of code or what type of functionality. Similarly, testers can select a test case based on the criteria keyed into the test database. You may want to classify test cases for unit tests, system tests, **Feature** tests, or qualification tests. Similarly, you can pull out the test cases that failed for the first testing phase and run only those test cases after **Defect**s are fixed.

The test database should contain links to a **Defect** tracking system as part of an integrated test environment. The test database should interface with an automated test execution environment.

Test Case Enhancement.   Test cases need to be reviewed periodically, particularly after a **Project** is completed. Test cases can have **Defect**s or be ineffective. Judging the effectiveness of test cases is a difficult task; however, it is necessary for efficient and effective testing. One piece of data that you can use is the performance of each test case. Periodically you need to review test case effectiveness by determining whether a test case found any **Defect**s in the past, is redundant, and still corresponds to the program specification. The **SoftwareProduct** specification may have been changed during the course of development or other changes may have occurred. Again, the idea is to minimize the number of test cases that you have to run without loosing test coverage.

Test Execution Tools

Test execution tools are for test execution activity and for comparing results after execution. A tool can drive the whole execution process by deciding if the test case passes or fails and then feeding the result back to the tool.

Capture and Play-back Tool.   A capture and play-back tool is useful if you are developing window-based software. Testing all graphical user interfaces (GUIs) or keystrokes in developed **SoftwareProduct**s is resource intensive. The idea is that a person runs a test case from a terminal. The tool records keystrokes or mouse movements that the test subject performs. Once a complete test sequence has been performed, the recorded movements can be replayed. It is the same concept of recording music and playing it back. Many capture and play-back tools come with their own language to write a script. The script languages are easy to learn and use. If the user writes a script, the entire test case can be developed without recording keystrokes.

These types of tools are widely available. Capture and play-back tools generate a script that is executed at test time. This can be used for regression testing by comparing test results to known correct results.

Test Driver.   Test driver tools supply inputs to **SoftwareProduct**s to stimulate operation. Test drivers tools are especially useful when many components need to be stimulated in a predefined sequence. These tools are useful in system test or qualification test phases. Unless a driver comes with the tool or tools that you are using, you may have to develop your own driver.

You may find it is easy to develop a driver using a script language that comes with a capture and play-back tool. We have developed a GUI test driver to exercise all **Feature**s of a GUI without requiring human intervention. Commercially available test drivers are mainly for GUI testing.

Data Compare Tools.   A data compare tool checks data bit by bit or character by character. When a capture and play-back tool is used, the output can be saved in a file. The data compare tool then compares the file bit by bit or character by character against output from a test. Recently, companies have developed software that compares GUI screens. The task of comparing GUI screens will generate a large data file. A 1-bit difference in the large file may not be significant. Since a computerized system does not have human flexibility, the tool will prompt the tester that a comparison failure has occurred when there is only a 1-bit difference. This may generate a lot of tasks that humans must later validate.

Data Generator.   A data generator tool produces random streams of input data for the program under test. It has been used in formulating data to test database or financial systems software. When a system takes a variety of input formats and the system has to be tested with many different formats of data, a data generator is useful.

A data generator is used in white-box testing. The tool analyzes the logic flow of the program and deduces the sets of input data that are necessary to achieve a specific criterion. Thus, the tool can be used to execute a particular path or a specific decision statement. Data generator tools can generate test data as part of test cases, but the tool cannot produce a complete set of test cases. Thus, you cannot use data generators to create complete test cases.

MANAGING TESTING ACTIVITIES AND RESULTS

How a test activity is managed may determine if the **Project** will be successful or not. Because testing is dynamic in nature, frequently the **Project** manager does not have a good grasp of the progress of the testing activity. Managers, in general, may be more interested in schedule and milestones than in testing. However, testing activity cannot be managed simply by schedule. The progress of **Defect** fixing based on monitoring test results determines test activity status. In the following sections, we will discuss the tools that facilitate managing test activity.

Test Activity Monitor Tools

Commercially available databases systems have **Feature**s that can prompt testers or managers if a test activity is not as scheduled. Intelligent agents to alert managers can be developed for the PAMPA tool described in Chapter 15. In this section, we will discuss **Defect** tracking systems.

Defect *Tracking Systems.* **Defect** tracking systems are used by many **Organization**s. Some are commercial off the shelf (COTS) and other are in-house developed tools. **Defect** tracking systems should gather the following basic material:

- **Defect**s number
- **Defect** category
- Date **Defect** was found
- How **Defect** was found
- Description of the environment containing the **Defect**
- Severity of **Defect**
- Who is responsible to correct the **Defect**
- Priority for fixing the **Defect**
- Date **Defect** was fixed
- Is another **Defect** related to this **Defect**
- Information about how the **Defect** was fixed
- Reproducibility of the **Defect**

The above information is useful for the current **Project** and future **Project**s to determine the reliability of the **SoftwareProduct,** as discussed in Chapter 11. In many cases, keeping track of **Defect**s, from the time a **Defect** is found till the time the **Defect** is fixed, involves more than one person. Thus, the tool has to be easy to use and accessible from multiple locations.

SUMMARY

We have discussed the software testing process and tools. The testing process should validate the software components or system at each stage of the software life cycle, as well as verify the final system with respect to requirements. The process should be executed intelligently and efficiently. For each software **Project**, you should create a test plan that covers the aspects of **SoftwareProduct Features** and **SoftwareProduct** validation requirement. Once a clear test plan is created, test methodology, strategy, tools, and techniques should be determined.

Selecting tools is an important aspect of the successful test process. A variety of tools is available, and each tool has its specific function and objective. Selecting appropriate tools based on your need could determine the efficiency and effectiveness of your entire test activities. Many references regarding available tools are available, and you should utilize these to select the most suitable tools for your environment. Tools can be integrated into a commercial CASE tool environment if it is applicable to your need. Since your resources are probably limited, you should formulate a methodology to efficiently test software when you select tools.

Monitoring test process may be considered to be time consuming. Assessment of your test process, however, allows you to manage your **Project** effectively. Any problem found during the software development cycle could have a direct effect on overall software quality. Monitoring test process and identifying problems, as well as finding **Defect**s at earlier stages, enables the **Project** to keep on schedule.

REFERENCES

[Boehm76]   Boehm, B. W., "Software Engineering," *IEEE Transaction on Computers,* Vol. C-25, No. 12, December 1976, pp. 1226–1241.

[Copi68]   Copi, I. M., *Introduction to Logic,* Macmillan, Inc., New York, 1968.

[DeMillo87]   Demillo, R. A., McCracken, W. M., Martin, R. J., and Passafiume, J. F., *Software Testing and Evaluation*, Benjamin Cummings Pub. Co., Menlo Park, CA, 1987.

[Humphrey89]   Humphrey, W. S., *Managing the Software Process,* Addison–Wesley Publishing Co., Reading, MA, 1989.

[Perry95]   Perry, W. E., *Effective Methods for Software Testing,* John Wiley & Sons, Inc., New York, 1995.

[Myers76]   Myers, G. J., *Software Reliability: Principles and Practices,* Wiley-Interscience, New York, 1976.

[Myers79]   Myers, G. J., *The Art of Software Testing*, John Wiley & Sons, Inc., New York, 1979.

[Yourdon92]   Edward Yourdon, *Decline and Fall of the American Programmer*, Yourdon Press, Englewood Cliffs, NJ, 1992, p. 8.

13
Usability

Usability is a fairly broad concept that basically refers to how easy it is for users to learn a system, how efficiently they can use it once they have learned it, and how pleasant it is to use. Also, the frequency and seriousness of user errors are normally considered to be constituent parts of usability.

R. L. Mack and J. Nielsen
[Mack94]

INTRODUCTION

Although software is the focus of this book, the approach taken in this chapter is that software and hardware are so interlaced that it makes no sense to separate them in a discussion of computer system **Usability**. From that perspective, we discuss three topics: the **Usability** problem, a definition of **Usability**, and the design for **Usability**. We sort through these topics in summary fashion and, in so doing, attempt to collect those kernels of knowledge that a reader can use and thereby make reviewing the chapter worthwhile.

THE USABILITY PROBLEM

Usability as a general concept refers to the ease with which a user can understand and use a system. To Scerbo, **Usability** refers to how well a person can interact with a product or operate a piece of equipment [Scerbo95]. The **Usability** of computers and associated software, although a relatively new concern, significantly increased in importance with growth in the general public's use of personal computers. With greater public use came an ever expanding number of users who complained about difficulties in understanding and using the systems that they purchased. In addition, companies, which invested considerable sums of money in computer technology, found later, to their dismay, that the technology was unused because it failed to support users in their work.

Booth describes it in this manner. While manufacturers sought to increase the numbers of things a computer can do (**Feature**s), users became steadily more confused and frustrated because they could not operate the systems. Too frequently, producers were absorbed in how to alleviate the consequences of **Usability** problems rather than how to keep **Usability** problems from occurring in the first place. Many **SoftwareProduct**s were abandoned not because they did not work but because users could not or would not use them. Booth summarizes the current status this way: "Today, we are just as capable of producing an unusable system as we have always been" [Booth90]. This being the case, the increased focus on **Usability** is a natural response to a necessity of the marketplace. As Dykstra indicates, software designers and manufacturers now must pay more attention to the user and provide a more usable **SoftwareProduct** [Dykstra93]. Producing a usable **SoftwareProduct** requires a common understanding of **Usability** and the attributes a **SoftwareProduct** must have to be usable.

DEFINITION OF USABILITY

Table 13.1 presents an early approach to defining **Usability** [Shackel86]. Shackel defines **Usability** in terms of four distinct attributes that should be measured during **Usability** evaluation. Booth identifies two limitations of the Shackel definition:

Table 13.1 Attributes for Usability Definition and Evaluation (Adapted from Shackel86)

1. *Effectiveness.* A better than some required level of performance (for example, speed and errors) by some required percentage of specified target range of users and within in some required proportion of the range of usage environments.

2. *Learnability.* Within some specified time from installation and start of user training based upon some specified amount of training and user support and within some specified relearning time for intermittent users.

3. *Flexibility.* Allowing adaptation to some specified percentage variation in tasks and/or environments beyond those first specified.

4. *Attitude.* Within acceptable levels of human cost in terms of tiredness, discomfort, frustration, and personal effort.

(1) flexibility is difficult to specify and communicate in a design environment, and (2) a fundamental attribute of **Usability**, usefulness, is not considered [Booth90]. Booth also suggests that the attribute flexibility be replaced with the attribute usefulness. He defines usefulness as an attribute that helps users to achieve their goals. Booth further explains that a system may be task effective, easy to learn, and well liked, but if the system functions fail to match a user's work tasks, it will not be used.

The **Usability** as a concept, as shown in Table 13.2, can be as broad as Gould's usability components, which include not only the end user but also programmers, system engineers, installation engineers, and support people [Gould88]. The latter approach appears to contain something for everyone and may not be as useful as the previous, but perhaps that is a judgment call for the software designer.

The International Standards Organization (ISO) defines usability as follows: "Usability [is] the degree to which users can achieve specific goals within a particular environment: effectively, efficiently, comfortably, and in an acceptable manner." Other definitions [Molich90, Yamada90, and Shackel91] suggest similar **Usability** attributes, such as utility, acceptability, learnability, likeability, effectiveness, operability, understandability, controllability, flexibility, and installability. Summarizing the current state of the **Usability** definition, Nielsen identifies five significant attributes: (1) learnability of the system, (2) efficiency of use once the system has been

Table 13.2   Usability Components (Adapted from Gould88)

System performance	Ability for **Customer**s to modify and extend
Reliability	Installation
Responsiveness	Packaging and unpacking
System functions	Installing
User interface	Field maintenance and serviceability
Organization	Advertising
Input/output hardware	Motivating **Customer**s to buy
For end user	Motivating user to use
Or other **Group**s	Support **Group** users
Reading materials	Marketing people
End User **Group**s	Trainers
Support **Group**s	Operators
Language translation	Maintenance workers
Reading materials	
User interface	
Outreach programs	
End user training	
On-line help system	
Hot lines	

learned, (3) ability of infrequent users to return to the system without having to re-learn, (4) frequency and seriousness of user errors, and (5) subjective user evaluation [Nielsen92]. However, the missing element of these definitions is the explicit identification what should be measured. An approach to supplying the missing element will be discussed in Chapter 14.

Booth provides a philosophical point of closure by suggesting that it "appears unlikely that a specifically agreed upon definition of **Usability** will emerge. . . . However, as the term is now in general use, and has entered the vocabulary of the media, it seems unlikely that it can be easily forgotten" [Booth90]. This being the case, perhaps Mack's definition [Mack94], which served as a point of departure in this discussion, provides the best understanding of **Usability** and the attributes that a **SoftwareProduct** must have to be usable.

DESIGNING FOR USABILITY

The fact that computers are difficult to learn and use presents a problem that will affect more and more people as computer use becomes even more prevalent. **Usability** design attempts to alleviate this problem, but designing for **Usability** can prove to be just as elusive as defining **Usability**. The problem with a **Usability** design approach may be that in the *final analysis,* one must design, build, and implement a system and then wait to see what happens. This is a point of view that not only cannot be tolerated; realistically, it must be rejected. Using data from systems already in the public domain is valuable, but certainly must not be the only source of data for designer/manufacturers, who need methodologies to evaluate systems early in the design process.

In the mid-1980s, four principles for **Usability** design that stress early design involvement evolved at IBM Research [Gould88]. These principles and their implementation in the design process are summarized by Gould: (1) start focus on the user early and continue that focus throughout the process; (2) start user testing early and continue to test throughout the process; (3) modify the design based on testing and repeat testing; and (4) all **Usability** attributes evolve in parallel under one focus with a single integrated focus.

Usability design implies quantification and computation, but the software development life cycle consists of a iterative series of definitions, assessments, and redefinition of specifications. Although the development cycle is difficult to predict and model, approaches to resolving these difficulties were presented in previous chapters. In regard to **Usability** design, three things can be emphasized: (1) a formal iterative design process must be adopted and followed; (2) on the whole, **Usability** depends on the interface; and (3) although still rather primitive in its current configuration, most professionals working in software development generally agree that **Usability** engineering still holds the key to assuring that a usable system emerges from the software development life cycle [Gould88,91]. The first two topics are explored further in subsections to follow. **Usability** engineering is discussed in Chapter 14.

FORMAL ITERATIVE DESIGN PROCESS FOR USABILITY _____

The technical literature contains several formal iterative approaches applicable to **Usability** design. Rather than attempting to describe these and show how each would be modified for application to **Usability** design, it is more useful to present an approach related specifically to software **Usability** design. Figure 13.1 [Williges87] is

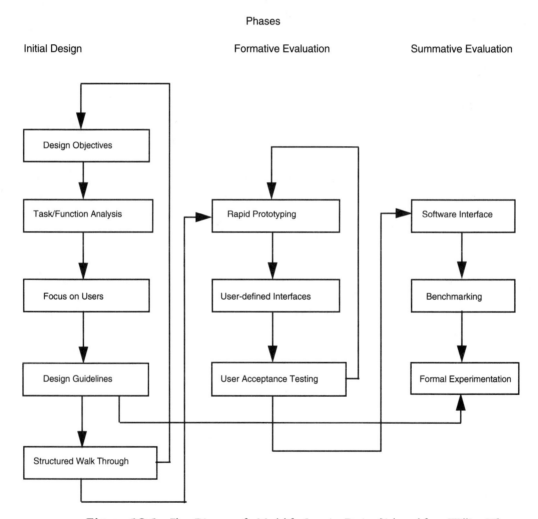

Figure 13.1   Flow Diagram of a Model for Iterative Design [Adapted from Williges87]

one example. Three phases including tasks for each phase are shown. For example, the Initial Design phase has five tasks associated with Design Objectives, Task/Function Analysis, Focus on Users, Design Guidelines, and Structured Walk Through. Tasks are repeated until outputs stabilize as inputs to the next phase, Formative Evaluation, where again an iterative process is followed to form the inputs to the third phase, Summative Evaluation.

INTERFACE

Most early computer systems provided only character-based presentations. Numeric input data were first, followed eventually by text. Keyboards served as input devices. CRTs and printers handled output. Graphical user interfaces arrived in the software community in the early 1980s. Both system types have several common design requirements.

Physical Factors

The output of a computer interface interacts primarily with the visual sense of a user. Meeting the visual requirements of a user is of first importance in design. The following recommendations are recognized guidelines for interface design (adapted from Bailey96).

1. *Luminance.* Luminance is the radiant intensity of a surface measured in millilamberts (mL). Given adequate contrast, any level above 25 mL is adequate. An upper limit for luminance must consider brightness.

2. *Brightness.* Brightness is a user's subjective impression of luminance. Good design provides a user with a brightness adjustment control, thereby permitting a user to set a comfortable level of brightness.

3. *Contrast.* Contrast is the ratio of background luminance minus figure luminance to the sum of background luminance and figure luminance. A contrast ratio between 88% and 94% is acceptable.

4. *Flicker.* Flicker is caused by the computer interface regenerating too slowly. A flicker rate of 60 Hz for monochromatic screen and 70+ Hz for color is acceptable.

5. *Resolution.* Resolution depends primarily on viewing distance. The visual angle subtended at the eye by a figure on the screen should be at least 15 arc minutes or at least 8 points in a pixel-based system.

6. *Character style.* Character style pertains to lettering and readability. Readability is best when a mixture of lower- and uppercase letters is used.

7. *Character height.* The preferred height for most reading tasks is between 15 and 20 arc minutes. Letter height should never be less than 10 arc minutes or more than 24 arc minutes.

8. *Character width and spacing.* Character width should be between 70% and 85% of character height. Spacing between characters should be at least 18% of character height.

9. *Interline spacing.* A distance of 66% of character height is preferred. A distance of less than 50% should be rejected.

Cognitive Factors

Given that the physical factors of design are acceptable, cognitive issues of the interface become of primary importance. Early work by Foley and co-workers formalizes the ways an interactive user interface can be described [Foley90]. Four levels are identified:

1. *Conceptual.* Describes the user's model of the interactive system.
2. *Semantic.* Describes the meanings conveyed both by the user's input and the computer's displayed output functions performed by the system. Semantic design tells what information is needed to perform each function and the result of performing it. Meanings are defined rather than forms or sequences, which are left to lower levels.
3. *Syntactic.* Describes the sequences of inputs and outputs. For the input, this means the rules by which sequences of words are formed into proper sentences.
4. *Lexical.* Deals with the binding of hardware actions to the hardware-independent words of the input and output languages.

Earlier, we pointed out that the user interface is often the dominant factor in determining the user satisfaction of a system. Couple this with the facts that different people have different reactions to the same set of screens and that there are few objective measures to evaluate a screen or a set of screens, the difficulties of **Usability** design become apparent. Like others, we suggest that it may be desirable to provide several different interfaces to the same set of operations. Such an ability would support various levels of system users (that is, novice to expert). In practice, however, it frequently is better to emphasize either the novice or the expert, because time frequently does not permit both.

Dialog Styles

User inputs to computers are of two basic types: control and data. The former tells the computer what to do and the latter identifies what to do it to. Both inputs are handled by an interactive interface. There are three basic interactive dialog styles:

command, direct manipulation and menu [Jacob90]. Although interfaces make use of various combinations of the three, it is useful to understand the distinctive characteristics of each.

1. *Command.* With command interfaces the user must create a requirement for the computer to do something. This requirement must be in a language with which the user is comfortable and proficient and that the computer understands. The completeness of the command language depends on several factors. Obviously, it is essential that the command language be sufficiently complete for the user to state exactly what is desired of the computer. With that as a given, it can be noted that experienced computer users are comfortable with an artificial language, while inexperienced users prefer a natural language. From a **Usability** standpoint, we feel that a natural-based language is preferable, but it should not be so sophisticated that it increases the complexity of the user's communication task and simultaneously reduces the efficiency of the command language processor.

2. *Direct manipulation.* These interfaces present objects on the screen, and users act upon these employing a standard list of actions. Other than the set of actions, there is no command language that the user must commit to memory. Although one advantage to direct manipulation interfaces is the relative ease by which they can be built using object-oriented languages, this does not necessarily contribute to **Usability**. An obvious disadvantage is identifying meaningful metaphors that represent objects in the problem domain and can be shown on the screen for visual acquisition by a user. The **Usability** of direct manipulation interfaces is best exploited with pointing devices rather than function keys and/or commands.

3. *Menu.* These interfaces provide a fixed set of choices from which a user makes a selection at each point in a dialog. With menus, users never have to remember a desired entry. All entries are presented on the screen, which only requires recognition. Novice users find menu-based interfaces beneficial; however, experienced users who know what they want can be frustrated by having to look over a whole list of choices before making an input. Long menus are undesirable. Menus should be limited to no more than six to seven items, arranged alphabetically. Vertical menus are preferred over horizontal. When there are many items to choose from, a hierarchy of trees should be developed such that a selection from one elicits another from which subchoices can be made.

Messages

Messages are employed by computers to provide feedback information to users. Content should be concise, accurate, and free from any requirement to access a document or reference for interpretation. The purpose of a message varies. It may indicate that an error has been made, it may be a prompt for more information, or it may provide the user with additional information. Message content may be text, icons, indicators, or combinations. The point is that messages should convey easily understood information. There is no minimum time for computer or message responses. Maximum time is considered to be between 3 to 5 seconds. A status bar should be provided as feedback to the user for response times in this latter range.

Graphical User Interface

The graphical user interface (GUI) initially was developed the Xerox Research Center at Palo Alto and subsequently promoted in the marketplace by the Apple Macintosh. Because of their pixel-based characteristics, monitors simultaneously display text, numbers, and graphics. Mouse/keyboard combinations are used for inputs and CRT monitors and laser printers for outputs. Although an expert, frequent user may prefer a well-designed command language as an interaction procedure, GUIs provide good ways to interact with a system for novice and intermittent users.

The design of graphical user interfaces, unlike character-based interfaces, makes use of style guides. These guides define the user interface, including its appearance and course of action. They provide design guidance related to commonly used GUI components such as windows, menus, and screen-based controls. The primary purpose of the style guides is to provide GUI consistency. The popular style guides include Apple's *Macintosh*, IBM's *Common User Access*, Microsoft's *Windows*, and Open Software's *Motiff.* The overwhelming acceptance of GUIs in the software community has led to the development of commercial tools enabling designers to quickly develop applications and **SoftwareProduct**s. Table 13.3 identifies the primary design components of **Individual** windows, multiple windows, and multiple-window coordination [Shneiderman92].

TABLE 13.3 Design Components of Individual and Multiple Windows (Adapted from Shneiderman92)

Window Type	Design Component
Individual	Titles, borders, scroll bars, open action, open place and size, close action, resize action, move action, and activation
Multiple	Multiple monitors, split displays, rapid display flipping, fixed space tiling, variable space tiling, nonspace tiling, piles of tiles, automatic panning, zooming, overlaps, and cascades
Multiple-window coordination	Synchronized scrolling, hierarchical browsing, direct selection, two-dimensional browsing, dependent-windows opening, dependent-windows closing, and save or open window slate

Interface Development Tools

Hix and Ryan claim that the emergence of user interface development tools has outstripped the systematic tool evaluation [Hix 92]. They evaluated four selected tools: Matesys' *ObjectScript*, Microsoft's *Visual Basic*, Asymetrix's *ToolBook*, and Macromind's *Director*. These four tools represent two of the most common platforms, *Macintosh* and *Windows 3.0*. A summary of their evaluation follows:

1. *ObjectScript.* This tool runs under Microsoft *Windows*. Of the four tools, it ranked the lowest in terms of both **Usability** and functionality. A ranking of strengths included boxes, forms, typed input strings, text, and output devices. Weaknesses were ranked as follows: animation, video, other hardware, audio, and transitions.

2. *Visual Basic.* This tool also runs under Microsoft *Windows*. In terms of **Usability** and functionality, it ranked only slightly higher that *ObjectScript*. Similarly, a ranking of its strengths included boxes, windows, forms, menus, and output devices, and its weaknesses were ranked as animation, video, other hardware, audio, and transitions.

3. *ToolBook.* Thus is a third tool that runs under Microsoft *Windows*. In terms of **Usability** and functionality, this tool rated much higher than *ObjectScript* and a little higher than *Visual Basic*. Its strong suits were ranked as follows: forms, text, boxes, output devices, and windows. Weaknesses were ranked as audio, video, other hardware, and input devices.

4. *Macromind Director.* This tool runs on an Apple Macintosh computer under Mac-OS. It had the highest rating of the four tools in both **Usability** and functionality. A ranking of its strong points included multimedia, output devices, transitions, forms, and animation. Weaknesses were ranked as input devices, audio, other interface attributes, and interface objects.

USER

To say that users vary is an oversimplification. Although the differences are too numerous to mention, it is advantageous to understand that not all **Individual** differences are important to **Usability** design. Having accepted this proposition, the question becomes what is important. Answers lie in resolving two other questions: (1) What is a reasonable taxonomy for user profiles? (2) What are the needs? Insight for resolving these questions has been offered as follows [Shneiderman92]:

1. *Novice or first-time user.* The vocabulary for developing the user's knowledge of the system should be restricted to a small number of familiar and consistently

used terms. The user should be given the capability to accomplish a few simple tasks coupled with informative feedback. Easy to understand error messages should be provided when errors occur. Minimize distraction from computer concepts and syntax. Manuals and step-by-step on-line tutorials will assist the user in learning the system. On-line help screens will be beneficial.

2. *Knowledgeable intermittent user.* Emphasize recognition, not recall, of the command language, menus, and other terminology. To ensure that tasks are being performed properly, use consistent sequences of actions, meaningful messages, and frequent prompts. Provide the user with a safety net to support exploration or use of partial commands. An on-line help screen will be beneficial to the user by plugging gaps in syntactic or computer semantic knowledge. Well-referenced manuals will also be helpful.

3. *Expert frequent user.* Remember that these users require rapid response time, less feedback, brief feedback, and the capability to accomplish actions with few keystrokes or selections. The capability to create macros or other abbreviated forms to reduce the number of steps in a sequence of commands is desired. Shortcuts through menus, abbreviations, and other accelerator forms are required.

User Tasks

Knowing the user is one step in the design process; knowing the tasks is another. A task may be defined as an activity contemplated by a user, for example, preparing a memorandum, using a word processor, or withdrawing a sum of money from an automatic teller machine. Just as it is important to understand the knowledge level of users, it is equally important to know how users prepare and plan for tasks. Schneider's early work provides a useful approach in this regard [Schneider82]. He suggests five stages, as follows:

Stage 1: Task analysis. User decomposes a single conceptual task into its component parts, determining the specific commands required for task completion. The user asks, "What are the steps and commands necessary to perform the overall task?"

Stage 2: Semantic analysis. Here the scope of the task is considered. The user asks, "What do I want to do in regard to definition of the data and control of the process?"

Stage 3: Syntactic analysis. This pertains to encoding the information; the correct function is chosen, and the semantics are understood. The user asks, "How do I do it?" The form of the computer interface affects this stage (command language, dialogues, menus, function keys, and so on).

Stage 4: System performance. This is the response of the system when the system is considered as a black box.

Stage 5: Response analysis. This pertains to the analysis and interpretation of the response produced by the system and is the final stage. The user asks, "What have I done?" The primary goal is to provide the user with relevant information; unnecessary information should be avoided. Verbosity and information content must be considered.

Psychological Decision Table.   Another useful way to view users and tasks and how they interact is provided by Simes and Sirsky in what they call the psychological decision table, as shown in Table 13.4 [Simes85]. The authors' interpretation of the table follows:

1. As the user's level of experience increases, the need to feel in control of the human–computer interaction increases.

2. As the user's experience level increases, the importance of the limitations in human information processing decreases.

3. As the user's experience level increases, the need for immediate closure decreases. Users will wait longer for a response without frustration.

4. As the frequency of use increases, the impact of sensory overstimulation decreases. Users can handle and interpret more diversified stimuli and at a faster rate.

5. As the complexity of the task increases, the user's need to control the interaction decreases. Frequent users will want more control over more complex tasks. The effects of the interaction between complexity of task and experience level of users are represented by the smaller arrow in parentheses.

6. As the complexity of the task increases, the importance of the limitations of human information processing increases. For frequent users, the importance of the limitations of human information processing is reduced, even when the

Table 13.4 Psychological Decision Table [Adapted from Simes85]

	Need to Control Interaction	Importance of Limitations of Human Information Processing	Need for Closure	Impact of Sensory overstimulation
Experience level	↑	↓	↓	↓
Complexity of use	↓ (↑)	↑ (↑)	↑	↑(↓)
Frequency of use	↑	↓	↓	↓

task is complex. This interaction between complexity of task, experience level of user, and human information processing is represented by the smaller arrow in parentheses.

7. As the complexity of the task increases, the need for closure increases. Complex tasks require more feedback since both the user's uncertainty and task ambiguity are higher. However, as the user's experience level and frequency of use increase, the need for closure decreases, even for tasks of increasing complexity. See smaller arrow in parentheses.

8. As the complexity of the task increases, the impact of sensory overstimulation increases. However, as frequency of use increase, the impact of sensory overstimulation decreases, even for more complex tasks. See smaller arrow in parentheses.

User Interactions with Software

Designing software systems also requires some basic understanding of how users interact with software. Mack contends that design insight may be gained by simulating user interactions. Interactions are simulated through a few simple questions [Mack92].

1. *What do users see?* What is the nature of the screens and screen flows? What is the visual information available for sight, including menu items, screen button labels, and application titles? What is the form and content of icon characteristics of graphical interface styles?

2. *Where is the focus of a user's attention?* What are the visual indications informing the user of an outcome and prompting for the next step?

3. *What do users need to know?* Knowledge influences what users see and plan to do. What does a user need to know to complete a series of task steps? How would they interpret visual prompts or interpret visual indications of an action outcome? Where and how would users acquire the necessary knowledge to use the software? What about past experience with other software? Would this past experience be helpful in the present situation?

4. *What do users need to do?* Given the layout of the interface objects, what do users need to do to accomplish a task in terms of the provided system methods? It would be useful for the designer to walk through the series of steps for accomplishing a goal in a preconceived task scenario, considering specific screens, screen flows, and actions. A crude assessment of effort could be determined by counting the number of steps. This number can be compared with alternative designs of this system, a predecessor system, or even competitor systems.

5. *What if users did the wrong thing at this point?* Just as it is useful to walk through a series of correct steps, it is also important to anticipate and evaluate incorrect

interpretations and actions. What are the errors a user might make in carrying out an action or interpreting a system feedback? How would users know that they made an error? What are the consequences of an error? How does a user recover from an error?

Combining the information found in the forgoing discussions of the software user taxonomy and user interaction with software will prove helpful in the design task. Although not offered as a complete answer to software design, a useful approach would be to anticipate user-level responses to the questions simulating interaction.

User Needs Analysis

An additional approach to design by understanding users and their tasks is a user needs analysis [Booth90]. A user needs analysis has a number of stages, and he identifies them as follows:

1. *User characterization.* There needs to be an understanding of who the users are, together with an appreciation of their relevant characteristics.

Table 13.5   User Characterization Checklist [Adapted from Booth90]

User Data	
Identify the target user **Group**	Proportion of males and females
Average age ranges	Cultural characteristics

Job Characteristics	
Job role description	Main activities
Main responsibilities	Reporting **Structure**
Reward **Structure**	Schedules
Status	Turnover rate

User Background	
Relevant education/knowledge/experience	Relevant skills
Relevant training	

Usage Constraints	
Voluntary versus mandatory use	Motivators versus demotivators

Personal Preferences and Traits	
Learning style	Interactional style
Esthetic preference	Personality traits
Physical traits	

Table 13.6   Task Analysis Checklist [Adapted from Booth90]

Goals
  Identify goals and list important supporting tasks and for each important task.

Task intrinsics
  Identifier information (identify the task uniquely)
  Inputs and outputs
  Transformational process
  Operational procedures and operational patterns
  Decision points
  Problem solving
  Planning
  Terminology
  Equipment

Task dependency and criticality
  Dependency on other tasks, systems, etc.
  Concurrent effects
  Criticality of task (linked to dependency)

Current user problems in performing task

Performance Criteria
  Speed/accuracy/quality

Task criteria
  Sequence of actions
  Frequency of actions
  Importance of actions
  Functional relationships between actions
  Availability of functions
  Flexibility of operation

User discretion
  Pace/priority/procedure

Task demands
  Physical demands
  Perceptual demands
  Cognitive demands
  Environmental demands
  Health and safety requirements

2. *Task analysis.* There needs to be an understanding of the user's goals and activities, as well as the tools that they use and the environments within which they work.

3. *Situational analysis.* There needs to be an appreciation of the situations that commonly arise as part of the user's normal activities.

4. *Acceptance criteria.* There needs to be an understanding of the user's requirements and preferences.

In the *user characterization* stage, the attempt is made to capture all the information possible about the target users (both primary and secondary) that is relevant to the proposed system. Booth says this is sometimes called product opportunity. Table 13.5 is Booth's checklist for this stage.

Task analysis here means identifying the user's goals and tasks. Goals mean the end result that a user wants to achieve. Tasks are the activities that the user must perform to achieve the goals. Table 13.6 is Booth's suggestion for a task analysis checklist.

Situational analysis entails an analysis of the situations that can arise in the work context and a consideration of how these might affect both the user's performance and the user's needs. The central question is the following: *If this situation arises, how will it affect the use of the system?* Knowing how then implies a requirement for mitigation. Table 13.7 is Booth's checklist for *situational analysis*.

Acceptance criteria suggest the importance of securing the users' own perceptions of their needs together with how the system matches these needs. These become user requirements, and these requirements become acceptance criteria for the system. If the system meets these requirements, it has a better chance of being accepted into the operational environment. A user needs analysis sets the

Table 13.7 Situational Analysis Checklist [Adapted from Booth90]: What Are the Likely Situations That Could Arise During System Use?

	Equipment
Does not meet performance target	Does not meet specification
Fails	
	Availability
Missing data	Missing materials
Missing personnel	Missing support
	Overloads
Too many people using resource	Too much data
Too many machines using resource	Too much information
Too much materials	
	Interruptions
Process breakdown	Things missed
Things forgotten	Restart required
	Surroundings
Change in physical environment	Change in social environment
	Policy
Changing laws	Changing rules
Changing standards	Changing guidelines

stage for design, as well as providing the criteria for testing **SoftwareProduct Usability**.

SUMMARY

In this chapter we discussed **Usability** in terms of three major topics. We began with a description of the *usability problem*. The **Usability** of computers and associated software, although a relatively new concern, significantly increased in importance with the growth in the general public's use of personal computers. With greater public use, there came an ever expanding number of users who complained about difficulties in understanding and using the systems that they purchased. Therefore, software designers and manufacturers must pay more attention to the user in order to provide a more usable **SoftwareProduct**.

We then focused on the second topic, a *definition of usability*. In its simplest sense, **Usability** refers to the ease with which a user can understand and use a system. More complex definitions that relate **Usability** to its attributes, components, and goals sometimes serve to complicate the issue. Given that fact, Mack and Nielsen [Mack94] offer the most helpful definition: "Usability is a fairly broad concept that basically refers to how easy it is for users to learn a system, how efficiently they can use it once they have learned it, and how pleasant it is to use. Also, the frequency and seriousness of user errors are normally considered to be constituent parts of usability."

In the discussion of *designing for usability*, we first emphasized the importance of a formal iterative design process. Attention was then given to interface factors, followed by a focus on such activities as knowing the user, user tasks, and understanding the interaction between users and tasks. In an attempt to tie these activities together for design, a process called a user needs analysis was introduced.

REFERENCES

[Bailey96]   Bailey, R. W., *Human Performance Engineering*, 3rd ed., Prentice Hall, Upper Saddle River, NJ, 1996.

[Booth90]   Booth, P., *An Introduction to Human–Computer Interaction*, LEA, Hove, East Sussex, U.K., 1990.

[Dykstra93]   Dykstra, D. J., *A Comparison of Heuristic Evaluation and Usability Testing: The Efficacy of a Domain-specific Heuristic Checklist*, an unpublished dissertation, Texas A&M University, College Station, TX, 1993.

[Foley90]   Foley, J. D., and Van Dam, A., Feiner, S. K., and Hughes, J. F., *Computer Graphic: Principles and Practice*, 2nd ed., Addison–Wesley Publishing Co., Reading, MA, 1990.

[Gould88] Gould, J., "How to Design Usable Systems," in Helander, M. (ed.), *Handbook of Human–Computer Interaction*, Elsevier Science Publishers, Amsterdam, 1988, pp. 757–789.

[Gould91] Gould, J., Boies, S. J., and Lewis, C., "Making Usable, Useful, Productivity Enhancing Computer Applications," *Communications of the ACM*, Vol. 34, No. 1, 1991, pp. 74–85.

[Hix92] Hix, D., and Ryan, T., "Evaluating User Interface Development Tools," *Proceedings of the Human Factors and Ergonomics Society*, 1992.

[Jacob90] Jacob, R., "Human Computer Interaction," in S. C. Shapiro (ed.), *Encyclopedia of Artificial Intelligence*, Wiley-Interscience, NY, 1990, pp. 383–388.

[Mack92] Mack, R. L., "Questioning Design: Toward Methods for Supporting User-centered Software Engineering," Lauer, T. W., Peacock, E., and Graesser, A. C., eds., *Questions and Information Systems*, LEA, Hillsdale, NJ, 1992.

[Mack94] Mack, R. L., and Nielsen, J., eds., Executive Summary, *Usability Inspection Methods,* John Wiley & Sons, NY, 1994.

[Molich90] Molich, R., and Nielsen, J., "Improving Human–Computer Dialogue: What Designers Know about Traditional Interface Design," *Communications of the ACM*, Vol. 33, No. 3, 1990, pp. 338–348.

[Nielsen92] Nielsen, J., "The Usability Engineering Life Cycle," *IEEE Computer*, Vol. 25, No. 3, 1992, pp. 12–22.

[Scerbo95] Scerbo, M. W., "Usability Testing," in J. Weiner, ed., *Research Techniques in Human Engineering*, Prentice Hall, Upper Saddle River, NJ, 1995.

[Schneider82] Schneider, M. L., and Rubinstein, R., "Models for the Design of Software User Assistance," in Badre, A., and Shneiderman, B., eds., *Directions in Human–Computer Interaction*, Ablex, Norwood, NJ, 1982.

[Shackel86] Shackel, B., "Ergonomics in the Design for Usability," in Harrison, M. D., and Monk, A. F., eds., *People and Computers: Designing for Usability, Proceedings of the Second Conference of the BCS HCI Specialist Group*, Cambridge University Press, New York, 1986.

[Shackel91] Shackel, B., "Usability—Context, Framework, Definition, Design and Evaluation," in Shackel, B., and Richardson, S. J., eds., *Human Factors for Informatics Usability*, Cambridge University Press, New York, 1991.

[Shneiderman92] Shneiderman, B., *Designing the User Interface*, 2nd ed., Addison–Wesley Publishing Co., Reading, MA, 1992.

[Simes85] Simes, D. K., and Sirsky, P. A., "Human Factors: An Exploration of the Psychology of Human–Computer Dialogs," in Hartson, H. R., ed., *Advances in Human–Computer Interaction*, Vol. 1, Ablex Publishing, Norwood, NJ, 1985.

[Williges87] Williges, R. C., Williges, B. H., and Elkerton, J., "Software Interface Design," in Salvendy, G., ed., *Handbook of Human Factors*, John Wiley & Sons, New York, 1987.

[Yamada90] Yamada, A., "Measuring Usability," *Proceedings of the 14th Annual International Computer Software and Applications Conference*, IEEE Computer Society Press, Los Alamitos, CA, 1990, pp. 68.

14
Usability Testing

The significant problems that we face cannot be solved at the same level of thinking that we were at when we created them.

A. Einstein

INTRODUCTION

Testing is essential to improving **Usability**. The purpose of this chapter is to identify and discuss the fundamental issues of **Usability** testing. The objective of testing, test variables, and **Usability** metrics are presented first. Test procedures include an examination of the number of participants, methods, **Usability** laboratories, and scenarios. These are then placed in the context of planning a **UsabilityTest**. The benefits we expect from a **UsabilityTest** are then described. We continue with a presentation of two **Usability** models that appear to have some promise in predicting **Usability** and conclude with a discussion of recent studies in **Usability** testing. This last topic introduces **Usability maxims**. In addition, a new method called a domain-specific heuristic checklist and a new automated environment for unobtrusively measuring the interaction between a user and a software application are discussed. We conclude the chapter with brief coverage of an emphasis called human technology, which is under national sponsorship and development in Japan. Human technology includes an approach to **Usability** evaluation unknown in the United States or anywhere else in the world.

BACKGROUND

In a response to the desire to make PCs more usable, developers have sought to formalize the process of *usability engineering* [Whiteside88]. They suggest a process founded on classical engineering techniques, which specify quantitatively in advance the **Feature**s a final **SoftwareProduct** to be engineered and produced must have.

Usability engineering requires testing. Although **Usability** engineering is accepted in the development process, several problems are recognized. The process requires analysis, computation, and evaluation, and herein lies a problem. An initial definition of specifications often depends on analytical methods, but the dilemma is that initial definition is only the beginning of the development process and consequently may not support the total process. Some authors suggest that analytical techniques beg the question by trying to collapse the process into a computation, but the fact is that the process may be too unpredictable, at that point, to be completely modeled by computation.

A second problem pertains to the time needed for **SoftwareProduct** testing. When the requirement is to design, produce, and market **SoftwareProduct**s on a schedule that ensures profitability, this often leaves little time for **Usability** evaluation. Time pressures too often lead to poor evaluations. A third problem is the development stage in which **Usability** testing can feasibly take place. Some investigators feel that the design of the system must be at or near "design freeze" for evaluation to occur. Obviously, **Usability** deficiencies found at this point during testing are often ignored because of the expense in correcting them. A fourth problem stresses that the essence of **Usability** is a user's act of choice to use a system, which suggests that it is not feasible to measure **Usability** in the laboratory. Forcing a person to use a system in order to assess its **Usability** destroys the best measure of **Usability**, that is, whether the system will be used. The following sections explore approaches to resolving these problems within the context of the objective and process of testing.

OBJECTIVE OF TESTING

Usability Defects

Although analytical techniques are useful in identifying system **Feature**s to be considered in design, it would be rare indeed for a system to reach design freeze and be manufactured without some **Usability** problems, that is, **Defect**s. Booth defines a **Usability Defect** as "anything in the **SoftwareProduct** which prevents a target user completing a target task with reasonable effort and within reasonable time" [Booth90]. These are attributes of a system that cause users difficulty. Since **Usabil-**

ity Defects may be considered analogous to problems in reliability and performance, they provide a focus on those **SoftwareProduct Feature**s that require attention and modification. Booth emphasizes, however, that this approach has its limitation and that limitation must be understood. Focusing only on the detail of **Usability** design **Defect**s, the larger issues of **Usability** may be missed, and it is some of the larger issues (for example, learnability and efficiency) that will ultimately determine whether software will be used in the work environment. Booth concludes, "This does not mean, however, that an approach that explicitly considers **Usability Defect**s is flawed." Rather, it is important that, in purpose, **Usability** testing must not concentrate on **Defect**s alone but also on the implications to **Usability** of those **Defect**s.

Purpose of Testing

Anticipating **Usability Defect**s and their implications during design is a difficult task. As a result, computer software/hardware manufacturers have attempted to incorporate **Usability** testing in the **SoftwareProduct** life cycle development. Given that **Usability** testing would then occur throughout the life cycle, the purpose and type of testing obviously vary. Table 14.1 is a slightly modified **Version** of Booth's conception of the purposes of **Usability** testing indexed by the development stage. As can be seen, testing occurs in the six life cycle phases from Analysis to Postrelease. The purpose of testing, as well as the **SoftwareProduct** status, varies according to phase. For example, in the Design Phase the purpose is to resolve problem conflicts,

TABLE 14.1 Usability **Testing: Phases, Purposes, and** SoftwareProduct **Status [Adapted from Booth90]**

Phases	**Purposes**	**SoftwareProduct Status**
Analysis	Set **Usability** objectives	Cognitive models
Investigation	Determine user needs	System functions
Design	Resolve problems/conflicts	Early paper and pencil concepts
	Answer questions	Physical and quantitative
Simulations	Debug	Prototypes
Manufacturer	Measure against objectives	Partial **SoftwareProduct**s
		Documentation
		Training manuals
Postrelease	Obtain sales/marketing data	Finished **SoftwareProduct**
	Provide inputs to next release	Competitor **SoftwareProduct**s
	Analysis of competitor	
	SoftwareProducts	

answer questions, and debug. **SoftwareProduct** Status is determined by paper and pencil tests, physical and quantitative simulations, and prototypes.

TEST VARIABLES

Obviously, no testing should be planned and conducted without a thorough understanding of the variables operating in test situations. Failure to give consideration to these compromises the interpretation of test results. Eason provides perhaps the best point of departure for classifying and understanding test variables. These are identified in Table 14.2. Eason concludes that the three classes of variables interact to influence whether a system is usable, not usable, or somewhere in between [Eason84]. When and how to use these depend on the conditions described in Table 14.1 and the ingenuity of the test planner. A brief summary of Eason's discussion follows.

System Functions

1. *Task match.* Pertains to the degree to which the information and functions provided by the system match the needs of the user. Does it do the job in terms of necessary functions and information needed by the user?

Table 14.2 Classification and Description of Test Variables

Independent Variables	
System functions	User characteristics
Task match	Knowledge
Ease of learning	Discretion
Ease of use	Motivation
Task characteristics	
Frequency	
Openness	

Dependent Variables	
User reaction	Negative outcomes
Implicit cost/benefit analysis	Restricted use
Positive outcomes	Nonuse
Good task–system match	Partial use
Continued user learning	Distant use

2. *Ease of learning.* Pertains to the effort required by the user to understand and operate the system.

3. *Ease of use.* Pertains to the effort required to operate a system once it has been mastered and understood by the user.

User Characteristics

1. *Knowledge.* Pertains to the amount and type of cognitive information that are applied from the user's storehouse of information to understand and operate the system. The fact is that the information may be applicable, not applicable, or somewhere in between.

2. *Discretion.* Pertains to the flexibility that the system provides the user to choose or not choose to use some function of the system.

3. *Motivation.* Pertains to a user's willingness to apply effort to understand and operate the system.

Task Characteristics

1. *Frequency.* Refers to the number of times a particular task is performed by a user during operation of the system. For infrequent tasks, users prefer prompts or memory aids, which may not be expected for frequent tasks.

2. *Openness.* Pertains to the degree to which a task can be modified. In open tasks, information needs of the user vary. If the same information is needed each time the task is performed, there is no need for an open task.

TEST PROCEDURES

Number of Participants

Opinions vary concerning the number of participants to use in a **UsabilityTest**. Some have found that by the second or third participant a majority of interface problems are identified [Nielsen90]. Virzi discovered that 4 to 5 participants were able to detect about 80% of the **Usability** problems [Virzi92]. More participants are required to detect 80% of the problems if the average likelihood of detection is 0.32 or lower [Lewis94]. Packenbush refers to a personal communication with R. Stimart with the User Interface Group at General Electric Information Services, Inc., indicating that his experience was that 8 to 12 participants will find 90% to 95% of the problems [Packenbush96]. Under this guidance, Packenbush compared two **Usability** testing methods, traditional and iterative, using 9 participants for each method of test. The number of participants appeared adequate, and the iterative test method proved superior to the traditional method.

These findings suggest that an optimum number of participants probably depends on the development cycle. Early in the development cycle, a small number (2 to 3) of participants is reasonable. That number would increase to a sample size of 4 to 7 at mid-cycle, and reach a maximum of 8 to 12 in the final stages of development.

Methods

Four basic methods have been identified to evaluate **Usability** [Nielsen90]. These are formal, empirical, heuristic, and automated. Some are more frequently used than others. A brief review of each is summarized here [Dykstra93].

Formal. These methods involve cognitive modeling of the user interface. One of the earliest and perhaps best known cognitive models is the Goals, Operators, Methods, and Selection Rules (GOMS). GOMS is a task procedural model that tries to specify in detail the knowledge, steps, procedures, and decisions necessary for skilled performance. Other methods for testing the human–computer interface include Task Action Grammar, SemNet, COGNET, Action–Effect Rules, and Programmable User Model.

Formal methods not only yield useful information about how people learn, plan, and solve problems, but they are also useful with fast prototyping techniques to evaluate the user interface throughout the design cycle. Formal methods benefit interface design and evaluation in several ways. Benefits include better defined design trade-offs, predictions of quantitative factors to perform tasks, more attention to issues of **Usability**, and the ability to constrain design space. Formal methods also have their shortcomings. There is the inability to address **Individual** differences, complexity and difficulty of designing the model, potential of being lost in detail and missing the big picture, and weakness in selecting an option among several options.

Empirical. This method involves observing and recording users as they perform human–computer tasks, and it is thought to be the most popular method employed by **Usability** engineers. Use is made of interviews and questionnaires, thinking aloud and protocol analysis, trouble analysis, scenarios, and field testing. Some of the apparent benefits of empirical methods include early problem identification, efficient data collection and detection of user difficulties, realistic information as to how a system is used, and assessment of goal accomplishment. Problems with empirical methods are also recognized. The validity of the empirical methods currently in practice have been questioned. **SoftwareProduct**s shown to usable in the laboratory may not be so in the field. Costs can be prohibitive. Empirical methods assume that subjects are "average" users, but the concept of an average user has been questioned. Attempts to reduce cost are being made by Nielsen, who argues for discount **Usability** [Nielsen91,95]. Mack and Nielsen make the case for inspection as a means of reducing costs [Mack93]. Several of the major software companies provide style guidelines for designing graphical user interfaces within their own operating systems [Sun Microsystems90, IBM91, Apple91, and Microsoft92].

Heuristic.   This method employs experts to evaluate a user interface by commenting on it. Evaluation is normally based on a small number of rules or heuristics. The most popular list comes from Molich and Nielsen [Molich90] and is shown in Table 14.3. The outcomes are (1) a list of **Usability** problems discovered by the experts for design correction and (2) good helps and intuitive visual layouts and reduced user need for documentation. Apparently, heuristic evaluation is intuitive, requires little to no planning, motivates evaluators, and can be used in any phase of the system design and development cycle. Given this last outcome, one of the major problems identified previously in **Usability** testing can be addressed. An obvious shortcoming is that the results are related to the number and experience of the evaluators.

Automated.   The automated method attempts to derive **Usability** information through data capture and analysis. The method can be divided into two fields of emphasis: implementing the procedures and policies of the heuristic method or analyzing the activity logs of the empirical method. Nielsen and Molich indicated that the automated approach is attractive, but its utility remains essentially unknown [Nielsen90]. To date, the automated method has been limited to a few rudimentary computerized evaluations of elements of the interface. A very recent automated approach that shows promise is discussed later.

Scenarios

Test scenarios are stories that describe how a **SoftwareProduct** is to be used. In the mind of the designer, those are the system models that include who will use the system, how it will be used, and anticipated problems that may confront the user. Sce-

TABLE 14.3   Nine Heuristics

1. Use a simple and natural dialog.	6. Provide clearly marked exits.
2. Speak the user's language.	7. Provide shortcuts.
3. Minimize the user's memory load.	8. Provide good error messages.
4. Be consistent.	9. Provide error prevention.
5. Provide feedback.	

narios are frequently used in some combination either in the **Usability** laboratory or the field, with the test methods described previously.

Usability **Laboratory**

The actual utility of any of the foregoing methods by **SoftwareProduct** designers and manufacturers in the design process is not well known. There is some evidence that these methods are related more to research methods than design. However, if and when they are used in a software design and development process, the company involved normally has a **Usability** laboratory. There are three common features of a typical **Usability** laboratory: (1) it includes two rooms separated by a two-way mirror; (2) participants work in one room that is normally decorated as a typical office equipped with video cameras that can be focused on the participant; and (3) the adjacent room is used by the experimenter for observation of the participant during work, and it is equipped with several monitors and some sort of mixing system that provides regular, split-screen, or overlay recording and a professional editing recorder. Most if not all of these features are shown in Figure 14.1, which is the layout and arrangement of the General Electric Information Services Laboratory in Rockville, Maryland.

Usability **METRICS**

The importance of measurement, coupled with an appropriate metric, is stressed in other chapters throughout this book. Measurement and metrics are no less important when it comes to **Usability** testing. Test variables that cannot be measured are of little value. Given this importance, a reasonable question is what are the available metrics for **UsabilityTest** measurement. Although several metrics may be found in a variety of sources, no simple single source exists. Table 14.4 was prepared in an effort to correct that situation. Selecting an appropriate metric for the variables identified in previous tables is left to the ingenuity of the developer.

PLANNING A **UsabilityTest**

Scerbo summarizes a planning process, adapted from Whiteside88, as follows [Scerbo95]:

1. *Identify the relevant attributes.* Although **SoftwareProduct**s can be characterized by several attributes, four common attributes of **Usability** are learnability, flexibility, intuitiveness, and likability.

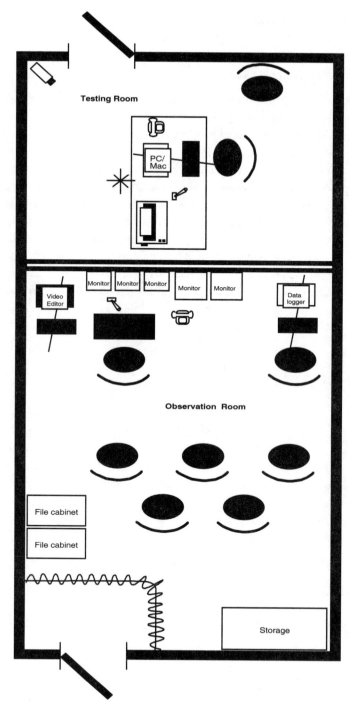

Figure 14.1   General Electric Information Services Laboratory in Rockville, Maryland

Table 14.4 Metrics and Associated References

Metrics	References
Error-free rate	[Lewis90]
Eye dwell time	[Graf87]
Eye scanning patterns	[Graf87]
Learning rate	[Yamada90]
Mean time between error actions	[Yamada90]
Number of errors	[Booth90]
Number of mistakes	[Norman83]
Number of misunderstandings	[Lewis86]
Number of mode errors	[Monk86]
Number of positive/critical statements	[Nielsen95]
Number of sidetracks from real task	[Nielsen93]
Number of slips	[Norman83]
Number of system features recalled	[Nielsen93]
Opinion questionnaires	[Brooke86]
Percentage of erroneous actions	[Carey91]
Statements of preference of one system over another	[Nielsen93]
Task completion time	[Whiteside88]
Time spent in committing errors	[Carey91]
Time spent seeking help	[Carey91]
Time to recover from errors	[Booth 90]
Time to relearn after a lapse	[Lewis90]
Types of errors	[Booth90]
Work rate	[Whiteside85]

2. *Specify measuring concepts.* The measuring concept is a plan for measurement. A concept of measurement must be specified for each relevant attribute, and specifying these concepts confirms that the attributes can be measured.

3. *Determine measuring methods.* The methods are the metrics that will be employed to assess the attributes. Each concept of measurement must have a corresponding metric.

4. *Set desired criterion levels.* A criterion level of performance is set for each attribute. This is the desired level of performance for the planned test.

5. *Set worst-case criterion levels.* A worst-case level of performance is set for each attribute. This is the lowest acceptable level of performance.

**Table 14.5   Sample Attribute Specification Table
[Adapted from Whiteside88]**

Attribute	Measuring Concept	Measuring Time	Planned Level	Worst Case	Optimal Level	Current Level
Learnability	On-line tutorial	Completion time	2 hr	3 hr	0	4 hr
Flexibility	Change default values	Number of errors	< 3	> 6	0	4
Intuitiveness	Use of help	Frequency of access	5	>10	2	?
Likability	Attitude survey	Likert scale	5 Positive	< 4 Negative	7 Very Positive	3 Negative

6. *Set optimal criterion levels.* An optimal level of performance is set for each attribute. This is a level of performance that might result from unlimited resources.

7. *Set current criterion levels.* A worst-case level of performance is set for each attribute. This specifies the present level of performance. The current level of performance may not be known until after the first **UsabilityTest**.

An example of a planned test based on the previous seven steps, given by Scerbo, is presented in Table 14.5. In this table, four attributes are identified, including for each a measuring concept, a measuring method, a planned level, a worst case, an optimal level, and a current level. Testing is an iterative process, because the desired levels of performance will seldom be achieved during an initial test. At this point, decisions must be made regarding whether a design change is to be recommended or if the original criteria were appropriate. If the original criteria were impractical, they must be adjusted. On the other hand, if they were realistic, design changes should be recommended. Implementing design change recommendations will depend on costs and resulting **Usability** benefits.

BENEFITS OF A UsabilityTest

A **UsabilityTest** results in recommendations for improving the use of a system. Implementing the recommendations can provide several benefits. Packenbush provides the following summary with references [Packenbush96].

1. *Increased user satisfaction and good reviews in major computer magazines that can make the software competitive and increase sales* [Nielsen93]. Nielsen reported that "a good review in a major magazine is worth $3 million of advertising, according to some companies."

2. *Saved money and resources due to decreased user training and user help support* [Karat90, Nielsen93]. Chris Peters, vice-president of the Office Product Unit at Microsoft, credits **Usability** testing with "halving the number of **Customer** calls per 'box' sold" [Cusumano95].

3. *Saved money and resources due to making product improvements before product commercialization.* The cost of changes to a released **SoftwareProduct** are four times higher than the cost of making the changes derived from **Usability** testing at the prototype stage [Karat90].

4. *Prevention of "feature creep."* The addition of too many unimportant and complex **Feature**s degrades rather then assists user performance [Cusumano95].

5. *Saved **customer** money and time.* Savings resulted from increased user productivity, decreased user errors, and decreased absenteeism and turnover [Karat90, Nielsen93].

Usability **MODELS**

Given the several metrics listed in Table 14.4, it would seem reasonable that there would be several models available for predicting **Usability**, but not so. The existence of several cognitive models such as GOMS [Card83], BNF [Reisner77], TAG [Payne86], CLG [Moran81], and GTNs [Kieras85], and others, should be acknowledged. However, it should be understood that they are limited in predicting **Usability**. Although a technical discussion of their limitations is outside the scope of this chapter, the practitioner who has attempted to use cognitive models to predict **Usability** is well aware of the problems. To the author's knowledge, there are only two quantitative models in existence for predicting **Usability**. One is a model developed by Mitta, and the second is a model developed Gutekunst. Each has its own special application to **Usability**.

Mitta developed and validated a methodology for quantifying **Usability** of an expert system [Mitta91]. It is a multivariate function for calculating a **Usability** score as an algebraic combination of measurements made of user perceptions and performance. The function was developed using a pair comparisons technique. The final form of the equation is as follows:

$$U = 0.21(S_1) + 0.24(S_2) + 0.22(O_1) + 0.05(O_2) + 0.16(O_3) + 0.12(O_4) \quad (14.1)$$

where U = **Usability** score
S_1 = confidence in a correct answer
S_2 = difficulty associated with problem solving by the system
O_1 = percentage of correct solutions

O_2 = number of responses in a consultation
O_3 = proportion of consultations where no solution was reached
O_4 = ratio of help requests to number of responses in a consultation

To use the methodology, Mitta suggests that measurements of user perception variables, S_i, be gathered using a Likert scale. Measurements of the user performance variables, O_i, may be directly obtained from users exercising the system in controlled tasks. The range of the **Usability** score is from 0 to 1, where the low end of the range represents low **Usability** and the upper end of the range represents high **Usability**.

Gutekunst developed and validated a model for predicting the **Usability** of a computer icon [Gutekunst96]. **Usability** is defined in terms of the ability of an icon to communicate its meaning to a user. The rationale is that the closer the meaning of an icon is to a user's interpretation of that icon, the more usable it will be. Gutekunst used a multivariate correlational technique to develop the following two equations for predicting **Usability** defined as communicativeness of an icon. Equation 14.2 applies to casual users, and equation 14.3 applies to experienced users.

$$C_{cas} = 0.924 - 0.202(X_1) - 0.139(X_2) + 0.174(X_3) \tag{14.2}$$

$$C_{exp} = 1.065 - 0.269(X_1) - 0.047(X_2) + 0.050(X_3) \tag{14.3}$$

where C_{cas} = casual user
        C_{exp} = experienced user
        X_1 = information
        X_2 = design quality
        X_3 = image function

Information is defined in terms of uncertainty and uses the classical information metric, bits of information. Both design quality and image function are determined through a special use of the semantic differential technique [Lin92]. The range of *C* is from 0 to 1, where low values represent low icon communicativeness and high values represent high icon communicativeness. Again, according to the rationale of the model, icon communicativeness is interchangeable with icon **Usability**.

RECENT STUDIES IN Usability TESTING

Recent trends in **Usability** testing bear watching. Three studies in particular are of special interest. One explores the question: is there a core set of **Usability maxim**s that most HCI practitioners use based on evaluation expertise accumulated from experience? A second deals with an alternative heuristic method of evaluation. The third proposes and tests an automated environment that unobtrusively records the interaction between a user and a software application. A fourth trend involves a development in Japan called Human Technology, which includes among other things **Usability** evaluation.

Usability Maxims

Lund suggests that many HCI designers have developed their own set of general HCI design maxims that they keep in working memory and use implicitly or explicitly from project to project [Lund97]. To explore the reality of the suggestion, Lund, using a forced choice technique, asked a small sample of highly experienced HCI design professionals to evaluate a well reviewed and edited list of maxims and assign to each a value of 1 to 5. A value of 5 represented greatest, and a value of 1 represented least. Two evaluations were obtained: 1) potential of the maxims to affect **Usability**, and 2) practicality of maxims for implementation. The maxims with the largest assigned values are presented in Table 14.6.

Lund concludes that although experienced HCI design professionals seem to feel that the foregoing lists of maxims have the greatest impact on **Usability**, no one seems to know how experts apply them. It is evident however that experience is required for their usage. He concludes that further research is needed to explore how maxims are used and how much experience is critical.

Table 14.6   HCI Usability Design Maxims [Adapted from Lund97]

Maxims Affecting Usability	Maxims for Practical Implementation
1. Know thy user, and you are not the user.	1. Make objects, actions, and options visible.
2. Things that look the same should act the same.	2. Minimize the amount of information a user must maintain in short term memory.
3. The information for the desicion needs to be there when the decision is needed.	3. Provide good error messages that are explained in plain language, precisely indicate the problem, and constructively suggest a solution.
4. Error messages should actually mean something to the user and tell the user how to fix the problem.	4. People should not have to remember information across a dialog.
5. Every action should have a reaction.	5. Provide the user with feedback and error correction capabilities.
6. Everyone makes mistakes, so every mistake should be fixable.	6. Testing, testing, testing.
7. Don't overload the user's buffers.	7. Support undo and redo.
8. Keep it simple.	8. No, you can't just explain it in the manual.

A Domain-specific Heuristic Checklist

Dykstra suggests that "there is some evidence that current heuristic sets may be of limited value, especially for experienced users of graphical user interfaces. Disinterest in heuristics is probably due to their global nature, as well as their lack of new information for the experienced **Usability** expert" [Dykstra93]. A major complaint leveled at heuristic sets is that they provide too few guidelines. However, providing too many guidelines is also a danger. Rather than dismissing heuristics, Dykstra argued for a middle ground. In his study, he proposes and tests an alternative heuristic method based on the concept of a domain-specific heuristic checklist. His contention is that the intended checklist will provide a mid-level of complexity, thereby avoiding the monotony of extensive guidelines and the generality of current heuristic sets.

In addition, he reasons that if the domain-specific checklist contains a portion of the knowledge expected of a domain expert, then fewer evaluators will be needed to discover a majority of the **Usability** problems. During the study, Dykstra made several comparisons in regard to the discovery of **Usability** problems: (1) software developers versus human factors **Usability** specialists, (2) domain-specific heuristic checklist versus Nielsen's nine heuristics, and (3) domain-specific heuristic checklist versus a "streamlined" discount laboratory evaluation.

The **SoftwareProduct** domain chosen for the study was on-line calendars. A formal five-step procedure was employed to develop the calendar checklist. The study was conducted in the **Usability** laboratory at the IBM facilities in Westlake, Texas. The participants were software developers and human factors specialists employed at the laboratory.

The results revealed that the participants using the calendar checklist found more total problems and a significantly higher percentage of user-oriented problems and severe problems than did the participants using the general heuristic method. Dykstra indicated that these results suggest that domain-specific checklists provide an improved heuristic approach. There were no differences between human factors **Usability** specialists and software developers in their ability to find user-oriented or severe problems. It was concluded also that, when time permits, heuristic testing is the best method. However, when heuristic testing is not feasible, "domain-specific heuristics may provide results approaching the effectiveness of the double specialist."

An Objective Usability Metric

Fleming formulated a system called the Usability Measurement Integrated Support Environment (UMISE) [Fleming95]. It consists of three component **Subsystem**s: monitoring, guidance, and analysis. The responsibility of the monitoring **Subsystem** is to measure the interaction between a user and an application in an unobtrusive and unintrusive manner. The tasks of instructing the user and gathering questionnaire data are automatically handled by the guidance **Subsystem**. Raw data from the monitoring **Subsystem** are output to the analysis **Subsystem,** where they are reduced and **Usability** metrics are extracted.

The X Window System, because it permits the interception and logging of keyboard and mouse activity, was selected for data monitoring. The monitoring and recording tasks are handled by XTrap, a public-domain software package. Fleming modified a part of XTrap called xtraout for final data collection.

Data analyses were accomplished using the Universal Quantification, Conditional Effect, Partial Order Planner (UCPOP), an AI planning agent [Barrett94]. Agents within the system are responsible for planning, activating, monitoring, and maintaining consistency. Goal selection triggers the formulation of a plan of actions to accomplish the goal. User actions are compared with the formulated action plan. If there is a match, the task is successful. If there is no match, an error is recorded, and a new plan of action is formulated on the basis of the user's current status.

The software selected for application of UMISE was *Mosaic*, a browser for the World Wide Web. The experiment consisted of first explaining to a user a series of tasks that make up a Mosiac operation and then asking the user to accomplish the operation. Data were collected during both the early learning sessions and the subsequent testing session. Fleming poses metrics for Nielsen's five heuristics [Nielsen92] and uses these as a basis for final data analysis. Table 14.7 depicts the five heuristics and Fleming's suggested metrics.

Results reveal that UMISE demonstrated the ability to answer unobtrusively the following questions: Did the user complete the required task? Did the user commit any errors? In so doing, it maps the answers to the abstract heuristics of Nielsen. It appears that a system such as UMISE has unusual potential for later stages of **Usability** testing.

Usability **Testing in Japan**

Price indicates that there has been a shift in product/service development in Japan. Japanese designers are moving away from engineering emphases on function, reliability, and cost savings to added value through human technology [Price94]. The concept of human technology is defined as "advanced technology that enhances perfor-

Table 14.7 Five Heuristics and Suggested Metrics

Heuristics	Metrics
Learnability	Error rate during learning trials
Relearnability	Error rate during later test trials
Frequency/severity of error	Deviations from the ideal actions of the planner
Efficiency	Ratio of user steps to goal to planner steps to goal
User satisfaction	Correlations of questionnaire data with other collected data

mance for humans in such areas as comfort, enjoyment, and **Usability**. This requires more attention to the characteristics of human factors." The approach is likely rooted in *Kansei* or human sensibility. Price says that "Kansei gives rise to terms such as *amenity* or *ambiance engineering, comfort engineering, susceptibility engineering,* and *ergolectronics.*" Human technology, the Japanese believe, will improve quality of life and give them a competitive advantage in the global marketplace.

On the basis of a $200 million, 8-year national research and development program, the Research Institute of Human Engineering for Quality of life (HQL) was formed. The mission is to develop technology and data to support industry in product design, where emphasis is given not only to performance and efficiency, but also to user sensory factors of familiarity and comfort. Price says:

> HQL has been commissioned to develop: (1) noninvasive physiological measurement technology for measuring physiological influences on the human body from external stimuli; (2) stimulated-environment technology that can generate and control heat, noise, light, and other external stimuli; and (3) correlation analysis technology to obtain statistical data on the correlations among external stimuli, physiological responses, and the senses. The results have ultimate application to the design and manufacture of products such as clothing that is comfortable to wear; chairs that are cozy to sit in; shoes that are easy to walk in; and working and living environments that produce minimal mental stress.

According to Price, **Usability** evaluation is becoming an important part of the interface design of Japanese products. It is destined to become a major activity in Japan because it is consistent with their shift to human technology. It takes no stretch of the imagination to believe that Japanese approaches to **Usability** evaluation will make use of the noninvasive physiological measurement technology currently under development, where concern will be given to user comfort as well as user efficiency. Interestingly enough, there are no known comparable approaches to **Usability** evaluation in the United States. Given this fact, it would be important, at least to conclude, that Human Technology as it relates to **Usability** evaluation in Japan bears close watching.

SUMMARY

Testing for **Usability** is discussed first in terms of the objective of testing. This is followed by a coverage of test variables and test procedures. Test procedures include an examination of number of participants, methods, **Usability** laboratories, and scenarios. Metrics for **Usability** are presented in a table listing the better-known metrics coupled with associated references. An example procedure for planning a **UsabilityTest** is given, followed by a discussion of **Usability** models. The last topic, recent studies in **Usability**, introduces **Usability** maxims and discusses a new method called a domain-specific heuristic checklist and a new automated environment for unobtrusively measuring the interaction between a user and a software application and converting the results to give a metric form to five heuristics suggested by Nielsen. The discussion concluded with a brief coverage of an emphasis called human technology, which is under national sponsorship and development in Japan. It includes an approach to **Usability** evaluation unknown in the United States or anywhere else in the world.

REFERENCES

[Apple91] Apple Computer, *Human Interface Guidelines: The Apple Desktop Interface*, Addison–Wesley Publishing Co., Reading, MA, 1991.

[Barrett94] Barrett, A., Golden, K., Penberthy, S., and Weld, D., *UCPOP User's Manual, Version 2.0*, Technical Report 93-09-06, Department of Computer Science and Engineering, University of Washington, Seattle, WA, 1994.

[Booth90] Booth, P., *An Introduction to Human–Computer Interaction*, LEA, Hove, East Sussex, 1990.

[Bovier90] Bovier, S., Kieras, D., and Polson, P., "The Acquisition and Performance of Text-editing Skill: A Cognitive Complexity Analysis," *Human–Computer Interaction*, 5, pp. 1–48.

[Brooke86] Brooke, J. B., "Usability Engineering in Office Production Environment," in Harrison, M. D., and Monk, A. F., eds., *People and Computers: Designing for Usability, Proceedings of the 2nd Conference of the BCS HCI Specialist Group*, Cambridge Press, New York, 1986.

[Card83] Card, S., Moran, T. P., and Newell, A., *The Psychology of Human–Computer Interaction*, LEA, Hillsdale, NJ, 1983.

[Carey91] Carey, T. M., "A Usability Requirements Model for Procurement Life Cycles," in Carey, T. M., ed., *Human Factors in Information Systems*, Ablex, Norwood, NJ, 1991, pp. 1–28.

[Cusumano95] Cusumano, M. A., and Selby, R. W., *Microsoft Secrets: How the World's Most Powerful Company Creates Technology, Shapes Markets, and Manages People*, Free Press, New York, 1995.

[Dykstra93] Dykstra, D. J., *A Comparison of Heuristic Evaluation and Usability Testing: The Efficacy of a Domain-specific Heuristic Checklist*, an unpublished dissertation, Texas A&M University, College Station, TX, 1993.

[Eason84] Eason, K. D., "Towards the Experimental Study of Usability," *Behavior and Information Technology*, Vol. 3, No. 2, 1984, pp. 219–224.

[Elkerton88] Elkerton, J., "Online Aiding for Human–Computer Interfaces," in Helander, M., ed., *Handbook of Human–Computer Interaction*, Elsevier, Amsterdam, 1988, pp. 345–364.

[Fleming95] Fleming, M. A., *A System for Objective Usability Metrics*, an unpublished dissertation, Texas A&M University, College Station, TX, 1995.

[Graf87]   Graf, W., Elsinger, P., and Krueger, H., "Methods for the Ergonomic Evaluation of Alphanumeric Computer-generated Displays," in Bullinger, H. J., and Shackel, B., eds., *Human–Computer Interact '87: Proceedings of the 2nd IFIP Conference on Human–Computer Interaction*, North Holland, Amsterdam, 1987.

[Gutekunst96]   Gutkunst, K. R., *A Predictive Model for Computer Icon Development*, an unpublished dissertation, Texas A&M University, College Station, TX, 1996.

[IBM91]   IBM, *System Application Architecture, Common User Access, Guide to Interface Design*, IBM, New York, 1991.

[Karat90]   Karat, C. M., "Cost–Benefit Analysis of Usability Engineering Techniques," *Proceedings of the Human Factors Society 34th Annual Meeting*, 1990, pp. 839–843.

[Kieras85]   Kieras, D. E., and Polson, P. G., "An Approach to the Formal Analysis of User Complexity," *International Journal of Man–Machine Studies*, Vol. 22, 1985, pp. 91–102.

[Lewis86]   Lewis, C., and Norman, D. A., "Designing for Error," in Norman, D. A., and Draper, S. W., eds., *User Centered System Design: New Perspective on Human–Computer Interaction*, LEA Associates, Hillsdale, NJ, 1986.

[Lewis90]   Lewis, J. R., Henry, S. C., and Mack, R. L., "Integrated Office Software Benchmarks: A Case Study," *Proceedings of Human–Computer Interaction: Interact '90*, Elsevier, Amsterdam, 1990, pp. 337–343.

[Lewis94]   Lewis, J. R., "Sample Sizes for Usability Studies: Additional Considerations," *Human Factors,* Vol. 36, No. 2, pp. 368–378.

[Lin92]   Lin, R., "An Application of the Semantic Differential to Icon Design," *Proceedings of the Human Factors and Ergonomics Society, 36 Annual Meeting*, Santa Monica, CA, 1992, pp. 336–340.

[Lund97]   Lund, A. M. "Expert Ratings of Usability Maxims," *Ergonomics in Design*, Vol. 5, No. 3, 1997, pp. 15–20.

[Mack93]   Mack, R., and Neilsen, J., "Usability Inspection Methods," *SIGCHI Bulletin*, Vol. 25, No. 1, 1993, pp. 28–33.

[Microsoft92]   Microsoft, *Windows Interface: An Application Design Guide*, Microsoft, Redmond, WA, 1992.

[Mitta91]   Mitta, D. A., "A Methodology for Quantifying Expert System Usability," *Human Factors*, Vol. 33, No. 2, 1991, pp. 233–245.

[Molich90]   Molich, R., and Nielsen, J., "Improving Human–Computer Dialogue: What Designers Know About Traditional Interface Design," *Communications of the ACM*, Vol. 33, No. 3, 1990, pp. 338–348.

[Monk86]   Monk, A. F., "Mode Errors: A User-centered Analysis and Some Preventative Measures Using Key-contingent Sound," *International Journal of Man–Machine Studies*, Vol. 24, 1986, pp. 313–327.

[Monk90]   Monk, A., "Action–Effect Rules: A Technique for Evaluating an Informal Specification against Principles," *Behavior and Information Technology*, Vol. 9, 1990, pp. 147–155.

[Moran81]   Moran, T. P., "The Command Language Grammar: A Representation for the User Interface of Interactive Computer Systems," *International Journal of Man–Machine Studies*, Vol. 15, No. 1, 1981, pp. 3–50.

[Nielsen90]   Nielsen, J., and Molich, R., "Heuristic Evaluation of User Interfaces," *Proceedings CHI '90*, ACM, New York, 1990, pp. 249–256.

[Nielsen91]   Nielsen, J., "Usability Metrics and Methodologies," *SIGCHI Bulletin*, Vol. 23, No. 2, 1991, pp. 37–39.

[Nielsen92]   Nielson, J., "The Usability Engineering Life Cycle," *IEEE Computer,* Vol. 25, No. 3, 1992, pp. 12–22.

[Nielsen93]   Nielsen, J., *Usability Engineering*, Academic Press, Boston, 1993.

[Nielsen95]   Nielsen, J., "Applying Discount Usability Engineering," *IEEE Software,* Vol. 12, No. 1, 1995, pp. 98–100.

[Norman83]   Norman, D. A., "Designs Rules Based on Analyses of Human Error," *Communications of the ACM*, Vol. 26, No. 4, 1983, pp. 254–258.

[Packenbush96]   Packenbush, S. J., *Participant Sample Size and Iterative Usability Testing*, an unpublished dissertation, Texas A&M University, College Station, TX, 1996.

[Payne86]   Payne, S. J., and Green, T. R. G., "Task–Action Grammars: A Model of the Mental Representations of Task Languages," *Human–Computer Interaction*, Vol. 2, 1986, pp. 93–133.

[Price94]   Price, H. E., "A Western View of Ergonomics in Japan," *Human Factors and Ergonomics Society Bulletin*, Vol. 37, No. 6, 1994, pp. 1–2.

[Reisner77]   Reisner, D. A., "The Use of Psychological Experimentation as an Aid to Development of a Query Language," *IEEE Transactions on Software Engineering*, Vol. SE-3, 1977, pp. 218–229.

[Scerbo95]   Scerbo, M. W., "Usability Testing," in Weimer, J., *Research Techniques in Human Engineering*, Prentice Hall, Upper Saddle River, NJ, 1995, pp. 72–111.

[Shackel91]   Shackel, B., "The Concept of Usability," *Proceedings of the IBM Software and Information Usability Symposium*, New York, 1981, pp. 1–30.

[Sun Microsystems90]   Sun Microsystems, *OPEN LOOK Graphical User Interface Application Style Guidelines*, Addison–Wesley Publishing Co., Reading, MA, 1990.

[Virzi92]   Virzi, R. A., "Refining the Test Phase of Usability Evaluation: How Many Subjects Is Enough?," *Human Factors*, Vol. 34, No. 4, 1992, pp. 457–468.

[Whitefield90]   Whitefield, A., "Human–Computer Models and Their Roles in the Design of Interactive Systems," in Falzon, P., ed., *Cognitive Ergonomics*, Academic Press, New York, 1990, pp. 7–25.

[Whiteside85]   Whiteside, J., Jones, S., Levy, P. S., and Wixon, D., "User Performance with Command, Menu and Iconic Interfaces," in Borman, L., and Curtis, W., eds., *Human Factors in Computer Systems II: Proceedings of the CHI '85 Conference*, North Holland, Amsterdam, 1985.

[Whiteside88]   Whiteside, J., Bennett, J., and Holtzblatt, K., "Usability Engineering: Our Experience and Evolution," in Helander, M., ed., *Handbook of Human–Computer Interaction*, Elsevier, Amsterdam, 1988, pp. 791–817.

[Yamada90]   Yamada, A., "Measuring Usability," *Proceedings of the 14th Annual International Computer Software and Applications Conference*, IEEE Computer Society Press, Los Alamitos, CA, 1990, p. 68.

Part Three

VISUALIZATION TOOL

15
Project Attribute Monitoring and Prediction Associate (PAMPA)

If an agent that could learn were available now, I would want it to take over certain functions for me. For instance, it would be very helpful if it could scan every project schedule, note the changes, and distinguish the ones I had to pay attention to from the ones I didn't. It would learn the criteria for what needed my attention: the size of the project, what other projects are dependent on it, the cause and the length of any delay. It would learn when a two-week slip could be ignored, and when such a slip indicates real trouble and I'd better look into it right away before it gets worse.

Bill Gates
[Gates95]

INTRODUCTION

Tools can be built to help to visualize software development projects. Agents that learn are not available to help to visualize software, but intelligent agents can be built to assist software project managers. We have created **PAMPA** (Project Attribute Monitoring and Prediction Associate) to help you to gather project information from any software development environment, save it in an understandable object/attribute format, view it using an inexpensive workstation that runs *Microsoft* Windows and Office, and supply input to expert system building tools used for creating intelligent agents. A CD (Compact Disc) is provided in the cover of this book for you to try an initial version of **PAMPA** to visualize your software **Project**. In this chapter we will give you an overview of **PAMPA**, describe an example of how it can be used to visualize a software **Project**, and explain how it can be used to control software **Project**s and improve software creation processes.

OVERVIEW

Projects often fail because management does not know true **Project** status. We know that software is harder to visualize than hardware. Brooks believes that in addition to being invisible it is unvisualizable [Brooks87]. In Chapter 1 a number of recent failed **Project**s were described. In one, neither Edward Esber, CEO of Ashton–Tate Corporation, nor his managers knew that their dBASE IV product was marred by thousands of errors until after they delivered a flawed product. Administrators of American Airlines spent $165 million before they realized that their replacement airline reservation system had major flaws. After spending $7 billion, the FAA ended up with a **Project** that was "out of control." The IRS spent $4 billion with nothing to show for it. In these cases, the true nature and pervasive extent of underlying **Project** problems remained invisible to the **Project** management until it was too late.

We are much more optimistic than Brooks. We believe that modern technology can be applied to software **Project**s to help managers to continuously visualize exactly what is occurring. In Chapters 3 and 5 through 9, a set of object classes was introduced that help **Project** personnel to visualize a software **Project**. As we did in Chapter 3, we will represent **Project** objects in *Microsoft* bold Arial font. Figure 15.1 displays objects that make up a software **Project**. **Supplier**s may provide COTS software in the form of **LicensedRunFile**s reusable software in the form of **ReusableSourceFile**s. The **Project Organization** develops and maintains the **SoftwareProduct**, which is used by the **Customer**s. Expenses of a software **Project** are normally dominated by personnel costs, which can be computed from **Salary** and **Assignment** records.

The **SoftwareProduct Feature**s and **DesignFile**s should be reflected in the **SourceFile**s created by a development team each time that they create a new **Version** of a **SoftwareProduct**. Thorough testing should be conducted to make sure that the **SoftwareProduct** is correct, complete, and usable. Tests run to validate **Feature**s and verify the design should be recorded as validation and verification test (**VAndVTest**s) records. Tests run to assure usability should be recorded as usability test (**UsabilityTest**) records. When a customer encounters trouble, trouble report records should be maintained to make sure that reported problems are resolved. Any test failures or problems identified in trouble reports that cannot be resolved should be logged as a record in a **Defect** tracking system. The **SoftwareProduct** objects in Figure 15.1 should mirror the actual **SoftwareProduct**.

We developed **PAMPA** to unobtrusively gather attribute values of objects from any arbitrary software development **Project**. A gatherer has been developed to gather

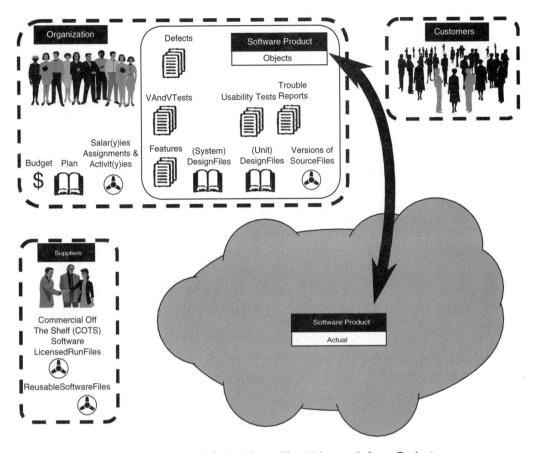

Figure 15.1 Objects That Make up a Software **Project**

data from a *Microsoft* Windows environments. Furthermore, gatherers can be written to extend this to a UNIX or other operating system environment. **PAMPA** can gather **Project** information from any software development environment that can share directories over a network to a *Microsoft* Windows client workstation. Figure 15.2 shows how **PAMPA** gathers data to represent the exact status of a software **Project**. Objects along with their attribute values are saved in the **PAMPA** database. A description of all **PAMPA** object classes, relationships, and attributes is given in Appendix A. You can use the **PAMPA** tool to

- monitor, measure, and calculate software **Project** attributes,
- generate management reports,
- generate two- and three-dimensional plots and radar plots,
- predict **Project** attributes,

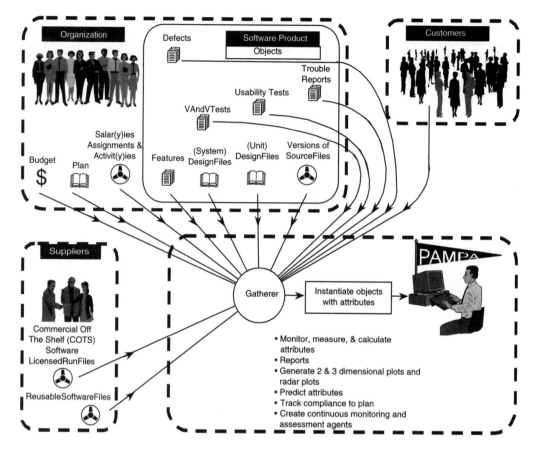

Figure 15.2   Project Attribute Monitoring and Predicting Associate (**PAMPA**)

- track **Project** compliance to the **Project** plan, and
- create agents to periodically or continuously monitor any one of your **Project**s.

In the next section we will describe a simple example of how **PAMPA** is used to visualize a software product.

Project **VISUALIZATION**

We have included in the cover of this book a CD that contains a simple version of the **PAMPA** tool that runs under *Microsoft* Windows that has *Microsoft* Office. A **PAMPA** users manual is provided in Appendix B. We will look at a **Project** implemented in C that uses the CLIPS (C Language Integrated Production System) expert system building tool to create intelligent agents. CLIPS was designed at NASA/Johnson Space Center with the specific purpose of providing high portability, low cost, and easy integration with external systems [Giarratano94]. We will show how the **PAMPA** tool can be used to view the sample **TSA SoftwareProduct**.

You would first use **PAMPA** to gather information about the **TSA Software-Product**. Figure 15.3 shows how the object editor can be used to view the **TSA Soft-wareProduct** tree. Notice that the eight **Versions v0.1** through **v0.8** were gathered. For demonstration purposes, let's assume that you are interested in version **v0.8**. If you click your mouse on the **Subsystem** icon under **Versions v0.8** in Figure 15.3, you would see an additional two levels of the tree. You then can scroll horizontally until you see the files related to CLIPS. Figure 15.4 shows the expanded **Subsystem** node for **v0.8** node of the **TSA SoftwareProduct** tree, where you see the CLIPS_OP.C **SourceFile** object node that is made up of the five **Chunk**s **gen_clips_data**, **gen_clips_results**, **select_tests**, **gen_clips_rules**, and **gen_ clips_parm**. Notice that in Figure 15.4 each of the **Chunk** names was truncated to 11 characters. The full name for the object appears in the status bar at the bottom of

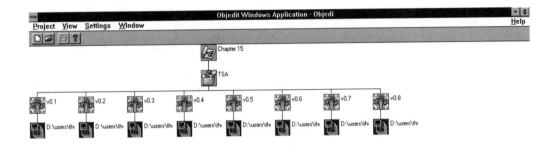

Figure 15.3 Sample **TSA SoftwareProduct** Tree

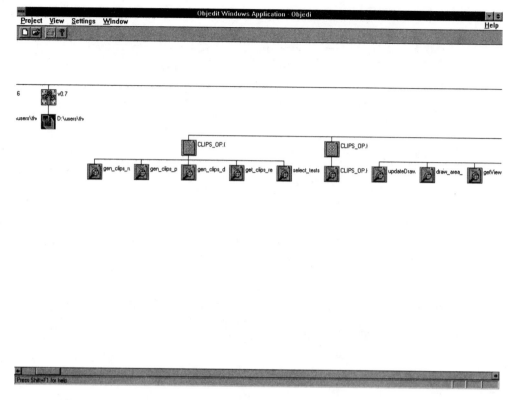

Figure 15.4   Expanded **Other** Node for **v0.8** Node of the **TSA SoftwareProduct** Tree

the screen whenever the mouse passes over the object. If you click on the **CLIPS_OP.C SourceFile** node, you can view its attributes as shown in Figure 15.5. Notice that 203 SLOCs were added to and 189 SLOCs were deleted from **CLIPS_OP.C.** By next clicking the **gen_clips_data Chunk** node icon, you can see its attributes as shown in Figure 15.6. Notice that it has 7,756 bytes, 41 compiler directive source statements, and 10 executable source statements.

Ideally, once you create a **SourceFile,** no **Rework** would be necessary. The amount of **Rework** is a function of the SLOCs that are added to and deleted from a **SourceFile.** Also, a well-documented program has a large ratio of comments to SLOCs. Figure 15.7 shows the values of **Volume** attributes $Adds_{\textbf{Calculate}}$, $Deletes_{\textbf{Calculate}}$, $CommentSLOC_{\textbf{Calculate}}$, and $SLOC_{\textbf{Calculate}}$ for **Version v0.8** of the **TSA SoftwareProduct.** You can see that the amount of **Rework** decreased from **Version v0.7** to **v0.8.** Also the comments are a very small proportion of the total **Volume** for each of the **Version**s.

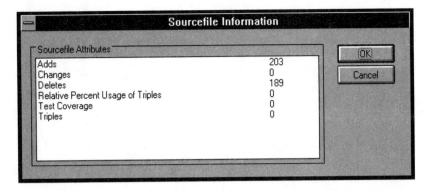

Figure 15.5 Values of Adds and Deletes Attributes in the **Rework** Class for **CLIPS_OP.C SourceFile** Object Node of the **TSA SoftwareProduct** Tree

We can now look at more details for **Version v0.8.** Figure 15.8 shows values of **Volume** attributes $Adds_{Calculate}$, $Deletes_{Calculate}$, $Chunks_{Calculate}$, $Comment$-$SLOC_{Calculate}$, and $SLOC_{Calculate}$ for each **SourceFile** in **Version v0.8** of the **TSA SoftwareProduct.** Eight of the 56 **SourceFile**s are listed alphabetically in Figure 15.8, which contains the attributes of CLIPS_OP.C. The other 49 can be seen on other screens. Of the **SourceFile**s in Figure 15.8, CLIPS_OP.C does seem to have a relative large amount of **Rework.** Instead of plotting the **SoftwareProduct SourceFile**s alphabetically, in Figure 15.9 we display them sorted in descending order by size of $Adds_{Calculate}$. Notice that CLIPS_OP.C is ranked fourth out of 56 **SourceFile**s.

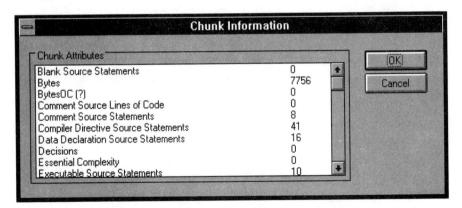

Figure 15.6 Values for **Volume** Attributes Bytes, CommentSS, CompilerDirectiveSS, and Decisions for **gen_clips_data Chunk** Node

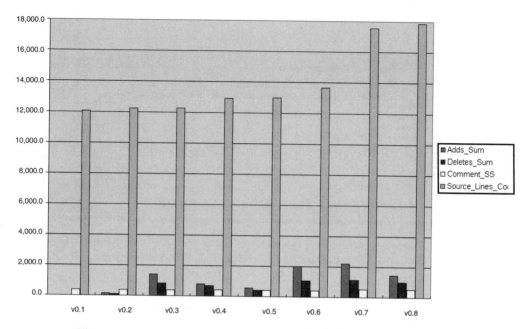

Figure 15.7 Values of **Volume** Attributes $Adds_{\text{Calculate}}$, $Deletes_{\text{Calculate}}$, $CommentSLOC_{\text{Calculate}}$, and $SLOC_{\text{Calculate}}$ for **Version v0.8** of the **TSA SoftwareProduct**

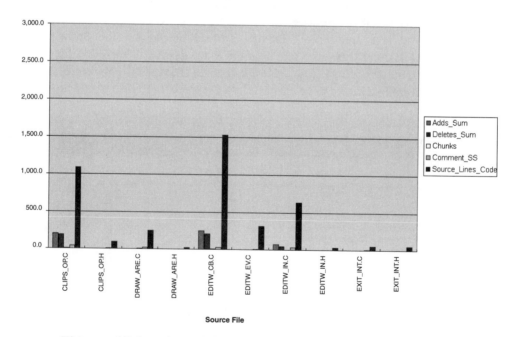

Figure 15.8 Values of **Volume** Attributes $Adds_{\text{Calculate}}$, $Deletes_{\text{Calculate}}$, $Chunks_{\text{Calculate}}$, $CommentSLOC_{\text{Calculate}}$, and $SLOC_{\text{Calculate}}$ for Each **SourceFile** in **Version v0.8** of the **TSA SoftwareProduct**

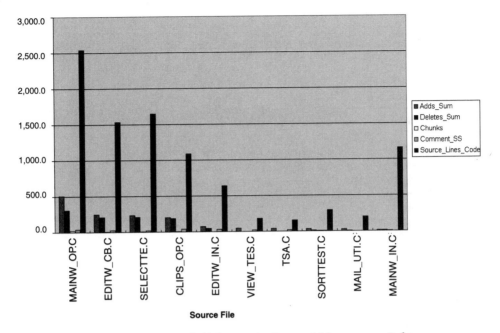

Figure 15.9 Values of **Volume** Attributes *Adds*_{Calculate}, *Deletes*_{Calculate}, *Chunks*_{Calculate}, *CommentSLOC*_{Calculate}, and *SLOC*_{Calculate} for Each **SourceFile** (Sorted by Value of *Adds*_{Calculate}) in **Version v0.8** of the **TSA SoftwareProduct**

While the plots show relative sizes of **SourceFile**s attributes, you may also like to see the numerical values in tabular form for each of the attributes. At your option, you can view the table that is used to create any **PAMPA** chart. Figure 15.10 displays the **SourceFile**s attributes sorted in detail by size of *Adds*_{Calculate} that were used to create Figure 15.9. You can see that only 16 of the **SourceFile**s had any *Adds*_{Calculate} or *Deletes*_{Calculate}. The others were stable and had no modifications for **Version v0.8**. This is reasonable for the **TSA SoftwareProduct,** which was in the later stages of the β test when the sample data were gathered. The values for CLIPS_OP.C are highlighted in the table. Notice that only 39 comment lines were used out of 1,088 total SLOCs. You may want to know how comments were distributed across each of the **Chunk**s within the CLIPS_OP.C **SourceFile.** Figure 15.11 shows the values of **Volume** attributes *CommentSS* and *SLOC* in **Chunk**s of **SourceFile** CLIPS_OP.C. Notice that each of the **Chunk**s has a relatively small number of comments.

Up to this point, we have only shown information using two-dimensional charts. You can portray attributes in three dimensions. Assume that you would like to see how *Adds*_{Calculate} varied for each **SourceFile** of each **Version**s. Figure 15.12 displays values of **Volume** attributes *Adds*_{Calculate} for each **SourceFile** in **Version**s **v0.1** through **v0.8** of the **TSA SoftwareProduct.** Notice that **CLIPS_OP.C** shows

Chart

	A	B	C	D	E	F
1	SRC_NAME	Adds_Sum	Deletes_Sum	Chunks	Comment_SS	Source_Lines_Code
2	MAINW_OP.C	506.0	307.0	22.0	41.0	2542.0
3	EDITW_CB.C	248.0	208.0	9.0	27.0	1535.0
4	SELECTTE.C	233.0	206.0	8.0	23.0	1644.0
5	CLIPS_OP.C	203.0	189.0	5.0	39.0	1088.0
6	EDITW_IN.C	72.0	47.0	2.0	31.0	642.0
7	VIEW_TES.C	47.0	3.0	2.0	19.0	178.0
8	TSA.C	39.0	3.0	3.0	17.0	156.0
9	SORTTEST.C	31.0	12.0	4.0	10.0	293.0
10	MAIL_UTI.C	26.0	7.0	3.0	2.0	198.0
11	MAINW_IN.C	16.0	13.0	5.0	0.0	1158.0
12	STRUCTUR.H	13.0	2.0	1.0	9.0	147.0
13	STATUS.C	12.0	5.0	4.0	2.0	96.0
14	MAINW_OP.H	6.0	0.0	1.0	1.0	60.0
15	TSA.H	6.0	1.0	1.0	4.0	36.0
16	DRAW_ARE.C	1.0	1.0	7.0	19.0	248.0
17	HELP_OPS.H	0.0	0.0	1.0	17.0	169.0
18	LOAD_FAC.C	0.0	0.0	3.0	3.0	418.0
19	LOAD_FAC.H	0.0	0.0	1.0	2.0	69.0

Figure 15.10   Table of Values for the Attributes Shown in Figure 15.9

initial $Adds_{\text{Calculate}}$ at **v0.3,** then has little activity for **v0.4** through **v0.5,** and then seems to have a relative constant level of $Adds_{\text{Calculate}}$ for versions **v0.6** through **v0.8**. By viewing the other **SourceFile**s, you notice that they have different patterns. The other ones have a single version where they are added to the system and then they have less activity for later versions. **CLIPS_OP.C**'s different behavior is from the fact that it is an embedded knowledge-based system where the source code is generated by a separate system. When external changes are made, the previous knowledge base has to be deleted to add the new one. Thus, for each version the $Adds_{\text{Calculate}}$ and $Deletes_{\text{Calculate}}$ were approximately equal.

Up to this point, we have been viewing a relative small number of attributes at a time. **PAMPA** allows you to evaluate a large number of attributes at a glance using radar charts like the one shown in Figure 15.13. The outer ring represents the maximum desired value for a **SourceFile** attribute. The inner ring represents the minimum desired value. The other connected plot represents the actual value for a given attribute relative to its minimum and maximum desired values. Figure 15.13 displays the values of relative minimum, actual, and maximum **SourceFile** attributes $Adds_{\text{Calculate}}$, $Deletes_{\text{Calculate}}$, $Chunks_{\text{Calculate}}$, $CommentSLOC_{\text{Calculate}}$, $CompilerDirectiveSS_{\text{Calculate}}$, $CyclomaticNumber_{\text{Calculate}}$, $NCSS_{\text{Calculate}}$,

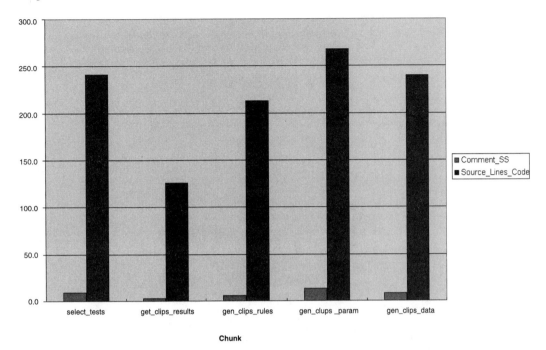

Figure 15.11 Values of **Volume** Attributes CommentSS and SLOC in **Chunk**s of **SourceFile** CLIPS_OP.C

*Operands*Calculate, *Operators*Calculate, *SLOC*Calculate, *UniqueSLOC*Calculate, *UniqueOperands*Calculate, and *UniqueOperators*Calculate for **CLIP_OP.C SourceFile**. Notice that the *Chunks*Calculate and *CommentSLOC*Calculate are both below the desired minimum and *SLOC*Calculate is above the desired maximum. A single function or *Chunks*Calculate of code should be kept small to reduce complexity. The average size to the *Chunks*Calculate in the **CLIP_OP.C SourceFile** is 1,088 ÷ 5 or 213 SLOCs average per chunk. A more desirable size would be in the 50 SLOCs range. The value of *CommentSLOC*Calculate is 39 SLOCs out of the 1,088 SLOCs or 3.6% of the CLIP_OP.C **SourceFile** is comments. To properly explain a program, usually at least 10% of the program SLOCs should be comments. The median size of a **TSA SourceFile** is 149 and the average size is 319 SLOCs. The **SourceFile**s that are larger than 1,000 SLOCs are slightly larger than desirable and should possibly be partitioned into smaller **SourceFile**s.

We have shown how **PAMPA** can be used to visualize the **TSA SoftwareProduct**. Only a small part of its capabilities has been demonstrated. A tree diagram of objects that comprise any **SoftwareProduct** can be drawn. The value of attributes for any node of the tree can be viewed. Any of the object attributes described in Appendix A can be plotted in two or three dimensions. Tables listing the numerical val-

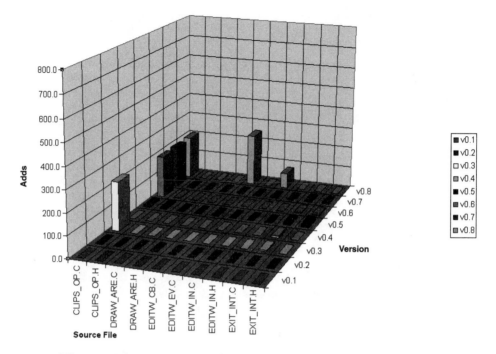

Figure 15.12 Values of **Volume** Attributes *Adds*Calculate for Each **SourceFile** in **Versions v0.1** through **v0.8** of the **TSA SoftwareProduct**

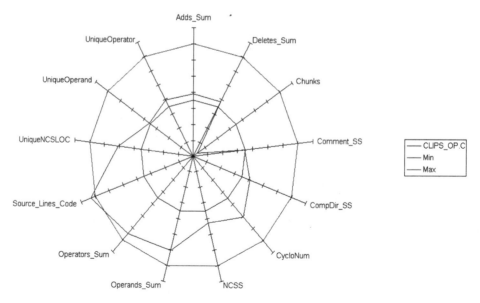

Figure 15.13 Values of Selected Relative Minimum, Actual, and Maximum **SourceFile** Attributes for CLIP_OP.C **SourceFile**

ues for an object attribute can be printed. Radar charts can be plotted to show how an attribute of an arbitrary object compares with its desired minimum or maximum.

CONTROL AND IMPROVEMENT CYCLES

To control **Project**s, managers must know the status of every aspect of the process. The primary method of gathering information about software **Project**s is to ask humans to manually produce status information. Manual procedures are fraught with inaccuracies and subjective interpretations of what should be accurate quantitative measurements. **PAMPA** removes the human from the gathering of information. Intelligent agents can be developed to gather and analyze **Project** data in a quantitative objective procedure that removes inaccuracies and inconsistencies from the monitoring, analyzing, and reporting processes.

Many of the software development **Project**s do not gather metrics because of the expenses involved with the metric gathering process. The **PAMPA** tool has reduced the cost to a minimum. By using intelligent agents, **PAMPA** can automatically on a periodic or continuous basis gather **Project** information in a local or distributed

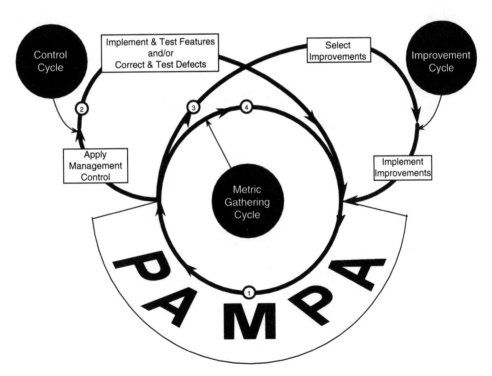

Figure 15.14 **PAMPA** interface to the dual control/improvement cycles

environment. Once the information has been gathered and stored in the database, information can be used as part of any **Project** software development control cycle, which was described in Figure 3.12 or as part of the continuous process improvement process described in Figure 3.15. In Figure 3.17, gathering of measurements and the analysis and prediction of attributes were shown as combined visualization stages of dual control/improvement cycles. In Figure 15.14, we show how the **PAMPA** tool can be used to perform the visualization stages activities for the dual control/improvement cycles. The overhead of operating the **PAMPA** tool can be held to a minimum. Automatic data gathering can be performed during nonpeak periods. By using agents, reports and alerts can be designed to automatically warn **Project** personnel of any anomaly that occurs within a software **Project**. The **PAMPA** tool is a step in the direction described by Bill Gates in 1995 when he described an agent that would take over certain management functions for him. By continually extending the **PAMPA** tool information gathering agents, object classes, prediction models, and agent knowledge bases, features can be developed to be helpful to managers of software **Project**s, from those manned by a small team to those with literally thousands of software professionals.

REFERENCES

[Gates95]   Gates, B., *The Road Ahead*, Viking Press, New York, 1995.

[Brooks87]   Brooks, Jr., F. P., "No Silver Bullet—Essence and Accidents of Software Engineering," *Computer*, Vol. 20, No. 4, April 1987, pp. 10–19.

[Giarrantano94]   Giarratano, J., and Riley, G., *Expert Systems—Principles and Programming*, PWS Publishing Company, Boston, 1994, 644 p.

Appendix A
PAMPA Object Classes

A software process can be divided into the following objects, each of which has relationships to other objects and attributes:

ProjectList
  Project
    Organization
      Areas
        Groups
          Individuals
            Salar(y)ies
            Assignments
            Activit(y)ies
    SoftwareProduct
      Features
      Defects
      Versions
        Subsystems
          RequirementsFiles
            Rework(RequirementsFile)
            Volume(RequirementsFile)
          DesignFiles
            Rework(DesignFile)
            Volume(DesignFile)
          DocumentFiles
            Rework(DocumentFile)
            Volume(DocumentFile)
          SourceFiles
            Chunks
              Volume(Chunk)

         Structure
        Rework(SourceFile)
      VAndVTests
      UsabilityTests
       Usability
Supplier
  ReusableSourceFiles
  LicensedRunFiles
Customer

In the following section, software process objects are listed alphabetically:

Activity
Area
Assignment
Chunk
Customer
Defect
DesignFile
DocumentFile
Features
Group
Individual
LicensedRunFile
Organization
Project
ProjectList
RequirementsFile
ReusableSourceFile
Rework(DesignFile)
Rework(DocumentFile)
Rework(RequirementsFile)
Rework(SourceFile)
Salary
SoftwareProduct
SourceFile
Structure
Subsystem
Supplier
Usability

UsabilityTest
VAndVTest
Version
Volume(Chunk)
Volume(DesignFile)
Volume(DocumentFile)
Volume(RequirementsFile)

In this section, software process objects are listed along with their relationships and attributes:

Activity
| Relationships |

Activit(y)ies are performed by an **Individual**.
Activit(y)ies are performed by a **Group**.
Activit(y)ies are performed by an **Area**.
Activit(y)ies are performed by an **Organization**.

| Attributes |

Strings:
  $Name_{Set}$
  $Description_{Set}$
  $StartDate_{Set}$
  $EndDate_{Set}$
  $PercentTimeOnActivity_{Set}$

Area
| Relationships |

An **Area** contains **Group**s.
An **Area** is managed by an **Individual**.
Areas are contained in an **Organization**.
An **Area** performs **Activit(y)**ies.
An **Area** employees **Individual**s.

| Attributes |

Set:
  $Name_{Set}$
Calculate:
  $AverageIndividualProductivity_{Calculate}$(average NCSS person per
  month)
  $DefectRate_{Calculate}$(Defects per 1,000 SLOC)

$Efficiency$**Calculate**

$Effort To Date$**Calculate** (in person-months)

$Productivity$**Calculate** (average NCSS per month)

$Speedup$**Calculate**

$Time$**Calculate** (time spent on project in person-months)

$TurmoilRate$**Calculate** (Turmoil per 1,000 SLOC)

   <u>Sum:</u>

  $Adds$**Calculate**

  $AreaGroups$**Calculate**

  $AreaIndividuals$**Calculate**

  $Bytes$**Calculate**

  $Changes$**Calculate**

  $Chunks$**Calculate**

  $Deletes$**Calculate**

  $GlobalVariables$**Calculate**

  $Knots$**Calculate**

  $NCSS$**Calculate**

  $Pairs$**Calculate**

  $SLOC$**Calculate**

  $SourceFileDefects$**Calculate**

  $SourceFiles$**Calculate**

  SS**Calculate**

  $Turmoil$**Calculate**

  $UniqueReferenceNCSS$**Calculate**

  $UniqueReferenceSS$**Calculate**

  <u>Average per source file:</u>

  $CyclomaticNumber$**Calculate**

  $EssentialComplexity$**Calculate**

  $InheritanceDepth$**Calculate**

  $NestingDepth$**Calculate**

  $Pairs$**Calculate**

  $RelativePercentageUsagePairs$**Calculate**

  $SourceLiveVariablesPerExecutableSS$**Calculate**

  $SpanLiveVariablesPerExecutableSS$**Calculate**

  $Spans$**Calculate**

  $ThresholdLiveVariablesPerExecutableSS$**Calculate**

  $Triples$**Calculate**

Assignment

| Relationships |

Assignments are related to an **Individual**.

| Attributes |

<u>Strings:</u>
   StartDate
   EndDate
   PercentTimeOnProject$(0 \leq \times \leq 1)$

Chunk

| Relationships |

Chunk contains **Structure**.
Chunk contains **Volume**.
Chunks are contained in **SourceFile**.

| Attributes |

<u>Strings:</u>
   Name

Customer

| Relationships |

Customers are related to a **Project**.

| Attributes |

<u>Set:</u>
   *Name*_{Set}
<u>Gather:</u>
   Performance
<u>Set:</u>
   *ExperienceLevel*_{Set}
   *Satisfaction*_{Set}

Defect

| Relationships |

SoftwareProduct contains **Defect**s.
Defects are located in **DesignFile**s.
Defects are located in **DocumentFile**s.
Defects are located in **RequirementsFile**s.
Defects are located in **SourceFile**s.
A **Defect** is owned by an **Individual**.

| Attributes |

<u>Set:</u>
   $Name_{Set}$
   $Description_{Set}$
   $Identification_{Set}(number)$
<u>Status:</u>
   <u>Plan</u>
   $Open_{Set}$ (date)
   $AllocateResources_{Set}$ (date)
   $V\&VTest_{Set}$ (date)
   $Close_{Set}$ (date)

DesignFile

| Relationships |

A **DesignFile** contains **Rework**.

A **DesignFile** contains **Volume**.

A **DesignFile** is authored by an **Individual**.

A **DesignFile** is owned by an **Individual**.

DesignFiles are contained in a **Subsystem**.

DesignFiles contain **Defect**s.

DesignFiles are related to **Feature**s.

| Attributes |

<u>Strings:</u>
   Name

DocumentFile

| Relationships |

A **DocumentFile** contains **Rework**.

A **DocumentFile** contains **Volume**.

A **DocumentFile** is authored by an **Individual**.

A **DocumentFile** is owned by an **Individual**.

DocumentFiles are contained in a **Subsystem**.

DocumentFiles contain **Defect**s.

DocumentFiles are related to **Feature**s.

| Attributes |

<u>Strings:</u>
   Name

Feature

| Relationships |

Features are contained in a **SoftwareProduct**.

A **Feature** is owned by an **Individual**.
Features are related to **DesignFile**s.
Features are related to **DocumentFile**s.
Features are related to **RequirementsFile**s.
Features are related to **SourceFile**s.
Features are related to **Subsystem**s.
Features are related to **VAndVTest**s.
Features are related to **UsabilityTest**s.

$\boxed{\text{Attributes}}$

Set:

$\quad$ *Name*$_{\textbf{Set}}$
$\quad$ *Description*$_{\textbf{Set}}$

Status:

$\quad$ Predictions:

$\quad\quad$ *PredictedVolume*$_{\textbf{Predict}}$(SLOC, SS, Function Points, Object Points, etc.)
$\quad\quad$ *PredictedEffort*$_{\textbf{Predict}}$(person-months)
$\quad\quad$ *PredictedSchedule*$_{\textbf{Predict}}$(months)
$\quad\quad$ *PlannedCompletion*$_{\textbf{Predict}}$(actual volume ÷ planned volume)
$\quad\quad$ *PredictedFullTimeEmployees*$_{\textbf{Predict}}$(full-time equivalent employees)
$\quad\quad$ *DefectEliminationRate*$_{\textbf{Predict}}$(defects eliminated ÷ person month)

$\quad$ Plan:

$\quad\quad$ *Volume*$_{\textbf{Set}}$(SLOC, SS, Function Points, Object Points, etc.)
$\quad\quad$ *Effort*$_{\textbf{Set}}$(person-months)
$\quad\quad$ *FullTimeEmployees*$_{\textbf{Set}}$(employee per phase)
$\quad\quad$ *Initial*$_{\textbf{Set}}$(date)
$\quad\quad$ *AllocateResources*$_{\textbf{Set}}$(date)
$\quad\quad$ *Requirements*$_{\textbf{Set}}$(date)
$\quad\quad$ *Design*$_{\textbf{Set}}$(date)
$\quad\quad$ *Implementation*$_{\textbf{Set}}$(date)
$\quad\quad$ *UnitTest*$_{\textbf{Set}}$(date)
$\quad\quad$ α*Test*$_{\textbf{Set}}$(date)
$\quad\quad$ β*Test*$_{\textbf{Set}}$(date)

$\quad$ Inferences:

$\quad\quad$ *FeaturesStabilizes*$_{\textbf{Infer}}$(date)
$\quad\quad$ *DesignStabilizes*$_{\textbf{Infer}}$(date)
$\quad\quad$ *DevelopmentCeases*$_{\textbf{Infer}}$(date)
$\quad\quad$ *V&VEnds*$_{\textbf{Infer}}$(date)
$\quad\quad$ *Installation*$_{\textbf{Infer}}$(date)
$\quad\quad$ *Turmoil*$_{\textbf{Infer}}$(SLOC)
$\quad\quad$ *InstallationVolume*$_{\textbf{Infer}}$(SLOC)

$CompletionRatio_{\textbf{Infer}}$(actual volume ÷ installation volume)
$DefectsRemaining_{\textbf{Infer}}$(defects)
$Quality_{\textbf{Infer}}$
$Reliability_{\textbf{Infer}}$
$Usability_{\textbf{Infer}}$

Group

Relationships

Groups are contained in an **Area**.
A **Group** is managed by an **Individual**.
A **Group** performs **Activit(y)**ies.
A **Group** employees **Individual**s.

Attributes

Set:
    $Name_{\textbf{Set}}$
Calculate:
    $AverageIndividualProductivity_{\textbf{Calculate}}$(average NCSS person per month)
    $DefectRate_{\textbf{Calculate}}$(Defects per 1,000 SLOC)
    $Efficiency_{\textbf{Calculate}}$
    $EffortToDate_{\textbf{Calculate}}$(in person-months)
    $Productivitity_{\textbf{Calculate}}$(average NCSS per month)
    $Speedup_{\textbf{Calculate}}$
    $Time_{\textbf{Calculate}}$(time spent on project in person-months)
    $TurmoilRate_{\textbf{Calculate}}$(Turmoil per 1,000 SLOC)
    Accumulation per version:
       Sum:
       $Adds_{\textbf{Calculate}}$
       $Bytes_{\textbf{Calculate}}$
       $Changes_{\textbf{Calculate}}$
       $Chunks_{\textbf{Calculate}}$
       $Deletes_{\textbf{Calculate}}$
       $GlobalVariables_{\textbf{Calculate}}$
       $GroupIndividuals_{\textbf{Calculate}}$
       $Knots_{\textbf{Calculate}}$
       $NCSS_{\textbf{Calculate}}$
       $Pairs_{\textbf{Calculate}}$
       $SLOC_{\textbf{Calculate}}$
       $SourceFileDefects_{\textbf{Calculate}}$
       $SourceFiles_{\textbf{Calculate}}$

$SS_{\text{Calculate}}$
$Turmoil_{\text{Calculate}}$
$UniqueReferenceNCSS_{\text{Calculate}}$
$UniqueReferenceSS_{\text{Calculate}}$
Average per source file:
$CyclomaticNumber_{\text{Calculate}}$
$EssentialComplexity_{\text{Calculate}}$
$InheritanceDepth_{\text{Calculate}}$
$NestingDepth_{\text{Calculate}}$
$Pairs_{\text{Calculate}}$
$RelativePercentageUsagePairs_{\text{Calculate}}$
$SourceLiveVariablesPerExecutableSS_{\text{Calculate}}$
$SpanLiveVariablesPerExecutableSS_{\text{Calculate}}$
$Spans_{\text{Calculate}}$
$ThresholdLiveVariablesPerExecutableSS_{\text{Calculate}}$
$Triples_{\text{Calculate}}$

Individual

Relationships

An **Individual** authors **DesignFile**s.
An **Individual** authors **DocumentFile**s.
An **Individual** authors **RequirementsFile**s.
An **Individual** authors **SourceFile**s.
An **Individual** authors **VAndVTest**s.
An **Individual** authors **UsabilityTest**s.
An **Individual** is related to **Assignment**s.
An **Individual** is related to **Salar(y)**ies.
An **Individual** manages a **Group**.
An **Individual** manages a **Project**.
An **Individual** manages an **Area**.
An **Individual** manages an **Organization**.
An **Individual** owns a **Project**.
An **Individual** owns **Defect**s.
An **Individual** owns **DesignFile**.
An **Individual** owns **DocumentFile**s.
An **Individual** owns **Subsystem**s.
An **Individual** owns **RequirementsFile**.
An **Individual** owns **SoftwareProduct**.
An **Individual** owns **SourceFile**s.
An **Individual** owns **VAndVTest**s.

An **Individual** owns **UsabilityTest**s.
An **Individual** owns **Version**s.
An **Individual** performs **Activit(y)**ies.
An **Individual** runs **VAndVTest**s.
An **Individual** runs **UsabilityTest**s.
An **Individual** works for a **Group**.
An **Individual** works for an **Area**.
An **Individual** works for an **Organization**.

  Attributes

Set:

  $EmployeeNumber_{Set}$
  $EmploymentDate_{Set}$
  $Experience_{Set}$(software development years)
  $FirstName_{Set}$
  $LastName_{Set}$
  $MiddleName_{Set}$
  $OverheadFactor_{Set}(\geq 1)$
  $Title_{Set}$

Calculate:

  $DefectRate_{Calculate}$(Defects per 1,000 SLOC)
  $EffortToDate_{Calculate}$(in person-months)
  $Productivity_{Calculate}$(average source lines of code per month)
  $Time_{Calculate}$(time spent on project in person-months)
  $TurmoilRate_{Calculate}$(Turmoil per 1,000 SLOC)

  Accumulation per version:

    Sum:

    $Adds_{Calculate}$
    $Bytes_{Calculate}$
    $Changes_{Calculate}$
    $Chunks_{Calculate}$
    $Deletes_{Calculate}$
    $GlobalVariables_{Calculate}$
    $Knots_{Calculate}$
    $NCSS_{Calculate}$
    $Pairs_{Calculate}$
    $SLOC_{Calculate}$
    $SourceFileDefects_{Calculate}$
    $SourceFiles_{Calculate}$
    $SS_{Calculate}$
    $Turmoil_{Calculate}$

*UniqueReferenceNCSS*_{Calculate}
$UniqueReferenceNCSS_{\text{Calculate}}$
$UniqueReferenceSS_{\text{Calculate}}$
<u>Average per source file:</u>
$CyclomaticNumber_{\text{Calculate}}$
$EssentialComplexity_{\text{Calculate}}$
$InheritanceDepth_{\text{Calculate}}$
$NestingDepth_{\text{Calculate}}$
$Pairs_{\text{Calculate}}$
$RelativePercentageUsagePairs_{\text{Calculate}}$
$SourceLiveVariablesPerExecutableSS_{\text{Calculate}}$
$SpanLiveVariablesPerExecutableSS_{\text{Calculate}}$
$Span_{\text{Calculate}}$
$ThresholdLiveVariablesPerExecutableSS_{\text{Calculate}}$
$Triples_{\text{Calculate}}$

LicensedRunFile

Relationships

LicensedRunFiles are provided by a **Supplier**.

Attributes

<u>Set:</u>
$Name_{\text{Set}}$

Organization

Relationships

An **Organization** contains **Area**s.
An **Organization** is managed by an **Individual**.
Organizations are related to **Project**s.
An **Organization** performs **Activit(y)**ies.
An **Organization** employees **Individual**s.

Attributes

<u>Set:</u>
$Name_{\text{Set}}$
<u>Calculate:</u>
$AverageIndividualProductivity_{\text{Calculate}}$(average NCSS person per month)
$DefectRate_{\text{Calculate}}$ (Defects per 1,000 SLOC)
$Efficiency_{\text{Calculate}}$
$EffortToDate_{\text{Calculate}}$ (in person-months)
$Productivity_{\text{Calculate}}$ (average NCSS per month)

$Speedup_{\textbf{Calculate}}$

$Time_{\textbf{Calculate}}$ (time spent on project in person-months)

$TurmoilRate_{\textbf{Calculate}}$ (Turmoil per 1,000 SLOC)

<u>Sum:</u>

$Adds_{\textbf{Calculate}}$

$Bytes_{\textbf{Calculate}}$

$Changes_{\textbf{Calculate}}$

$Chunks_{\textbf{Calculate}}$

$Deletes_{\textbf{Calculate}}$

$GlobalVariables_{\textbf{Calculate}}$

$Knots_{\textbf{Calculate}}$

$NCSS_{\textbf{Calculate}}$

$OrganizationAreas_{\textbf{Calculate}}$

$OrganizationGroups_{\textbf{Calculate}}$

$OrganizationIndividuals_{\textbf{Calculate}}$

$Pairs_{\textbf{Calculate}}$

$SLOC_{\textbf{Calculate}}$

$SourceFileDefects_{\textbf{Calculate}}$

$SourceFiles_{\textbf{Calculate}}$

$SS_{\textbf{Calculate}}$

$Turmoil_{\textbf{Calculate}}$

$UniqueReferenceNCSS_{\textbf{Calculate}}$

$UniqueReferenceSS_{\textbf{Calculate}}$

<u>Average per source file:</u>

$CyclomaticNumber_{\textbf{Calculate}}$

$EssentialComplexity_{\textbf{Calculate}}$

$InheritanceDepth_{\textbf{Calculate}}$

$NestingDepth_{\textbf{Calculate}}$

$Pairs_{\textbf{Calculate}}$

$RelativePercentageUsagePairs_{\textbf{Calculate}}$

$SourceLiveVariablesPerExecutableSS_{\textbf{Calculate}}$

$SpanLiveVariablesPerExecutableSS_{\textbf{Calculate}}$

$Span_{\textbf{Calculate}}$

$ThresholdLiveVariablesPerExecutableSS_{\textbf{Calculate}}$

$Triples_{\textbf{Calculate}}$

Project

| Relationships |

Projects are contained in a **ProjectList**.

A **Project** is related to **Organization**s.

A **Project** is related to a **SoftwareProduct.**
A **Project** is related to **Supplier**s.
A **Project** is related to **Customer**s.
A **Project** is managed by an **Individual**.
A **Project** is owned by an **Individual**.

Attributes

Set:

*Name*_{**Set**}

*Overhead*_{**Set**}

Calculate:

*Cost*_{**Calculate**}
*EffortToDate*_{**Calculate**} (person-months)
*HeadCount*_{**Calculate**} (persons)
*FullTimeEquivalent*_{**Calculate**} (persons)
*TimeToDate*_{**Calculate**} (months)

ProjectList

Relationships

A **ProjectList** contains **Project**s.

Attributes

Set:

*Name*_{**Set**}

RequirementsFile

Relationships

A **RequirementsFile** contains **Rework**.
A **RequirementsFile** contains **Volume**.
A **RequirementsFile** is authored by an **Individual**.
A **RequirementsFile** is owned by an **Individual**.
RequirementsFiles are contained in a **Subsystem**.
RequirementsFiles contain **Defect**s.
RequirementsFiles are related to **Feature**s.

Attributes

Strings:

Name

ReusableSourceFile

Relationships

ReusableSourceFiles are provided by a **Supplier**.

| Attributes |

Set:

   $Name_{Set}$

Rework

| Relationships |

Rework contains attributes of a **DesignFile.**
Rework contains attributes of a **DocumentFile.**
Rework contains attributes of a **RequirementsFile.**
Rework contains attributes of a **SourceFile.**

| Attributes |

Gather:

   Adds
   Changes
   Deletes

Calculate:

   $Turmoil_{Calculate}$

Salary

| Relationships |

Salar(y)ies are related to an **Individual**.

| Attributes |

   $Amount_{Set}$
   $EffectiveDate_{Set}$

SoftwareProduct

| Relationships |

A **SoftwareProduct** is related to a **Project**.
A **SoftwareProduct** is owned by an **Individual**.
A **SoftwareProduct** contains **Feature**s.
A **SoftwareProduct** contains **Defect**s.
A **SoftwareProduct** contains **Version**s.

| Attributes |

Set:

   $Name_{Set}$

SourceFile

| Relationships |

A **SourceFile** contains **Chunk**s.

A **SourceFile** contains **Rework**.
A **SourceFile** is authored by an **Individual**.
A **SourceFile** is owned by an **Individual**.
SourceFiles are contained in a **Subsystem**.
SourceFiles contain **Defect**s.
SourceFiles are related to **Feature**s.

<u>Attributes</u>

<u>Status:</u>

   <u>Predictions:</u>

      *Volume*_{**Predict**}(SLOC or SS)

   <u>Plan(Set):</u>

      *Volume*_{**Set**}(SLOC or SS)
      *Initial*_{**Set**}(date)
      *Implementation*_{**Set**}(date)
      *UnitTest*_{**Set**}(date)

   Inferences:

      *DesignStabilizes*_{**Infer**}(date)
      *DevelopmentCeases*_{**Infer**}(date)
      *V&VEnds*_{**Infer**}(date)
      *ShipVolume*_{**Infer**}(SLOC)
      *CompletionRatio*_{**Infer**}*(actual volume ÷ ship volume)*
      *DefectsRemaining*_{**Infer**}*(defects)*
      *Reliability*_{**Infer**}

<u>Strings:</u>

   *Language*_{**Infer**}
   Name

<u>Gather:</u>

   RelativePercentageUsageTriples
   TestCoverage(branches tested ÷ total branches)
   Triples

<u>Calculate:</u>

   *CyclomaticNumber*_{**Calculate**}
   *EssentialComplexity*_{**Calculate**}
   *FanIn*_{**Calculate**}
   *FanOut*_{**Calculate**}
   *InformationFlow1*_{**Calculate**}
   *InformationFlow2*_{**Calculate**}
   *InformationFlow3*_{**Calculate**}

   Accumulation:

   *Bytes*_{**Calculate**}

$BytesOC_{\text{Calculate}}$

$CommentSLOC_{\text{Calculate}}$

$Chunks_{\text{Calculate}}$

$GlobalVariables_{\text{Calculate}}$

$Knots_{\text{Calculate}}$

$NCSLOC_{\text{Calculate}}$

$NCSS_{\text{Calculate}}$

$Pairs_{\text{Calculate}}$

$SLOC_{\text{Calculate}}$

$SS_{\text{Calculate}}$

$Turmoil_{\text{Calculate}}$

$UniqueReferenceNCSLOC_{\text{Calculate}}$

$UniqueReferenceSLOC_{\text{Calculate}}$

$VolumeSoftSci_{\text{Calculate}}$

Average per chunk:

$AverageBytes_{\text{Calculate}}$

$AverageInheritanceDepth_{\text{Calculate}}$

$AverageNCSLOC_{\text{Calculate}}$

$AverageNCSS_{\text{Calculate}}$

$AverageNestingDepth_{\text{Calculate}}$

$AveragePairs_{\text{Calculate}}$

$AverageRelativePercentageUsagePairs_{\text{Calculate}}$

$AverageSLOC_{\text{Calculate}}$

$AverageSpanLiveVariablesPerExecutableSS_{\text{Calculate}}$

$AverageSpans_{\text{Calculate}}$

$AverageSS_{\text{Calculate}}$

$AverageThresholdLiveVariablesPerExecutableSS_{\text{Calculate}}$

$AverageSourceLiveVariablesPerExecutableSS_{\text{Calculate}}$

Structure

$\boxed{\text{Relationships}}$

Structure contains attributes of a **Chunk.**

$\boxed{\text{Attributes}}$

Gather:

EssentialComplexity

InheritanceDepth

Knots

NestingDepth

Pairs

RelativePercentageUsagePairs

SpanLiveVariables
Spans
ThresholdLiveVariables
Variables

Set:

$n1_{Set}$(Threshold for threshold live variables)

Calculate

$CyclomaticNumber_{Calculate}$
$SourceLiveVariables_{Calculate}$
$SourceLiveVariablesPerExecutableSS_{Calculate}$
$SpanLiveVariablesPerExecutableSS_{Calculate}$
$ThresholdLiveVariablesPerExecutableSS_{Calculate}$

Subsystem

Relationships

A **Subsystem** contains **RequirementsFile**s.
A **Subsystem** contains **DesignFile**s.
A **Subsystem** contains **DocumentFile**s.
A **Subsystem** contains **SourceFile**s.
A **Subsystem** is owned by an **Individual.**
Subsystems are related to **Features.**
Subsystems are contained in a **Version.**

Attributes

Set:

$Name_{Set}$

Status:

Predictions:

$PredictedVolume_{Predict}$(SLOC, SS, Function Points, Object Points, etc.)
$PredictedEffort_{Predict}$(person-months)
$PredictedSchedule_{Predict}$(months)
$PlannedCompletion_{Predict}$(actual volume ÷ planned volume)
$PredictedFullTimeEmployees_{Predict}$(full-time equivalent employees)
$DefectEliminationRate_{Predict}$(defects eliminated ÷ person month)

Plan

$Volume_{Set}$(SLOC, SS, Function Points, Object Points, etc.)
$Effort_{Set}$(person-months)
$FullTimeEmployees_{Set}$(employee per phase)
$Initial_{Set}$(date)
$AllocateResources_{Set}$(date)
$Requirements_{Set}$(date)

$Design_{Set}$(date)
$Implementation_{Set}$(date)
$UnitTest_{Set}$(date)
$\alpha Test_{Set}$(date)
$\beta Test_{Set}$(date)
Inferences:
$FeaturesStabilizes_{Infer}$(date)
$DesignStabilizes_{Infer}$(date)
$DevelopmentCeases_{Infer}$(date)
$V\&VEnds_{Infer}$(date)
$Ship_{Infer}$(date)
$Turmoil_{Infer}$(SLOC)
$ShipVolume_{Infer}$(SLOC)
$CompletionRatio_{Infer}$(actual volume ÷ ship volume)
$DefectsRemaining_{Infer}$(defects)
$Quality_{Infer}$
$Reliability_{Infer}$
$Usability_{Infer}$

Gather:
$TestCoverage$(branches tested ÷ total branches)
Calculate:
$CyclomaticNumber_{Calculate}$
$EssentialComplexity_{Calculate}$
Accumulation:
$Adds_{Calculate}$
$Bytes_{Calculate}$
$BytesOC_{Calculate}$
$CommentSLOC_{Calculate}$
$Changes_{Calculate}$
$Chunks_{Calculate}$
$Deletes_{Calculate}$
$GlobalVariables_{Calculate}$
$Knots_{Calculate}$
$NCSLOC_{Calculate}$
$NCSS_{Calculate}$
$Pairs_{Calculate}$
$SLOC_{Calculate}$
$SS_{Calculate}$
$Turmoil_{Calculate}$
$UniqueReferenceNCSLOC_{Calculate}$

$UniqueReferenceSLOC_{\textbf{Calculate}}$
$VolumeSoftSci_{\textbf{Calculate}}$

Supplier

| Relationships |

Suppliers are related to a **Project.**
Supplier provides **ReusableSourceFiles.**
Supplier provides **LicensedRunFiles.**

| Attributes |

Set:
    $Name_{\textbf{Set}}$

Usability

| Relationships |

Usability contains attributes of a **UsabilityTest.**

| Attributes |

Gather:
    Responses
    HelpRequests
    Efficiency
Set:
    $Confidence_{\textbf{Set}}$
    $Difficulty_{\textbf{Set}}$
Forecast:
    Infer:
      $SolutionCorrectness_{\textbf{Infer}}$
      $Solution_{\textbf{Infer}}(\text{YES/NO})$

UsabilityTest

| Relationships |

A **UsabilityTest** is authored by an **Individual.**
A **UsabilityTest** is owned by an **Individual.**
A **UsabilityTest** is run by an **Individual.**
UsabilityTest attributes are contained in **Usability.**
UsabilityTests are related to a **Version.**
UsabilityTests are related to **Features.**

| Attributes |

    Name

    Date
    Description
    Configuration
    InputFiles
    TestStartDateTime
    TestEndDateTime
    EngineerTime
    TechnicianTime
    Status(Failed/Passed, i. e., Usability Test is ready or not ready to be run)
    Duration

VAndVTest

| Relationships |

A **VAndVTest** is authored by an **Individual**.
A **VAndVTest** is owned by an **Individual**.
A **VAndVTest** is run by an **Individual**.
A **VAndVTest** is related to a **Version**.
VAndVTests are related to **Feature**s.

| Attributes |

Strings:
    Configuration
    Name
    Description
    Status(Failed/Passed, i. e., Test is ready or not ready to be run)
    Failure(YES/NO)
Gather:
    Date
    InputFiles
    TestStartDateTime
    TestEndDateTime
    EngineerTime
    TechnicianTime
    Duration
    CoverageVector(% by source)

Version

| Relationships |

A **Version** contains **Subsystem**s.
A **Version** contains **VAndVTest**s.

A **Version** contains **UsabilityTest**s.

A **Version** is owned by an **Individual**.

Versions are contained in a **SoftwareProduct**.

Attributes

Status:

Predictions:

PredictedVolume$_{\mathbf{Predict}}$(SLOC, SS, Function Points, Object Points, etc.)
PredictedEffort$_{\mathbf{Predict}}$(person-months)
PredictedSchedule$_{\mathbf{Predict}}$(months)
PlannedCompletion$_{\mathbf{Predict}}$(actual volume ÷ planned volume)
PredictedFullTimeEmployees$_{\mathbf{Predict}}$(full-time equivalent employees)
DefectEliminationRate$_{\mathbf{Predict}}$(defects eliminated ÷ person month)

Plan:

Volume$_{\mathbf{Set}}$(SLOC, SS, Function Points, Object Points, etc.)
Effort$_{\mathbf{Set}}$(person-months)
FullTimeEmployees$_{\mathbf{Set}}$(employee per phase)
Initial$_{\mathbf{Set}}$(date)
AllocateResources$_{\mathbf{Set}}$(date)
Requirements$_{\mathbf{Set}}$(date)
Design$_{\mathbf{Set}}$(date)
Implementation$_{\mathbf{Set}}$(date)
UnitTest$_{\mathbf{Set}}$(date)
α*Test*$_{\mathbf{Set}}$(date)
β*Test*$_{\mathbf{Set}}$(date)

Inferences:

FeaturesStabilizes$_{\mathbf{Infer}}$(date)
DesignStabilizes$_{\mathbf{Infer}}$(date)
DevelopmentCeases$_{\mathbf{Infer}}$(date)
V&VEnds$_{\mathbf{Infer}}$(date)
Ship$_{\mathbf{Infer}}$(date)
Turmoil$_{\mathbf{Infer}}$(SLOC)
ShipVolume$_{\mathbf{Infer}}$(SLOC)
CompletionRatio$_{\mathbf{Infer}}$(actual volume ÷ ship volume)
DefectsRemaining$_{\mathbf{Infer}}$(defects)
Quality$_{\mathbf{Infer}}$
Reliability$_{\mathbf{Infer}}$
Usability$_{\mathbf{Infer}}$

Strings:

PreviousVersionIdentification
SourceDir

VersionIdentification

<u>Gather:</u>

TestCoverage(branches tested ÷ total branches)

VersionCreated(date)

<u>Calculate:</u>

*AverageIndividualProductivity*_{Calculate}(average NCSS person per month)

*DefectRate*_{Calculate} (Defects per 1,000 SLOC)

*Efficiency*_{Calculate}

*EffortToDate*_{Calculate} (in person-months)

*Productivity*_{Calculate} (average NCSS per month)

*Speedup*_{Calculate}

*Time*_{Calculate} (time spent on project in person-months)

*TurmoilRate*_{Calculate} (Turmoil per 1,000 SLOC)

*CyclomaticNumber*_{Calculate}

*EssentialComplexity*_{Calculate}

<u>Accumulation:</u>

*Adds*_{Calculate}

*Bytes*_{Calculate}

*BytesOC*_{Calculate}

*CommentSLOC*_{Calculate}

*Changes*_{Calculate}

*Chunks*_{Calculate}

*Deletes*_{Calculate}

*EquivalentSize1*_{Calculate}

*EquivalentSize2*_{Calculate}

*EquivalentSize3*_{Calculate}

*GlobalVariables*_{Calculate}

*Knots*_{Calculate}

*NCSS*_{Calculate}

*Pairs*_{Calculate}

*SLOC*_{Calculate}

*SS*_{Calculate}

*Turmoil*_{Calculate}

*UniqueReferenceNCSLOC*_{Calculate}

*UniqueReferenceSLOC*_{Calculate}

*VolumeSoftSci*_{Calculate}

Volume(Chunk)

| Relationships |

Volume contains attributes of a **Chunk.**

| Attributes |

Gather:
  BlankSS
  Bytes
  BytesOC
  CommentSLOC
  CommentSS
  CompilerDirectiveSS
  DataDeclarationSS
  Decisions
  ExecutableSS
  Operands
  Operators
  SLOC
  UniqueNCSLOC
  UniqueOperands
  UniqueOperators
  UniqueReferenceNCSLOC(Unique compared to a unique library-based
  NCSLOC list)
  UniqueReferenceSLOC(Unique compared to a unique library-based
  SLOC list)
  UniqueSLOC
  UniqueSS

Set:
  $CodeModifiedCode_{Set}$(% of total effort to code modified code)
  $DesignModifiedCode_{Set}$(% of total effort to design modified code)
  $IntegrationModifiedCode_{Set}$(% of total effort to integration modified
  code)
  $k1_{Set}$(Bailey and Basili used a value of 0.2)
  $k2_{Set}$(Thebaut used a value of 0.857)
  $ModifiedCode_{Set}$(% of code modified)

Calculate:
  $CommentBytesOC_{Calculate}$
  $Length_{Calculate}$
  $NCSS_{Calculate}$
  $NCSLOC_{Calculate}$
  $SS_{Calculate}$
  $Vocabulary_{Calculate}$
  $VolumeSoftSci_{Calculate}$

Volume(DesignFile, DocumentFile, RequirementsFile)

Relationships

Volume contains attributes of a **DesignFile.**
Volume contains attributes of a **DocumentFile.**
Volume contains attributes of a **RequirementsFile.**

Attributes

Gather:
   Bytes
   SS
   UniqueReferenceSS(Unique compared to a unique library-based SS list)

Appendix B
PAMPA
═══ Users Manual ═══

SECTION 1—INSTALLATION AND SETUP

- Installing PAMPA
- Deinstalling PAMPA
- Installing and Configuring ODBC
- PAMPA Manuals

This section provides detailed instructions for installing and configuring PAMPA. Details are also provided on how to access and print the manuals that are installed along with the PAMPA programs.

STATEMENT OF COPYRIGHT
AND LIMITATIONS OF LIABILITY

Disclaimer: The authors make no warranty or representation, either express or implied, with respect to this software product, including its quality, merchantability, or fitness for a particular purpose. In no event will the authors be liable for direct, indirect, special, incidental, or consequential damages arising out of the use or inability to use the software, even if the authors have been advised of the possibility of such damages.

INSTALLING PAMPA

1. Make sure that you have Windows NT 3.5x or later or Windows 95 installed on your computer. The Microsoft environment must have Excel 97 and Access 97.
2. Make sure that Microsoft Windows is running.
3. Insert the PAMPA CD into the appropriate CD drive.
4. To run the setup program do one of the following:

   - If your computer uses Windows NT 3.5x or later, choose **Run** from the Program Manager **File** menu, type D:\pampa.exe, and click **OK** or press ENTER.
   - If your computer uses Windows 95 or Windows NT 4.0, click the **Start** button, choose **Run**, type D:\pampa.exe, and click **OK** or press ENTER.

5. The installation will automatically prompt you for an ODBC data source. Choose the file name in C:\pampa\pampa.mdb and system database option.
6. After setup is successful, you are returned to Windows.
7. If you have any questions or problems in the setup of PAMPA, please contact the Software Process Improvement Laboratory, Texas A&M University. Tel: (409) 845-0608.

DEINSTALLING PAMPA

1. To keep the ODBC drivers but remove files in the PAMPA application, choose the **Custom** option instead of the **Automatic** option during the deinstallation process.
2. The menu will prompt you to select the files to deinstall. To keep the ODBC drivers, do not remove any files installed in the Windows directory.
3. Use the Deinstall icon in Windows NT or the Control Panel Add&Remove Program for Windows 95 to remove the program.

INSTALLING AND CONFIGURING ODBC (OPTIONAL) _____

ODBC Update Installation

Install the 32-bit version of Microsoft ODBC Driver Update Pack 2.0 within Windows.

- Before setting up ODBC, close any open applications that are running with the exception of the Program Manager.
- Insert Microsoft ODBC Database Drivers Disk #1. Setup in the appropriate floppy drive.
- Choose **Run** from the Program Manager File menu, type A:\SETUP, and click **OK** or press ENTER.
- Follow the instructions displayed in the Setup program's dialog boxes.
- Select the drivers that you want to install from the list and then choose **OK**.

    Note: You MUST install the updated Microsoft Access driver. The other drivers are optional.

- If the install program displays error or warning boxes stating that a newer version of the driver is already on the hard drive, do NOT install the driver from the Update Pack over it.
- If the install program displays error or warning boxes stating that some files were already in use and could not be overwritten, follow the instructions to retry or install it over again. Make sure that there are no open applications except the Program Manager.

ODBC Data Source Setup (Optional)

- After the installation of the ODBC Drivers is complete, you can add one or more data sources for the drivers you installed. To add a data source, first start the ODBC program by either double-clicking the item within the new Program Group or within the Control Panel. (*Note:* For Windows NT 4.0 or Windows 95 users, start the ODBC program by using the **Start** button. Choose ODBC or Control Panel). Once ODBC has been started, choose *Add* in the Data Source dialog box.
- In the Add Data Source dialog box, select the Microsoft Access Driver (*.mdb) from the installed ODBC drivers list and choose **OK**.
- In the ODBC Microsoft Access Setup dialog box, enter the following information to set up the data source; then choose **OK**.
- Data Source Name: pampadb.

- Use the Select button to select PAMPA.MDB from the directory PAMPA was installed into.
- If the install program displays a warning box stating that the data source named "pampadb" already exists, choose Yes to replace it with this definition.
- In Data Sources dialog box, choose **Close** to finish ODBC setup.
- After setup is successful, you are returned to Windows.

PAMPA MANUALS

- Once setup is complete and you have returned to Windows, look in your newly created PAMPA group. You will see an icon labeled "PAMPA Manuals." By double-clicking on this icon you will unpack the current manuals into your C:\temp directory. You can either view them from this directory or move them to your newly created PAMPA directory.
- Once you are done viewing them, you may delete them and simply reuse the icon again the next time you wish to view the manuals.

SECTION 2—PAMPA TUTORIAL

- Introduction to PAMPA
- Setting up Your Project
- Gathering Project Data
- Plotting the Project Data

This section of the PAMPA manual will introduce you to the capabilities of the system and show you how to create and measure a software development project. This step by step tutorial provides enough information to get started with PAMPA right away, while the later sections provide a more detailed reference to the capabilities of PAMPA.

INTRODUCTION TO PAMPA

Project Attribute Monitoring and Prediction Associate (PAMPA) is designed to support the planning and management of a software development project. PAMPA is primarily used to gather information about a project's coding effort on a regular basis during development. This information can then be displayed in a variety of formats, providing a manager with an overview of the project complexity, effort, and progress.

PAMPA can gather project source files from both UNIX and MS-Windows environments. PAMPA then parses the source files and stores the resulting software metrics in a database. This gathering and measurement process is supported by the *Object Editor* component of PAMPA. The Object Editor is used to create a description of the development organization, its people and its product(s). As the development of a software product proceeds, PAMPA gathers and measures the source files on a regular basis. These measures can then be used by the project manager to visualize the development project, gauge progress, and identify problem areas.

The rest of this section will guide you through the process of setting up, measuring, and reviewing a sample project. To support this effort, sample code files are provided with the PAMPA distribution. When you complete this section, you will be ready to set up and measure an actual software development project.

SETTING UP YOUR PROJECT

The first task is to define the project that will be monitored and enter relevant information about the project into the PAMPA database. The PAMPA Object Editor is the tool used to implement the PAMPA Object Classes in a readily accessible visual structure. Elements in the PAMPA Object Classes represent products of a software development project and are graphically displayed and manipulated by the Object Editor. The hierarchy of object icons represents the organizational structure of the software project.

Start the PAMPA Object Editor by double-clicking on the Object Editor icon in the PAMPA program group. Select **New** from the **Project** menu, or press the new document icon on the toolbar. For a project name, enter *Example* in the name entry field. Click the **OK** button to create the project. The Object Editor will display the first object associated with your new project, as shown in Figure B2.1.

Click the project object with the right mouse button to bring up the menu associated with a project object, as shown in Figure B2.1. This menu allows you to modify the project object or create several other objects associated with a project. Click **New** item and then the **SoftwareProduct** item of the submenu. A software product object represents one of the primary deliverables of the software development effort. Give the software product object the name *MyProduct*. At this point, we are ready to begin gathering and measuring product source files.

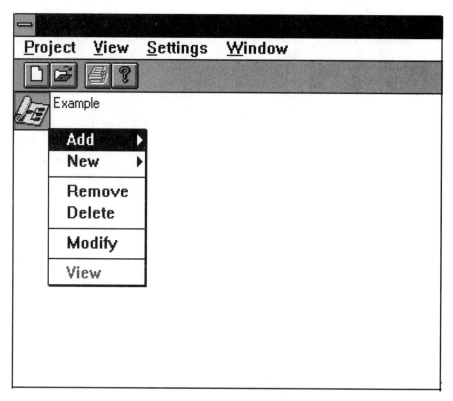

Figure B2.1   Sample Project Object

GATHERING PROJECT DATA

The PAMPA Object Editor has a built-in parser that can make various measurements on the source code files that belong to a software development project. Measurement can be performed in place if the source files are stored in a directory accessible to PAMPA. Alternatively, PAMPA can copy the source files to a working directory directly or by using the ftp protocol.

The Data Gatherer extension of the Object Editor is used to designate and optionally copy project source files. For this example, we will directly measure sample files that are supplied with PAMPA when it is installed. We will assume that the project files were gathered on a weekly basis and placed into separate local directories.

Right-click the software product icon and then select **New** and **Version** from the object menu. The Data Gatherer dialog box will be displayed, as shown in Figure B2.2. The Data Gathering dialog provides a File Manager-like interface to define the directory in which source files are kept. Use this dialog to select the VERSION1 subdirectory of the EXAMPLES directory in the PAMPA distribution, as shown in

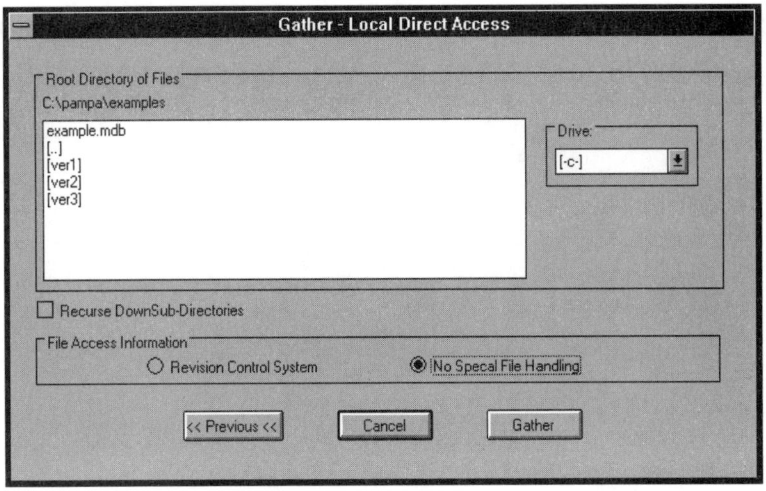

Figure B2.2   Data Gatherer Dialog

Figure B2.3. A default installation of PAMPA would make the source path D:\PAMPA\EXAMPLES\VERSION1. Click the **No Special File Handling** option button and click the **Gather** button to begin the process of measuring source files and entering the measures into the database.

PAMPA will display a progress bar as it measures the source files within the directory you have selected. When measurement is complete, PAMPA will display a version object. Double-click this object to expand it out, as shown in Figure B2.4.

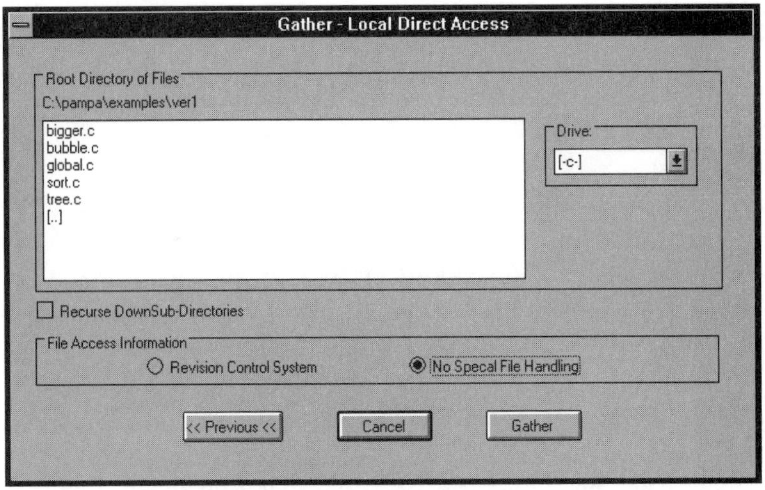

Figure B2.3   Selecting the Source Directory

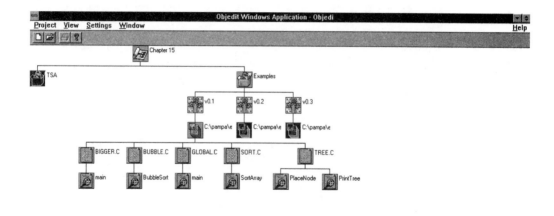

Figure B2.4   Version 1 Source Tree

PAMPA displays a tree of File and Chunk objects that belong to the selected Version object. If you select **View** from the right-button menu of either of these objects, PAMPA will display a tabular form that shows the metrics for the selected File or Chunk object. The next section will show you how to plot this information in various ways.

For now, return to the SoftwareProduct objects and select **New** and **Version** from its right-button menu. Repeat the above steps to create two more versions using the D:\PAMPA\EXAMPLES\VERSION2 and D:\PAMPA\EXAMPLES\VERSION3 directories. When you have finished gathering source file measures from these three directories, exit the PAMPA Object Editor.

PLOTTING THE PROJECT DATA

Double-click on the Metric Plot Generator icon in the PAMPA program group to view the project data that you have gathered. Select the **Enable Macros** button on the Microsoft Excel dialog. The initial dialog (Figure B2.5) of the Metric Plot

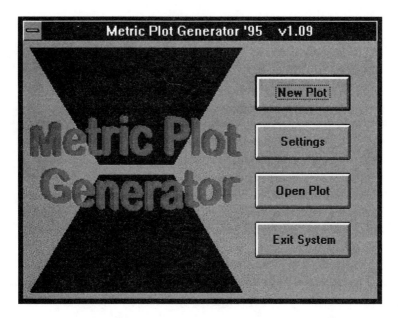

Figure B2.5   Initial Dialog of Metric Plot Generator

Generator contains four buttons. Click on the **New Plot** button. In the New Plot dialog, select the Sample Project that you just created from the Project pull-down list; then click the **Next** button. In the Software Product Dialog, select Sample from the SoftwareProduct pull-down list, and then click the **Next** button. The next set of dialogs will determine what is plotted on the display. We will view three different plots of the data that you created in the earlier sections.

For the first example, we will plot source file metrics using a two-dimensional graphic plot. Begin by selecting the *Example* project in the first dialog and the *MyProduct* product in the second dialog. In the Plot Specification dialog (Figure B2.6), select the **2-D Bar Chart** radiobutton and the **Source File** radiobutton. The next dialog allows you to select which version of the source files to plot. Use the pull-down menu to select version 0.3, the last version you measured. The Metrics dialog will display a list of measures that can be plotted for File objects. First press the **Deselect All** button; then click on *CommentSS* and *SLOC* list items, as shown in Figure B2.7. This will allow you to compare the size of each file in the Sample Project and the ratio of comment to noncomment statements in each file.

Click the **Next** button to display the final plot dialog. This dialog allows you to change the way in which metrics are displayed (Sort By) or to change the title and other parameters on the plot. For now, simply click the **Finish** button to view the plot shown in Figure B2.8. Note that if all the files would not fit on a single plot chart a set of tab buttons is provided so that you can switch among sets of files. The

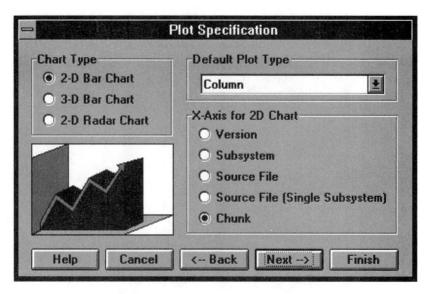

Figure B2.6   Plot Specification Dialog

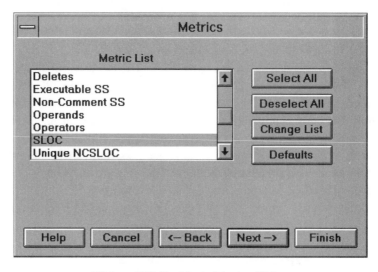

Figure B2.7   Metric Selection Dialog

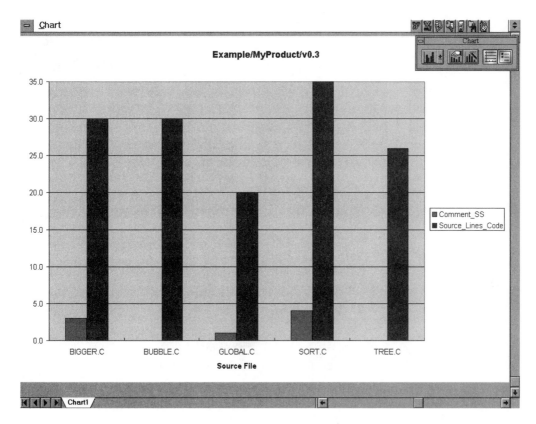

Figure B2.8 Two-dimensional Plot

files are ordered by filename, since we did not select a particular sorting order by metric.

Select **Return** from the **Chart** menu at the top of the plot display to return to the last dialog. Click the **Sort Descending** radiobutton and choose *SLOC* from the **Sort By** pull-down list. Click the **Finish** button. The new plot will arrange the sample files by *SLOC*, from highest to lowest. Note the first two files and then redisplay the plot sorted by CommentSS.

For the second example, we will plot file-related metrics, by version, using a three-dimensional plot format. This format allows you to see how a given metric changes across versions gathered during the project lifetime. Select **Return** from the **Chart** menu; then press the **Back** button until you return to the Plot Specification dialog. Select the **3-D Bar Chart** and **Source File** radiobuttons and then press the **Next** button. Select *SLOC* in the Metrics dialog. In the final dialog press the **Finish** button to view the graph shown in Figure B2.9.

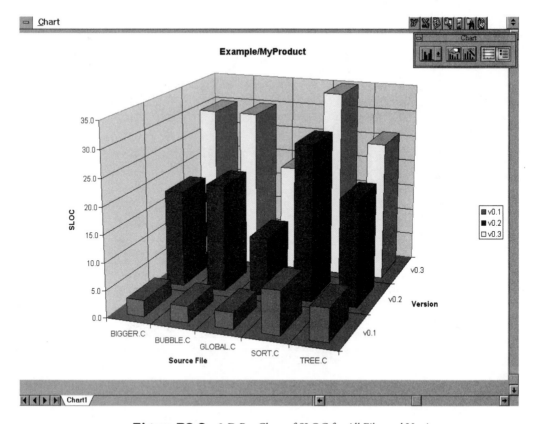

Figure B2.9   3-D Bar Chart of SLOC for All Files and Versions

For the third example, we will plot file-related metrics using a radar diagram. Once again, select **Return** from the **Chart** menu and then press **Back** to return to the Plot Specification dialog. Click the **2-D Radar Chart** and **Source File** radiobuttons. The next dialog prompts for a version number. The next dialog prompts for a specific source file name. Select *SORT.C* from the pull-down menu and then proceed to the Metric dialog. Select the metrics *Adds, Deletes, Chunks, Operators, Operands,* and *SLOC.* Proceed to the final dialog and plot the result, as shown in Figure B2.10.

The Radar plot shows multiple metrics for a single source file. Each metric axis is normalized to provide a balanced view. Typical min and max values for each metric are also displayed. The Radar plot is useful when checking to see if a source file falls within established limits or to compare one source file to another.

Try experimenting with the various options in each of the plot setup dialogs of the Metric Plot Generator. Section 4 of the User Manual is a detailed reference on dialogs and plots if you need more information. Exit the Metric Plot Generator by using the **Cancel** button to return to the initial welcome screen; then click **Exit System**.

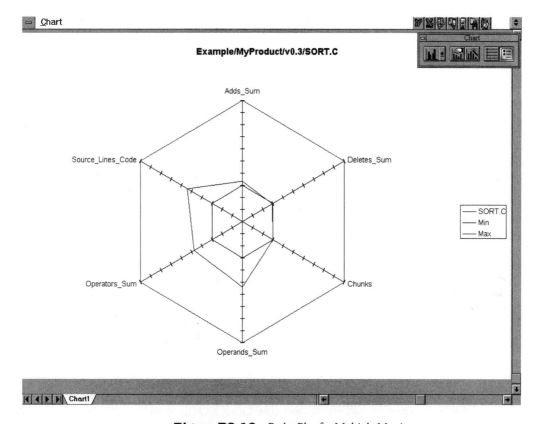

Figure B2.10 Radar Plot for Multiple Metrics

SECTION 3—OBJECT EDITOR REFERENCE

- Introduction
- Creating a Project
- The Icon Menu
- Creating the Project Tree

This section of the PAMPA manual provides a reference for the PAMPA Object Editor.

INTRODUCTION

The Pampa Object Editor is a tool used to implement the Pampa Object Classes in a readily accessible structure. Its purpose is to allow the user to lay out his or her entire project using the Pampa Object Classes. The user can then easily keep track of any changes that occur in their project. This document will guide you through the essential steps necessary to create your own project in the Pampa Object Editor.

CREATING A PROJECT

To start Pampa, locate the PAMPA folder in the Windows Program Manager and double-click on it. This will open up the PAMPA window (see Figure B3.1). In the window, there will be an icon called Object Editor. Double-click on this icon and the Pampa Object Editor will load up.

To start out, you must first create a project. Locate the command on the menu bar labeled **Project**. Click on it, and you will be given a menu with the commands **New** or **Open**. To create a new project, select **New**. A dialog box will then appear. It will ask you to input the name of the project and the overhead factor. When you are done inputting this information, click **OK** and an icon will appear with your project's name on it. This icon represents your project. It will be the root of the tree structure to which all the information about the project will be connected.

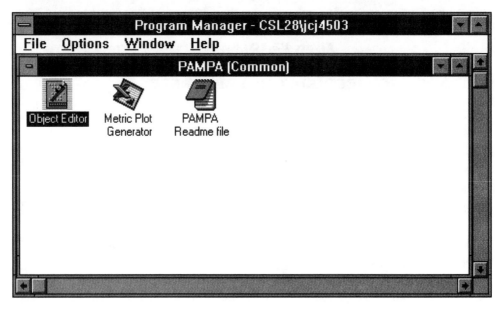

Figure B3.1   PAMPA Window

THE ICON MENU

An icon contains all the information for the particular object that it is representing. To view or modify this information, right click on the icon. It will give you the menu shown in Figure B3.2.

  Six commands are featured in the menu: *Add, New, Remove, Delete, Modify,* and *View*. The menu will not always have all six commands in it, depending on the object you select. For example, you can only *View* Sourcefiles and Chunks. If the object you have selected does not support a command, then that command will either not appear in the menu or be grayed out.

CREATING THE PROJECT TREE

To begin creating the project tree, bring up the menu on the project icon and click on **New**. Four object classes will be listed: Supplier, Organization, SoftwareProduct, and Customer (see Figure B3.3). These are the four object classes that are associated with the Project object. When we create these objects, we can then create any of the

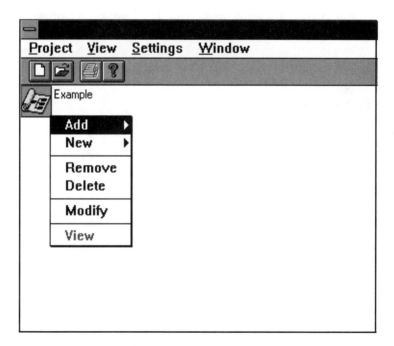

Figure B3.2 Object Menu

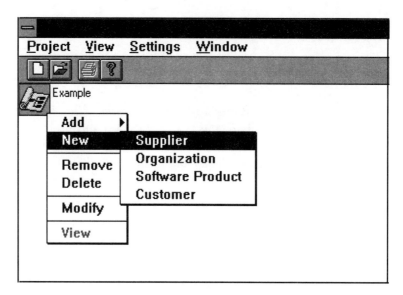

Figure B3.3   Object Classes Associated with Project

object classes associated with the new object. It is important to note that you can create two objects of the same object class. For example, if CompanyA and CompanyB are both working on the same project, then you can add two Organization objects. One would contain information for CompanyA, and the other would contain information for CompanyB.

The Supplier

When you choose to create a Supplier object, the program will bring up a dialog box and ask you to input the name of the supplier. After typing in the name of the supplier, click on **OK** and the Supplier icon will appear below your Project icon. Two classes are contained in the Supplier object: ReusableSourceFile and LicensedRunFile.

  Reusable Source File. You may create a ReusableSourceFile object from the Supplier icon. A dialog box will appear asking for the name of the file. Type in the Reusable Source File name and click on **OK**. The ReusableSourceFile icon will appear below the Supplier icon.

  COTS Run File. You may create a COTSRunFile object from the Supplier icon as shown in Figure B3.4. A dialog box will appear asking for the name of the file. Type in the COTS Run File name and click on **OK**. The COTS Run File icon will appear below the Supplier icon.

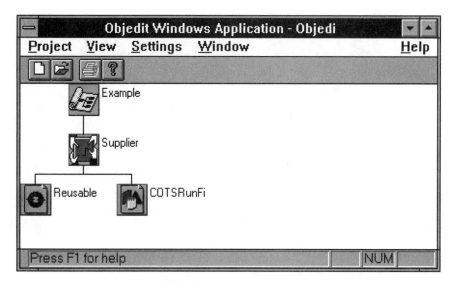

Figure B3.4   Sample Supplier Tree

The Organization

An Organization is a specific company that is working on the project. When you choose to create an Organization object, the program will bring up a dialog box and ask you to input the name of the organization. After typing in the name of the organization, click on **OK** and the Organization icon will appear below the Project icon. One class is contained within the Organization object: Area.

Area.   An Area would be a specific part of the Organization that is working on the project. You may create an Area object from the Organization icon. A dialog box will appear asking for the name of the Area. Type in the Area name and click on **OK**. The Area icon will appear below the Organization icon. One class is contained within the Area object: Group.

Group.   A Group is a specific group of people in an Area that is working on the project. You may create a Group object from the Area icon. A dialog box will appear asking for the name of the Group. Type in the Group name and then click on **OK** and the Group icon will appear below the Area icon. One class is contained within the Group object: Individual.

Individual.   An Individual is a specific member of a Group. You may create an Individual object from the Group icon. When you create an Individual, a dialog box will appear asking you to input information about the employee (see

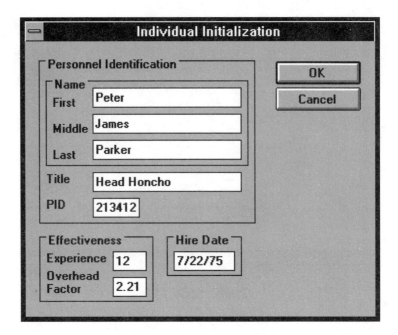

Figure B3.5   Individual Menu with Sample Data

Figure B3.5). You will need to know the following information about the Individual: first name, middle name, last name, title, personal identification number, experience, overhead factor, and hire date. If you do not have some of the information required, you can leave it blank. You can modify the object later when you do have the missing information by using the **Modify** command.

The Sample Organization Tree is illustrated by Figure B3.6.

Software Product

The SoftwareProduct is the actual program that you are writing for the project. When you choose to create a SoftwareProduct object, the program will bring up a dialog box and ask you to input the name of the SoftwareProduct. After typing in the name of the organization, click on **OK** and the SoftwareProduct icon will appear below the Project icon. Two classes are contained within the SoftwareProduct object: Defect and Version.

Defect.   The Defect object keeps track of all defects in the SoftwareProduct. When you choose to create a new Defect, the program will bring up a dialog box and ask you to input the name of the Defect. After typing in the name, click on **OK** and the Defect icon will appear below the SoftwareProduct icon.

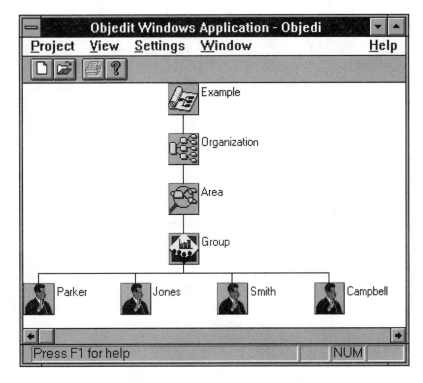

Figure B3.6 Sample Organization Tree

Version. The Version is the current version of the software project that you are working on. The first time you create a Version object, it will be labeled v0.1. Subsequent Versions will be labeled in increments of 0.1. Therefore, the second Version object created will be labeled v0.2. When you attempt to create a Version, you will initiate the Data Gatherer. This program will allow you to specify the files that you wish to parse. For more information on the use of the Data Gatherer, refer to Section 2 User Manual. One class is contained within the Version object: Path.

Path. The path is automatically detected and created by the program when you create a Version and gather files. This will specify the path of the Sourcefile. The status bar at the bottom of the page shows the complete path listing. One class is contained within the Path object: SourceFile.

Source File. The Source Files are the files that contain the uncompiled C code needed to build the SoftwareProduct. Usually, there will be several SourceFile objects in the project tree, one for each C file. Each SourceFile object label will correspond to the name of the file that is associated with it. By clicking on the **View** button, you will be able to see information about the selected SourceFile (see Figure B3.7). The infor-

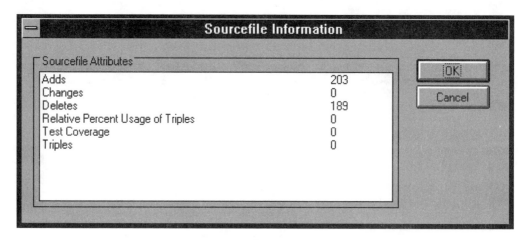

Figure B3.7 SourceFile Information Screen

mation that you can currently get from the PAMPA Object Editor is Bytes, Adds, and Deletes. The Adds and Deletes metrics will generate positive integer values for source files occurring in two or more versions. Otherwise, they will have a 0 attributed to them. All the other metrics will also be listed in the dialog box. They will have a 0 listed by them, meaning that that particular metric has not yet been implemented.

Chunks. The Chunks are the chunks of code inside the corresponding Source-File. These objects will also be labeled according to the name of the SourceFile associated with them. Each Chunk icon will be located directly below the SourceFile icon that it corresponds with. By clicking on the **View** button, you will be able to see infor-

Chunk Attributes	
Operands	29
Operators	22
Pairs	0
Source Lines of Code	20
Span Live Variables	0
Spans	0
Threshold Live Variables	0
Unique Non-comment Source Lines of Code	19
Unique Non-comment Source Statements	19
Unique Operands	9

Figure B3.8 Chunk Information Screen

mation about the selected Chunk (see Figure B3.8). The information that you can currently get from the program is Blank Source Statements, Compiler Directives, and Source Lines of Code.

The Sample Software Product Tree is illustrated by Figure B3.9.

The Customer

The Customer is the person or organization who is purchasing your product. When you choose to create a Customer object (Figure B3.10), the program will bring up a dialog box and ask you to input the Name, Experience Level, and Satisfaction of the Customer. After typing this in, click on **OK** and the Customer icon will appear below the Project icon.

Completion of a Project Tree

Congratulations! You have just finished building your first project tree. When you are done creating your tree, you may exit the Pampa Object Editor by clicking on **Exit** under the **Project** command on the menu bar. All your information has

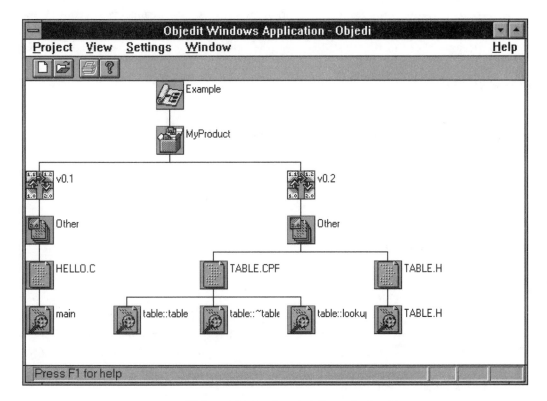

Figure B3.9 Sample Software Product Tree

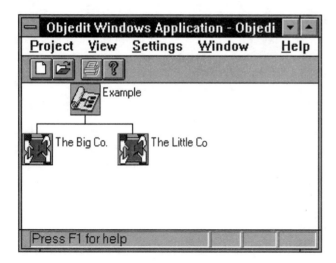

Figure B3.10   Sample Customer
Tree

already been stored in the PAMPA database. When you run the Pampa Object
Editor again, you may open up the project you just made by selecting Open
under the Project command. A dialog box will appear with a list of all the current
projects stored in the database. Select the project name that you want to work with
and click on **OK**. The current project tree will then appear and you can begin
to work.

SECTION 4—METRIC PLOT GENERATOR REFERENCE

- Dialog Reference
- Plot Reference
- Limitations and Problems

This section documents the Metric Plot Generator portion of PAMPA.

DIALOG REFERENCE

This section of the document describes the Metric Plot Generator dialogs and interface controls. This documentation will serve as a preliminary help reference for users
of the Metric Plot Generator. General descriptions of the dialogs and screens that
users encounter will be given.

Terminology

The dialog shown in Figure B4.1 will illustrate some of the terminology used throughout the *User Reference*. Labels on the various dialog controls indicate the terminology that will be used in describing the functionality of that control in this documentation. The controls are named by the label appearing above or adjacent to them, along with the type of control, as depicted in Figure B4.1.

Metric Plot Generator Main Dialog

The Metric Plot Generator Main Dialog found in Figure B4.2 is the first dialog that the user will encounter if the Metric Plot Generator is able to load up and initialize itself correctly. If this dialog does not appear when the Metric Plot Generator application is initiated, look for any error messages produced and then use the *Metric Plot Generator Error Messages* section of this manual to determine the source of the problem. This dialog allows the user to create new plots, select program settings, open previously defined plots, or exit the system.

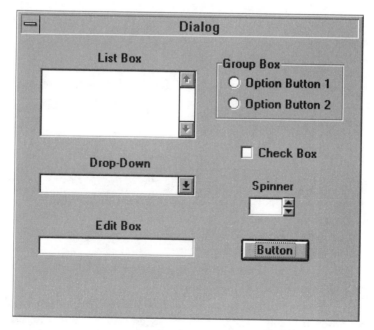

Figure B4.1   Terminology of Dialogs

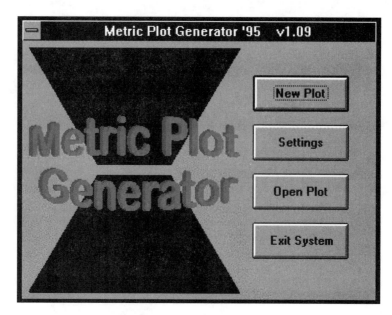

Figure B4.2   Metric Plot Generator Main Dialog

New Plot Button.   Pressing this button takes the user to the *New Plot Dialog*. This allows the user to create a new plot by responding to a collection of dialogs presented.

Settings Button.   Pressing this button takes the user to the *Settings Dialog*. This allows the user to configure various program settings using a collection of dialog windows.

Open Plot Button.   Pressing this button causes the File Open Dialog shown in Figure B4.3 to appear. This dialog allows the user to select a file for a previously saved plot. By default, only those files with the *plt* extension will appear. Hence, it is advantageous to make sure that you save all plots with the *plt* extension. The validity of the file will be checked and an error message will appear if the file selected is not a valid plot file.

Press the *OK* button when the appropriate file has been selected, or press **Cancel** to abort the open plot operation.

If a valid plot file has been selected, the plot will automatically be created without prompting the user for any further response. In this way, saving a plot that will need to be reproduced at a later time provides very efficient plot generation.

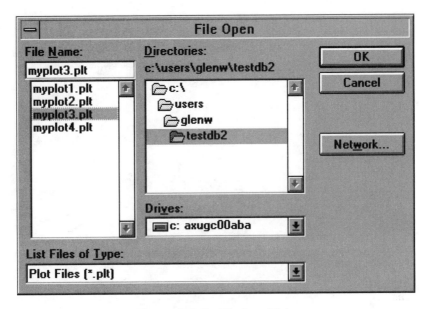

Figure B4.3   File Open Dialog

Exit System Button.   Pressing this button will exit the Metric Plot Generator and terminate the current session. All necessary data relevant to a Metric Plot Generator session are stored so that they are available for future sessions.

New Plot Dialog

The New Plot Dialog shown in Figure B4.4 will appear when the *New Plot Button* is pressed.

Project Drop-Down

This drop-down allows the user to select from a list of projects that are currently defined in the PAMPA database.

Project Category Group Box

This group of option buttons allows the user to select the type of project category for the plot. The available options are described next.

Software Product Option Button.   This option button allows the user to produce a plot based on the software product data currently defined in the PAMPA database.

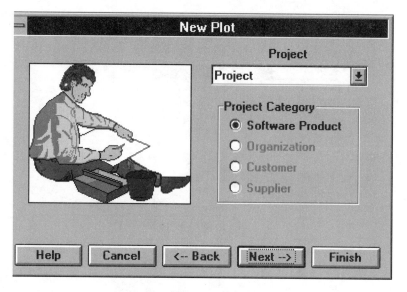

Figure B4.4   New Plot Dialog

Organization Option Button.   Not yet supported.

Customer Option Button.   Not yet supported.

Supplier Options Button.   Not yet supported.

Sequence Buttons

The collection of buttons found on the bottom of the New Plot Dialog is common to almost all dialogs in the Metric Plot Generator interface. Given next is a general description of these buttons.

Help Button.   Not yet supported. In future versions, this button will invoke the Windows help file viewer.

Cancel Button.   Aborts the current construction of a new plot and sends the user back to the Metric Plot Generator Main Dialog.

Back Button.   This button sends the user to the previous screen that was presented.

    Next Button. This button sends the user to the next screen that is applicable for the current dialog control selections. See Figure B4.15 for the 15 Metric Plot Generator Dialog sequence.

    Finish Button. This button sends the user to the *Plot Preferences Dialog*. This button provides a way to bypass any subsequent dialog screens for the current plot being constructed. Caution must be used with this button. Any information needed from subsequent dialogs is taken from the controls that were set the last time that those dialogs appeared to the user. In order to be certain that all necessary information has been provided for a new plot, use the *Next Button* to answer all relevant questions on the dialogs.

Software Product Dialog

The Software Product Dialog shown in Figure B4.5 appears when the user selects the *Software Product Option Button* on the *New Plot Dialog* and then presses the *Next Button*. This dialog allows the user to specify criterion for the purpose of producing a plot based on software product data. The dialog consists of a drop-down list for specifying a particular software product and option buttons for the software category.

Figure B4.5 Software Product Dialog

Software Product Drop-Down

This drop-down allows the user to select from a list of software products currently defined in the PAMPA database for the project selected on the *New Plot Dialog.*

Software Category Group Box

This group contains option buttons that allow the user to select the software category for the plot.

Versions Option Button.   This option button allows the user to produce a plot based on the software product version data currently defined in the PAMPA database. This is the current default option.

Defects Option Button.   Not yet supported.

Plot Specification Dialog

The Plot Specification Dialog shown in Figure B4.6 appears when the user selects the *Versions Option Button* on the *Software Product Dialog* and then presses the *Next Button.* This dialog allows the user to specify the plot type for a software product plot. The dialog consists of two option button groups.

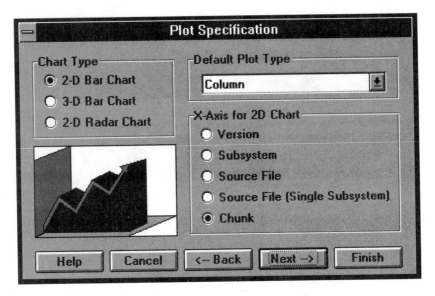

Figure B4.6   Plot Specification Dialog

Chart Type Group Box

This group of option buttons selects the configuration for the plot.

2-D Bar Chart Option Button. This button configures a two-dimensional bar chart. Version, Subsystem, Source File, Source File (Single Subsystem), and Chunk are the available options for the *x* axis of a two-dimensional bar chart.

3-D Bar Chart Option Button. This button configures a three-dimensional (or multiple *x* axis) bar chart. Subsystem, Source File, Source File (Single Subsystem), and Chunk are the available options for the *x* axis of a three-dimensional bar chart.

2-D Radar Chart Option Button. This button configures a two-dimensional radar chart. Version, Subsystem, and Source File are the available options for the source of a two-dimensional radar chart.

X Axis for 2D Chart Group Box

This group box contains five option buttons: Version, Subsystem, Source File, Source File (Single Subsystem), and Chunk. These are the available options for the *x* axis of a two-dimensional chart.

X Axis for 3D Chart Group Box

This group box contains four active option buttons: Subsystem, Source File, Source File (Single Subsystem), and Chunk. These are the available options for the *x* axis of a three-dimensional chart.

Radar Chart Item Group Box

This group box contains three active option buttons: Version, Subsystem, and Source File. These are the available options for the source of a two-dimensional radar chart.

Version Dialog

The Version Dialog shown in Figure B4.7 appears when the user selects a plot type from the *Plot Specification Dialog* that requires the selection of a specific version. This dialog allows the user to specify a version for a software product plot. The dialog consists of a drop-down list.

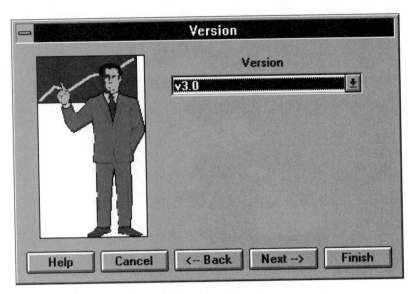

Figure B4.7 Version Dialog

Version Drop-Down

This drop-down allows the user to specify a particular version from a list of versions currently defined in the PAMPA database for a software product.

Subsystem Dialog

The Subsystem Dialog shown in Figure B4.8 appears when the user selects a plot type from the *Plot Specification Dialog* that requires the selection of a specific subsystem. This dialog allows the user to specify subsystem criterion for a software product plot. The dialog consists of a single drop-down list.

Subsystem Drop-Down

This drop-down allows the user to specify a particular subsystem from a list of subsystems currently defined in the PAMPA database for a software product.

Source File Dialog

The Source File Dialog shown in Figure B4.9 appears when the user selects a plot type from the *Plot Specification Dialog* that requires the selection of a specific source file. This dialog allows the user to specify source file criterion for a software product plot. The dialog consists of a single drop-down box.

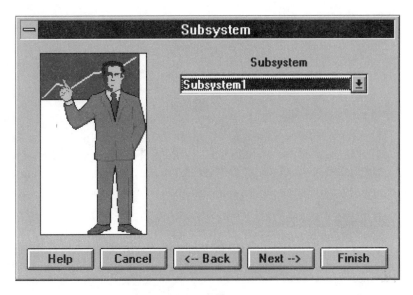

Figure B4.8   Subsystem Dialog

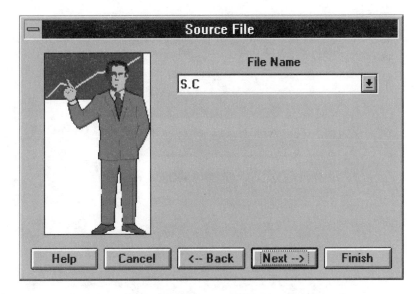

Figure B4.9   Source File Dialog

File Name Drop-Down

This drop-down allows the user to specify a particular file name from a list of file names currently defined in the PAMPA database for a software product.

Metrics Dialog

The Metrics Dialog shown in Figure B4.10 allows the user to specify which metrics are to be plotted for the plot type selected. This dialog consists of a single list box containing relevant metrics and buttons that perform special operations.

Metrics List Box

This list box is automatically filled with the user-defined set of metrics for the particular plot type. This list can be changed by using the *Change List Button* and *Defaults Button*.

     If a two-dimensional plot has been specified, the metrics list box functions in a multiselect mode. The user can specify the set of metrics to plot by simply clicking on them using the mouse. An entry that is selected will be highlighted. The entry can be deselected by clicking on the metric again with the mouse.

     If a three-dimensional plot has been specified, the metrics list box functions in a single-select mode. The user can only select a single metric from the list of metrics currently in the box.

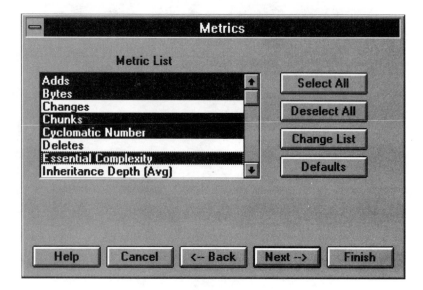

Figure B4.10   Metrics Dialog

Select All Button. This button selects all the entries currently in the *Metrics List Box*. This button is not enabled if a three-dimensional plot has been specified.

Deselect All Button. This button deselects all the entries currently in the *Metrics List Box*. This button is not enabled if a three-dimensional plot has been specified.

Note: Due to a bug in the Visual Basic interface code for list boxes, if the user has clicked on a metric in the *Metric List Box* before pressing the *Deselect All Button*, a single entry (that is, the last entry that was selected) will remain selected.

Change List Button. Pressing this button brings up the *Metric List Configuration Dialog* and allows the user to configure the set of metrics that appears in the *Metrics List Box*. See the section for the *Metric List Configuration Dialog* for more information.

Default Button. Pressing this button resets the *Metrics List Box* by filling it with a predefined set of metrics for the particular type of plot.

Metric List Configuration Dialog

The Metric List Configuration Dialog shown in Figure B4.11 appears when the *Change List Button* is pressed on the Metrics Dialog. This dialog allows the user to configure which metrics will appear in the *Metric List Box* on the *Metrics Dialog*. The

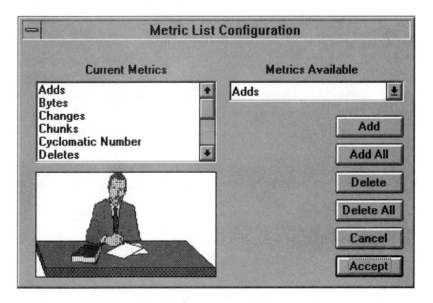

Figure B4.11   Metric List Configuration Dialog

configuration is saved so that each time the particular plot type is used this same set of metrics will appear.

This dialog has a list box for the current metric list configuration, a drop-down for the metrics that are available, and a button to execute various list configuration operations.

Current Metrics List Box

This list box is simply a copy of the metrics currently found in the *Metrics List Box* on the *Metrics Dialog*. This list can be edited by using the buttons on the right-hand side of the dialog.

Metrics Available Drop-Down

This drop-down contains the metrics that are available for the particular plot type specified. Note that each plot type will have a different set of metrics available.

Add Button.   This button adds the item currently selected in *Metrics Available Drop-Down* to the *Current Metrics List Box*. Note that if an entry already appears in the current list this button does not duplicate the entry. In addition, the entry is placed into the current list in alphabetical order.

Add All Button.   This button adds all the metrics in the available list into the current list. No entries will be duplicated.

Delete Button.   This button deletes the selected metrics from the current list. Select metrics by clicking on the entry in the *Current Metrics List Box* with the mouse. Pressing this button when no metric is selected has no effect.

Delete All Button.   This button deletes all the metrics in the current list. Note that at least one metric must be added to the current list before the *Accept Button* is pressed or this dialog will have no effect on the original metric list.

Cancel Button.   This button aborts the current metric list configuration and restores the original metric list. Pressing this button also returns the user back to the *Metrics Dialog*.

Accept Button.   This button accepts the metric list in the *Current Metrics List Box* and updates the *Metric List Box* on the *Metrics Dialog*. Note that if the current metric list is empty the original metric list is restored. Pressing this button returns the user to the *Metrics Dialog*.

Plot Preferences Dialog

The Plot Preferences Dialog shown in Figure B4.12 is the last dialog presented before the plot is actually produced. This dialog also appears when the *Finish Button* is pressed from any other dialog. This dialog allows the user to control how the plot will appear after it is constructed. The user can configure how the returned data will be sorted before the plot is created. In addition, the user can set special charting parameters and labels.

Sorting Group Box

This group contains option buttons that allow the user to specify how the data returned from the PAMPA database will be sorted prior to plot construction.

Sort Ascending Option Button. Selecting this option button will sort the data returned from the PAMPA database in ascending order according to the field specified in the *Sort By Drop-Down*.

Sort Descending Option Button. Selecting this option button will sort the data returned from the PAMPA database in descending order according to the field specified in the *Sort By Drop-Down*.

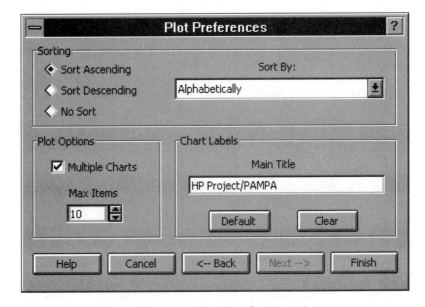

Figure B4.12   Plot Preferences Dialog

No Sort Option Button.   Selecting this option button disables the *Sort By Drop-Down* and causes no sort to be performed on the returned data.

Sort By Drop-Down

This drop-down specifies the field on which the data returned from the PAMPA database will be sorted. This control is disabled if the *No Sort Option Button* is selected.

The list for this control is automatically generated from the metrics selected in the *Metrics List Box* on the *Metrics Dialog*. The user can sort the data alphabetically based on the grouping for the plot by selecting the **Alphabetically** item in the list. In addition, the user can sort the data by size in bytes by selecting the **Size (Bytes)** item of the list.

Note: The **Size (Bytes)** entry only appears when the **Bytes** metric has not been selected in the *Metric List Box* on the *Metric Dialog*.

Plot Options Group Box

This group contains controls that allow the user to specify how charts are to be produced in the case that too much data is returned for a single chart.

Multiple Charts Check Box

Checking this check box allows the Metric Plot Generator to produce multiple charts if the data returned from the PAMPA database are too lengthy for a single chart. The Metric Plot Generator automatically produces as many charts as necessary to plot all data returned if this box is checked. If the box is not checked, only a single chart will be produced.

Max Items Spinner

This spinner allows the user to specify the maximum number of items to plot on a single chart. The user can either click on the spinner to set the value or enter the value manually with the keyboard.

This control is useful if a large number of data items are returned from the PAMPA database. Use this control to limit the number of items used for the *x* axis of the plot. By using this control in conjunction with the *Multiple Charts Check Box*, the user can produce a series of charts to display a large amount of data from the PAMPA database.

Caution: If you specify a value smaller than the number of data items returned from the PAMPA database, the Metric Plot Generator will truncate the extraneous data items. In general, plots with more than 20 items will appear too crowded to be meaningful.

Chart Labels Group Box

This group contains controls for setting the main title of the charts produced by the Metric Plot Generator.

Chart Title Edit Box

This edit box will initially contain the default title generated automatically by the Metric Plot Generator from current settings of the dialogs. You can manually edit the title by clicking on the edit box and using the keyboard.

Default Button.   This button causes the Metric Plot Generator to automatically regenerate the chart title. Use this button if you want to restore the title that initially appeared in the *Chart Title Edit Box*.
Warning: Pressing this button will cause any information previously entered into the *Chart Title Edit Box* to be lost.

Clear Button.   Press this button to clear out the *Chart Title Edit Box*. This is useful for entering user-defined titles.

Next Button.   This button is greyed-out and is unselectable.

Settings Dialog

The Settings Dialog shown in Figure B4.13 will appear when the *Settings Button* on the Metric Plot Generator main dialog is pressed. This dialog allows the user to select which dialogs to skip and sets the maximum and minimum values for radar charts.

Skip Dialogs Check Boxes

These check boxes allow the user to select dialogs that can be skipped whenever possible. If the dialog is skipped, the Metric Plot Generator uses the default or last configuration of the dialog. For example, if *New Plot Dialog* is checked, the New Plot Dialog will be skipped and the last project and project category will be used to generate the graph.

Radar Chart Min/Max Buttons.   Pressing one of the three Radar Chart Min/Max buttons will open a dialog similar to the example dialog in Figure B4.14. The *Radar Chart Min/Max Dialog* allows the user to change the minimum and maximum ranges for radar chart plots. The Metric list box is used to select the desired

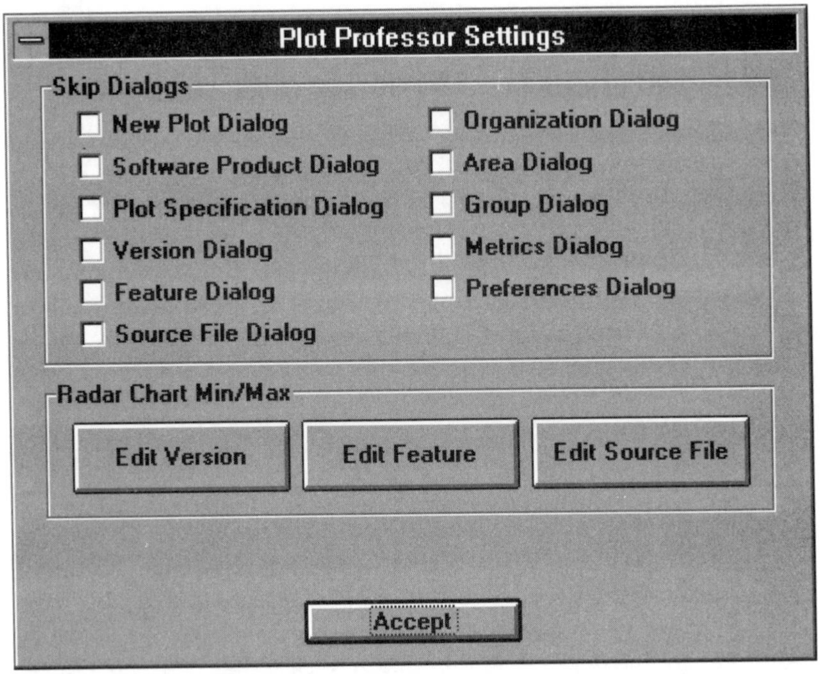

Figure B4.13   Settings Dialog

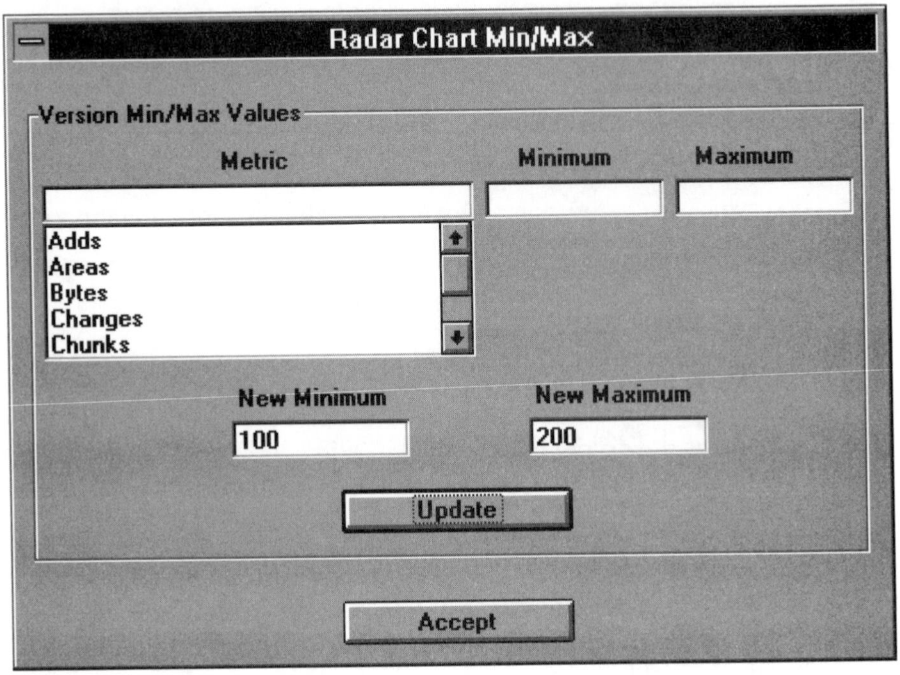

Figure B4.14   Radar Chart Min/Max Dialog

metric. The current minimum and maximum values for the selected metric appear in the Minimum and Maximum list boxes. To change the minimum or maximum value, type the new value in the New Minimum or New Maximum list box. Then press the Update button for the changes to take effect. When finished, pressing the Accept button returns the user to the *Settings Dialog*.

Table B.4.1 Error Messages

Error Message	Description
The project you have selected has no software products	The PAMPA database has no software products that match the project that you have selected.
The product you have selected has no versions	The PAMPA database has no versions that match the software product that you have selected.
The version you have selected has no features	The PAMPA database has no features that match the version that you have selected.
No data returned from query	The Metric Plot Generator was unsuccessful in generating the desired plot or no data were returned from the PAMPA database.
Could not open ODBC data source	The Metric Plot Generator was unable to connect to the PAMPA database. Make sure that the Windows ODBC facility is configured correctly and that the PAMPA database is not being used by another application.
Could not execute SQL query on data source	The Metric Plot Generator was unable to execute a query on the PAMPA database.
Could not retrieve query results from data source	The Metric Plot Generator was unable to retrieve the query results from the PAMPA database.
ODBC data source is invalid	An invalid data source has been specified as the PAMPA database. Make sure that the Windows ODBC facility is configured properly.
Could not get necessary database information	The Metric Plot Generator could not get the necessary initialization data from the PAMPA database. Check to make sure that the Windows ODBC facility has been configured properly and that the PAMPA database tables have been initialized.
Invalid plot file was selected	User tried to open an invalid plot file. Make sure that this file is one that was previously created using the Save Menu Item from the Chart Menu.
The option you have selected is not yet supported by this system	User selected a feature or option that has not yet been implemented by the Metric Plot Generator. These features will be available in future versions of the Metric Plot Generator

Accept Button.   The Accept button stores the new settings and opens the *Metric Plot Generator Main Dialog.*

Metric Plot Generator Error Messages

Whenever possible, the Metric Plot Generator tries to recover from errors by displaying an error message and continuing with the application. However, during initialization of the system, if Metric Plot Generator cannot obtain all necessary information, the application will abort.

Table B4.1 provides a listing of some error messages that may appear during execution of the Metric Plot Generator. If you do not find the error message listed there, then it is a run-time error message produced by Excel. Most run-time errors will abort the current plot-building sequence and return the user back to the Metric Plot Generator *Main Dialog.*

PLOT REFERENCE

This section explains the different plot types in the Metric Plot Generator and how to manipulate plots after they have been created.

Sequence Flow Chart

This section describes the sequence of dialogs that will appear depending on the responses made to the Metric Plot Generator dialogs. The flow chart shown in Figure B4.15 describes the sequence of dialogs that will appear as the user traverses through the Metric Plot Generator interface. The yellow boxes denote the dialogs that will appear on the screen. Blue boxes denote user responses to the dialog controls. Finally, red boxes denote the actual plot construction that takes place without user intervention.

The red boxes also indicate the type of plot that will be produced. The user can produce the same plot type by following the flow chart from the New Plot Dialog and making the appropriate responses to the Metric Plot Generator dialogs. These plot types are described next.

Plot Type 1 *(Note: This plot type is not implemented currently)*

- Two-dimensional
- Single organization
- **All Areas** selected → horizontal axis by area
- **All Groups** selected → single area; horizontal axis by group
- Otherwise → single area, single group; horizontal axis by individual

Metric Plot Generator Dialog Sequence

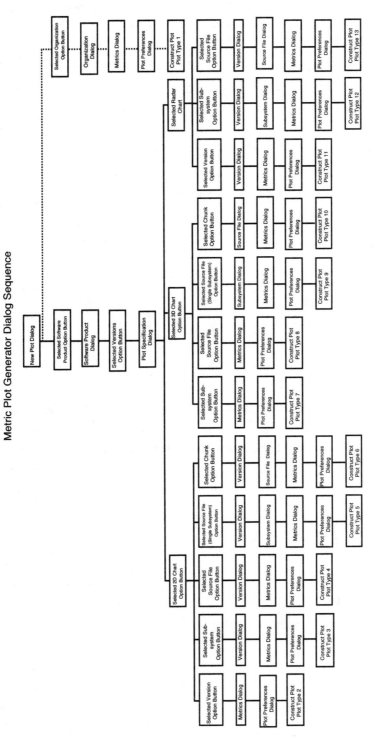

Figure B4.15 Metric Plot Generator Dialog Sequence

Plot Type 2

- Two-dimensional
- Single project, single software product
- Horizontal axis by version

Plot Type 3

- Two-dimensional
- Single project, single software product, single version
- Horizontal axis by feature

Plot Type 4

- Two-dimensional
- Single project, single software product, single version
- Horizontal axis by source file

Plot Type 5

- Two-dimensional
- Single project, single software product, single version, single feature
- Horizontal axis by source file

Plot Type 6

- Two-dimensional
- Single project, single software product, single version, single source file
- Horizontal axis by chunk

Plot Type 7

- Three-dimensional
- Single project, single software product
- Horizontal axis by subsystem

Plot Type 8

- Three-dimensional
- Single project, single software product
- Horizontal axis by source file

Plot Type 9

- Three-dimensional
- Single project, single software product, single subsystem
- Horizontal axis by source file

Plot Type 10

- Three-dimensional
- Single project, single software product, single source file
- Horizontal axis by chunk

Plot Type 11

- Radar chart
- Single project, single software product, single version

Plot Type 12

- Radar chart
- Single project, single software product, single version, single subsystem

Plot Type 13

- Radar chart
- Single project, single software product, single version, single source file

Plot Window

The Plot Window shown in Figure B4.16 displays the plot constructed by the Metric Plot Generator. This window is simply another Excel workbook used for the purpose of creating and displaying new charts. This window consists of a chart menu bar, window scroll bars, chart tabs, and the actual plot.

Chart Menu Bar

This menu bar contains items that allow the user to save plots, print plots, show plot data, make plots editable, and return to the Metric Plot Generator dialogs.

Save Menu Item

Selecting this menu item causes the File Save As Dialog shown in Figure B4.17 to appear. This dialog is used to save the current plot, which can later be re-created using the *Open Plot Button* on the Metric Plot Generator *Main Dialog*.

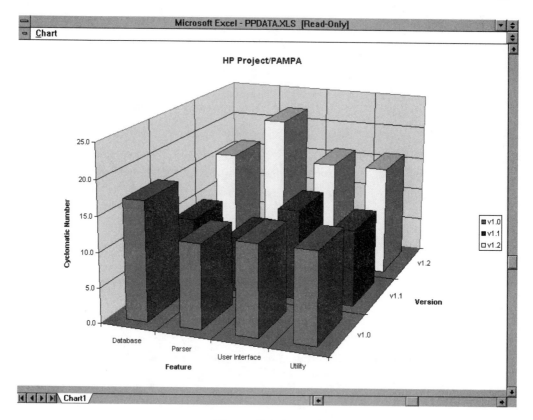

Figure B4.16   Plot Window

The user should save the plot with a *plt* extension so that this file will automatically appear in the *File Open Dialog*. Note that only the plot query definition is saved, not the actual charts. This means that as the PAMPA database is altered a saved plot may produce differing charts.

The *Save Menu Item* allows the user to construct a set of plots using the Metric Plot Generator dialogs and then recall them at a later time using the open plot feature. This eliminates the need to re-create a plot definition each time that the Metric Plot Generator is used.

Print Menu Item

Selecting this menu item brings up the *Excel Print Preview Screen*. The user can manipulate the printing parameters of the current chart by using the buttons located at the top of the screen. Print the plot by pressing the *Print Button*. Abort the print operation by pressing the *Close Button*.

Note: The current chart is sent to the *default printer* for Windows. Configure the default printer using the Print Manager.

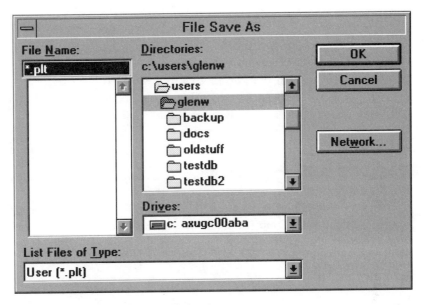

Figure B4.17   File Save As Dialog

Show Data Menu Item

Selecting this menu item allows the user to view the data sheet from which the graph is generated. To hide this data sheet, simply select Show Data again.

Locked Menu Item

This menu item allows the user to lock or unlock the charts found in the current plot. If this menu item is checked, the charts cannot be altered using the built-in features of Excel. If this menu item is not checked, then all charts in the current plot can be altered by using the built-in format tools of Excel.

Each aspect of the chart can be changed by unchecking the *Locked Menu Item* and then using the right mouse button to click on the desired chart object. Excel pops up a menu that allows the user to change the chart appearance.

Return Menu Item

Selecting this menu item takes the user back to the Metric Plot Generator *Main Dialog*. The current plot is not automatically saved, so the user must use the *Save Menu Item* to save the plot if desired.

Note: Use only the *Return Menu Item* to close the current plot and return to the Metric Plot Generator *Main Dialog*. Closing the window in any other way will cause the Metric Plot Generator to behave abnormally.

Plot Window With Multiple Charts

The Plot Window with Multiple Charts shown in Figure B4.18 gives an example of how the Metric Plot Generator displays a plot with multiple charts. For this plot, the *Max Items Spinner* on the *Plot Preferences Dialog* has been set to 8 and the *Multi-Chart Check Box* has been selected. The user can tab through all the charts produced by using the sheet tabs on the bottom of the window.

LIMITATIONS AND PROBLEMS

This section describes some of the limitations and problems that have been encountered during the development of the Metric Plot Generator interface. Future versions of the Metric Plot Generator will attempt to solve these problems.

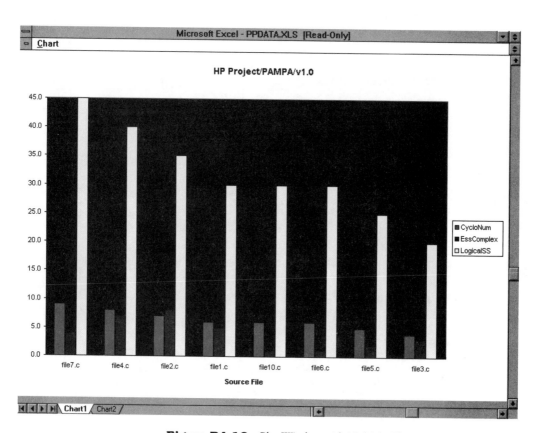

Figure B4.18 Plot Window with Multiple Charts

Averages per Source File

Many of the metrics listed for the various plot types are calculated based on averages per source file. It turns out that this is a very difficult calculation to make due to the structure of the PAMPA database tables.

The problem arises because the tables that store the source file and chunk data are joined when calculating metric data. This join results in a table that has a number of entries limited by the number of chunks that match the query criterion. The aggregate function AVG used in SQL queries works by performing a summation of the data based on the specified grouping and then dividing by the number of entries in the table. Thus, averages per chunk are easy to calculate using the aggregate AVG, but averages per source file are not so trivial.

Count Metrics

Another problem arises when trying to calculate counts such as the number of source files for a particular feature or groups in a particular area. The source of this problem is similar to that of the averaging issue described above. Due to the redundant entries of the joined table, it becomes difficult to use the aggregate SQL function COUNT to calculate these metrics.

More information and solutions to these problems should be available in future versions of the Metric Plot Generator.

INDEX

α test, 80
$f_{C_{MAXIMUM}}$, 235
K_{Effort_1}, 171
β, 200
β test, 80, 82, 353
η_1, 125
η_2, 125
a, 177
a_1, 137

A

AA, 138
AAS, 12
accountability, 91
acknowledgment learning stage, 58
activities, 91
Activity, 106
Adds, 106, 113, 124, 160
*Adds*_{Calculate}, 350
Advanced Automation System (AAS), 12
AFNOR, 35
aggregation, 109
Agresti, W.W., 66
Air Force Academy, 227
Alberts, D.S., 75
Albrecht, A.J. 74, 133, 173, 241
Alpha AXP program, 9
Amdahl Corporation, 73
America On Line, 12
American Airlines, 11, 47, 346
American National Standards Institute (ANSI), 33, 35
American Society for Testing and Materials (ASTM), 34
amount of documentation, 220
Amount, 107
AMR, 11
Analysis phase, 75, 82
analytic methods,178
analyze and predict stage, 62
ANSI, 34
Apple, 328, 339
Application Composition Model, 134
application generator, 82

architecture/risk resolution, 192
Area, 49, 109, 215
Aron, J. D., 66
Ashton-Tate, 11, 47, 346
assembler language, 226, 241
assessment program, 26, 29
*AssessmentAassimilation*_{Set}, 138
Assignment, 49, 106, 215, 346
Association Française de Normalisation (AFNOR), 35
association, 108
ASTM, 34
AT&T Bell Laboratories, 7, 47
AT&T Network Systems, 7, 9, 47
AT&T, 9, 23, 58
AT, 138
attribute value, 347
attributes, 48, 106, 347
authors, 116, 119
*Automatic Translated*_{Set}, 138
average duration of a work interruption, 185, 233
average months of progress per month for *n* **Project**s, 210
average number of software developers, 203
average time to regain a train of thought after an interruption, 185, 233
*AverageProgress*_n, 210
awareness stage, 42

B

b, 177
Badre, A., 321
Baecker, R.M., 254
Bailey, J.W., 239
Bailey, R.W., 309
Baldrige award criteria four element framework, 30
Baldrige award criteria seven categories, 30
Baldrige award, 22
Baldrige score, 42
Banker, R.D., 77
Barrett, A., 337
base-line estimator, 177
Basic level effort model, 188
Basili, V.R., 239

LICENSE AGREEMENT AND LIMITED WARRANTY

READ THE FOLLOWING TERMS AND CONDITIONS CAREFULLY BEFORE OPENING THIS CD PACKAGE, PAMPA. THIS LEGAL DOCUMENT IS AN AGREEMENT BETWEEN YOU AND PRENTICE-HALL, INC. (THE "COMPANY"). BY OPENING THIS SEALED CD PACKAGE, YOU ARE AGREEING TO BE BOUND BY THESE TERMS AND CONDITIONS. IF YOU DO NOT AGREE WITH THESE TERMS AND CONDITIONS, DO NOT OPEN THE CD PACKAGE. PROMPTLY RETURN THE UNOPENED CD PACKAGE AND ALL ACCOMPANYING ITEMS TO THE PLACE YOU OBTAINED THEM FOR A FULL REFUND OF ANY SUMS YOU HAVE PAID.

1. **GRANT OF LICENSE:** In consideration of your purchase of this book, and your agreement to abide by the terms and conditions of this Agreement, the Company grants to you a nonexclusive right to use and display the copy of the enclosed software program (hereinafter the "SOFTWARE") on a single computer (i.e., with a single CPU) at a single location so long as you comply with the terms of this Agreement. The Company reserves all rights not expressly granted to you under this Agreement.

2. **OWNERSHIP OF SOFTWARE:** You own only the magnetic or physical media (the enclosed CD) on which the SOFTWARE is recorded or fixed, but the Company and the software developers retain all the rights, title, and ownership to the SOFTWARE recorded on the original CD copy(ies) and all subsequent copies of the SOFTWARE, regardless of the form or media on which the original or other copies may exist. This license is not a sale of the original SOFTWARE or any copy to you.

3. **COPY RESTRICTIONS:** This SOFTWARE and the accompanying printed materials and user manual (the "Documentation") are the subject of copyright. The individual programs on the CD are copyrighted by the Texas Engineering Experiment Station. If you intend to use one of these programs, you must read and follow its accompanying license agreement. You may not copy the Documentation or the SOFTWARE, except that you may make a single copy of the SOFTWARE for backup or archival purposes only. You may be held legally responsible for any copying or copyright infringement which is caused or encouraged by your failure to abide by the terms of this restriction.

4. **USE RESTRICTIONS:** You may not network the SOFTWARE or otherwise use it on more than one computer or computer terminal at the same time. You may physically transfer the SOFTWARE from one computer to another provided that the SOFTWARE is used on only one computer at a time. You may not distribute copies of the SOFTWARE or Documentation to others. You may not reverse engineer, disassemble, decompile, modify, adapt, translate, or create derivative works based on the SOFTWARE or the Documentation without the prior written consent of the Company.

5. **TRANSFER RESTRICTIONS:** The enclosed SOFTWARE is licensed only to you and may not be transferred to any one else without the prior written consent of the Company. Any unauthorized transfer of the SOFTWARE shall result in the immediate termination of this Agreement.

6. **TERMINATION:** This license is effective until terminated. This license will terminate automatically without notice from the Company and become null and void if you fail to comply with any provisions or limitations of this license. Upon termination, you shall destroy the Documentation and all copies of the SOFTWARE. All provisions of this Agreement as to warranties, limitation of liability, remedies or damages, and our ownership rights shall survive termination.

7. **MISCELLANEOUS:** This Agreement shall be construed in accordance with the laws of the United States of America and the State of New York and shall benefit the Company, its affiliates, and assignees.

8. **LIMITED WARRANTY AND DISCLAIMER OF WARRANTY:** The Company warrants that the SOFTWARE, when properly used in accordance with the Documentation, will operate in substantial conformity with the description of the SOFTWARE set forth in the Documentation. The Company does not warrant that the SOFTWARE will meet your requirements or that the operation of the SOFTWARE will be uninterrupted or error-free. The Company warrants that the media

on which the SOFTWARE is delivered shall be free from defects in materials and workmanship under normal use for a period of thirty (30) days from the date of your purchase. Your only remedy and the Company's only obligation under these limited warranties is, at the Company's option, return of the warranted item for a refund of any amounts paid by you or replacement of the item. Any replacement of SOFTWARE or media under the warranties shall not extend the original warranty period. The limited warranty set forth above shall not apply to any SOFTWARE which the Company determines in good faith has been subject to misuse, neglect, improper installation, repair, alteration, or damage by you. EXCEPT FOR THE EXPRESSED WARRANTIES SET FORTH ABOVE, THE COMPANY DISCLAIMS ALL WARRANTIES, EXPRESS OR IMPLIED, INCLUDING WITHOUT LIMITATION, THE IMPLIED WARRANTIES OF MERCHANTABILITY AND FITNESS FOR A PARTICULAR PURPOSE. EXCEPT FOR THE EXPRESS WARRANTY SET FORTH ABOVE, THE COMPANY DOES NOT WARRANT, GUARANTEE, OR MAKE ANY REPRESENTATION REGARDING THE USE OR THE RESULTS OF THE USE OF THE SOFTWARE IN TERMS OF ITS CORRECTNESS, ACCURACY, RELIABILITY, CURRENTNESS, OR OTHERWISE.

IN NO EVENT, SHALL THE COMPANY OR ITS EMPLOYEES, AGENTS, SUPPLIERS, OR CONTRACTORS BE LIABLE FOR ANY INCIDENTAL, INDIRECT, SPECIAL, OR CONSEQUENTIAL DAMAGES ARISING OUT OF OR IN CONNECTION WITH THE LICENSE GRANTED UNDER THIS AGREEMENT, OR FOR LOSS OF USE, LOSS OF DATA, LOSS OF INCOME OR PROFIT, OR OTHER LOSSES, SUSTAINED AS A RESULT OF INJURY TO ANY PERSON, OR LOSS OF OR DAMAGE TO PROPERTY, OR CLAIMS OF THIRD PARTIES, EVEN IF THE COMPANY OR AN AUTHORIZED REPRESENTATIVE OF THE COMPANY HAS BEEN ADVISED OF THE POSSIBILITY OF SUCH DAMAGES. IN NO EVENT SHALL LIABILITY OF THE COMPANY FOR DAMAGES WITH RESPECT TO THE SOFTWARE EXCEED THE AMOUNTS ACTUALLY PAID BY YOU, IF ANY, FOR THE SOFTWARE.

SOME JURISDICTIONS DO NOT ALLOW THE LIMITATION OF IMPLIED WARRANTIES OR LIABILITY FOR INCIDENTAL, INDIRECT, SPECIAL, OR CONSEQUENTIAL DAMAGES, SO THE ABOVE LIMITATIONS MAY NOT ALWAYS APPLY. THE WARRANTIES IN THIS AGREEMENT GIVE YOU SPECIFIC LEGAL RIGHTS AND YOU MAY ALSO HAVE OTHER RIGHTS WHICH VARY IN ACCORDANCE WITH LOCAL LAW.

ACKNOWLEDGMENT

YOU ACKNOWLEDGE THAT YOU HAVE READ THIS AGREEMENT, UNDERSTAND IT, AND AGREE TO BE BOUND BY ITS TERMS AND CONDITIONS. YOU ALSO AGREE THAT THIS AGREEMENT IS THE COMPLETE AND EXCLUSIVE STATEMENT OF THE AGREEMENT BETWEEN YOU AND THE COMPANY AND SUPERSEDES ALL PROPOSALS OR PRIOR AGREEMENTS, ORAL, OR WRITTEN, AND ANY OTHER COMMUNICATIONS BETWEEN YOU AND THE COMPANY OR ANY REPRESENTATIVE OF THE COMPANY RELATING TO THE SUBJECT MATTER OF THIS AGREEMENT.

Should you have any questions concerning this Agreement or if you wish to contact the Company for any reason, please contact in writing at the address below.

Robin Short
Prentice Hall PTR
One Lake Street
Upper Saddle River, New Jersey 07458

How to Use the CD-ROM for *Software Measurement:* *A Visualization Toolkit for Project Control and Process Improvement*

INSTALLING PAMPA

1. Make sure that you have Windows NT 3.5x or later or Windows 95 installed on your computer. The Microsoft environment must have Excel 97 and Access 97.
2. Make sure that Microsoft Windows is running.
3. Insert the PAMPA CD into the appropriate CD drive.
4. To run the setup program do one of the following:

   - If your computer uses Windows NT 3.5x or later, choose **Run** from the Program Manager **File** menu, type D:\pampa.exe, and click **OK** or press ENTER.
   - If your computer uses Windows 95 or Windows NT 4.0, click the **Start** button, choose **Run,** type D:\pampa.exe, and click **OK** or press ENTER.

5. The installation will automatically prompt you for an ODBC data source. Choose the file name in C:\pampa\pampa.mdb and system database option.
6. After setup is successful, you are returned to Windows.

PAMPA SOFTWARE UPDATES

Updates to the PAMPA software system are available, free of charge, over the Internet at URL:

http://www.cs.tamu.edu/research/SPI/pampa/